DISCLOSURE DILEMMAS

Medical Law and Ethics

Series Editor
Sheila McLean, Director of the Institute of Law and Ethics in Medicine, School of Law, University of Glasgow

The 21st century seems likely to witness some of the most major developments in medicine and healthcare ever seen. At the same time, the debate about the extent to which science and/or medicine should lead the moral agenda continues, as do questions about the appropriate role for law.

This series brings together some of the best contemporary academic commentators to tackle these dilemmas in a challenging, informed and inquiring manner. The scope of the series is purposely wide, including contributions from a variety of disciplines such as law, philosophy and social sciences.

Other titles in the series

The Child As Vulnerable Patient
Protection and Empowerment
Lynn Hagger
ISBN 978-0-7546-7252-4

Critical Interventions in the Ethics of Healthcare
Challenging the Principle of Autonomy in Bioethics
Edited by Stuart J. Murray and Dave Holmes
ISBN 978-0-7546-7396-5

Law, Mind and Brain
Edited by Michael Freeman and Oliver R. Goodenough
ISBN 978-0-7546-7013-1

Speaking for the Dead
The Human Body in Biology and Medicine
D. Gareth Jones and Maja I. Whitaker
ISBN 978-0-7546-7452-8

The Jurisdiction of Medical Law
Kenneth Veitch
ISBN 978-0-7546-4944-1

Disclosure Dilemmas

Ethics of Genetic Prognosis after the 'Right to Know/Not to Know' Debate

Edited by

CHRISTOPH REHMANN-SUTTER
University of Lübeck, Germany

HANSJAKOB MÜLLER
University of Basel, Switzerland

Routledge
Taylor & Francis Group
LONDON AND NEW YORK

First published 2009 by Ashgate Publishing

2 Park Square, Milton Park, Abingdon, Oxfordshire OX14 4RN
52 Vanderbilt Avenue, New York, NY 10017

Routledge is an imprint of the Taylor & Francis Group, an informa business

First issued in paperback 2020

British Library Cataloguing in Publication Data
Disclosure dilemmas : ethics of genetic prognosis after the
'right to know/not to know' debate. -- (Medical law and
ethics)
1. Medical genetics--Moral and ethical aspects. 2. Genetic
screening--Moral and ethical aspects. 3. Disclosure of
information--Law and legislation. 4. Confidential
communications--Physicians. 5. Informed consent (Medical
law) 6. Genetic disorders--Patients--Psychology.
I. Series II. Rehmann-Sutter, Christoph, 1959- III. Müller,
Hj. (Hansjakob)
174.2'96042-dc22

Library of Congress Cataloging-in-Publication Data
Disclosure dilemmas : ethics of genetic prognosis after the 'right to know/not
to know' debate / [edited] by Christoph Rehmann-Sutter and Hansjakob Müller.
p. cm. -- (Medical law and ethics)
Includes bibliographical references and index.
ISBN 978-0-7546-7451-1
1. Genetic screening--Law and legislation. 2. Genetic counseling--Law and legislation.
3. Medical ethics. I. Rehmann-Sutter, Christoph, 1959- II.
Müller, Hj. (Hansjakob)

K3611.G46D575 2009
344.04'196--dc22

2009002176

ISBN 978-0-7546-7451-1 (hbk)
ISBN 978-0-367-60312-0 (pbk)

Contents

List of Figures and Tables *ix*
Notes on Contributors *xi*
Acknowledgements *xix*

Introduction 1
Christoph Rehmann-Sutter and Hansjakob Müller

PART 1 SETTING THE SCENE

1 The Right to Know and the Right Not to Know – Ten Years On 9
Ruth Chadwick

2 Genetic Counselling:
Placing the Room in Context 19
Barbara Katz Rothman

3 Genetic Counselling:
Clinical Settings and Constraints 25
Hansjakob Müller

PART 2 CASES AND ISSUES

4 Prevention of Harmful False Diagnosis versus Threat by
Disclosure of an Inheritable Disease – A Medical Case 39
David Winkler and Philippe Lyrer

4a Communication Yes, but How – and What? Commentary to
the Case Presented by David Winkler and Philippe Lyrer 45
Christoph Rehmann-Sutter

5 The Need for an Ethics of Kinship:
Decision Stories and Patients' Context 53
Rouven Porz

6 Testing for Susceptibility Genes: A Cautionary Tale 65
Margaret Lock

7 'If Only I Had (Not) Known That': About Risk-Individualization, Chance-Specification and the Loss of Certainty of Not-Knowing 85
Tjeerd Tymstra

8 The Symbolic Fallout of Gene Talk: Replacing the Person with Manageable Constructs 97
Silja Samerski

9 Predictive Genetic Testing of Adolescents at Risk of Inherited Arrhythmic Death 113
Jane Kaye, Michael Parker and Edward Blair

PART 3 RESPONSIBILITIES

10 How Legal Frameworks Construct Patterns of Liability in Genetic Counselling: An International Perspective 131
Daniel Wied, Susanne Listl and Maximilian Seibl

11 Responsibility Towards Relatives 153
Michael Steel

12 Careful Communication of 'Bad News': The Cancer Experience 167
Wolf Langewitz

13 The Responsibility of the Truth-Teller 183
Thomas Cerny

14 Practising Informed Choice: Decision Making and Prenatal Risk Assessment – The Danish Experience 191
Nete Schwennesen, Lene Koch and Mette Nordahl Svendsen

15 Receiving and Interpreting Information: A Joint Enterprise 205
Jackie Leach Scully

16 Without Disclosure, No Informed Choice 219
Peter Miny

17 Allowing Agency: An Ethical Model for Communicating Personal Genetic Information 231
Christoph Rehmann-Sutter

Conclusions 261
Christoph Rehmann-Sutter and Hansjakob Müller

Index *269*

List of Figures and Tables

Figures

4.1	Cranial CT with multiple cerebral calcification foci (arrows), characteristic for HSA	41
6.1	Lifetime risk curves for use in the education and counselling protocol for women with genotypes ε3/ε4 and ε4/ε4, for the individual concerned and their first-degree relatives, compared with the general population	73
16.1	Decision options for the prenatal risk assessment and diagnosis of aneuploidy	223

Tables

3.1	Reasons for applying for genetic counselling	29
3.2	The main elements of genetic counselling	30
17.1	Genetic counselling model of practice – postulated tenets and goals	241

Notes on Contributors

Edward Blair is Lead Clinician and Consultant in Clinical Genetics at the Oxford Radcliffe Hospitals NHS Trust, Oxford. He has a long-standing interest in cardiovascular genetics and the monogenic causes of sudden cardiac death. He has undertaken basic genetic research at the University of Oxford Department of Cardiovascular Medicine and with colleagues there uncovered novel disease mechanisms in HCM as well as providing the first description of mutations in AMPK in HCM patients. Dr Blair continues an active clinical commitment in cardiovascular genetics through the ORH and the Oxford Biomedical Research Centre.

Thomas Cerny is Professor of Medical Oncology at the University of Berne and Head of Oncology-Hematology at the Kantonsspital St Gallen, Switzerland. He studied Medicine at the University of Bern and was trained as a Medical Oncologist at the Christie Hospital and Patterson Institutes, University of Manchester, UK. He is especially involved in new drug development, anti-nicotine vaccination and palliative care development and has experience in studies of unorthodox medicine in oncology. He has a special interest in political and ethical issues regarding cancer prevention and early detection programs, access to best cancer care, fair pricing of new drugs and implementation of quality assessment in cancer treatment through cancer networks. He is Acting President of the Swiss Cancer League.

Ruth Chadwick is Director of the ESRC (Economic and Social Sciences Research Council) Centre for Economic and Social Aspects of Genomics (Cesagen), Cardiff University, UK. She holds a Link Chair between Cardiff Law School and the School of English, Communication and Philosophy (ENCAP). She has coordinated a number of projects funded by the European Commission, including the EUROSCREEN projects (1994–6; 1996–9) and co-edits the journal *Bioethics* and the online journal *Genomics, Society and Policy*. She is Chair of the Human Genome Organisation Ethics Committee and has served as a member of several policy-making and advisory bodies, including the Panel of Eminent Ethical Experts of the Food and Agriculture Organisation of the United Nations (FAO), and the UK Advisory Committee on Novel Foods and Processes (ACNFP). She was Editor-in-Chief of the award-winning *Encyclopedia of Applied Ethics* (1998), of which a second edition is now being prepared. She is an Academician of the Academy of Social Sciences and a Fellow of the Hastings Center, New York; of the Royal Society of Arts; and of the Royal Society of Medicine. In 2005 she was the winner of the World Technology Network Award for Ethics for her work on the relationship between scientific developments and ethical frameworks.

Jane Kaye is a Wellcome Trust Research Fellow in Law at the Ethox Centre, University of Oxford. She obtained her degrees from the Australian National University (BA), University of Melbourne (LL B) and University of Oxford (D.Phil.). She was admitted to practice as a solicitor/barrister by the Australian Capital Territory Supreme Court in 1997. She is a member of the Faculty of Law, University of Oxford. Her research in the area of law and genetics focuses on the development of innovative technologies and the legal issues of intellectual property rights, privacy, confidentiality, data protection and negligence, as well as the broader issues of the public interest, global governance and regulation. Her socio-legal research is based on issues that have implications for clinical and medical research practice. She is involved in a number of expert committees focusing on the issues surrounding biobanks within Europe and internationally.

Lene Koch is Professor of History of Reproductive and Genetic Technologies at the University of Copenhagen, Denmark and Head of the Unit of Health Services Research at the Institute of Public Health. She studied English and American Studies (MA) and History (BA) at the University of Copenhagen. She has a PhD in Women's Studies (Women and In Vitro Fertilisation, 1989) and is D.Phil. in History (Eugenics and Compulsory Sterilisation in Denmark, 2000). She was a member of the Danish Ethical Council from 1994–2000 and since 2007 a member of the Danish Royal Society of Science and Letters. Her work concerns the history and sociology of genetic and reproductive technology with special reference to the political and ethical aspects. She has published widely on these issues <http://www.pubhealth.ku.dk/stf/ansatte/leko/>.

Wolf Langewitz is Professor of Internal Medicine at the University of Basel and Deputy Head of the Department of Psychosomatic Medicine. He studied medicine at the Universities of Freiburg i. Brsg. and Berlin. After a year in Pathology, he trained as an Internist at the University of Bonn (D), Board Certificate 1986, and in 1990 he received a degree in Psychotherapy. From 1990 until now he has worked at the Department of Psychosomatic Medicine, and was head of the department from 1998–2007. Since 1996 he has been co-editor of the German textbook *Uexküll: Lehrbuch der Psychosomatischen Medizin* (Elsevier: Munich, 2003). In 2006 he was elected President of the European Association for Communication in Health Care (EACH). Since 2008 he has also been Visiting Professor at the Faculty of Communication in Health Care at the University of Lugano (Head: Professor P. Schultz). His research interests include theoretical questions of the interplay of mind and body in psychosomatic medicine, application of semiotic and phenomenological thinking in medicine, physician patient communication and somatoform disorders. A list of his publications can be found at <www.psychosomatik-basel.ch>.

Susanne Listl is Academic Assistant to Professor Dr Andreas Spickhoff, Chair for Civil Law, Private International Law, Comparative Law and Civil Procedure Law. She studied both Medicine and Law at the University of Regensburg and received a doctorate in Medicine in 2008 for a thesis on comparative legal backgrounds of transfusion medicine in Europe. After having passed the first judicial state examination in 2005, she is currently in her final year of practical training in judicial work. Among transfusion law, her research interests encompass medical malpractice law, pharmaceutical law, bioethics and institutional review boards, as well as physicians' professional regulations.

Margaret Lock is Marjorie Bronfman, Professor Emerita in Social Studies in Medicine, and is affiliated with the Department of Social Studies of Medicine and the Department of Anthropology at McGill University. She is a Fellow of the Royal Society of Canada and an Officier de L'Ordre national du Québec. Lock was awarded the Prix Du Québec, domaine Sciences Humaines in 1997 and in the same year the Wellcome Medal of the Royal Anthropological Society of Great Britain. In 2002 she received the Canada Council for the Arts Molson Prize, in 2005 the Canada Council for the Arts Killam Prize, and in the same year she was awarded a Trudeau Fellowship. In 2007 she received the Gold Medal for Research from the Social Sciences and Humanities Research Council of Canada (SSHRC). She is the author and/or co-editor of 14 books and has published over 190 articles. Her monographs *Encounters with Aging: Mythologies of Menopause in Japan and North America* and *Twice Dead: Organ Transplants and the Reinvention of Death* have each won several awards. She is currently working on two books. One is in connection with the genetics of Alzheimer's disease and the social ramifications of testing for susceptibility genes. The second, co-authored, book documents the global circulation of biomedical technologies and their impacts at local sites.

Philippe Lyrer is a Consulting Neurologist at the University Hospital Basel. He is Associate Professor of Neurology and leads the stroke programme. He studied medicine at the University of Basel and got his MD in 1983. He accomplished his training in Clinical Neurology in 1992. In 1992 he was also Visiting Research Fellow at the University of London Ontario, Canada. His research interests are dedicated to the pathophysiology, diagnosis and treatment of cerebrovascular diseases. He is the President of the Swiss Cerebrovascular Working Group (Zerebrovaskuläe Arbeitsgruppe der Schweiz, ZAS) and a member of the European Stroke Council. The ZAS issues guidelines for diagnosis and treatment of stroke and promotes research in all fields of cerebrovascular diseases.

Peter Miny is Interim Head of the Division of Medical Genetics at the University Children's Hospital in Basel where he has held an appointment since 1995. After medical school and three years of general clinical work in various hospitals, he received his formal training in Medical Genetics at the Institute of Human Genetics, University of Münster, Germany. He is board certified as a medical geneticist and laboratory director and is involved in teaching Medical Genetics at the University of Basel Medical School. His special research interests are in prenatal diagnosis of genetic conditions and clinical genetics. He is currently Co-President of the Swiss Society of Medical Genetics and member of an expert commission on genetic testing appointed by the Swiss Federal Council.

Hansjakob Müller, MD, is Professor Emeritus of Medical Genetics at the University of Basel and former Head of the Division of Medical Genetics belonging to the University Children's Hospital and the Department of Biomedicine where he serves now as a consultant. His major research interests include hereditary cancer and many aspects of clinical genetics including ethical questions. He was/is a member of several professional bodies and organisations in the field of human genetics and biomedicine. In addition, he served as a member of ethical commissions of the European Council and the Swiss Academy of Medical Sciences. Currently, he is a member of the Swiss National Ethics Commission for Human Medicine.

Michael Parker is Professor of Bioethics at the University of Oxford and Director of the Ethox Centre. His research activities include leading a programme of embedded bioethics research on ethical and social dimensions of international consortial genomic epidemiological research into severe malaria in childhood in 20 sites, most in malaria-endemic developing countries, (MalariaGEN, funded by the Gates Foundation and the Wellcome Trust); carrying out research into ethical issues arising in the development and use of e-science and Grid technologies for medical research using medical records (funded by the Medical Research Council); carrying out multidisciplinary social science, ethical and legal research on the governance of genetic databases (funded by the Wellcome Trust); and facilitating the Genethics Club, a national deliberative ethics forum in clinical genetics.

Rouven Porz is a biologist and philosopher and is and is currently Head of the Ethics Unit at the Inselspital (University Hospital) in Bern, Switzerland. He is working in a qualitative interview study, investigating patients‘ perspectives in IVF and their ideas about egg sharing, embryo donation, human embryonic stem cell research from an ethical point of view. He did his PhD in Bioethics on the Absurdity of Genetic Testing. This research work was carried out in Basel at the Unit for Ethics in Biosciences, working in a qualitative interview study on genetic diagnosis, with Jackie Leach Scully and Christoph Rehmann-Sutter. He is the Editor of the EACME newsletter (European Association of Centres of Medical Ethics, with Guy Widdershoven) and Visiting Research Fellow at the Institute for Biomedical Ethics in Zürich, Switzerland. His research interests include genetic diagnosis, genomics, stem cell research and, from an ethical point of view, narrative reconstruction of life stories, boundary situations and existentialism. He has a strong interest in ethical methodologies, mainly focusing on questions of how to bridge empirical investigation and normative argumentation.

Christoph Rehmann-Sutter is Professor of Theory and Ethics in the Biosciences at the University of Lübeck, Germany. He first studied Molecular Biology and then Philosophy and Sociology in Basel, Freiburg i. Brsg. and Darmstadt. From 1997 to 1998 he was Research Fellow at the University of California Berkeley. From 2001 to 2009 he was elected President of the Swiss National Advisory Commission on Biomedical Ethics, which gives recommendations to the Swiss Government and Parliament. Since 2008 he has also been Visiting Professor at the London School of Economics and Political Science (LSE). His research interests include basic theoretical questions of philosophical and interdisciplinary bioethics, ethical questions of gene therapy, genomics, embryo research and governance issues of biotechnology.

Barbara Katz Rothman is Professor of Sociology at the City University of New York, where she also serves on the Faculties of Public Health, Disability Studies and Women's Studies. Her books include *The Tentative Pregnancy*; *In Labor* and *Laboring On* (with Wendy Simonds); *Recreating Motherhood*; *The Book Of Life* and *Weaving A Family*. She is the recipient of the Jesse Bernard Award of the American Sociological Association and the Lee Founders Award of the Society for the Study of Social Problems. She has served as a Leverhulme Professor at Plymouth University in the UK; a Visiting Professor at the University of Osnabrueck in Germany and a Fulbright Professor at the University of Groningen in the Netherlands.

Silja Samerski is Assistant Professor at the Institute for Sociology and Social Psychology at the Leibniz University of Hannover, Germany. She studied Biology and Philosophy in Tübingen and Bremen and earned a PhD in the Social Sciences with a thesis on '*Die verrechnete Hoffnung. Von der selbstbestimmten Entscheidung durch genetische Beratung*' ('The Mathematisation of Hope. On Autonomous Decision-Making Through Genetic Counseling'). She is a collaborator in an interdisciplinary circle of scholars who analyze the sociogenesis of modern myths, such as the belief that the consumption of medicine leads to health or the management of risks to a foreseeable future. Her own research focuses on the latent and symbolic functions of genetic literacy and professional counselling. She has just completed a project in collaboration with Barbara Duden on the social and cultural effects of the 'release of genetic terms' into everyday language.

Nete Schwennesen is a PhD Fellow at the University of Copenhagen, Institute of Public Health, where she is working on a project about the social implications of prenatal risk assessment. She holds a MA in Social and Political Science from Aalborg and Copenhagen University, Denmark, and a MA in Contemporary Sociology from University of Lancaster, UK. In 2005 she was a Marie Curie Fellow at the Science and Technology Studies Unit (SATSU), University of York, UK. Her research interests include the social implications of new reproductive and genetic technologies, the ethics of risk assessment in the context of reproduction and science and technology studies (STS).

Jackie Leach Scully is currently Senior Lecturer in the School of Geography, Politics and Sociology at Newcastle University. Her first degree was in Biochemistry at the University of Oxford followed by a PhD in Cellular Pathology at the University of Cambridge. She then pursued research at ISREC, the Swiss Experimental Cancer Research Institute, and at the University of Basel. Her primary research focus has been in bioethics since she joined the Unit for Ethics in the Biosciences in 1995. She is Honorary Visiting Fellow at the ECAV Academy of the Arts, Valais, Switzerland, and Honorary Senior Lecturer in the Faculty of Medicine, University of Sydney, Australia. Her research interests cover the broad area of moral reasoning and identity, genetic and reproductive medicine, disability, feminist bioethics, empirical methodologies in bioethics and psychoanalytic theory applied to bioethical issues.

Maximilian Seibl is Academic Assistant to Professor Dr Andreas Spickhoff, Chair for Civil Law, Private International Law, Comparative Law and Procedural Law at the University of Regensburg. He studied Law in Regensburg and is currently working on his doctoral thesis concerning 'The burden of proof with respect to factual elements in private international law provisions'. He has also published essays on legal problems of medical and health care law.

Michael Steel is Emeritus Professor in Medical Science at the Bute Medical School, University of St Andrews, Scotland and Honorary Consultant in Clinical Genetics for Lothian and Tayside Health Boards. He received his medical education at Edinburgh and was, for many years, on the staff of the UK Medical Research Council's Human Genetics Unit in Edinburgh, latterly as Assistant Director. His particular interests have been in the clinical and molecular genetics of cancer, initially studying the interactions between Epstien Barr virus and human lymphoid cells that give rise to Burkitt's Lymphoma, but since the late 1980s he has concentrated on familial breast cancer, both at the fundamental molecular and the clinical level. He has contributed to the establishment, operation and evaluation of outpatient clinics for women at increased familial risk in Edinburgh and Dundee and has published many reports based on this experience, often in collaboration with other centres in the UK and across Europe. He has been a member of the UK Gene Therapy Advisory Committee and sits on the board of several Medical Research Charities.

Mette Nordahl Svendsen is Assistant Professor at the Department of Health Services Research, Institute of Public Health, University of Copenhagen. She holds an MA and PhD in anthropology. Her main research interests concern relationships between health policies, clinical and scientific practices, and the lives of patients in the context of new genetic and reproductive technologies. She has carried out ethnographic studies on cancer genetics counselling and testing and on embryo donations to human embryonic stem cell research. She is currently working on a research project about patient participation in pharmacogenomics research. She has published her work in a number of social science journals, such as *Medical Anthropology*, *Social Studies of Science* and *Body and Society*.

Tjeerd Tymstra is a Medical Sociologist at the University Medical Centre Groningen, The Netherlands. His research interest is in the study of the psychosocial impact of new medical technologies (reproductive technologies, screening procedures, organ donation and transplantation). His recent publications concern the subject 'Society and Genomics'.

Daniel Wied is Academic Assistant to Professor Dr Andreas Spickhoff, Chair for Civil Law, Private International Law, Comparative Law and Procedural Law at the University of Regensburg. He earned his first law degree at the University of Regensburg in 2004 and passed the Bavarian bar exam in 2006 after a 2-year compulsory clerkship program. He then studied at the University of Oxford where he earned a postgraduate law degree (M.jur.) in 2007. He has published articles on general civil law issues. Since 2007 he has been pursuing his doctorate thesis on characterization issues in European and German Procedural Law.

David Winkler, MD, PhD, is a board-certified neurologist specializing in electroencephalography and electromyography. He graduated from Basel University and holds a PhD in neurobiology. His research is focused on neurodegenerative disorders.

Acknowledgements

The editors thank the Käthe Zingg-Schwichtenberg Fonds and the Swiss Academy of the Medical Sciences for generous financial support. The Swiss National Science Foundation funded a bioethical research project *Time as a contextual element in ethical decision-making in the field of genetic diagnostics* (11-64956.01 and 101311-10306), which was carried out at the Unit of Ethics in the Biosciences, University of Basel by Jackie Leach Scully, Rouven Porz and Christoph Rehmann-Sutter. This project provided the intellectual framework, in which Hansjakob Müller's initial idea for the book could develop. At different stages of the conception and materialization of the book (first as an international conference on a sunny spring day in 2001 at Wenkenhof in Riehen near Basel, then through the invitation and inclusion of new authors), the supportive and inspiring collaboration of Irina Miletskaja, Rouven Porz and Franziska Genitsch was indispensable. Rowena Joy Smith, Jackie Leach Scully and Monica Buckland reviewed the English of several chapters. Special thanks go to Gabriela Brahier, who guided the manuscript carefully and with the necessary patience through the final steps. In 1997, Ruth Chadwick, Mairi Levitt and Darren Shickle edited a book in the Avebury Series in Philosophy for Ashgate on the ethical and philosophical implications of genetic screening, with the title *The Right to Know and the Right Not to Know*. We are grateful to Ashgate for accepting and producing our new volume that takes a fresh look, a decade on, at some of the same topics. Our special thanks go to Carolyn Court, Alison Kirk, Kate Brown and many other supportive staff at Ashgate, and to two helpful external reviewers.

Introduction

Christoph Rehmann-Sutter and Hansjakob Müller

'Why did you make me see what I can't change anyway?'
(Friedrich Schiller, *Kassandra*, 1802, line 53 f. – our translation)

In many cases, genetic testing and screening can provide diagnostic information for improving health care. But the logic of the genes implies that diagnoses may be pre-emptive. Genetic information may be essentially prognostic information; its practical implications may be diverse and only partly predictable. The genome can rarely be 'read' (a difficult term in this context) in such a clear way that future events of health and disease can be forecast with security. Rather, in most cases the information takes the form of probabilities. This partial knowledge can clearly be useful; but because it is, at the same time, a new non-knowledge it can also be difficult to interpret and to handle. Furthermore, there may be stakeholders other than the patient themself involved: at-risk family members, carers, even institutions with interests. The construction, disclosure and exchange of personal genetic information that reveals things about one's likely future in terms of potential disease is an emerging new space of 'biosociality' (Paul Rabinow's term; cf. Rose 2007) in which ethical dilemmas arise.

We all sometimes grapple with fate, with what we see as the unchangeable and often unforeseeable course of events. To tame the unpredictable by foreseeing and understanding the future has been a powerful motive throughout history for the advancement of the sciences and technologies (Toulmin 1961). However, divining the future has also been a reason to turn to auguries, prophets and clairvoyants of many kinds, some of them very dubious. Omens, unlucky black cats and lucky horseshoes have also served in attempts to tame the unpredictable. One of the outcomes of the scientific and rational strand in the development of foresight-and-understanding tools is modern genetics and genomics. Today, personal genetic information of various forms and relevance for predicting the future is becoming available with increasing ease. Genetic tests are now being used to divine the future and to plan lives. Here, genetics meets the complexities of social life.

The medical value of personal genetic information is equivalent to its potential for preventing disease. But its personal utility is often ambiguous and ambivalent. Predictive genetic information, when known, can have a profound impact on those who request or get it. A truth, once it has been told, cannot be untold. And it is often unclear to those involved exactly what 'the truth' is when it comes to test results. There may be different 'truths' in the raw data, and there is a potential for over- and misinterpretation. Professional expertise is needed. Genetic counselling has been developed to accompany genetics. And genetic counsellors or medical geneticists have developed a rich technical literature about, and ethical reflection on, the ambivalences and dilemmas that arise in their practice.

This interdisciplinary book starts from the professional discourse about 'disclosure dilemmas' in genetic counselling, but goes beyond the professional ethics of genetic counsellors. It brings together and confronts the new contributions of social scientists, philosophers, lawyers, medical doctors, geneticists and bioethicists who reflect on disclosure dilemmas from different angles and with different expertise and complementary experiences. The idea for the book included the aim of enlarging the focus of bioethical discussions about disclosure dilemmas. New problems have arisen that were not visible 10 years ago, problems which perhaps only become apparent if one adopts a patient's perspective and investigates how dilemmas 'feel' if experienced in their concrete, local settings and histories. Some of the new issues relate to recent developments in science, technology and medical practice. Many more diseases can now be tested for, with the number of available tests rapidly increasing. Tests cover not only monogenetic but also multifactorial diseases, some of them very common disorders such as diabetes, obesity, heart diseases or cancers. It should soon be possible to test for some psychiatric disorders. One striking example of recent developments is the introduction of routine risk assessment based on ultrasound and maternal blood in prenatal diagnosis. Before offering an invasive genetic test to the pregnant woman, the risk assessment is provided as an element of informed decision making. But this changed much more for the women concerned than just the amount of information available.

Recent publications in bioethics have indicated a need for further interdisciplinary research and discussion about genetic dilemmas. From many possible examples we mention Monica Konrad (2005), who did in-depth interviews with families affected by Huntington's disease. She demonstrates how 'the exchange of genetic information between kin entails unresolved processes of moral decision making within and across the generations' (4). This may be unsurprising, but her study shows clearly that bioethics can only meet the local understandings of what knowledge is 'good' to know and what knowledge is 'bad' to tell and share with others, in the context of a close understanding of subjective illness experiences that can not be provided by 'thin' descriptions in case vignettes or theoretical imagination. This opens a new field for empirically-based bioethics that takes the perspectives of participants into account and treats patients as moral pioneers, to use Rayna Rapp's term.

A second groundbreaking contribution is the book by Neil C. Manson and Onora O'Neill (2007). They attempt to rethink informed consent in bioethics on the basis of a developed theoretical approach to 'information' that goes beyond the assumption that information is 'something' (meaning, ideas) that can be conveyed or transferred from one mind to the other. Information is better understood as the result of processes of interaction and communication involving both sides of the encounter. This account of information was first developed in genetics (by

Susan Oyama) and it sheds new light on the processes of communicating genetic information between geneticists and patients or clients.

Thirdly, the relationship between ethical theory and the application of ethical principles to individual cases has long been one of the standard issues of medical ethics. The normal approach in bioethics textbooks is the anthology, in which the student is offered a collection of ethical theories (Kantian deontology, utilitarianism, contract theory, care ethics, virtue morality and others) to pick from. The recent book edited by Richard Ashcroft et al. (2005) turns the relation between case and theory around. They present one clinical case (from medical genetics) and analyze it with the help of different ethical approaches. This impressively demonstrates the particular power, and also the limits, of each approach in terms of this one case. In the end, we see that it is not so important whether the philosophical search for 'the best' ethical theory ever gives a conclusive result. The integration of many methods to bear on the complexities of the genetics case is much more powerful, and delivers a much more comprehensive understanding of the ethical terrain than one single approach. The (overly) predominant liberal individualism mainstream bioethics (Crosthwaite 1998; Rehmann-Sutter, forthcoming) should therefore be complemented with other approaches on the level of case discussions.

The term 'disclosure' does not assume that there is a single true content, one piece of stable information in the outcome of a test that could be disclosed or concealed. The ethical dilemmas that are opened by the acts of disclosure and non-disclosure also include the dilemmas of the interpreters, whether they are on the providing or the receiving end of the disclosing relationship. But the use of genetic data is today not confined to the clinical context to ascertain diagnoses, to avoid the birth of a child with severe genetic diseases, to improve the viability of transferred embryos or to plan appropriate preventive measures. More recently, genetic information is also offered directly to consumers by companies who advertise and offer genetic services over the Internet. 'Personal genomics' is the new idea. Thanks to the collapsing costs of gene analysis and the dramatic success of mapping DNA variants linked to common diseases, there is great excitement and also great concern and controversy about for-profit services advertised by specialized companies with slogans like 'We check your genome for $300'. In the future, the costs of mapping will decrease further and the number of freely testable mutations will increase. In December 2007, the British Human Genetics Commission issued a report entitled *More Genes Direct*, identifying 27 companies who already market genetic tests directly to consumers.

But the number of *clinically* testable conditions rises each month as well. According to the NIH funded 'Genetests' website <www.genetests.org>, there are now (March 2009) tests for 1,422 diseases clinically available, 200 more than only one year before, those still under research not counted. In medical genetics, we see the rapidly growing availability of *personal* genetic information with major prognostic impact for people's health.

Due to the inclusion of common diseases to the list of the testable conditions, the issue of disclosing or not disclosing genetic information is now relevant to a much larger number of people. This has political implications because it affects concepts of preventive medicine and health policy. The 'oracle of DNA' – Nancy Wexler (1989) has suggested this illuminating metaphor – has opened its doors for all, at least for all those who can afford it; not just those who have reason to believe that they are in a situation of higher-than-average risk, but also those who just want to 'face the truth' about their own genetic constitution. New questions arise about 'identity', the 'self' or 'authenticity'. We have reason to believe that all of our bodies carry a distinct and personal mix of genetic risk factors. Human existence with the limits and frailties, the finitude and contingency of vital embodiment, is re-described in the language of correlation coefficients, risk rates or mutation acronyms.

In 1989, Wexler wrote: 'The most disquieting dilemma provoked by genetic advances is the capacity to prophesy before we can prevent' (430). This remains true for many genetic conditions like Huntington's disease. But for other conditions preventive measures are indeed available, sometimes even cures. Many cancers can be kept under control, if they are diagnosed early enough. The more genetic risk factors for 'common' conditions, like diabetes or cardiovascular disease, become pre-symptomatically detectable, the less true it is that we can only forecast but not prevent or treat. The corresponding disclosure dilemmas become sometimes easier to resolve, but sometimes even more complex.

But not all of this is new. Human embodiment, the existential condition of our life on earth, has always placed us within a peculiar dialectic: the dialectic of control and assent, of activity and passivity, of acting and suffering. Phenomenologists have seen that the voluntary emerges from a background of the involuntary and remains in relation with it (Ricoeur 1963). Life itself, the gift of birth, our predispositions, our unconscious, are all beyond control, but they make it possible for us to control other parts of our existence: to be active in some ways, to have lively impulses or feelings, to have intentions and be ethically responsible. Our genes play into this dialectic. Genetic information is incorporated (literally) into a pre-existing corporeality. The old dialectic of control and assent that was always present in human condition is currently being reconfigured within the codes of genetics. Genetics therefore does not pose a completely new challenge for human existence. But it offers a new code, with new frameworks of understanding, new constellations of social risk factors and new possibilities of meaning. And it constructs new forms of knowledge, embedded in political and social contexts with their particular corporate interests and power structures (Rose 2007).

Genetic knowledge, once it becomes available to the individual, often does not provide the desired certainty. It appears in the form of statistical correlations, probable outcomes and risks, and may therefore also cause new uncertainties. (Will I be affected? Will my child be affected?) The evidence of the genetic oracle is ambiguous – as oracles always are. But nonetheless, it is possible to get bits and pieces of information about invisible limits, tendencies and capabilities of our bodies, and for many of us these bits and pieces seem irresistible to get or to disclose. The knowledge also (re)connects people – kin or complete strangers –

who share the same mutations in new bio-social relationships and challenges their moral perceptions of the situations that emerge. Avoiding the rhetoric of 'genetic exceptionalism', and drawing on an expanded field of bioethical, sociological and anthropological research, this book sets a new agenda for discussing the ethics of disclosing prognostic genetic information. The bioethical discussion of the handling and disclosure of personal genetic information was initially dominated by the concept of individual rights, especially the right to know and not to know, developing the normative ideal of value-neutrality and non-directive genetic counselling. With the advance of empirical studies in bioethics that have given insights into the experiences of people, both professionals and non-professionals, who are personally involved, the limitations of these rights-based approaches have become more visible. This is one reason that led us to the production of this book.

Another reason is the essential two-sidedness of disclosure. Disclosure is an interaction between somebody who receives and another who provides information. When it comes to genetic information, the person requesting disclosure may be the same person that the requested information is about. But it can also be about somebody else, for example, a child. In contributing to awareness and reflection about the ethical issues that arise around possible and actual disclosures, then, this book necessarily takes a decisively multi-perspective approach. The dilemmas are no longer just those of the provider (the doctor's or the counsellor). They are, fundamentally, the client's dilemmas as well. And the dilemmas of one party may be influenced by the anticipated dilemmas of the other: I am faced with a dilemma because I think that you will be in a dilemma, if I ... Dilemmas enter a dialogical structure.

References

Ashcroft, R. et al. (2005), *Case Analysis in Clinical Ethics* (Cambridge: Cambridge University Press).

Chadwick, R. et al. (1997), *The Right to Know and the Right Not to Know* (Aldershot: Ashgate).

Crosthwaite, J. (1998), 'Gender and Bioethics', in H. Kuhse and P. Singer (eds), *A Companion to Bioethics* (Oxford: Blackwell), 32–40.

Human Genetics Commission (2007), *More Genes Direct. A Report on Developments in the Availability, Marketing and Regulation of Genetic Tests Supplied Directly to the Public.* London <www.hgc.gov.uk>.

Konrad, M. (2005), *Narrating the New Predictive Genetics. Ethics, Ethnography and Science* (Cambridge: Cambridge University Press).

Manson, N.C. and O'Neill, O. (2007), *Rethinking Informed Consent in Bioethics* (Cambridge: Cambridge University Press).

Ricoeur, P. (1963), *Le Volontaire et l'involontaire* (Paris: Aubier).

Rehmann-Sutter, C. (forthcoming), '"... it is her problem; not ours." – Contributions of Feminist Bioethics to the Mainstream', in J.L. Scully et al. (eds), *Feminist Bioethics* (Baltimore: Johns Hopkins University Press).

Rose, N. (2007), *The Politics of Life Itself. Biomedicine, Power, and Subjectivity in the Twenty-first Century* (Princeton: Princeton University Press).

Toulmin, S. (1961), *Foresight and Understanding. An Enquiry into the Aims of Science* (Indianapolis: Indiana University Press).

Wexler, N.S. (1989), 'The Oracle of DNA', in L.P. Rowland et al. (eds), *Molecular Genetics in Diseases of Brain, Nerve and Muscle* (Oxford: Oxford University Press), 428–442.

PART 1
Setting the Scene

The Right to Know and the Right Not to Know is the title of a collection of chapters, edited by Ruth Chadwick, Mairi Levitt and Darren Shickle 12 years ago, on the ethical and philosophical implications of genetic screening (Avebury Series of Philosophy, Ashgate 1997). This book shaped the discussion and gained wide academic reputation. The first chapter of the present book is written by the first editor of the former, philosopher *Ruth Chadwick*. She outlines the main trends through which the debates have moved since the publication of her earlier book, and exposes a catalogue of problems to be discussed when considering a new set of ethical perspectives and approaches, all retaining the right to know and the right not to know as a key entrance formula for identifying and understanding ethical issues of genetic testing and screening.

Barbara Katz Rothman opens a sociological perspective on the evaluation of ethical issues in genetic counselling. It cannot be taken for granted, she writes, that some aspects are highlighted as 'ethical dilemmas' while others remain just ordinary practice. The social construction that precedes the philosophical analysis has to be recognized in the bioethical analysis. She raises the question of why the right to know or not to know is the appropriate or even unique frame for understanding the nature of such dilemmas.

Hansjakob Müller, as a practitioner of medical genetics in Switzerland, visualizes the framework in which genetic counselling usually takes place. He defines the necessary requirements for good genetic counselling from a professional perspective, and observes that in everyday medical routine there are many difficulties and constraints due to institutional limits, and lack of time, financial resources and also of knowledge to fulfil high ethical standards. Pre-symptomatic (predictive) tests should only be made available via consultation though a doctor experienced in this field. Laypersons, who are often also emotionally involved, are not capable of defining the correct indication for a genetic test, and are also not competent in the interpretation of the emerging results.

Chapter 1

The Right to Know and the Right Not to Know – Ten Years On

Ruth Chadwick

Over ten years ago, 1997 saw the publication of *The Right to Know and the Right Not to Know*, edited by myself together with Mairi Levitt and Darren Shickle (Chadwick et al. 1997). Although it was in fact one of the outputs of the Euroscreen project funded by the European Commission (Euroscreen 1, 1994–6; Euroscreen 2, 1996–9), it had not been planned at the outset: the theme emerged from our work towards other objectives. Explicit discussion of this theme, although discussed in relation to specific dilemmas, for example, concerning what circumstances, if any, justify disclosure in genetic counselling, was at the time less prominent than it has since become. In this chapter I attempt to outline the main trends and ways in which the debate has moved on in the intervening time. These ways can, I think, be classified into three groups, arising from changes in *context*, changes in *issues* and changes in *ethical approaches*.

Changes in Context

The first contextual change that must be mentioned is the completion of the mapping and sequencing of the human genome. This is important for the right to know and the right not to know in at least two ways. First, attention turned to the significance of the information that had been produced, and also returned to issues of genetic determinism, The discovery that humans have far fewer genes than had previously been supposed – only about 25,000 instead of 100,000 – led to the suggestion that genetic determinism had been proved false, in so far as the genes themselves could not explain the complexity of human beings. Any discussion of the right to know and the right not to know has to have regard to all these issues as a backdrop, because if genes *did* determine then that might affect the arguments concerning rights to know and not to know. In addition to the human genome, the sequencing of the genomes of other species has facilitated the development of comparative genomics, which affects the context in which we come to terms with information in the human genome.

The second contextual factor is the development of new or enhancement of existing technologies. There have been developments in preimplantation genetic diagnosis, but also considerable advances in sequencing technologies, facilitating multiplex testing and the move towards whole genome sequencing of individuals. Thus the scope of what can be tested for and when has been considerably enlarged.

The third contextual factor, which has arguably affected the debate as much if not more than any of the others, has been the development of large-scale population genetic research involving the establishment of biobanks. Alongside the much discussed national initiatives planned or launched, for example in Iceland, Estonia and the United Kingdom, there has been increasing recognition of the scale of biobanking of different kinds, including disease-specific collections, regional collections and international initiatives. In addition to biobanks that include sample collections, moreover, other kinds of databases have to be considered, such as those involved in the Human Variome Project, examining the mutations in the genome. The Ethics Committee of the Human Genome Organisation defined a human genomic database in the following way, which makes clear the variety of databases that might be at stake:

> A genomic database is a collection of data arranged in a systematic way so as to be searchable. Genomic data can include inter alia, nucleic acid and protein sequence variants (including neutral polymorphisms, susceptibility alleles to various phenotypes, pathogenic mutations), and polymorphic haplotypes. (Human Genome Organisation 2002)

These developments have at the very least added a new dimension to the right to know and the right not to know discussion. The general features of the change might be characterized in different ways. Elsewhere, I have written about the move out of the clinic and into the public arena; the move from 'I' to 'we' in discussion of the issues (Chadwick 2004). The ongoing tension between the interests of the individual and the collective has been played out afresh in relation to biobanks. It has been suggested that as far as ethical discussion is concerned, the traditional focus on the individual has been replaced by a new focus on public health ethics (see, for example, Knoppers 2005). This claim needs to be treated with caution, especially in its relevance to the topic of this chapter. There are other reasons, beyond public health genetics, that account for a greater focus on public health: concerns about the rising incidence of obesity for example. Beyond that, however, bioethics has arguably always dealt with public health issues: the ongoing debates about allocation of health care resources are a case in point. The debates about the scope of bioethics aside, however, it remains the case that discussions of biobanks and ethics have challenged ethical thinking in relation to the rights claims of individuals. This trend promises to become even more intense in line with developments towards the linking of national biobanks to form international initiatives. These at the very least add a layer of complexity to the protection of the individual rights at stake.

The fourth contextual change to which I wish to draw attention refers to social and political developments beyond the genome itself. This has at least two aspects.

First, in the post 9/11 world, concerns about security have had a significant impact upon debates about privacy. The extent to which there can and should be a trade-off between privacy and other values such as security is a live issue not only in genomics but also in relation to such developments as biometric identification technologies. This is requiring scholars to revisit the concept of privacy itself.

Lastly, but not least, the extent to which debates about science have become public debates, has increased over the last 10 years, with the increasing recognition that public engagement should move upstream. This phenomenon is related to the right to know/not to know debate in so far as the public or different publics might claim a right to know what options are on the table at a much earlier stage than the downstream offer of a test. Rather, it might be argued that their awareness of, and input to, the discussion of the relevant issues should take place at the stage when decisions are being taken about research that will ultimately lead to the offer of particular tests.

Changes in Issues

Despite all these changes in context, it would be inaccurate to say that there has been a wholesale change in the issues now being confronted regarding the right to know and the right not to know – some of the dilemmas remain in place – the issue of what to do in the light of a finding of non-paternity, for example, remains. It is important to recognize, however, the areas in which new issues have emerged.

In the Clinic: Carrier Status

As regards issues in the clinic, a question that has become more prominent relates to carrier status, in relation to both newborn screening and preimplantation diagnosis. In the past, carrier status was largely of relevance to the reproductive decisions of couples. They may have wanted to know their carrier status before proceeding to a pregnancy, or, if both were carriers, have been anxious to find out if a foetus had inherited a recessive gene from both parents. A termination of a pregnancy would not typically have been sought, or even been an option on the table, for carrier status. Where preimplantation diagnosis is available, however, the selection of an embryo without carrier status is a possibility. This is even further away from the idea of having the children God gives, spoken of eloquently by Jørgen Husted in the 1997 volume (Husted 1997), than was previously the case. The more that carrier status is held to be relevant in contexts such as this, however, the more it may appear to be relevant in others. Thus in the case of newborn screening there is an issue as to whether parents have a right to know the carrier status of their child, even though the rationale for newborn screening is to detect conditions for which early treatment can be offered. The issues surrounding newborn screening, whether or not for carrier status, are also affected by developments in multiplex testing – to what extent is the parent's right to know, as well as the child's present and future rights, related to the range of conditions for which screening is offered?

Biobanks

In relation to population genomic research involving biobanks, one of the most prominent emerging issues has been the extent to which individuals have the right to feedback regarding results from research on their samples. There are at least two distinct questions – the actual policies of biobank initiatives, on the one hand, and the principles involved, on the other. Biobanks in different countries have taken different stances on this, so the discussion here will be limited to the kinds of arguments appealed to. Considerations in favour of the view that individuals either do not or should not be regarded as having such a right include, first, that the information is likely to be of little value to the individual. Raw research data may not provide information of any real benefit: it may be unclear what the significance is. From an ethical point of view, an argument against a *right* also follows from the informed consent, involved – if individuals have agreed to participate knowing that there is to be no feedback, then they do not have a right to it – there is no legitimate expectation of a contractual or quasi-contractual sort. Based on considerations of this sort, there is a view that information provided about research on samples provided to biobanks should be limited to general research results, and not to specific information.

On the other hand, however, whatever the facts of the informed consent, there is a moral argument for a residual obligation to offer feedback of the following sort. If A has information which could be potentially life-saving to, or even significantly relevant to the future health of, person B, then A has a moral obligation to offer that information. While this could be argued against by appealing, for example, to a purported moral difference between harming B and not going out of one's way to help B, the context in which the information is sought and possessed arguably affects the issues. These individuals have volunteered to participate for the public good – if information is discovered which is material to their welfare, to withhold it could be construed not only as an omission but also as a harm. If they are displaying solidarity to their community, are there not moral considerations of solidarity for supporting them in return?

This discussion is integrally linked to another, the issues concerning how information gathered by biobanking initiatives is held and stored, including the specifics of anonymization and coding. Much has been written about the very confusing terminology surrounding these questions (Knoppers and Saginur 2005). Simply, the main issues relevant to the right to know and the right not to know debate turn on the extent to which it is possible to link data to identifiable individuals. If it is not, then the previous issue, concerning feedback, would not even arise, for it would not be possible to trace the particular individual involved.

If samples are completely anonymized, and it is not possible to link the data to be gleaned from them to individuals, then their value in research terms is considerably reduced. But as has been frequently pointed out, where DNA is concerned there is no such thing as complete loss of identifiability – DNA is, after all, despite ongoing debates about its usefulness in the forensic context, one of the primary identifiers, if not *the* primary one. It has been argued that, while it is commonplace to promise privacy to those who contribute to a biobank, in exchange for their participation, this is a promise that cannot be kept, because of the inherent properties of DNA in relation to identification mentioned above, in addition to increasingly sophisticated techniques of data mining (Lunshof et al. 2008).

Where there is less than complete anonymization, however, another issue arises, beyond that of the individual's right or otherwise to feedback on their data – and this is the question of who else has the right to access the data. There are questions here about, for example, the access of commercial companies and other third parties to data that have been collected as a public resource.

What of the right *not* to know in relation to population research? This might appear to be a non-issue – it appears from what has been said already that as far as the individual is concerned, the burden of proof is upon those who would seek to know, or seek to disclose, rather than the other way round. However, this is not clear cut. In so far as population genetic research produces results which characterize groups in particular ways, then individuals may be made aware of factors which they would have preferred not to know about, in so far as they identify with a group in question.

Identity

These considerations raise the very large issue of the role of identity in the right to know and right not to know debates. It was suggested in the 1997 volume that there may be a right not to know genetic information on the grounds that it may constitute a threat to the individual's sense of their identity. Despite the fact that genetic determinism has taken a knock in the light of the results of the Human Genome Project, genetic information may still be *perceived* as a very important constituent of individual or collective identity (Chadwick 1999). Developments in the last decade have arguably added new ways in which, and increased the extent to which, this is the case.

Collective identity, for example, may be affected in a variety of ways. A prominent example has been the arguments put forward by disability rights organizations in opposition to the characterization of particular conditions as disorders, combined with the seeking of measures to 'cure' them. There are at least two strands of thought to be disentangled here. The first is the concern that attempts to eliminate or cure genetic conditions will lead to a society that is less tolerant of disability. This is typically countered by an argument that the object of these attempts is not the people but the conditions. At this point the second strand comes into play, which is that it is not possible to distinguish these two elements, because their identity is dependent upon their genetic condition.

Beyond the relatively familiar debates surrounding genetic conditions of a health-affecting sort, however, other developments such as behavioural genomics and genetic ancestry tracing can have far-reaching implications for individuals' sense of themselves and have the potential to affect social and political rights in addition to their relevance to the right to know and not to know. Comparative genomics has further identity implications: for our self-identity *as a species* in relation to others. This may be perceived as threatening in some way, as is the prospect, for some, of hybrid embryos.

Personal Health

One promised outcome of population genomic research has been personalized health advice, in the context of both medication and nutrition. Pharmacogenomics aims to identify the genetic factors involved in drug response and to facilitate the avoidance of adverse drug reactions. Nutrigenomics plays an analogous role in relation to food and food ingredients, enabling personalized nutritional advice for optimum health. In the case of pharmacogenomics, the argument for a right to know is clear: it makes sense to say that if someone's genetic make-up is such that they have a higher than normal risk of responding adversely to a particular drug, then they have a right to know that they should not take it. It has also been argued that this kind of genetic information is less sensitive than other types of genetic information – the fact that someone should not take drug B has less potential to be damaging, if disclosed inappropriately, than information that they have a genetic predisposition to developing a late onset condition, for example. However, this argument depends on the assumption that the drug-related information is not linked or linkable to other more sensitive information, in the following way. While it might appear that the right *not* to know argument would not apply in relation to susceptibility to drug toxicity, in the event of multiplex testing, however, it might in principle be possible to test at the same time for predisposition to a disease and for susceptibility to toxicity for the recommended treatment. Then the question arises as to whether having this information is a benefit or a burden, because this could be, in effect, analogous to the situation where there is *no* treatment available. In such a case the argument for a right not to know does come into play.

In principle, in the context of nutrigenomics, there is also an argument for a right to know diet-related genetic information in so far as it could be of benefit to health prospects. However, there is more scepticism about the value of the information in nutrigenomics (Müller and Kersten 2003). Whereas drugs are well characterized substances acting on specific targets in the body, foodstuffs are far more complicated, and the difficulty of establishing reliable associations is therefore greater. Nevertheless even in the pharmacogenomics context there has been concern about achieving sufficient statistical power to ensure the reliability and replicability of association studies, and calls for oversight of these (Human Genome Organisation 2007).

While the prospect of tailored dietary advice may seem attractive, there are also arguments for a right not to know here. While some may see the provision of such personal information as empowering, there may be concerns about political agendas behind it, such as putting responsibility for health squarely on the shoulders of individuals. This is an issue, for example, in the light of the purported obesity problem. Providing individuals with information, including genetic information, may be promoted in the name of choice, but there is a question as to whether what is at stake is the freedom to make *any* choice or whether there is a presupposition that there is a 'right' choice, leading to being held responsible for wrong choices in particular.

One concern about the turn towards personalized health advice based on genetic information is that it represents a 'boutique' model of health care which fits with societies which demonstrate an individualistic culture and sufficient resources to afford it (Daar and Singer 2005). It has been argued, however, that pharmacogenomics, in particular, may have important benefits for developing countries, perhaps by resuscitating drugs which have been taken off the market on the ground of adverse reactions. In the light of population genetic research they may be found to be suitable for specific population groups (Daar and Singer 2005; Human Genome Organisation 2007). Here we find a potential 'right to know' argument that is not based on individualism, but rather a group right to information which will facilitate access to medicines.

Public Goods

This type of argument is in line with patterns of argument that emphasize the genome as the common heritage of humanity, or genomics as a global public good (see, for example, Chadwick and Wilson 2004). The thrust of this type of thinking is to move away from thinking in terms of the rights of the individual person, and the rights of commercial entities, to seek a just and equitable distribution of the benefits of genomic research. In so far as the Human Genome Project produces knowledge that is a potential benefit, the argument goes, this should be available to all; and this depends on access to knowledge. It therefore can be seen as a type of right to know argument.

Whole Genome Sequencing

Another new development is the prospect of whole genome sequencing made possible by the new developments in technology. The new generation of sequencing technologies massively increases the density of analyses that can be performed in a single run, as compared with conventional sequencing. But what is meant by 'whole genome' here?

> Clearly for diagnostic purposes the vast majority of the genome is not particularly useful since no meaningful clinical interpretation can be applied to most variation

> detected. We could define 'whole genome' as all the coding exons in the genome or perhaps more usefully a subset of these we are interested in for diagnostic investigation. (Mattocks 2008, 49)

While for the near future targeted investigations are likely to remain necessary, the prospect of whole genome sequencing changes the scope of what is talked about in the right to know and right not to know debate. While there have always been issues concerning disclosure of incidental findings (for example, non-paternity), the possibilities of whole genome sequencing open up the prospect of knowing everything in the genome. There is of course a question about the extent to which the volume of information will be meaningful, at least in the early stages of this development, but are there grounds for thinking that the privacy concerns are increased? If there is concern about access to knowledge about one's genome, does the volume of information that may be accessed give rise to a parallel increase in the concerns about privacy? There may be concerns influenced by a residual genetic determinist view, that to know someone's genome is to know everything about the person. Different ways to counter this particular concern are available. One is to argue against genetic determinism, already arguably undermined; another is to try to allay concerns about privacy. The advent of 'celebrity genomes' are one instance of this: where key figures willingly publish their genomes to illustrate a different attitude towards privacy and disclosure, but such plans have not been met without some alarm (Check 2007).

Changes in Ethical Approaches

It is not necessary to subscribe to full-blown genetic exceptionalism to take the view that there have been developments in ethical thinking alongside the developments in genomics and in the social and political context in which these have taken place. In the early nineties the issues surrounding disclosure and rights to know and not to know tended to fall into two main types: conflicts of interest in the genetic counselling setting, where one person's reluctance to disclose information might have implications for another's right to know it; and situations where an individual had to deal with predictive information, concerning which they would prefer not to have knowledge. So discussion turned on the circumstances in which it could be right to disclose; and choice in relation to tests. The ethical considerations at stake included, primarily, individual autonomy, confidentiality and beneficence. In the 1997 volume, for example, Jørgen Husted drew attention to two conceptions of autonomy, a 'thin' one which was typically used to support the benefits of genetic information; and a 'thick' one which supported a right not to know (Husted 1997).

The arguments of the time are still rehearsed in different contexts, but I want to draw attention to two trends since that time. The first is towards a greater emphasis on solidarity and equity. Thus the HUGO Statement on Pharmacogenomics, Solidarity and Equity states:

> the Committee considers it urgent that the ethical principles of solidarity and equity be given increased attention:
>
> > Solidarity: Because of shared vulnerabilities, people have common interests and moral responsibilities to each other. Willingness to share information and to participate in research is a praiseworthy contribution to society.
> >
> > Equity: To reduce health inequalities between different populations, and to work towards equal access to care is an important prerequisite for implementing genomic knowledge for the benefit of society. (Human Genome Organisation 2007)

This emphasis is thus on information sharing rather than on greater protection of individual rights.

The second, not unrelated. trend is towards rethinking the concept of privacy. In 1997 Tony McGleenan asked if there should be a genetic privacy law. In a different context, it has been claimed that even if we could rely on public institutions to adhere completely to regulations on data protection, there is still a need to look at the issues in different ways. In the genomics context, there has been a suggestion that emphasis on privacy should be replaced by the concept of open consent (Lunshof et al. 2008). The concept of open consent is used in the context of the Personal Genome Project, which aims to build a framework for the development and evaluation of personal genome technologies. Towards this end, open consent implies that research participants accept that their data may be included in an open access database with no guarantees of privacy and confidentiality (Lunshof et al. 2008).

Prospects for the Future

So how is the debate on the right to know and the right not to know likely to develop? The pace of development of the technologies is very fast: ethical thinking is faced with the move towards greater 'personalization', on the one hand, and more global developments, on the other, in relation both to the facilitating of international biobanks (requiring thinking about harmonization of standards and ethics) and to claims for sharing the benefits that genomics has to offer on a global scale. The discussion of rights to know and not to know has to be continually renegotiated in the light of these interests in tension.

References

Chadwick, R. et al. (eds) (1997), *The Right to Know and the Right Not to Know* (Aldershot: Avebury).

Chadwick, R. (1999), 'Gene Therapy and Personal Identity', in G.K. Becker (ed.), *The Moral Status of Persons: Perspectives on Bioethics* (Amsterdam: Rodopi), 183–94.

Chadwick, R. (2004), 'Telling the truth about genomics', *Communication and Medicine* 1:2, 193–199.

Chadwick, R. and Wilson, S. (2004) 'Genomic databases as global public goods?' *Res Publica* 10:2, 23–24.

Check, E. (2007), 'Celebrity genomes alarm researchers', *Nature* 447, 358–9.

Daar, A. and Singer, P. (2005), 'Pharmacogenetics and geographical ancestry: Implications for drug development and global health', *Nature Reviews Genetics* 6, 241–246.

Human Genome Organisation (HUGO) (2002), *Statement on Human Genomic Databases* (London: HUGO).

Human Genome Organisation (HUGO) (2007), *Statement on Pharmacogenomics, Solidarity and Equity* (London: HUGO).

Husted, J. (1997), 'Autonomy and a Right Not to Know', in R. Chadwick et al. (eds), *The Right to Know and the Right Not to Know* (Aldershot: Avebury).

Knoppers, B.M. (2005), 'Of genomics and public health: Building public "goods"?', *Canadian Medical Association Journal* 173:10, 1185–6.

Knoppers, B.M. and Saginur, M. (2005), 'The babel of genetic data terminology', *Nature Biotechnology* 23:8, 925–927.

Lunshof, J. et al. (2008), 'From genetic privacy to open consent', *Nature Reviews Genetics* 9, 406–11.

Mattocks, C. (2008), 'Diagnostic application of new sequencing technologies', *Newsletter of the British Society for Human Genetics*, 28 February, 47–50.

McGleenan, T. (1997), 'Should There be a Genetic Privacy Law?', in R. Chadwick et al. (eds), *The Right to Know and the Right Not to Know* (Aldershot: Avebury).

Müller, M. and Kersten, S. (2003), 'Nutrigenomics, goals and strategies', *Nature Reviews Genetics* 4, 315–22.

Chapter 2
Genetic Counselling: Placing the Room in Context

Barbara Katz Rothman

The Metaphor of the Room

Think of the new genetics as a room. (It's not a perfect metaphor – there are none – but bear with me a moment.) Now think of all of the critics of the new genetics as having come into that room through various doorways. Some came in through public health: they were working on public health issues and this room caught their attention. Some came in via medical sociology. A huge number came in through the doorway of bioethics, peering down at their beneficence/non-maleficence/justice/autonomy grid, trying to map this new room on to that scheme. Quite a few came in via feminism. I personally came through a nearby door, midwifery, leaning up against the feminist door but never quite merged. Some came rolling, limping, helping each other through the door of disability. The historians had a door, with eugenics almost blocking the way. And there are more: cultural studies, media studies, psychiatry and psychology, science studies, environmentalism – the list goes on. Each of these are 'contexts', ways of placing and understanding the new genetics and the genetic counselling that goes on in that room.

The door that I came in encouraged me to look at prenatal testing and see the woman in the room, the pregnant woman, as the centre, the heart of what was happening. Her joy, pain, suffering, relief, anguish, fear, desperation, hope – it was her experience that was at the centre of the room I saw (Katz Rothman 1986). Not so for most Americans and maybe not so for most people outside of that midwifery-world-view. Most saw the fetus there in the centre, and the pregnant woman in whom it resides as variously a barrier, conduit, threat or protector.

Defining Ethical Problems

When we look in that room, the space in the new genetics where genetic counselling takes place, some of what happens is understood to be ethically problematic. When I think about the ethical issues in genetic counselling, what most interests me is how some things get defined as 'ethical dilemmas' and other things as ordinary practice, ordinary facts of life. In the context of the US, anything that has anything whatsoever to do with abortion is definitionally an ethical or moral dilemma. The fetus, it seems, is at the ethical centre of the American universe. When I was a teenager, we often used the word 'moral' to refer to sexuality. To be virginal, was to be moral. Some girls were very moral and some were just totally immoral, which meant that they 'went all the way'. If we talked about some girl being not so moral, no one thought that perhaps she had injured someone, or was a thief – it was completely obvious to us all that we were talking about her sexual conduct. The naïvetè, the narrow-mindedness, the just plain-old silliness of that is of course striking to me now – but hardly more so than when the word 'ethical' is a code for abortion.

When prenatal testing was first introduced, it was immediately understood to raise 'ethical dilemmas' because it involved abortion. What I have seen in my years of work on prenatal diagnosis is that if a woman was not going to consider abortion, then prenatal testing was seen as 'just information'. This might raise any number of concerns about what the information might mean to her, to her family and to the forthcoming child. For so many of these conditions no treatment, before or after birth, exists and no clear management path opens up. Parents learn the baby will have or may develop eventually this-or-that condition, and they must make of it what they will. But ethicists seemed to be able to ignore all of that, as long as abortion was not involved. The problems were 'psychological', sometimes 'medical', but not 'ethical'.

When you enter that room through the door marked 'access to information', the entire debate appears to be about a right to know, and – to a considerably smaller extent – a right not to know certain things. The right to have or not have information in the context of a pregnancy is – most especially in the context of the US, forever entangled in the abortion debate. Moving the discussion from the right to information about a fetus to information about a born child effectively bypassed the abortion discussion: once the child is born and among us, there is a powerful drive towards information. Even when very little good can come of that information, information per se is a widely held value in American and European society. As a new parent, gathering information about the child becomes an unquestioned good.

Beyond Abortion: Newborn Screening

That is the path through which newborn screening has so easily slipped into practice. Rachel Grob, who is doing one of the first major studies of the impact of newborn screening (Grob 2005) points out that newborn screening is the single most widely utilized form of genetic testing in the US, with more than four million infants being tested each year. That means that four million families are tested, because for many of these conditions it is only when an affected baby is born into the family that parents and extended kin learn that future children are at risk.

Newborn screening started, as such things usually do, with one useful and interesting medical breakthrough. Robert Guthrie developed a laboratory procedure that enabled screening for Phenylketonuria, known more usually as 'PKU'. PKU is a metabolic disorder. Infants born with this condition cannot metabolize the ordinary phenylalanines of milk, and become severely mentally retarded. With a special – and very restricted – diet introduced immediately after birth, the damage can be prevented. If one waits till symptoms appear, the damage will be irreparable. With Guthrie's test, newborn diagnosis was possible, and the mental retardation caused by PKU became preventable.

With heavy lobbying by groups such as the March of Dimes, and those representing people with mental retardation, something really astonishing happened. The test, a 'heel stick' – blood drawn from the heel of a newborn baby within a couple of days after birth – became not just one more routine medical procedure, but something entirely new in the US: a legally mandated test for a non-infectious disease. The ordinary medical standards for a diagnostic intervention are entirely bypassed: informed consent, any information or any consent for that matter, is not necessary. Consent is not required, and a refusal of consent is not an option. Whatever the parents' opinions, the test will be done. So the law states.

That is where the situation stood for quite some time. And then came the genetics revolution. More and more genetic conditions became diagnosable, and more of those conditions were added to the various state lists for newborn screening. In the US, each state makes its own laws covering medical practice. Just a couple of years ago, an average of eight conditions were required for newborn screening. Between 2004 and 2005, Grob found it jumped up to an average of 20 – and no end is in sight. As the genetic testing technology develops, it is easily imaginable that each newborn will soon be tested for hundreds of conditions.

And isn't that a good thing? Is there a reason one would refuse PKU testing after all? It seems so straightforward, so unproblematic ethically. With newborn screening there is no question of abortion, no fetus to be saved or to be spared a life of suffering. There is only a baby to be protected.

But once the mechanism was in place for state-mandated, required screening, it was (one can see with hindsight) inevitable that the conditions to be screened for would expand. And expand. Parents are given more 'information' with less useful intervention available, less counselling in place, less support of all kinds. Rachel Grob, in her work, has focused mostly on Cystic Fibrosis screening. CF is a good example of everything PKU was not. CF is not one disease with one genetic cause, but a cluster of conditions with a variety of presentations. It is not preventable with one (yes drastic, but quite clear and simple to understand) preventative measure. With CF the genetic test gives one only guesses about what condition the baby will be in. Some babies are symptomatic even before birth, with pregnancy-related conditions raising the possibility of the diagnosis; some have, years after the newborn screening diagnosis, been retroactively 'undiagnosed', parents told that while genotypically the child has CF, phenotypically there is no disease there.

Grob's work, and work that she, Martine Hackett and I are currently doing (Katz Rothman et al. 2006), studies the paths by which states added more and more conditions to the list for required screening. If a baby in one state is diagnosed and parents feel that was a good thing, legislators in neighbouring states are pushed to add the condition to the list. One well-known or politically active person has a child with a particular condition, and the pressure is on to add that to the list as well. The original logic was only to test for things that were preventable with interventions that had to be started early. The logic began to fade away as personal stories took over and more and more conditions got added. At some point, given how many and varied the conditions on the list are, it becomes only reasonable to add this one more and that one more – and so it goes. With the technological developments for testing increasing, but the confidence in genetic predictability decreasing, we are at a funny moment. We will know more and more about less and less, have more and more genetic diagnostic results with less and less certain prognosis.

That is a problem, I think most would agree. But is it an ethical dilemma? The language of 'dilemmas' asks us to look for choice-points, places where decisions can be made about gathering, disclosing or using information. State-mandated newborn screening bypasses all of that: what is left is a mopping-up operation. The genetic counselling that is done after a newborn diagnosis is not about choices and decisions. Or at least not about choices for this particular child. It may well be that one of the latent functions of newborn screening – perhaps intended and perhaps not overtly intended – will be to prevent the births of later babies with the same condition. And that, of course, brings us round back again to the abortion question. If one of the purposes or one of the unintended consequences of newborn screening is to encourage prenatal diagnosis and selective abortion in future pregnancies, then I believe it will be seen, in the American context certainly, as an ethical concern.

It may well be, my conspiratorially sensitized mind thinks, that prevention of later births is indeed the basis on which newborn screening is being developed to such a degree. A programme to prevent the births of diagnosed fetuses with particular potential disabilities is simply out of the question in the US today. But mine is not a welcoming, loving, caring society, that offers all of its people the things they need to have a rich and full life. Mine is not a country that welcomes each baby by meeting its needs, but one that expects individual parents to do what they can without much help from the state. People are asked to have only the children that they can 'afford'. Mothers on public assistance who have another child are told that they cannot expect the state to take care of feeding or housing it. Can it really be that this same country welcomes the (expensive, resource-consuming) sick or disabled children of poor parents?

So one possibility is that newborn screening is a eugenics program in some fairly effective disguise. The newborns screened are not the real target, but rather it is the decisions their mothers make about future pregnancies that are at issue. It need not be one or the other, of course – newborn screening is a well-meaning if sometimes muddled attempt to help the diagnosed babies lead healthier lives. But we know that there are many, many other things we could be doing if our goal was the health of children. Do we want our children to be healthy? There is no question.

We each want what is best for our children. And how can we do that? There are of course many ways. Consider how little children, low to the ground as they are, are disproportionately the victims of cars. They get run over. We know these accidents occur right in their very neighbourhoods, even their own driveways. My husband once ran over a tricycle in our driveway, and I will never forget the sight of that empty mangled little trike – and what it might have meant.

But if I suggest that perhaps we should separate our residential space from cars, provide, say, centralized parking a few streets away, in America certainly, people think I am being foolish, utopian, unrealistic. Search for a gene that causes (less) damage and (fewer) deaths of little children than do cars, and that makes great sense. Find such a gene and it seems reasonable to start testing newborns so that we can try to treat it as best we can, as early as we can. Because of course we want to prevent the suffering of little children. But rearrange the parking? Get real! Do you know what that would cost? A revived public health movement is beginning again to move towards an ecological perspective, seeing infant mortality in particular as a health issue that has economic causes, and to move towards advocacy – political action as public health (private communication, Hackett 2006). We know that the best indicator of infant outcome is not the mother's genetic code, but her postal or 'zip' code – a good indicator of her socio-economic status. Want to improve infant health around the world? End poverty!

That is not the mainstream agenda. So it is not just the concern for health that drives the search for genetic causes of diseases in newborns, just as it was not the concern for health that drove the push for prenatal testing. The state – each individual state in the US, and the state as the larger concept of government – acts in its own economic interests. In the US, the economic interests of the state in prenatal diagnosis and selective abortion were blocked by the profound anti-abortion sentiment found in the US, by the Christian Right that supported the government that worked so hard to minimize its responsibility for the poor and the sick, and by the whole horrific history of eugenics. Newborn screening offers a neat way around that political problem, slipping in as no kind of dilemma at all, simply as ordinary practice, good medicine. The genetic counselling begins with the current child, with seemingly no ethical questions at all, only 'medical' ones – how best to treat, what symptoms to look for and what to expect of the genetic condition that has been diagnosed. Counselling for later pregnancies, with all of the ethical dilemmas that it is known to have, comes in after.

Beyond the Room

So let us go back now and open the door to the room: a woman is sitting there. Maybe she has a fetus growing in her now, maybe she has a new baby in her arms or waiting at home, maybe she has a hope of another baby to come some day. The genetic counsellor has the test results, the reading of the code, the molecular possibilities for any and all of those babies. The born one has a particular condition, the unborn one will have it, the one not-yet-conceived risks it. What goes on in that room is the interface of molecular genetics, economics, love, hope and fear.

I have been looking in that room, studying genetic screening, for over 20 years now. You would think, by now, I would know what to tell the woman and what to tell the counsellor, how to help them. And it is certainly the case that I have had plenty of opportunity to see counsellors behaving badly in there – pressuring women to have tests they do not want, tricking them into doing things they may well regret. And, while I have far more sympathy for the position they are in, I have also seen women behaving badly in that room, rejecting well-intentioned helpful advice without even considering it, blaming the bearer of bad tidings, refusing to 'face reality'. So yes, I do have some ideas about how these players could perhaps be kinder to each other in that room. But to me, as a sociologist, that just isn't the issue. Neither the women – and children and men – being tested nor the counsellors who advise or 'non-directively inform' them have much control over the things that really matter. They cannot do much to fix broken bodies, and less to fix broken worlds. In a society and a world that does not care for all of its people, that does not allow its mothers to love their babies no matter how damaged, expensive or difficult they may be, nothing the genetic counsellor can do is really going to make much difference.

The door the sociologist enters asks us to see where the room is placed. Sociology asks to consider the context always, to take what C. Wright Mills called the leap of the 'Sociological Imagination' (1959), to see the ways that individuals are placed in societies, to see that we each live in a moment of historical time and place. If we are going to make it a better world, it is not going to happen inside the room.

References

Grob, R. (2005), *Testing Baby*, revised Doctoral Dissertation (City University of New York).

Katz Rothman, B. (1986), *The Tentative Pregnancy. Prenatal Diagnosis and the Future of Motherhood* (New York: The Viking Press).

Katz Rothman, B. et al. (2006–2008), *Heel Sticks and Amnios: Disjunctures and Discrepancies in Prenatal and Newborn Genetic Screening*, A Health Investigators Award Project of the Robert Wood Johnson Foundation.

Mills, C.W. (1959), *The Sociological Imagination* (New York: Oxford University Press).

Chapter 3
Genetic Counselling: Clinical Settings and Constraints

Hansjakob Müller

This chapter describes the principal aims and requirements of genetic counselling from the point of view of a medical geneticist. Disclosure dilemmas can occur because doctors ask themselves, in the light of the increasing number of genetic tests and the growing demand for autonomy of the people seeking counselling, whether they may be placing an unbearable burden on these persons, with all the freedom of choice and personal responsibility this autonomy entails.

Introduction

With a few exceptions[1] the term 'genetic counselling' is employed by the medical community and also appears in legal texts or guidelines of various international and national institutions, without a clear concept or in-depth definition of what it really signifies. There are a number of reasons for this lack of clarity. Opinions are divided on the content and purpose of genetic counselling. For some, the medical and scientific aspects should be emphasized, for others, the psycho-social implications are more important. Opinions also differ as to who is entitled to offer genetic counselling: should it be only doctors with more or less clearly defined specialized qualifications or other staff that have the necessary qualifications but are from the nursing, psychology or social sciences sector? In the USA, genetic

1 For example, Switzerland's *Federal Law on Genetic Testing of Humans* describes genetic counselling in general (Art. 14) as non-directive and skilled. (1) Counselling should only take into account the individual and familial situation of the person concerned, not general social interests. It should consider possible psychological and social implications of a test result for the person concerned and her or his family (2). (3) The person concerned, or, if they are not competent, the legal representative must be informed in particular about (a) goal, nature and validity of the examination and the possibility of further measures, (b) eventual risks of an examination and frequency as well as nature of the disorder to be diagnosed; (c) the possibility of an unexpected result of the examination; (d) possible physical and psychological burdens; (e) the possibility that costs for examination and measures to be covered; (f) the possibilities of getting support related to implications of the results; (g) the significance of the diagnosed disorder as well as the available prophylactic of therapeutical measures.

counsellors are certified by the American Board of Genetic Counseling.[2] Since a patient's understanding of the results and consequences of a genetic analysis forms an integral part of genetic testing, the European organization EuroGentest[3] also aims to improve the quality of genetic counselling services. The Council of Europe is expected to publish, in the near future, recommendations on the impact of genetics on the health care services and training of health care professionals. The intent is to profit from progress of modern genetics within the health systems of all member states.

Furthermore, a new era of medicine, know as 'molecular medicine' or 'biomedicine', has just begun in which we are constantly increasing our genetic knowledge about human health and disease on a molecular, that is biochemical, level. The more we understand about human genetics, the greater its impact on health care will be. As a consequence of this development the number of genetic analyses increases. These tests are not only used for diagnosing and classifying an illness that has already manifested in a subject, but also for the prevention of such disorders (prenatal and presymptomatic diagnosis). Moreover, genetic tests are a precondition for so-called 'personalized medicine', which aims at selecting and apportioning medication in accordance with the patient's individual characteristics in order to improve efficiency and to avoid undesirable side effects. It is therefore hardly surprising that even genetic counsellors are beginning to specialize: some focus on questions concerning prenatal diagnostics and reproductive medicine or paediatrics (dysmorphology, mental retardation, sensory impairments, metabolic disorders), and others concentrate on adult medicine (adult-onset disorders such as Huntington disease, myotonic dystrophy) or cancer genetics (hereditary breast-ovarian cancer, hereditary colorectal cancer).

The growing importance of genetics in medicine is recognized worldwide, as can be judged from the large number of scientific publications or the high attendance figures at genetic meetings. However, conditions for providing adequate medical care with a stronger emphasis on genetics differ greatly between countries. These differences apply first to the educational background of the entire staff involved in medical care, the availability of genetic counsellors with the appropriate training and of institutions specializing in medical genetics. Importantly the attitude of the medical staff and the public towards genetics also plays a part. Recent advances in genetics give rise to numerous hopes and promises for new medical treatments. However, fear is increased of a future characterized by exorbitant genetic testing and discrimination on the grounds of genetic characteristics. Of special concern is the testing of embryos, fetuses and children who may become the objects of unprofessional and unnecessary examinations that are carried out only to satisfy the curiosity and desires of parents.

Hence, the importance and the availability of genetic counselling should not be discussed only from a theoretical point of view, but should also take the practical

2 <http://www.abgc.net/>.

3 <http://www.eurogentest.org>.

implications and feasibility of such services into account. Idealized concepts, however attractive they may sound, lead to demands that cannot be fulfilled in the foreseeable future.

A Short History of Human Genetics and Genetic Counselling

Observations regarding the influence of heredity are as old as mankind itself. Scientifically based genetics began only in 1865 with the appearance of two publications: One by the Augustinian monk Johann Gregor Mendel (1822–1884) described the hereditary transmission of the characteristics of peas. The other by the doctor and mathematician Francis Galton (1822–1911) considered the transmission of human mental and character traits. Both scientists were well ahead of their contemporaries, because they did not only collect their findings but also classified them in a mathematical order, drawing up statistics for the first time. In the second half of the last century, technical innovations enormously accelerated scientific progress in the field of medical genetics. The advances included procedures for preparing and analyzing chromosomes, cell culture technology and somatic cell genetics, gene technology and above all modern bioinformatics (research in silico), which has opened up a whole range of new possibilities (McKusick 2001).

Advances in the perception and understanding of genetic phenomena have always been accompanied by eugenic considerations. This is hardly surprising, since such ideas were derived from the empirical experience gained from the breeding of animals and the cultivation of plants. Around 1900, Francis Galton, a cousin of Charles Darwin, and his fellow doctors feared that the future existence of mankind was threatened by the weakening of natural selection and that unfavourable hereditary dispositions would therefore increase. This led to the opinion that there existed not only a right but a duty to recommend 'eugenic' measures, which went as far as the forced sterilization of certain groups of people. The physician Alfred Ploetz (1860–1940) invented the German term 'Rassenhygiene' (racial hygiene) (Müller-Hill 1984). For him, this term described that part of medicine that is concerned with the 'hygiene' of the human race, as opposed to the then increasingly popular term 'general hygiene', which refers to the health of the individual person. The terrible events in Nazi-Germany show the extent of the scandalous aberrations to which scientists and doctors can be prone if they conform to the prevailing political climate.

The recognition of genetic counselling as a medical discipline in its own right is relatively recent, although the practice of offering genetic advice actually goes back a long way. For instance, the Babylonian Talmud, which was completed in the seventh century AD, contains a clear instruction that a mother must refuse the ritual circumcision of her son if two other sons have already died as a result of the rite (because uncontrollable bleeding equals haemophilia). Charles Davenport (1866–1944) of the Eugenics Records Office in New York began to give genetic advice as early as 1910. The first genetic counselling clinics were opened in the

US, in Michigan in 1940 and in Minnesota in 1941. In the UK, the Hospital for Sick Children in London set up the first such clinic in 1946. Sheldon C. Reed (1910–2003) coined the term 'genetic counselling' in 1947 and defined the following three requirements: 1) knowledge of human genetics; 2) respect for sensitivities, attitudes and reactions of clients; 3) teach and provide genetic information to the full extent known (Reed 1955). In 1975 the American Society of Human Genetics (ASHG) published a definition of genetic counselling which was to be adopted on repeated occasions later on. It implies a communication process and stipulates patient autonomy as the guiding principle. At the time, this attitude constituted a genuine paradigm shift. The paternalistic stance, which was aimed at preventing serious disabilities, was replaced by an individual, more psycho-social outlook. Genetic counselling was adapted to meet the needs and interests of individual counsellees and their families (see below).

Applied human genetics has thus experienced several paradigm shifts within a short time period. The aim of eugenics was to improve hereditary dispositions in the population by means of forced measures and direct influence. In the 1960s, it was prevention that became the main objective of genetics, employing a paternalistic approach aimed at reducing individual suffering and ensuring an economic use of resources (Hagard and Carter 1976). Today, emphasis is placed on providing decision-making guidance by means of non-directive counselling. However, this approach gives rise to the question of whether such a large degree of autonomy and individual responsibility does not place an unbearable burden on the counsellees. Is the idealized neutral transmission of medical and genetic information indeed feasible and desirable, especially considering the fact that we know only very little about the phenotypical impact of genomic variations/mutations and in most cases we cannot be sure of the efficiency and feasibility of the options we have at our disposal to combat such effects? It therefore becomes increasingly urgent to find solutions to the problem of disclosure dilemmas.

The Essence of Genetic Counselling

The field of genetic counselling is expanding rapidly, and the discipline is evolving more and more into a unique, multi-facetted component of health care service. Table 3.1 summarizes the indications for genetic counselling. The questions can have many different facets, such as diagnosis, cause, prognosis of a genetic disability/hereditary disorder in the patient as well as in an unborn or already born child, risk of development of the disease in a person whose family has a specific disease disposition, indication and performance of genetic laboratory testing, options to combat the genetic 'destiny' (preventive measures, management of severe symptoms, gene therapy).

Table 3.1 Reasons for applying for genetic counselling

Reasons for applying for genetic counselling
Congenital defects; inherited deformities
Mental retardation; problems at school
Disturbance of growth and development
Disorders of sexual development
Neurological and muscular diseases, severe sensory disorders
Metabolic disorders
Diseases of the blood (anaemias, impaired coagulation)
Tumour diseases occurring early, multifocal and/or in several family members
Prenatal screening/diagnostics
Inability to conceive/repeated spontaneous miscarriages
Marriage between members of the same family
Exposure to mutagenic and teratogenic substances (medication, viruses, radiation)

The most crucial step in any genetic consultation is to establish the correct diagnosis of a disorder or the predisposition that may lie behind it. If the diagnosis is incorrect, inappropriate or even misleading information could be given, leading to tragic consequences. Reaching a reliable diagnosis of a genetic disorder usually involves three fundamental steps: 1) recording an individual and family history; 2) carrying out a clinical examination; and 3) undertaking meaningful laboratory tests, including chromosome and molecular genetics analysis as well as other clinical investigations, for example with imaging procedures.

Peter Harper gives a succinct description of the multi-facetted aspects of genetic counselling (2004). Genetic counselling is the process by which patients or relatives at risk of a disorder that may be hereditary are advised of the consequences of the disorder, the probability of developing or transmitting it and the ways in which this may be prevented, avoided or ameliorated. A list of the individual elements of the processes can perhaps provide a clear idea of the substance of this definition (see Table 3.2). If possible, genetic counselling should include all the issues mentioned in this list. It should be characterized by communication, comprehension, care and confidentiality.

Table 3.2 The main elements of genetic counselling

- Definition of the needs and expectations of the counsellees, recognition of false perceptions
- Recording of individual and family case histories, if necessary including information on religious beliefs, social and ethnic background
- Drafting of a genealogical tree (at least a complete recording of first and second degree relatives)
- Evaluation of the existing clinical findings and clinical examination to clarify and/or specify the diagnosis (perhaps even including other family members)
- Clarification of the possibility of laboratory tests in order to identify the disposition that may lie behind the disease
- Listing of the medical aspects of the disorder in question (diagnosis, development of the disease, types of treatment), if necessary by means of a thorough literature research, including internet searches
- Recognition of inheritance patterns (significance, traceability and genetic transmission of the assumed disposition), identification of possible exogenous influences (teratogens, mutagens) and risk estimation
- Communication of the medical and genetic situation with empathy and explanation of the possible significance of the disease for the individuals concerned and, if applicable, their families
- Information on and discussion of available options and further measures, including legal implications and obligations of health insurance companies and health insurance funds
- Coordination of laboratory examinations and continuing medical care by contacting the general practitioner and the specialists required
- Support for decision-making and for the decisions made
- Documentation of the genetic counselling and written summary (counselling letter) for the counsellees and the experts involved

With regard to ethical issues, the action guides described in the book *The principles of Bioethics* (2001, first published in 1979) by Tom Beauchamp and James Childress have won broad acceptance. Procedural methods for specific situations can be defined and justified with the aid of four basic principles, although contradictions may occur regarding the interpretation of individual cases. The four principles are autonomy, beneficence, non-maleficence and justice.

Respect for autonomy stipulates a freedom of decision on the part of the counsellee and a right to privacy. Not only the right of self-determination (informed consent), but also the right not to know must be guaranteed. However, autonomy does not just mean that everyone can do or not do what they want to at the moment, but that every person assumes the responsibility for their own actions after the consultation. In their daily work, genetic counsellors are quite often confronted by individuals who do not seek autonomy at all. Instead they seek a counsellor who takes some of the responsibility off their shoulders and as an expert in the field actually makes specific suggestions as to what they should do. In addition, autonomy is also considerably restricted by directives and/or recommendations of relevant professional associations and other organizations.

The principle of beneficence demands acting in the patient's best interest, that is, providing the best possible care. This includes adequate, careful information about the counsellees, a perceptive recording of their individual situation and ensuring that patients receive the best possible assistance for the decisions they have to make for their own future and that of their families (coping). Care may also sometimes mean withholding certain information that would only cause confusion and anxiety.

Non-maleficence implies that counsellees should be in an improved condition following the consultation. Genuine quality checks of the counselling methods, the genetic diagnostic tests and the subsequent treatment all help to ensure that the interests of the patients are protected. It is also important to carefully prepare the patient for the discovery of a predisposition to a disease and to suggest effective preventive measures.

Justice signifies ensuring that all patients have equal access to genetic counselling and diagnostics, and a fair distribution of resources. Furthermore, a diagnosed disposition must not lead to discrimination of the person concerned.

One of the starting points for the search for legal rules applicable to genetic testing and screening may be found in the Convention for the Protection of Human Rights and Fundamental Freedoms of the Council of Europe. The legal provisions governing genetic counselling is discussed by Steel (this volume) and Wied et al. (this volume).

Preconditions for Genetic Counselling

The request for genetic counselling and testing must be voluntary. Genetic tests reveal something very personal that may determine not only the patient's own destiny, but also that of their relatives, especially their children. The importance of confidence and trust between the counsellee and the health professional can never be underestimated. Counsellees and counsellors must therefore be on the same 'wavelength' during the consultation.

The genetic counsellors are medical experts who are expected to have a multitude of other abilities apart from a profound knowledge of their speciality. They must prepare themself thoroughly for the consultation and take the necessary time to respond adequately to the counsellee's questions. In so doing, they must accept their attitudes and opinions. If requested, they can also voice their own personal point of view. They must communicate complex medical and genetic information in a scientifically correct manner, but also in a way that is easily comprehensible, balanced and truthful. This requires didactic skills. Since they work as part of a wider health care team, they must be on open, collegial terms with the other members of the team. They must never make condescending remarks about the observations of other members of the health care team. The genetic counsellor often has to play the role of patient advocate.

Counsellees are entitled to request other consultations or diagnostic tests, if necessary from another source (second opinion). In this book, several authors discuss the implications of this right. Counsellees should also be informed about self-support groups, which exist in large numbers today and which can offer considerable support and companionship. When they are first confronted with the diagnosis of a rare hereditary disease, people may feel very isolated. Within the support group they can find people who empathize, have specific knowledge of the disease and show solidarity.

Genetic registers provide a useful means of ensuring that effective contact can be maintained with all such relevant family members. However, there are strong and widespread reservations against such tools. The practice of creating and administrating genetic registers should be subjected to a systematic review.

Because of the complexity of all the issues discussed, the genetic counselling consultations must be thoroughly documented.

Constraints

Often the general public has only a moderate amount of knowledge of genetics. Unfortunately, media reports on genetic issues are not objective in many cases, and even in scientific journals new findings are frequently described in an exaggerated fashion. Science can never perform miracles. It is therefore desirable to provide the public with reliable information about genetic counselling and genetic testing.

Medical and genetic research has made such progress over the last few years that the amount of data and knowledge available can no longer be mastered by one person alone. The chief physician who knows everything no longer exists. Genetic services should bring together multidisciplinary groups of various medical and non-medical disciplines because close cooperation between all the experts that are involved in the care of an individual person is becoming more and more indispensable. Currently, this type of teamwork still needs to be fine-tuned in some cases. In many places, the team still lacks a pilot who can guide the counsellee from one expert to the next.

Primary care providers should have the necessary knowledge and skill to identify persons/patients with genetic problems, which is often not the case. They have to refer them to the appropriate genetic services. In-depth education in genetics should be given to the various groups of professionals involved in the medical care of the people concerned (physicians, human biologists, nurses, pharmacists, social workers, clinical psychologists and especially genetic counsellors). Existing specialist genetic centres thereby play a leading role in the dissemination of genetic knowledge and developments across the rest of health care services.

Genetic tests provide specific data on the characteristics of the genome. If the analysis was performed in a technically correct manner and analytical validity is ensured, this information can be accepted as reproducible and reliable. However, laboratory results must then be transformed into genetic information. This is only possible if the tests were performed in accordance with a clearly defined medical indication ensuring the best possible degree of clinical validity, that is, the relationship between the text results and the clinical status. Genetic tests must therefore be authorized by a specialist who can evaluate the significance of the resulting genetic data. A final point is the question of clinical utility, the likelihood that the test results will have a favourable impact for the person tested. In this context, ethical, psycho-social and legal issues are also of considerable importance in addition to purely medical concerns.

No individual laboratory on its own has the capacity to perform reliable analyses for all rare diseases for which genetic tests are already available (see OMIM: Online Mendelian Inheritance in Man and OMIM statistics).[4] If the appropriate tests for these diseases are not performed regularly the experience that is necessary to ensure adequate quality assurance is lacking. Genetic centres should therefore be encouraged to develop international cooperation for rare genetic diseases in order to have access to reliable clinical and laboratory resources.

Diagnostic problems arise as a consequence of many genetic phenomena including allelic diversity or heterogeneity. If the disorder in question is associated with genetic heterogeneity, which means that more than one mutated gene can be involved in its cause, the precise nature of the disorder often cannot be easily identified. A classical example of this is retinopathia pigmentosa, which can show autosomal-dominant, autosomal-recessive and even X-linked-recessive inheritance. Various factors, such as reduced penetrance or variable expressivity of the predisposition, can complicate the calculation of the recurrence risk. It is difficult for both laymen and experts to appreciate a risk that is described in percentage points or decimal fractions. This situation can change rapidly, for example if a sibling falls ill. The factor that influences the parents' decision whether to have another child is the nature of the long-term burden, or the severity of the disorder associated with the risk, but not a precise numerical value.

Since our current knowledge concerning underlying predispositions to many diseases is still limited, storage of DNA material from white blood cell samples is generally recommended. However, as developments in understanding of genes or other functional elements within the genome and their role in health and disease, as well as of testing methodologies, are likely to increase dramatically it is impossible to accurately predict the type of results which will be obtained from such sources in the future and to foresee them in the informed consent documents.

---

4 <http://www.ncbi.nlm.nih.gov/omim/>.

Most people are referred by a general practitioner or clinical specialist following a diagnosis (see Table 3.1). Others seek advice when they become aware of the presence of a genetic disorder in their family. Unlike in traditional everyday medical practice, where patients consult a doctor with the aim to eliminate or at least alleviate their discomfort, the objective of the care in medical genetics must often be discussed with the patient beforehand. Frequently, the genetic counsellor is only consulted during a pregnancy, when screening tests have hinted at the presence of a genetically determined disability in the embryo or fetus. Patients referred to genetic counsellors often have only a vague idea of the purpose of a consultation and are unaware of why they were referred to the counselling clinic. Therefore, the first contact, the first conversation must be undertaken with great care.

The actual counselling can also be made more difficult by competition between the various disciplines concerned with treating patients with genetic problems. Who is finally responsible for counselling? The training and further education programmes offered by the relevant medical associations are not very transparent with regard to the required quality profile of a genetic consultation and are seldom adequately developed.

It has to be recognized that genetic counselling requires time. For both the counsellee and the counsellor it represents a considerable medical, genetic and also psychological and perhaps even an ethical challenge. The duration of the consultation should be commensurate with the issues and the aims at stake. The counsellees need to feel that an expert is finally taking the time to discuss the multifaceted aspects of a disease disposition with them in a manner that is comprehensible to a layperson. If necessary, additional consultations should be offered. Unfortunately, the time budget for the consultation is limited for obvious reasons, such as, for example, the workload of the counsellor and the costs allocated by health insurance funds. Genetic counselling touches very deeply on human emotions of guilt, grief and fear, and on deeply felt moral beliefs. Partners and their relatives can make mutually unjustified accusations. In many cultures, hereditary diseases are felt to be a real reason for shame. It is not rare for people to decide against a genetic consultation because they fear that the process and its findings may stigmatize them as outsiders.

Relatives must not be contacted without the explicit consent of the counsellees, unless under certain conditions it is permitted by law. It happens quite often that a counsellee, for reasons of unjustified guilt or shame, or because of difficult family relationships, is not prepared to inform their relatives about findings that may be very relevant for their heath, too.

It is difficult to ensure that all genetic counselling services fulfil the same quality standards. The counsellor has an obligation to regularly attend further education courses and their supervision is desirable. The outcome of a genetic consultation is difficult to grasp, despite frequent attempts to do so. The majority of the counsellees who have attended a genetic counselling clinic have a reasonable recall of the information given, especially if this was reinforced by a personal letter. However, confusion may occur since the counsellees can be confronted with other views forwarded by family members or other parties.

Genetic Tests Supplied Directly to the Public

The number of genetic tests on the open market is constantly increasing, which leads to concerns regarding the test's efficacy, utility or its implication for individuals and their families. Special types of disclosure problems arise with respect to over the counter genetic tests. Usually, the test providers produce scientifically sound and detailed reports. The problem is that the tested subjects and even their physicians lack understanding of the meaning of the produced results. Often, there is no clear indication to undertake these analyses. Thus, unjustified fears are provoked or false security is obtained. Pre-symptomatic (predictive) tests in particular should only be made available via a consultation through a doctor and like prescription medicines, should not be advertised directly to the public. Provision of better information to the public in schools or the media about genetic examinations and medical genetics as a whole would be the best way to allay widespread concerns about self examinations.

References

ASHG (American Society of Human Genetics, ad hoc Committee on Genetic Counselling) (1975), 'Genetic counselling', *American Journal of Human Genetics* 27, 240–242.

Beauchamp, T.L. and Childress, J.E. (2001), *Principles of Biomedical Ethics* (5th edition) (Oxford: Oxford University Press).

Galton, F. (1865), 'Hereditary trait and character', *Macmillan's Magazine* 12, 157.

Hagard, S. and Carter, F.A. (1976), 'Preventing the birth of infants with Down Syndrome: A cost-benefit analysis', *British Medical Journal* 1, 753.

Harper, P.S. (2004), *Practical Genetic Counselling* (6th edition) (London: Arnold).

HCG (Human Genetics Commission) (2007), *More Genes Direct.*

McKusick, V.A. (2001), 'The anatomy of the human genome: A neo-vesalian basis for medicine in the 21st century', *Journal of the American Medical Association* 286, 2289–2295.

Mendel, J.G. (1865), 'Versuche über Pflanzen-Hybride', *Verhandlungen des naturforschenden Vereins in Brünn (Brno)* 4, 3–47.

Müller, H. (2005), *Gentests. Antworten zu Fragen aus der medizinischen Praxis* (Basel: Karger).

Müller-Hill, B. (1984), *Tödliche Wissenschaft. Die Aussonderung von Juden, Zigeunern und Geisteskranken* (Hamburg: Rowohlt).

Reed, S.C. (1955), *Counseling in Medical Genetics* (Philadelphia: WB Sanders).

PART 2
Cases and Issues

New aspects of a practice can best be seen when exploring the concrete circumstances of individual cases. The reality of cases *does not* teach *us* how to answer ethical questions, but which concerns and problems are important for those involved and need to be thought about. Ethical thinking in the field of genetic testing needs information about cases from those who share experiences, in order to decide which questions should be asked. We see these as 'issues' for which established social practices and routines has not found a solution that is unquestionably good for all, and therefore demand ethical reflection. Those issues cannot be fully anticipated by theoretical thinking. The contributors in the following second part of the book have investigated the practices in which predictive genetics is concretely involved.

David Winkler and *Philippe Lyrer*, two medical doctors, report an authentic experience. They present the case of patient John S. whose disease – hereditary systemic angiopathy – could only be diagnosed by genetic evidence after previous, in hindsight unnecessary, treatment and invasive examinations (including brain biopsy) due to a previous false diagnosis. They faced the ethical dilemma of unrequested disclosure of this finding to three cousins who were at risk but had not yet developed symptoms, and knew nothing of the nature of the disease to which they were susceptible. Disclosure, in this case, could prevent a future repeated false diagnosis. This is an interesting constellation because it turns the attention away from highlighting the question of whether the not-yet-patient has a right to know and to the process of communication. Given that they do have a right to know in such circumstances, the question is still how to communicate with them, how to disclose. There may be possibilities one has not yet thought of, and there may be allies within the family able to minimize or prevent damage to those who might suffer from a knowledge that is a potential benefit but also a burden. The ethics of communication also concerns the content of the message to be given. – In a commentary to the case, *Christoph Rehmann-Sutter* explores these aspects from an ethical point of view.

Genetic counselling is a professional practice, but it is also a relationship connecting (at least) two people. The professional's perspective needs to be complemented by those of the patients. *Rouven Porz* reports from an empirical bioethics project where qualitative in-depth interviews were conducted with persons who had been offered a genetic test, in order to explore the situation of genetic decision making from the perspectives of those directly concerned, that is, the decision makers themselves. They are entangled in specific networks of familial relationships. And they see those relationships as meaningful in the light of the experienced history and in the light of narratives that are predominant in the family. In order to reflect on these familial contexts systematically, he outlines the necessity of an 'ethics of kinship' that can take into account the complexity of contextual factors influencing the situation of the patients and that bear on the communication of personal genetic information.

Genetic testing has moved beyond the relatively rare monogenetic diseases and entered the vast field of multigenetic common diseases, where technical and ethical questions of different sorts arise. *Margaret Lock*, herself a medical anthropologist, takes the example of Alzheimer's disease in which genetically-based risk estimates are particularly ambiguous and difficult to assess. She concludes that in such situations, routine testing is questionable from a medical and also from an ethical point of view.

Another rather cautionary approach is taken by psychologist *Tjeerd Tymstra*. He starts from the observation that in many circumstances it may be psychologically and rationally difficult to reject testing offers because of the fear that one may regret it afterwards. Many patients want to be sure, at some point in the future, that they had tried everything to avoid a disease. This mechanism, however, can lead patients into a contrary situation where they may also regret having gone forward: 'If I only had not known that.' The increased possibilities of early detection of diseases or susceptibilities for diseases have side effects. They individualize the risk in public health systems and they are responsible for a loss of certainty in social life.

Anthropologist *Silja Samerski* deconstructs gene talk. She bases her analysis on an empirical study of cancer genetic counselling sessions and focuses on the symbolic effects of genetic discourse, pointing out epistemic misunderstandings. Contrary to current thinking in genomics, in this context risks are explained and understood as personal threats and statistical correlations as 'genes for' a disease. Genes, in popular talk, are seen as things and causes, which may lead a patient to feel that the mutated gene is a threat from within the body.

In a final interdisciplinary chapter, *Jane Kaye* (a lawyer), *Michael Parker* (a bioethicist) and *Edward Blair* (a medical geneticist) discuss the question of whether adolescents at risk of inherited arrhythmic death should be tested genetically and they present two clinical scenarios. In one case the child wants to be tested; in the other, the parents want the child to be tested. In their discussion of the possible ways of helping the family to come to a good resolution the authors differentiate the focus of professionals who work to some common ground within the family, and the focus of the law, which offers a statement of principle.

Chapter 4

Prevention of Harmful False Diagnosis versus Threat by Disclosure of an Inheritable Disease – A Medical Case

David Winkler and Philippe Lyrer

The Case[1]

It was shortly before John S.'s 40th birthday that he was hospitalized due to a sudden weakness of his left arm and leg. J.S. was a married salesman without children and had just moved into a newly constructed villa. During the previous years, J.S. had suffered from various minor health problems: recurrent episodes of diarrhoea led to a duodenal biopsy, diagnosis of celiac disease and a gluten free diet. Liver biopsy was taken due to persistently elevated liver enzymes and showed foci of hepatic fibrosis. A severe episode of his chronic migraine-like headaches preceded his acute left-sided palsy. Cerebral CT scans revealed a tumour-like right parietal mass lesion and multiple cerebral calcifications with perifocal edema also seen in MRI studies.

While PET studies would have been compatible with a malignant tumorous lesion, brain biopsy ruled out a malignoma and showed coagulation necrosis, calcifications and perivascular inflammation. Muscle biopsy performed due to muscle atrophy and pain showed several obliterated vessels. Diagnosis of a systemic microvasculitis was established. J.S. was set on high-dose steroids and cyclophosphamide pulse therapy. His left-sided hemiparesis significantly improved after steroid administration. Two months later, a retinal artery occlusion occurred and he suffered from recurrent febrile episodes with pleural effusions. Immunosuppressive therapy was considered insufficient and changed to azathioprine, pulse therapy with intravenous immunoglobulines and later methotrexate.

J.S. was still working part time as a salesman and two years had passed, when he had his first epileptic seizure. A CT scan revealed a new calcified left frontal mass lesion. Tuberous sclerosis was considered as a differential diagnosis due to the multiple cerebral calcifications. J.S. was then asked repeatedly about his family history. He had not had any contact with family members for years. His parents had died more than a decade ago; his half-brother emigrated and he lost

1 Names and locations changed for reasons of anonymity.

contact. Family history therefore remained unclear. Due to the threat of the new left-sided cerebral mass lesion causing symptomatic epileptic seizures, a second brain biopsy was performed, documenting similar findings to the previous one. Again, J.S. was asked about his family history. He told us that his mother had died more than 20 years ago after an episode of psychiatric illness. J.S. did not know any details about her disease, as he lived apart from her in those days. We were able to find J.S.'s mother's case history in our hospital's archives, dating 25 years back – it read exactly like the case history of J.S.

She underwent brain, liver, skin and lymph node biopsies that showed almost identical findings to those obtained from her son. She suffered from a progressive disease that could not be classified and caused multiple invasive investigations and inadequate treatment. Interestingly, there was a letter from a US neurologist in her case history, asking for further information on her disease. This neurologist was treating J.S.'s uncle, who emigrated to the US in his childhood and seemed to be suffering from a similar disease to his sister, J.S.'s mother. We contacted this neurologist. He remembered this particular case and still had the 25-year-old CT scans of J.S.'s uncle N.S. He agreed to send us further information if the widow of N.S. would give her consent. This elderly lady was very interested in helping us to extend our knowledge about the disease of her husband and her nephew. The case history of N.S. was almost identical to the two cases we had seen. His cranial CT scan also showed multiple cerebral calcifications (see Figure 4.1, arrows indicate multiple small calcification foci). Diagnosis of a hereditary systemic angiopathy (HSA) then became definite (Winkler et al. 2008). Differential diagnosis included CADASIL (Joutel et al. 1996), Aicardi-Goutieres-syndrome (Aicardi and Goutieres 1984) and tuberous sclerosis, but they would not explain hepato- and nephrosclerosis. The protein losing enteropathy was in favour of Rambaud's syndrome (Rambaud et al. 1986), but so far only female patients have been described with this disease. The HSA of the family S most resembled the hereditary endotheliopathies with cerebral involvement such as CRV (Weil et al. 1999), HERNS (Jen et al. 1997) and HRV (Terwindt et al. 1998) that have been linked to chromosome 3p21 (Ophoff et al. 2001). However, none of these syndromes includes all systemic findings of our patients with nephropathy, hepatopathy and myopathy, so we considered HSA to be a variant with a broader, systemic organ involvement. Like his mother and his uncle, J.S. unfortunately died in his mid-forties due to disease progression with recurrent seizures, cognitive decline, progressive enteropathy and hepato-renal dysfunction.

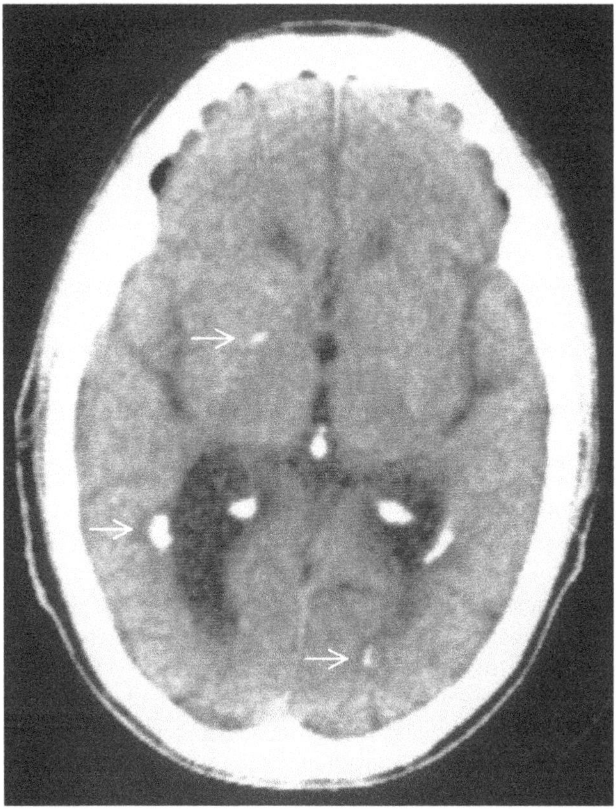

Figure 4.1 Cranial CT with multiple cerebral calcification foci (arrows), characteristic for HSA

The Dilemma

J.S.'s aunt has three sons at a critical age for developing the first symptoms of potentially inherited HSA. Is there a need to inform these sons at risk about the possibility of having inherited HSA? How should one inform, whom and when? After our own experiences with HSA, we might feel an urge to forward the information about a possible inheritable disease to the patients at risk, their relatives or their family practitioner for the following reasons: J.S.'s diagnosis was delayed by more than five years after the first brain biopsy. During this time he underwent multiple diagnostic interventions with considerable morbidity, including a second brain biopsy. He was mistreated with harmful drugs, such as different immunosuppressant drugs, due to a misleading diagnosis of vasculitis.

This may have accelerated his hepato-renal dysfunction. J.S.'s mother also underwent multiple biopsies and harmful mistreatments before dying from the disease without a correct diagnosis. In contrast, with knowledge of the family history of HSA, we might have diagnosed the disease with a simple CT scan and a single biopsy proving vasculopathic changes.

On the other hand, we must recognize that there are currently no curative treatment options for HSA. The disease has a poor prognosis with a life expectancy of 5 to 10 years after first symptoms. An early diagnosis of HSA might have negative socio-economic effects for the patients due to insurance limitations and difficulties at work. J.S. maintained a partial working ability even after multiple biopsies and on immunosuppressive drugs, still believing in a potential cure. Informing the sons at risk about their potential inheritance of this fatal disease might cause them to live in a state of permanent threat and fear. Can we thus balance the threat of a potential disease and the loss of hope if or when the disease manifests in its early stage versus the prevention of potential substantial harm? Do we even know how high the risk of a potential inheritance is for these sons? The inheritance seems to be autosomal-dominant, so that the sons have a 50 per cent risk each of having inherited the disease causing gene. But as only *mater semper certa est*, N.S. might not be the father of these sons and they may not be at risk at all. Further, we do not have a genetic test at hand, so we cannot advise the sons at risk with regards to family planning unless they show characteristic disease symptoms themselves.

We presented the disclosure question to our ethical advisor. In a detailed discussion of the dilemma we balanced arguments for and against disclosure. We physicians, as well as the ethical advisor, considered a complete withholding of information from the sons to be unethical, due to the potential significant harm caused by unnecessary diagnostic measures and mistreatment. On the other hand, we wanted to avoid the creation of an unnecessary persistent threat to the possibly healthy sons. We agreed that the best compromise would be to inform J.S.'s elderly aunt about the potential risk to her sons, as we had already established good contact with her and we considered her capable of handling the information.

As the aunt was living in the US, we had to transmit the information by telephone, although a personal meeting of course would have been preferable. In our telephone conversation, we first informed her about the course of our patient J.S., the diagnostic difficulties and the unfortunately currently limited therapeutic options. We explained that J.S. exhibited similar findings to her husband and that her earlier help by providing data on her husband's case history was crucial for us to establish a correct diagnosis for our patient. We stated that they both might have suffered from the same hereditary disease. The aunt understood that there might be a potential risk of her sons developing HSA. We explained that we are unable to define the theoretical risk to her sons precisely, but that we consider it a very positive fact that they do not exhibit symptoms yet. The aunt recognized the need for an information transfer in case the sons developed symptoms compatible with HSA. She agreed to keep this information confidential to avoid unnecessary threat to her sons, and only to disclose it if and when her sons showed symptoms of the disease. She would also leave a note about our communication in her deceased husband's medical dossier, so that her sons might have the information at hand, in case she passed away. She was grateful that we had contacted her and that she was provided with our knowledge, although we could offer neither specific diagnostic or therapeutic options yet.

Amazingly, while this manuscript was under final preparation, the genetic basis of hereditary systemic angiopathies has been solved by a Dutch/US team (Richards et al. 2007). Thus, advances in medical research that may suddenly offer new diagnostic or even therapeutic approaches add a further dimension to ethical aspects of counselling patients or their family members.

The history of the family S shows that disclosure dilemmas can occur outside the setting of genetic testing, prenatal diagnostics or legal dilemmas, such as patients forbidding physicians to inform their relatives. Disclosure dilemmas may evolve from diseases such as HSA, for which neither genetic testing nor specific treatment are available at the time of presentation – but would the dilemma be substantially different if we had a genetic test for this rare disease at hand? An important problem in the case of the family S is the disrupted family situation that prevents the individual patients from having knowledge about their relatives' experiences. Even though J.S. was repeatedly asked about his family history, only years after the onset of his disease did his physicians learn about his mother's disease. It seems to be a characteristic effect of familial neuro-psychiatric disorders that they provoke patients to separate from their roots and hinder them from communicating their disease openly to relatives. In such cases, healthy family members may take the responsibility of carrying the knowledge to the next generation.

Abbreviations

HSA = hereditary systemic angiopathy; HERNS = hereditary endotheliopathy with retinopathy, nephropathy, and stroke; CRV = cerebroretinal vasculopathy; HVR = hereditary vascular retinopathy; CADASIL = cerebral autosomal-dominant arteriopathy with subcortical infarcts and leukoencephalopathy; CT = Computed tomography; MRI = Magnetic resonance imaging.

References

Aicardi, J. and Goutieres, F. (1984), 'A progressive familial encephalopathy in infancy with calcifications of the basal ganglia and chronic cerebrospinal fluid lymphocytosis', *Annals of Neurology* 15, 49–54.

Jen, J. et al. (1997), 'Hereditary endotheliopathy with retinopathy, nephropathy, and stroke (herns)', *Neurology* 49, 1322–1330.

Joutel, A. et al. (1996), 'Notch3 mutations in cadasil, a hereditary adult-onset condition causing stroke and dementia', *Nature* 383, 707–710.

Ophoff, R.A. et al. (2001), 'Hereditary vascular retinopathy, cerebroretinal vasculopathy, and hereditary endotheliopathy with retinopathy, nephropathy, and stroke map to a single locus on chromosome 3p21.1-p21.3', *American Journal of Human Genetics* 69, 447–453.

Rambaud, J.C. et al. (1986), 'Digestive tract and renal small vessel hyalinosis, idiopathic nonarteriosclerotic intracerebral calcifications, retinal ischemic syndrome, and phenotypic abnormalities. A new familial syndrome', *Gastroenterology* 90, 930–938.

Richards, A. et al. (2007), 'C-terminal truncations in human 3'-5' DNA exonuclease trex1 cause autosomal dominant retinal vasculopathy with cerebral leukodystrophy', *Nature Genetics* 39, 1068–1070.

Terwindt, G.M. et al. (1998), 'Clinical and genetic analysis of a large dutch family with autosomal dominant vascular retinopathy, migraine and raynaud's phenomenon', *Brain* 121 (Pt 2), 303–316.

Weil, S. et al. (1999), 'Cerebroretinal vasculopathy mimicking a brain tumor: A case of a rare hereditary syndrome', *Neurology* 53, 629–631.

Winkler, D.T. et al. (2008), 'Hereditary systemic angiopathy (hsa) with cerebral calcifications, retinopathy, progressive nephropathy, and hepatopathy', *Journal of Neurology* 255, 77–88.

Chapter 4a

Communication Yes, but How – and What? Commentary to the Case Presented by David Winkler and Philippe Lyrer

Christoph Rehmann-Sutter

David Winkler contacted me before making the phone call to his late patient J.S.'s aunt in the US, and we discussed the situation in detail, trying to look at it from as many angles as possible. That finding a way of communicating the information was necessary was intuitively clear to both of us, but it was not clear how and to whom the information should be disclosed. I remember that at the beginning of the conversation we understood the question to be: how should the information that the relatives of J.S. are at risk of developing hereditary systemic angiopathy (HSA) be communicated? Should it be communicated at all to the two brothers that might be affected, or to anybody else? The option of a telephone call to J.S.'s aunt was clear, but it was unclear whether it was the right thing to do. There might be other options as well, perhaps better ones.

But towards the end of our conversation we discovered that it was not clear *what* should be said: should the message be that the two cousins are at risk of developing HSA, perhaps combined with an explanation of the Mendelian risk pattern? Or would it be better, perhaps even enough, to tell them about the discovered similarity of the diagnostic results between their father (the aunt's late husband) and J.S.? The message in the first option is a derivation of the message in the second option. The existence of a risk is the conclusion drawn from the discovery of the similarities in the diagnostic pattern. But from the point of view of those informed, it is perhaps a different kind of message. The second version is perhaps easier to deal with, because it stays closer to the doctor's direct experiences. And it is a message that does not tell somebody something about their fate, although it could be read as leading to precisely such a conclusion. Perhaps it would be different if the cousins (or their mother) drew the conclusion themselves, or asked for it, instead of a doctor they did not know personally coming up with it directly, out of the blue, from Europe.

My intuition told me that some way of telling them was necessary. The explanation I gave was that I sympathized with Dr Winkler's aim to help prevent a misdiagnosis and consequently harmful mistreatments if one of the sons developed symptoms of HSA. It was a responsible doctor's wish to use the knowledge that he had acquired during the treatment of one of his patients – knowledge that would have helped his patient considerably if available in time – to prevent similar (major) harm for other family members. Part of Dr Winkler's motivation, as I understood it, was to prevent the painful and harmful effects of the probable misdiagnosis and mistreatment, the other part was to prevent medicine from acting in the wrong way and causing (instead of preventing, treating and alleviating) harm. The first part of the motivation was therapeutic: to help to prevent people suffering from a disease wherever possible. The second part of the motivation was connected with a sense of medical responsibility: the feeling that harm caused by medicine is even worse (from a doctor's point of view) than harm caused by other factors. The move to inform J.S.'s aunt would be a doubly preventive act: prevention of harm and prevention of a breach of the core principle of medical ethics: *nihil nocere* – don't harm your patients.

At the end of the conversation, after talking through all the possibilities and their implications, and after the email exchange that followed, I believed that Dr Winkler's proposal to contact the aunt was right (or the best option within what seemed possible). And I thought it was essential to tell her about the discovery of the similar diagnoses that led to the very probable conclusion that *J.S.'s disease was the same as that of her late husband.* She needed to understand this in case her sons developed symptoms associated with HSA, at which point they would need the information about HSA, but not necessarily before. She should be in a position to take precautions to ensure that this information is available to her sons, even after her eventual death. But at the start of the conversation the message for her should *not* be: 'Your son's are at risk of HSA and you should tell them.'

This was a relatively smooth and gentle approach. It did all that was necessary but not more than was necessary. And it was carefully done to avoid collateral harm. Dr Winkler told me afterwards that the telephone conversation with J.S.'s aunt went well.

The case did not seem difficult, but it was still complex. I spontaneously invited Dr Winkler to write an account of this case for the book on Disclosure Dilemmas that I was co-editing, because it seemed to be instructive – at least it was for me. Here I try to present the considerations that led to my conclusions in a more organized way, while discussing some of the more general questions that appear in the case.

Unsolicited Disclosure

One of the ethical problems with unsolicited disclosure of information about a disease-related genetic mutation to relatives is that their right to have access to informed consent is taken away (Kohut et al. 2007). The disclosure is 'unsolicited' (Husted 1997, 58), but the ethical relevance of this obvious fact was not very clear in this case, because it depended on to whom information was given and which information was provided.

If the cousins were contacted (perhaps through J.S.'s aunt) this concern would be greater than if the aunt were contacted. The aunt would learn, without soliciting the information, that her late husband's disease was a genetic condition, and also that his true disease stayed undiagnosed for a long time. She would also learn that her sons are at risk of inheriting the condition. But she would not learn something about her own health. It is information that allows her to prevent misdiagnosis and mistreatment of her sons. Clearly, the disease itself develops independently from the acts of communication. But the suffering caused by the disease and by the medical treatment of the disease would be considerably worse if the genetic pattern were not recognized in time. With the right information in her hands, the aunt can act as a caring mother and spare her sons unnecessary suffering, in the not unlikely case that they are affected by the hard lot of HSA.

However, the information that her sons might be affected by the same disease that her husband suffered from so much, and which eventually took his life, may also cause her psychological distress. She could suffer from anxiety about the health of her sons as a result of her knowledge about the disease's inheritability. Perhaps she was already anxious, because she suspected that the disease might have an inheritable component. The medical information would make a concrete risk out of this suspicion, but the anxiety might be outweighed by the possibility of preventing even worse things from happening.

After receiving the information, the aunt will also face a disclosure decision herself. Should she tell her sons? When? How? Should she keep this important information about life and death secret? Will the sons sense that she knows something, or that something is wrong? Will it affect their relationship? This is also a relevant aspect of the decision about whether and how to inform: the person informed may face a new disclosure dilemma themself. Genetic knowledge has implications beyond the patient as an individual, it 'affects more than ego; it is profoundly relational' (Konrad 2005, 13). The relationality of genetics is sequential in the sense that it may apply to relatives, to relatives of the relatives, to relatives of the relatives of the relatives, and so on. Each disclosure (depending on the condition and the genetic relationships in the interrelated net of families) may open new opportunities and disclosure dilemmas. In our case, the knowledge did not concern J.S.'s aunt herself, but it nevertheless affected her situation deeply, and it opened a way to the possible carriers of the gene.

In the literature, the problem of unsolicited disclosure is often treated as a matter of principle. Jørgen Husted (1997) discusses the consequences of a 'thin' conception of autonomy as opposed to those of a 'thick' one. Both conceptions agree that: 'Autonomy is the running of one's own life according to one's own lights: People are said to be autonomous to the extent to which they are able to fashion their own lives, and to some extent their own destiny, by the exercise of their own faculties in successive choices during their lives' (59). Autonomy as independence is common to both conceptions. This thin conception (introduced with reference to John Harris (1985)) assumes that, ideally, an agent is maximally autonomous, having 1) maximal control of desires and actions; 2) no defects of reasoning; and 3) all the information at hand. The preferences and wishes that will lead them are 'something given'. Autonomy means that an agent can act accordingly, knowing about the situation and not suffering from constraints. This approach would endorse unsolicited disclosure on the grounds that it violates autonomy only in a formal sense, but respects and even enhances it in a substantial sense: Disclosure enables an agent to make choices (reproductive choices and other life plans). Compared to this, the formal sense (taking away a right to informed consent) is less important for the person concerned than the substantive sense. Therefore the information ought to be given.

In a 'thick' conception of autonomy, however, unsolicited disclosure to relatives is not so unproblematic. This conception takes autonomy as self-determination in a fuller sense. The assumption is that wishes and preferences are *not* to be 'considered as given and outside the reach of critical evaluation. What makes self-determination possible is the unique capacity of the human person for reflective self-evaluation, for considering what they want their motivations to be, for forming higher-order wants and preferences defining what they for themselves find it *worth being* and *worth doing* in life' (62). Accordingly, the counsellor's role is to make a real choice possible. Their role is not just to provide information and to leave the counsellee alone with the decision, to act according to their wishes or preferences. These wishes or preferences might not be clear for the person concerned, not something 'given', and they might wish to discuss these options and their implications with the counsellor in more depth. Clarification of wishes or preferences belongs to the field of ethical reflection and is also relevant for the counsellor's practice. The doctor's role is: 'To help clarify the values, possibilities and consequences and, so far as possible, create valuable options suited to the individual's unique situation' (63).

The 'thick' conception of autonomy, which Husted clearly prefers, views unsolicited disclosure as a 'mixed blessing'. It can lead a person into a situation of 'morally forced choices' (Husted 1997, 67), accepting undesirable alternatives.

But whether this holds true depends on the situation. If we look at the alternatives that open up for J.S.'s aunt after receiving the information that the father of her sons might have passed the gene to them, there are no draconian alternatives she might be forced into. The information will be troubling for her, but she will be put into a position to choose whether, when and how to pass it to her sons. This is a serious matter, but we can anticipate that she can understand it as part of her role as a responsible mother. The doctor takes her capacity to act responsibly towards her sons seriously.

Knowledge as Burden and Chance

It is very difficult to tell in general whether genetic knowledge represents a burden and/or chances. In her anthropological study of different situations of genetic 'foreknowledge', Monica Konrad has demonstrated that the understanding of knowledge as burden and chance can better be clarified by following the 'local moralities of information disclosure' than by following some external criteria (Konrad 2005, 4).

The dilemmas that are ethically pertinent are *local* in two senses. First, the value of knowledge (positive and negative) depends on the particular situation. In our case, the value of avoiding harm caused by a probable misdiagnosis is pertinent, as is the age of the sons, their situation in life, and so on. Second, the dilemma is also local in the sense that the participants in the situation are the true moral experts. It is they who can see how to act: J.S.'s aunt, but also eventually her two sons. In a certain way this changes the position of the counsellor (in our case, J.S.'s doctor in Switzerland). He is no longer an outsider in the situation, but he participates in it. He is also one of the local actors, in his own situation, with his own understanding of professional excellence (and weakness) in carrying out his role as a good doctor. His situation, he learns, connects him to J.S.'s family, and therefore the relationship to the aunt becomes important – a relationship that is already established by an earlier request.

But there are also the limits of anticipatory knowledge to consider. Foreknowledge is difficult, but the evaluation of the value of foreknowledge is even more difficult, because it is in a sense 'foretelling foreknowledge', as Monica Konrad (2005, 61) has suggestively named it. It is about doubled foreknowledge. The practice under ethical scrutiny involves doubled foretelling and is therefore prone to doubled uncertainty.

I believe that one way of coping with this situation ethically is to recognize the subsequent persons in the whole chain of events as ethically reflecting actors. It is not possible for J.S.'s doctor to anticipate what will be right or wrong from their perspectives. This would be a form of moral paternalism, a kind of paternalism that is even more problematic than medical paternalism because, as Husted has rightly pointed out in his conclusion, medical professionals have no professional expertise at all regarding moral decisions. They can pass the ball to another person, and in doing so they must reflect on all the implications that this pass has, as far as they are able to see. But then they no longer have the ball, and they need to leave it up to those who do.

Beyond Rights and Duties

This example shows the limits of a vocabulary of rights and duties when understanding the different dimensions of ethical responsibility that people experience. But what is the problem with framing the dilemma of responsibility as a dilemma of a right to know/not to know on the one hand, and a right to know/duty to know on the other? Contrary to Konrad's suggestion I think it is less a problem of individualism – she sees the problem in the discrepancy between individualist premises and the obvious relational nature of genetic information (2005, 88) – and more a problem of abstraction of the rights/duties vocabulary.

In the case of J.S., the doctor said to me at the beginning of our conversation that he felt obliged to disclose, and also that he felt that the relatives had a right to be informed in order to prevent a misdiagnosis. And during our discussion I could not see a valid counterargument. For both of us, the doctor's obligation to disclose and the relatives' right to be informed were already established. But the relatives may also have a right to be spared too much intrusion from an unknown doctor in Europe, since family members have not been in close contact with each other. The cousins did not ask for the information, they might not want to know it in advance and, because there is no way of preventing the disease, it is unclear whether they have an interest in receiving it right now. With regard to the aunt, however, the situation was different. She was imagined as a caring person who is not indifferent to the fate of her sons. She could be seen as having an interest in getting the information, and an interest in not knowing it could not reasonably be imagined. This given, it was still not entirely clear how to proceed. Hence, the allocation of rights and obligations is not sufficient to clarify what it is best to do, or which strategy of communication should be chosen.

I would not claim that rights are irrelevant. They can form the basis for a more detailed assessment. The right to know and the right not to know can be present at the same time and lead to a contradiction. The cousins did have a right to know and *also* a right not to know. The right to know was a right to be spared from a misdiagnosis. And the right not to know was a right to be spared from unsolicited and unhelpful foreknowledge. The doctor had the means to fulfil the right to be spared a misdiagnosis. Therefore he felt himself under obligation to provide the information to those concerned. But this was only the beginning of his search for the right strategy. What he could not know was whether the sons would want to know everything now in order to make other kinds of decisions, such as choosing a prenatal diagnosis if they wanted children. There were many unknowns, and the challenge was to act under uncertainty.

A major problem with unsolicited disclosure is its irreversibility. Once you have told, you cannot un-tell. Knowledge cannot be annihilated; the cat, once freed, will not return into the bag. And it is very difficult to tell somebody that there is information about their health available without already disclosing its essential content. The strategy chosen – to contact the aunt only and not to ask her for the addresses of her sons – had the advantage of allowing room for reversibility. The aunt, knowing the situation of her sons, can decide in her own way, and even make other arrangements later if the situation changes in any relevant aspect. This might be important also in other cases: A communication plan can deliberately split the decision into small steps and share them among different people, enabling them to participate actively in a relational construction of responsibility in communicating genetic risks. Each 'micro-decision' (Scully et al. 2007) builds some reversibility into the process. And each bit of reversibility is a chance to include more aspects and perspectives in the decision process. It makes the *process*, which is the sum of the contributions of several actors, more responsive.

References

Harris, J. (1985), *The Value of Life* (London: Routledge).

Husted, J. (1997), 'Autonomy and a Right Not to Know', in R. Chadwick et al. (eds), *The Right to Know and the Right Not to Know* (Aldershot: Ashgate), 55–68.

Kohut, K. et al. (2007), 'Should healthcare providers have a duty to warn family members of individuals with an HNPCC-causing mutation? A survey of patients from the ontario familial colon cancer registry', *Journal of Medical Genetics* 44, 404–407.

Konrad, M. (2005), *Narrating the New Predictive Genetics. Ethics, Ethnography and Science* (Cambridge: Cambridge University Press).

Scully, J.L. et al. (2007), 'You don't make genetic test decisions from one day to the next', *Bioethics* 21:4, 208–217.

Chapter 5
The Need for an Ethics of Kinship: Decision Stories and Patients' Context

Rouven Porz

Introduction

This chapter focuses on the patients' perspectives in genetic diagnosis. Patients' accounts give an insight into decision situations that might differ significantly from the doctors', counsellors' or ethicists' perspectives. As genetic testing is a rapidly growing field of molecular biomedicine, it is likely that more and more patients will be facing situations in which they have to decide for or against a genetic diagnosis. This chapter is based on empirical data from a qualitative study that was carried out in Switzerland between 2002 and 2005. An interpretative phenomenological analysis of our interview data showed that patients rarely perceive their test decision as a single discrete decision. Rather, they use time to protect their moral agency (Scully et al. 2007; Scully 2006; Rehmann-Sutter 2006 and 2008). In their interview stories they talked about decision processes, steps and time spans. In addition they emphasized the difficulty and absurdity of some of the test situations (Porz et al. 2008). And they particularly emphasized the role of their family and friends, thus making it clear that a decision to take a genetic test is linked to a number of contextual factors.

Emphasis on these contextual factors also presents the discipline of bioethics in a new light. If the family relationship plays such a great role in genetic tests, then bioethics must make suggestions of how to harness this interwoven kinship in genetic counselling. From a bioethical viewpoint, a new form of kinship ethics is suggested. The conceptualization of such a kinship ethics would make it possible to describe more precisely the disclosure dilemma of the patients affected.

I first provide a brief glimpse of the focus and methodology the qualitative interview study to which I primarily refer (1). In the next step I follow the decision stories of two participants in our study, using specific quotations from the interviews (2).[1] The complexity of the contextual factors in both cases leads to the conclusion that bioethics must develop a kind of subdiscipline of kinship ethics in order to rise adequately to the challenges of genetic counselling (3).

---

1 Some of the material in this chapter is published in Rommetveit and Porz (2009) and Porz and Scully (2009).

Our Qualitative Study: Investigating Decision Making in Genetic Diagnosis

The qualitative interview study from which I take my examples was carried out in 2002–2005 by the Unit for Ethics in Biosciences at the University of Basel. The study was entitled, 'Time as a contextual element in ethical decision making in the field of genetic diagnosis.' The study's methodology and results have been published in detail elsewhere.[2] The primary research objective of the study was to investigate situations in which decisions about genetic diagnosis were made, from the perspectives of the people affected: a particular substantive focus directed to the temporal aspects of this decision. The rationale for the study was the (widely accepted) observation that the perspective of the people actually affected has so far been given little attention in the ethical discourse on genetic tests.

A total of 25 interviews were carried out, with participants who had experienced four different fields of genetic investigation. In the first, we interviewed people who had had to decide whether or not to take genetic tests to ascertain their predisposition to familial forms of cancer; a second area involved interviews with carriers tested for the recessively inherited condition cystic fibrosis; third, families affected by the genetic disease Huntington's Chorea were interviewed. Finally we also included women exposed to prenatal diagnosis in the study. In part this was because, although not routinely considered as genetic testing, the standard prenatal diagnostic applications such as amniocentesis and chorionic villus biopsy examine the genetic material chromosomal form, and can therefore be described as genetic tests (SAMW 2004, 9); in addition, while carrying out our study it quickly became clear that these prenatal diagnostic techniques were also perceived as a form of genetic test by the women concerned.

The semi-structured interviews were conducted and the transcripts evaluated followed the methods developed in *Grounded Theory* for qualitative research (see Glaser and Strauss 1998; Charmaz 2003). We also used interpretative phenomenological analysis (IPA), as developed by Jonathan A. Smith (2003). The objective of IPA is to gain insight into phenomena as experienced by affected individuals in their life worlds without applying previously established analytic categories.

Our qualitative methodology makes no claim to statistical representation. This is clear from the present text, as only two interview stories are used to provide the empirical basis of our ethical considerations. My discussion will nevertheless show that exemplary individual cases can also have implications that are accessible to a more general ethical reflection. This procedure belongs to the field of empirical ethics: the interpretational results obtained from empirical interview data are set in

2 The research group was composed of Jackie Leach Scully, Rouven Porz and Christoph Rehmann-Sutter, Swiss National Science Foundation, 1114-64956.01. See Porz et al. 2002; for the results see Scully et al. 2007; see also the chapters by Scully and Rehmann-Sutter in this volume. Do also compare the citations in the introduction.

relation to the normative discourse of bioethics (Widdershoven and van der Scheer 2004; Molewijk et al. 2004; Porz et al. 2008).

Examining the results of our study it quickly became clear that decisions about genetic tests are often not simple 'yes' or 'no' decisions, but rather reflect a decision-making 'process' that confronted the person concerned with life situations that were often difficult and unpredictable. It also became apparent that life circumstances, contextual factors and the personal biographies of the persons concerned play a great role in the processes leading to their decision. To make this clear, two interview stories from our study are presented in more detail below. The complexity of the genetic test situation is apparent in both stories.

Decision Stories and Patients' Context

The first story I present takes place within the context of a family affected by colon cancer. However, our interviewee – Suzanne – unexpectedly developed breast cancer, and underwent a predictive test for colon cancer at the same time as her breast cancer treatment. The second story is situated within a family context of Huntington's disease. Our interviewee – Daria – cannot make up her mind whether she wants to know about her Huntington status. In the end she decides against the predictive test.[3]

Suzanne – Imprisoned in Her Genes

The interview with Suzanne took place in spring 2003 at the University of Basel. Her interview story recounted the development of her breast cancer and the predictive genetic test she had taken to find out about any possible predisposition to colon cancer. The additional predictive genetic test was suggested to her while she was receiving treatment for breast cancer, as her father, grandfather and great-grandfather had all died of colon cancer. At the time of the interview, Suzanne's illness and her genetic test were a few years in the past and she was now 38 years old. She first explained to us that she had never expected to get breast cancer, as all her paternal relations had died of colon cancer. Since the age of 20, she had been having preventive examinations to detect the first signs of colon cancer. Then suddenly came breast cancer:

> I was completely shocked, disoriented, powerless, confused, I was choking, and I had the sense of being in a nightmare, It was a hammer blow right into my face. … From one day to the next your life is no longer what it was … Well, you get wrenched out of it. Suddenly everything is simply different. Death is in the next room.

3 The names of the participants have been changed.

It was not just the diagnosis of cancer that threw her off balance, but also the additional genetic test for possible predisposition to colon cancer, while she was having treatment for breast cancer:

> Yes, it got worse for a while, with the genetic test. That's clear. … I was then more afraid, I thought, now I'm also going to get colon cancer. And I asked myself: have I got other mutations as well? Genetic mutations?

At that point she was burdened not just with the breast cancer, but also with the result of the genetic test, which indicated that there was a high level of probability she would also develop colon cancer. We asked her why, in the difficult situation of having breast cancer, she had decided to have an additional predictive genetic test at all:

> I was thinking, what other genes are also defective? And I struggled for a long time to cope with this. And I also wanted to take on something like a new identity. I had the feeling that I should change my life, I cut my hair off. I had the feeling I should get a new job [pause, she laughs] – yes, it's complicated. Well, I really struggled with myself, I wanted a new identity, I didn't want to be the person I was any more.

Her decision to take the test thus took place in a phase of her life when she was no longer certain of her own identity. She was bewildered because of her breast cancer, and because of her family context of cancer she automatically related all her considerations to her genes. She thought she had to be particularly careful in general, because of her dangerous family history:

> Yes, for example, food: I thought I should eat only raw food, because of my colon. I would only be allowed to eat wholemeal products. If I ate something that wasn't so healthy, I had a bad conscience, and I smoked and if I had smoked a cigarette I then had a bad conscience, and I couldn't enjoy anything anymore. I even thought there was something in vegetables that could set off cancer, and … Like, if I am riding my bicycle behind a car and breathing in the exhaust gases, I had the feeling, now I'm going to get lung cancer.

It is important to note here that she did not yet have colon cancer, but she appeared to be almost certain that she would develop colon cancer or some other form of cancer if she did not take extreme care. At the same time a sort of social estrangement from her surroundings took place:

> Well, I had the feeling that I was some kind of outsider. I had the feeling, I'm no longer one of the people, the 'normal people' in inverted commas. For example, if we were out with friends, going for a meal, they could all be so easygoing,

> smoke, drink wine, and I had the feeling, I can't do this any more, I don't belong here any more, and nobody understands me.

She would like to have reassured her friends that she still 'belonged', but she did not know how to tell her friends about her decision to take the additional genetic test. What could she have said?

> But somehow, most people I tell about the genetic test don't understand it. Even those who then ask about it. But hardly anyone asks. Well, that is depressing.

Suzanne further emphasized that at that time she also became distanced from her husband – not, however, because she felt misunderstood, but that she was distancing herself so as not to burden him with her 'fears':

> [I had a dream in which] I saw my funeral, I read my own death notice and was thinking, oh, how long do I still have to live? And I couldn't tell my husband about it. Because I would have burdened him with that as well. … If I had told my husband what I was afraid of like that, he would perhaps also have been troubled with it.

Obviously she was worried that her husband would be 'troubled' by her fantasies about her death. She thought that she might get help from her brother, since he was carrying similar genes and perhaps had the same problems. He then also had a predictive genetic test for colon cancer. Her brother's result, however, was negative, and at that moment Suzanne once again feels alone with her genetic self-definition:

> At that moment I was a bit jealous. OK, I was of course happy for him, but I felt abandoned again with the whole thing.

Suzanne's quotations make clear that that one thing the genetic test did was to shut her out of her normal life. She felt socially alienated (see Porz and Scully 2009; Porz 2008). In these quotes, as in the entire interview, it becomes clear that all her considerations, both about the breast cancer and the additional predictive genetic test, were always with reference to her genetic make-up. She simply takes it as given that, as part of her colon cancer family, she will be at the mercy of these hereditary determinants. She explains her decision to take the genetic test by saying she wanted to find out more about her genes. The question that must be asked here is whether the genetic counselling should not have shown her that the timing of her genetic test was obviously a bad choice – after all, she was undergoing chemotherapy for breast cancer at the time and was likely to have her attention focused on that, and not on the possible future repercussions of knowing her genetic status for colon cancer risk. The fact that all her paternal relations had died of colon cancer may not of itself be sufficient reason to lead one's whole life under the Damocles' sword of one's own genes.

Daria – Facing a Family Tragedy

Daria was 30 years old at the time of the interview in 2004. She had a mother who was already suffering from the symptoms of Huntington's disease. Huntington's disease is a dominantly inherited, severe, late-onset neurological disorder, causing disturbances in motor function and sometimes alterations of the personality as well, and leads ultimately to death. If one parent has the disease, children face a 50 per cent risk of developing it too. Thus, the genetic test can provide children in Huntington's families with the predictive knowledge of whether they belong to the 50 per cent affected or to the 50 per cent who do not carry the Huntington allele and have therefore 'escaped' the disease. Daria, then, was facing the difficult decision of whether to undergo predictive genetic testing to find out if she would develop the disease. Would she belong to the one 50 per cent or the other? After a long period of reflection she decided not to take the predictive test, but rather *wait* and see whether she developed symptoms of the disease.

During the interview it became clear that, for a long time, Daria had been unaware of the presence of Huntington in her family, nor had she been familiar with the term. When she was very young she vaguely realized that her grandfather suffered from a strange illness, but at that time in her life the problem did not have a name. And although Daria had learned about genetics and inheritance at school, she did not possess any specific knowledge about Huntington's. As she was only 18-years-old at that time, she was not particularly worried about ageing or age-related disease. In the interview she said:

> That was very far away for me, well, I just thought, if it is inherited, one day, I should think about it …

Therefore, due both to her youth and to a lack of family knowledge, she was initially able to ignore the problem of the family disease. But, of course, that did not make the disease go away. Some years later, through one singular event, the problem re-emerged with full force. By the age of 28, her grandfather had died, and his strange and unknown disease seemed to have gone with him. Daria was not living at home any more, and she saw her mother only once in a while for short visits. On a shopping trip, as the two of them were in a shoe shop, Daria realized that her mother was unable to walk properly Suddenly, she was reminded of the strange disease her grandfather had suffered from:

> I went shopping with her and I realized that she had difficulties walking. Her feet did not hit the ground properly, and suddenly it was clear to me: my mum was affected. She had the family disease.

In a way, in this shoe shop Daria lost her innocence with regard to the disease: it could no longer be ignored. She entered a phase of alarm and awareness, suddenly realizing that the strange disease could also have an effect on her life. After this episode she was in complete despair. She did not dare to talk to her mother about her observation in the shop, and she also withdrew from her own friends. She realized that her mother now had her grandfather's condition, and that this proved it was heritable. Searching the Internet for information, she tried to find out more about the disease. This went on for a year, during which she fell deeper into isolation and despair. Looking back, she says of this time:

> Well, I could hardly bear the weekends anymore, I was really alone, crying, asking myself: Will I get the disease? How will I cope with that? Why me? What should I do with my life? What have I done to deserve this?

Searching the Internet, she remembered the term 'Huntington'. Obviously at some point in the past, nurses or doctors had used the word to describe her grandfather's disease. She now developed the expectation that she would also get the disease. For some months she was convinced that she was fated to get it. And without having talked to anybody, her self-diagnosed fate soon encompassed all of her normal concerns, plans and goals:

> I was really desperate, then, because it [the possible disease] simply concerned every subject of my life, and then I was really badly off. And, yes, what about children? I mean, until then that had never really been a thing that I thought about much, but then it suddenly became an important thing. And what about sports, further education, and so on? What about hobbies? Coordination is really important in my hobbies. I dance, I do aerobics, and so it was really a major theme for me. And I was almost unable to cope.

Meanwhile, her mother's disease situation was getting worse. The mother was told by her doctor about her possibility of having Huntington's disease, and the doctor suggested a genetic test was now available to confirm the diagnosis. The mother quite quickly decided to go for the genetic test. Although she had received genetic counselling the information had been hard for her to understand, and she was not fully aware of the consequences that her test result would have for her children. Only a few weeks later the mother was tested positive, knowing for sure now that she was suffering from Huntington's. And so the obscure family disease was finally given its proper name.

At this point, Daria started to talk to her mother about the disease. She also started to talk to her brother and her father. Although she still did not know what to do, communication with her family improved, and she began taking a more active stance towards the disease. In view of her mother's test procedure, Daria had also been told about the possibility of conducting a predictive test for herself. However, having already spent some months in despair, she did not go for the test immediately, but undertook a series of other steps: she went to a psychologist; she tried to improve her health insurance; she then went to another genetic counsellor, then to another doctor; and finally, she decided against the genetic test. In the end, the process of making the decision had taken place over a period of two difficult years. Her retrospective explanation sounds very reasonable:

> I then decided not to go for the test. Somehow, it was very easy then, suddenly. Huntington's will always be part of my family. I will have to take care of my mother. My brother might have it sometime. So what is the use of the predictive test now? Whether I get it or not – it will be part of my family anyway! I will have to deal with it anyway.

According to commonly held bioethical notions about autonomous decision making, Daria's story has a simple structure: After a period of not knowing about the family disease, she found out what it was – Huntington's. She gathered information and then decided against taking the test. But hang on: What about her long phases of despair and her breakdown at the weekends? What about her hopes and life plans that she saw vanishing in the face of the possibility of this disease? What about her communication impasse with her family? She obviously did not make the decision in one step, but rather gradually renegotiated her life in the face of possible tragedy (Rommetveit and Porz 2009). This tragedy is linked to her family context, another good reason to point to the need for a kinship ethics.

The Need for an Ethics of Kinship

I am adopting the term 'kinship ethics' from Monica Konrad, who in her book *Narrating the New Predictive Genetics* (2005) writes about predictive genetic tests from the viewpoint of social anthropology. In her book, Konrad also refers to Huntington's disease and describes the 'new genetic family' (ibid., 143), which must negotiate the taking of a pre-symptomatic test within the family. She, too, emphasizes the life world of these families, and expresses them through the term 'home truths' (ibid., 59 ff.). She indicates new issues of the guilt and responsibility of future parents, and among other things points out divergences from more traditional ideas of kinship (ibid., 145). It does not do justice to the complexity of the genetic counselling situation if the individual family member is considered separately from their relations. Thus, new forms of kinship dependencies arise.

The new kinship relationship, as became clear in the quotes from the interviews is uncommon in western societies which from a sociological viewpoint have become highly individualized in terms of their values and goals (Beck and Beck-Gernsheim 1994, 10 ff.). With the medicalized emphasis of genetics, the relational family membership is reassigned a completely new value. One may object that genetics relates only to the relational situations within one family, and sociology primarily to couples who live together or become a family through marriage. But the married couple too enters the field of the 'new genetic family' as soon as they plan to have their own children. The genetic information of the future child can no longer be assigned to a single individual, but is conditioned by the genetic make-up of both parents. As Monica Konrad says: 'Because genetic information is not simply information about an individual person but necessarily reveals knowledge about one's biological relations, the new genetics can be said to literalize kinship as webs of biological relatedness' (2005, 153).

If kinship here leads literally to a web of biological relatedness, then at the same time, mutual dependencies also occur: 'Heredity … is made lively as social anatomies of interdependence' (ibid.).

Such dependencies in earlier times found expression in the saying, 'Blood is thicker than water'; this now sounds anachronistic, but genetic diagnostics confront us with the same core message of this saying, albeit in a new packaging. Put another way, one could say: 'Genetic constitution is thicker than our ideal of the atomized individual.' The genetic constitution determines family membership in terms of molecular genetics.

In the west, multiple generations of one family no longer commonly live under one roof. Grown children live in other cities, parents divorce and find new partners, have new children with the new partners – the increase in patchwork families cannot be ignored (cf. Bernstein 1990; Maihofer et al. 2001). It is therefore all the more interesting that it is precisely these genetic diseases that give a new emphasis to an old tradition: the value of kinship is once again brought into prominent light. However far away one lives, emotionally or geographically, from one's father, mother, brother, sister, son or daughter, even if a growing patchwork family means one perhaps no longer has any contact to one's biological father, a decision to take a genetic test places the person concerned unavoidably in a relation of direct kinship – whether I have been socialized with these relations or not. This is shown clearly in Suzanne's story, in her referring to her paternal relations and in her unfulfilled hope that her genetic brother could be a support for her.

Daria's interview story also demonstrates a new feeling of belonging to a family. In her special case, it was as if she almost did not care, in the end, whether *she* herself would one day fall ill or one of her direct *relations*. Daria's new conception of her family might be explained like this: in confronting the familial disease, the idea of her family as a whole was more important to her than her role as an individual in this family. I infer that we need a kind of kinship ethics to be able to fully consider this problem area from an ethical standpoint. But what are the problematic areas that such a kinship ethics would need to cover? Here are some suggestions:

1. Time: Relatedness crosses and pervades generations. A kinship ethics must be capable of incorporating time dimensions in the ethical consideration. It must ask how the dimension of time affects genetic knowledge and counselling.

2. Location: The context of the genetic counselling situation acquires an additional complexity in terms of the location of the relations, if new contact to old relations has to be established, perhaps with relations who are geographically scattered – and therefore may also be living in different social situations.
3. Tradition: The clear trend towards individualization was linked to a turning away from the classical model of the extended family. An emphasis on the foundation of kinship, however, brings the genetically determined belonging to a family into a new light. The self-concept of *Homo sapiens* can be expressed by a new term (Porz 2008, 335 ff.): considered genetically, the human being becomes *Homo affinitas (relatedness).*
4. Loyalty: *Homo affinitas* is confronted with decisions of how to deal with the responsibilities of kinship networks – particularly when its affiliations are communicated by means of a genetic test. I argue that instead of talking only of confidentiality, autonomy or data protection, a kinship ethics must also interrogate such terms as loyalty towards family members, or the limits to private identity. Passing on, or alternatively keeping silent about, genetic information may thus develop into an issue of loyalty or disloyalty.

Although at this point these issues cannot be further developed, the four central issues of time, location, tradition and loyalty at least provide a hermeneutical basis for a new reorientation of genetic counselling. In counselling it is obviously not sufficient just to recognize the new role of the family as such. There needs to be a hermeneutic investigation of how the role of the family is to be understood from the patient's point of view; what values and standards are mobilized, and by whom; and what a consideration of kinship structures would signify for the discipline of bioethics. If bioethics is to give guidance in the context of real-life families, models of behaviour must be identified and examined in such family structures, the dynamics of which go far beyond the modes of action of single individuals.

Acknowledgement

I thank my colleagues Jackie Leach Scully and Christoph Rehmann-Sutter for their support in this work and for their helpful comments. Our interview study 'Time as a contextual element in ethical decision making in the field of genetic diagnosis' was funded by the Swiss National Science Foundation, SNSF. I am grateful to Monica Buckland-Hofstetter for linguistic assistance and to Gaby Brahier for her editorial work. Parts of this chapter were written at the Foundation Brocher in Geneva, Switzerland. Thanks also to the Brocher support and to their team of wonderful people.

References

Beck, U. and Beck-Gernsheim, E. (1994), *Riskante Freiheiten. Individualisierung in Modernen Gesellschaften* (Frankfurt am Main: Suhrkamp).

Bernstein, A.C. (1990), *Die Patchwork-Familie* (Zürich: Kreuz).

Charmaz, K. (2003), 'Grounded Theory', in J.A. Smith (ed.), *Qualitative Psychology* (London: Sage), 81–110.

Glaser, B. and Strauss, A. (1998), *Grounded Theory: Strategien Qualitativer Forschung* (Bern: Verlag Hans Huber).

Konrad, M. (2005), *Narrating the New Predictive Genetics. Ethics, Ethnography and Science* (Cambridge: Cambridge University Press).

Maihofer, A. et al. (2001), *Wandel der Familie. Zukunft der Generationen*, Heinz Böckler-Stiftung, Arbeitspapier 48.

Molewijk, B. et al. (2004), 'Empirical data and moral theory. A plea for integrated empirical ethics', *Medicine, Health Care and Philosophy* 7, 55–69.

Porz, R. et al. (2002), 'Welche Rolle spielt der Faktor Zeit bei Entscheidungsprozessen zu genetischen Tests?', *Medizinische Genetik* 4, 382–384.

Porz, R. (2008), *Zwischen Entscheidung and Entfremdung. Die Patientenperspektive in der Gendiagnostik and Albert Camus' Konzepte zum Absurden* (Paderborn: Mentis).

Porz, R. et al. (2008), 'The Absurd in the Field of Genetic Diagnosis', in M. Orme et al. (eds), *Albert Camus in the 21st Century* (Amsterdam: Rodopi), 157–168.

Porz, R. and Scully, J.L. (2009), 'Entfremdung and Absurdität? Die prädiktive Gendiagnostik aus der Patientenperspektive', in S. Dungs et al. (eds), *Biotechnologien in sozialen und medizinischen Disziplinen and Professionen. Neue gesellschaftliche Leitbilder and soziale Praxen.*

Rehmann-Sutter, C. (2006), 'Die Empfindung von Schuld and die Ethik der Retro-spektive', in G. Pfleiderer et al. (ed.), *Zeithorizonte des Ethischen – Zur Bedeutung der Temporalität in der Fundamental- and bioethics* (Stuttgart: Kohlhammer), 103–122.

Rehmann-Sutter, C. (2008), 'Genetics, A Practical Anthropology', in M. Düwell et al. (ed.), *The Contigent Nature of Life* (Dordrecht: Springer).

Rommetveit, K. and Porz, R. (2009), 'Tragedy and grenzsituationen in genetic prediction', *Medicine, Health Care and Philosophy* 12:1, 9–16.

Schweizerische Akademie der Medizinischen Wissenschaften (SAMW) (2004), *Genetische Untersuchungen im medizinischen Alltag.*

Scully, J.L. (2006), 'Time, Tests and Moral Space', in G. Pfleiderer et al. (ed.), *Zeithorizonte des Ethischen – Zur Bedeutung der Temporalität in der Fundamental- and Bioethics* (Stuttgart: Kohlhammer), 151–164.

Scully, J.L. et al. (2007), 'You don't make genetic test decisions from one day to the next: Using time to preserve moral space', *Bioethics* 21:4, 208–217.

Smith, J.A. (2003), 'Interpretative Phenomenological Analysis', in J.A. Smith (ed.), *Qualitative Psychology* (London: Sage), 51–80.

Widdershoven, G. and Van der Scheer, L. (2004), 'Integrated empirical ethics: Loss of normativity?', *Medicine, Health Care and Philosophy* 7, 71–79.

Chapter 6
Testing for Susceptibility Genes: A Cautionary Tale

Margaret Lock

In a 1997 article entitled 'Plundered Memories', published in the now defunct journal *The Sciences*, Zaven Khachaturian, the Director of the Ronald and Nancy Reagan Research Institute of the Alzheimer's Association had this to say:

> Some critics ask whether genetic research is worth the resources it consumes and the anguish it will bring to those who test positive for a harmful gene – when a cure still seems so far away. In my view, however, the genetic approach is on the right track, and I think the continuing research on Alzheimer's disease may soon confirm that belief. Those of us in the front lines of the fight against Alzheimer's have never been closer to unmasking this mysterious thief, the robber of the very thing that makes human beings unique. (Khachaturian 1997, 21)

In the same year, 1997, John Hardy, who researches the genetics of Alzheimer's disease (AD), and is currently Chief of the Laboratory of Neurogenetics at the National Institute of Aging (NIA) of the US argued: 'We now know several *causes* (emphasis added) of Alzheimer's disease (all of them genetic).' Hardy had in mind both early-onset AD, in which genes with an autosomally dominant mode of transmission are invariably involved, *and* late-onset AD in which the implicated susceptibility gene functions in a non-Mendelian manner and is estimated to be involved in only somewhere between 30 per cent and 60 per cent of the disease incidence. Hardy cannot be faulted for underestimating the complexity of action of this latter gene, given that his comment was made nearly a decade ago, and he went on to declare, '… The unofficial "goal" of the NIA is to have some form of effective therapy by the year 2000 and this goal may yet be realized' (1997). At the time Hardy was perhaps justified in assuming that the new genetic insights could well bring about therapeutic advances but, as is well known, effective medication for AD has yet to be found, even though research into the genetics of dementia has accelerated exponentially since the end of the twentieth century.

In this chapter I will first present a rather simplified overview of the current state of knowledge about the genetics of AD, with emphasis on the common, late-onset form of the disease. The second half of the chapter will be devoted to a discussion of genetic testing for Alzheimer's including presentation of some findings from a controlled trial in which first degree relatives of Alzheimer patients are being given their APOE test results and then followed for a year to monitor any effects this knowledge may have had on their lives. The APOE gene, one form of which is associated with being at increased risk for late-onset AD, is not a Mendelian gene, but rather a susceptibility gene. As the following section will show, APOE provides an excellent example of a gene strongly associated with an adult-onset complex disease, but that is neither necessary nor sufficient to cause the disease. It is, therefore, of importance to examine how information about the effects of the gene are imparted to individuals considered to be at risk, and how they respond to genotyping. The findings from open-ended interviews, to be discussed below, with individuals who come from families where AD has been diagnosed, strongly suggest that after learning one's genotype, feelings of uncertainty about the future, and who in the family will get AD, persist. However, people do not exhibit undue anxiety about something that may happen 20 years down the road, nor do they become consumed by their 'genetic identity.' On the contrary, many simply forget their test results entirely.

The Genetics of Alzheimer's Disease

Alois Alzheimer originally observed what is now known as 'early-onset' AD. This form of dementia occurs in only approximately 170 extended families worldwide (although the number may increase with further research), has long been thought of as a 'genetic disease' and is associated with three specific, genetic mutations all of which have been mapped (St. George-Hyslop 2000). Early-onset AD usually (but not inevitably) manifests itself somewhere between the ages of 35 and 60, progresses relatively quickly to death, and accounts for between 2 per cent and 5 per cent of all diagnosed cases of the disease. It is of note that it is not strictly true to claim that the gene *determines* even this autosomal dominant form of the disease, because the age of onset for identical twins can vary by as much as a decade (Tilley et al. 1998).

In 1993 the first publication appeared explicitly making an association between the APOE gene and an increased risk for the common, late-onset form of AD (Corder et al. 1993). This finding forced some revisions of the received wisdom of the time – namely that AD in older people is 'sporadic', and does not 'run in families'. The APOE gene, present in all mammals, is located in humans on chromosome 19, and is essential for lipid metabolism. This gene manifests itself in three forms that are universally distributed, APOEε2, APOEε3 and APOEε4, and evidence from over 100 laboratories indicates that it is the APOEε4 allele that puts individuals at increased risk for AD. Between 14 per cent and 16 per cent of Caucasian populations (the most extensively studied population) carry at least one ε4 allele, however, it is unanimously agreed that the presence of the allele is neither necessary nor sufficient to cause the disease, for reasons that are as yet very poorly understood and it is estimated that at least 50 per cent of ε4 carriers never succumb to AD.

Research in connection with the allele shows that when it *is* implicated in AD, exactly the same final biological pathway is involved as that set in motion by the autosomal dominant genes associated with the early-onset form of the disease; but the biological changes in which APOEε4 in its homozygous form is implicated become manifest later in life, usually between the ages of 65 and 75 (Selkoe 2002). For individuals who are heterozygous and have only one ε4 allele, the age of onset is later. Given that somewhere between 30 per cent and 60 per cent of patients diagnosed with late-onset AD do not have the APOEε4 allele (Myers et al. 1996), there must be at least one other, and probably several more pathways to AD. It is assumed that such pathways are constituted by mutually interactive genes and non-coding DNA, in conjunction with environmental factors, internal and/or external to the body. These alternative pathways become evident late in life, usually after the age of 70, but they too result in the same final common pathway as that for early-onset AD and APOEε4-linked AD, with the characteristic pathological signs that can only be seen at autopsy – plaques, tangles and cell loss in the brain. Because, in addition to APOEε4, it is assumed that several more genes must be implicated in late-onset AD, intensive gene hunting continues unabated.

The current situation has recently been summarized by two neurogeneticists as follows: 'First, and most importantly, the heritability of AD is high … this had been demonstrated in various studies … over the past decades.' But, these experts go on to note: 'Most of the research currently being done has faulty methodology, lacks replication, and is inattentive to haplotype structure' (Bertram and Tanzi 2004, R135). Using the citation index PubMed, Bertram and Tanzi show that in 2003 alone a total of 1037 studies were carried out on the genetics of AD, out of which 55 analyzed genes were reported to have a positive association with increased risk for the disease, while 68 tested negative. Candidate genes have been examined on every single chromosome and mitochondrial DNA has also been investigated. These authors conclude with a caveat: 'While the genetic association per se [of APOEε4 with AD] has been extremely well established … there is no consensus as to *how* this association translates pathophysiologically' nor how it functions in conjunction with the other numerous candidate genes (Bertram and Tanzi 2004, R137).

Until recently, because the disease is limited to older people, and because researchers thought that it was sporadic in origin, pedigree studies with large extended families have not been carried out in connection with late-onset AD. Now that the results of such research are beginning to accrue, the inconclusive nature of knowledge about APOE is glaringly evident. The more such articles are published, a clear impression is created that too much weight may have been given by researchers to the contribution of the APOEε4 allele to AD, although at the same time research continues to show that this allele is indeed regularly implicated in both familial and sporadic forms of AD, and also in heart disease. The biological anthropologist, Alan Templeton, is particularly critical of the conclusions drawn by most researchers into APOE function. He points out that genomes are 'commonly organized into clusters of functionally related genes' and that APOE is part of one such cluster. Templeton argues that when this type of gene is associated by linkage with a specific phenotype great caution is called for, because the gene may simply be a marker for another gene or genes located nearby on the same, clustered segment of DNA that may actually be contributing to the pathology (Templeton 1998, 376).

Even given the obvious complexity, the genetic epidemiologist, Richard Mayeux commenting on the genetics of AD in a recent New Yorker article, made it clear that he does not believe we will be held back too much longer by the current knowledge deficit: 'A decade from now your doctor will look up your gene profile and decide whether you have a high risk for Alzheimer's, and then give you a prophylactic treatment of some sort.' He adds: 'Right now, you don't know what the hell to do!' (Halpern 2005).

Despite this optimism, population research in connection with the genetics of both early- and late-onset AD suggests that no straightforward solution is in sight. This type of research has amply demonstrated that genes are shape-shifters without peer, the products of evolutionary and recent human history, possibly of toxic environments and, at times, of serendipitous mutations. Most epidemiological research into the genetics of AD has been carried out since the early 1990s, when the significance of the ApoE ε4 allele was first identified but, as noted above, these studies have been confined largely to so-called Caucasian populations (Growdon 1997; Korovaitseva et al. 2001; Roses 1998; Saunders 2000; Silverman et al. 2003). Even though the methodology has been criticized, this research makes it clear that the relationship between ApoEε4 and AD incidence is probably significantly weaker than commonly suggested. One community-based study found that 85 per cent of elderly homozygous ε4 individuals whose average age was 81 showed no sign of dementia when given the standard tests for cognitive functioning (Hyman et al. 1996).

Adding to the uncertainties, ApoE ε4 has been shown to work in unexpected ways in specific populations. Among Pygmies, Bushmen, Lapps and other groups of people whose subsistence economy was until relatively recently predominantly that of hunting and gathering, possession of an ApoEε4 genotype *apparently* protects against AD. This finding holds when controlled for age (Corbo and Scacchi 1999). Low rates of AD have been reported for parts of Nigeria, and the presence of an ε4 allele does not appear to place individuals at increased risk. On the other hand, ApoEε4 is significantly associated with dementia among African Americans, although less so than in Caucasian populations (Farrer et al. 2000). Once again, the methodology of this research has been criticized, but the data appear sufficiently robust to conclude that risk-reducing factors (in Africa) *and* risk-enhancing factors (in North America) must be implicated, among them other genes, their protein products, diet, environment and quite possibly yet other variables.

It is evident that basic science and epidemiological findings about late-onset AD are subject to continual revision and are far from conclusive. It is no surprise, then, that current guidelines about genetic testing for APOE status do not support its routinization in clinical care, but it is possible that this may change in the not too distant future. Very recently *The Pharmacogenetics Journal* presented preliminary findings concerning a new drug, Rosiglitazone (Risner et al. 2006) This drug alters glucose metabolism in the brain and, it is reported, has a positive effect on cognitive functioning, but only on those patients with mild to moderate AD who are APOEε3. This finding, by the team of Allan Roses, the same researcher who first reported that APOEε4 puts individuals at increased risk for AD, and who is now the CEO of the pharmaceutical company GlaxoSmithKline, suggests that, *should* this drug move successfully through clinical trials, AD genotyping will likely become routinized in clinical settings. Other researchers are working on similar drugs believed to function differentially according to genotype.

Embodying a Predisposition

Edward Yoxen (1982) suggested over two decades ago that newfound abilities to detect 'pre-symptomatically ill' individuals would ensure that virtually all of us would be subject to increased medical surveillance in the near future. Among the technologies designed to assist in making predictions about the future that Yoxen had in mind were genetic testing and screening. The relentless pace of technological development in connection with molecular biology and the hype and public acclaim that accompany much of it, have caused concern among many critical commentators (see for example Duster 1990). It has been suggested that social scientists and bioethicists, may collude in the hype by 'over-sensationalizing' the potential of such technologies to transform society at large (Franklin 1995, 178). This is certainly the case at times, but it is becoming increasingly clear that Yoxen's statement about medical surveillance was not hyperbolic.

Many years ago Lippman created the concept of 'geneticization' to characterize her concern about the introduction of molecular genetics into the clinic 'in which differences between individuals are reduced to their DNA codes' (1992, 1470). She argued that an indirect reinforcement of racism, social inequalities and discrimination of various kinds is likely to result from a newly rekindled conflation of social realities and an essentialized biology grounded in small differences in DNA sequences among individuals (for evidence of this see, for example, Draper 1991; Duster 1990; Parens and Asch 1999; Paul and Spencer 1995). Lippman further argued that we might well be witnessing an incipient neo-eugenics, a consequence of the voluntary termination of pregnancies on the basis of results obtained from fetal genetic testing. Other writers have made similar comments, noting that what in the early twentieth century was enforced by the state through involuntary sterilization programs is now carried out under the rubric of individual choice (see, for example, Kitcher 1996).

Increasingly nuanced investigation of the way that people respond to and are affected by the introduction of molecular genetics into the clinic and public health screening programs are being carried out (Kerr et al. 1998; Michie et al. 1995). This shift in emphasis that parallels other social science research in connection with the public understanding of science more generally, shows clearly how individuals and families are profoundly affected by genetic testing (Hallowell 1999; Novas and Rose 2000), and in families where lethal childhood diseases are common, parents frequently become politicized in order to advance research that may help overcome the particular disease that affects their family (Heath et al. 2004; Rapp 2003).

In contrast, other studies have documented the way in which individuals actively interpret available knowledge about molecular genetics, and how they frequently exhibit resistance to using genetic explanations alone to account for the illnesses that 'run' in their families (Condit 1999; Lock et al. 2006). Furthermore, when genetic information is incorporated into accounts about illness causation, such information supplements previously held notions of kinship, heredity and health. For example, Cox and McKellin (1999, 130), writing about Huntington's disease, have shown that lay understandings of heredity conflict with theories of Mendelian genetics because scientific explanations prove to be inadequate for families dealing with the lived experience of genetic risk. They argue, on the basis of empirical findings: 'Theories of Mendelian inheritance frame risk in static, objective terms. They abstract risk from the messiness of human contingency and biography' (1999, 140). Their findings show graphically how at certain junctures in an individual's life cycle – notably when making decisions about reproduction – knowledge obtained from genetic testing is recognized as useful but, in general, factors such as social proximity to an affected family member and the family's inter-subjective construction of risk are the most significant forms of knowledge that inform everyday life. Kerr suggests that it is reasonable to assume that lay people are their own authority when it comes to appreciating and understanding how exactly genetics may shape their lives (Kerr et al. 1998).

To date, almost all social science research into the social ramifications of the new genetics has concentrated on the impact of transmitting information about mutant genes with a highly predictable (but not fully so) mode of Mendelian transmission. This commentary is exceedingly rich, and has set a high standard for future research. However, the creation and transmission of knowledge about susceptibility genes associated with complex diseases such as the APOE gene poses a challenge that far exceeds what we have been confronted with to date. For one thing, as suggested above, molecular biology, population genetics and clinical practice are riddled with competing discourses that must be analyzed in their own terms as part of a reflexive approach (Lock 2005).

It is now recognized among virtually all involved researchers that there is no simple correspondence between genotype and phenotype and, for complex traits, 'usually only a weak (and often variable) correlation between genotype and phenotype' (Nijhout 2001, 129). The philosopher of biology, Lenny Moss, notes that as a developmental resource a gene is 'ontologically on the same plane as any number of other biomolecules' (2004, 47). And biologist Steven Rose argues: 'The functioning cell, as a unit, constrains the properties of its individual components. The whole has primacy over its parts' (1997, 169). The contents of human cells –

DNA, RNA, enzymes, proteins and other key molecules including important regulatory ions, mutually interact throughout the life course of individuals, in a dynamic molecular mix. This interaction is influenced by micro-environments – intra and extra cellular – and by macro-environments external to the body. Disruptions in this complex cell machinery, stimulated toxins and stressors of various kinds, as well as by the process of aging, result in temporary fluctuations or else outright pathology, and eventually death of the organism.

In the case of Mendelian diseases, a basic grasp of the relevant scientific knowledge means that individuals understand how transmission of genes is accomplished and, further, that such genes have high penetrance – in other words having either one or two copies of such a gene leads to predictable outcomes (although age of onset and severity often cannot be predicted). Knowledge about the presence of one or two copies of a specific mutational gene, together with information about average age of onset of the disease, can then be drawn on to make crucial family decisions, most often in connection with reproduction.

The situation is quite different with susceptibility genes because estimates of risk are based on calculations of probability that have low explanatory power. Adding to the complexity, professional understanding about the molecular genetics of complex disease is for the most part 'knowledge-in-flux,' with the result that the variables on which estimates of probability are made are subject to revision. We are not dealing with 'matters of fact', but with information that is both provisional and probabilistic, and that must, of course, be translated into estimates presumed relevant for individual cases. Given the complexity involved it is fair to question, I believe, whether such estimates are of any value to individuals in their daily lives.

Genetic Testing for Late-onset Alzheimer's Disease

Even though official guidelines are currently opposed to routine testing for the APOE gene, several private companies offer testing (the US-based Athena diagnostics holds the patent for APOE testing), and an 'Early Alert Alzheimer's Home Screening Test' kit is marketed directly to consumers (Kier and Molinari 2003). Furthermore, a strong argument is being made among certain neurologists that individuals diagnosed with Mild Cognitive Impairment (believed to be a sign of incipient AD) should be routinely tested for their APOE status. Recent research suggests that although by no means everyone diagnosed with MCI 'converts' to AD, those diagnosed individuals who also have the ε4 allele are at much greater risk for conversion, and should be identified as early as possible (Farlow et al. 2004). In addition to testing carried out in these settings, an NIH-approved randomized controlled trial involving APOE testing that goes under the name of REVEAL (Risk Evaluation and Education for Alzheimer's disease) is in progress. Families where one or more members have been diagnosed with AD are subjects for this research. Findings from ethnographic interviews with 65 of these research subjects will be presented in the last section of this chapter.

The REVEAL trial was originally a three-sited project involving 162 subjects at Boston University Medical School; Case Western Reserve, Cleveland and Cornell University Medical School, New York, but has been extended to include Howard University in Washington DC. Subjects were recruited either through systematic ascertainment from American AD research registries kept at the respective medical schools, or through self-referral at each site (Cupples et al. 2004). Upon recruitment into Phase 1 of the project, research subjects were randomized into intervention and control groups. In the original three-sited sample everyone self-identified as 'white' and the majority are women. Participants are highly educated, with a mean of 17 years of education. The Howard sample identify themselves as African Americans and also have a high mean education level, of 15 plus years. All participants reported that they are highly motivated and eager to assist with medical research into AD. Upon recruitment they were required to attend an educational session about AD in the form of a PowerPoint presentation, with emphasis on theories about causation of AD, including estimates of genetic susceptibility based on gender, family history and genotype, after which they were asked to return to the research site at a later date for a blood draw. People in the intervention arm were informed a few weeks later about their APOE status. People assigned to be controls were not given this information until after the study was completed, more than a year later. Reactions of the subjects to APOE testing were systematically monitored by means of three follow-up structured interviews conducted by genetic counsellors over the course of 12 months, and then compared with the reactions of individuals in the control group. In phase II of the project, at four sites, everyone was given their APOE status from the outset and both clinicians and counsellors were involved in disclosing APOE status to research subjects.[1] A subset of 65 individuals were interviewed by a small group of anthropologists, including myself.[2] These individuals volunteered to return after the completion of the basic REVEAL study to participate in hour-long open-ended interviews. This is the first comprehensive study of risk disclosure in connection with a susceptibility gene and is, therefore, of considerable interest.

---

1 The initial intake for REVEAL II was 446 subjects, 326 of whom were randomized into the trial. After the blood draw, several subjects dropped out or were screened out leaving 280 people who were informed of their APOE status, only 255 of whom continued through to completion of the 12-month follow-up interview.

2 Janalyn Prest and Stephanie Lloyd, affiliated with the Anthropology department at McGill University, acted as research assistants and conducted and coded most of the qualitative interviews from Phase I of the REVEAL study. Heather Lindstrom, in the Anthropology department at Case Western Reserve also conducted some interviews. Julia Freeman and Gillian Chilibeck, Anthropology department, McGill University, conducted the interviews at Howard University and transcribed and coded the data.

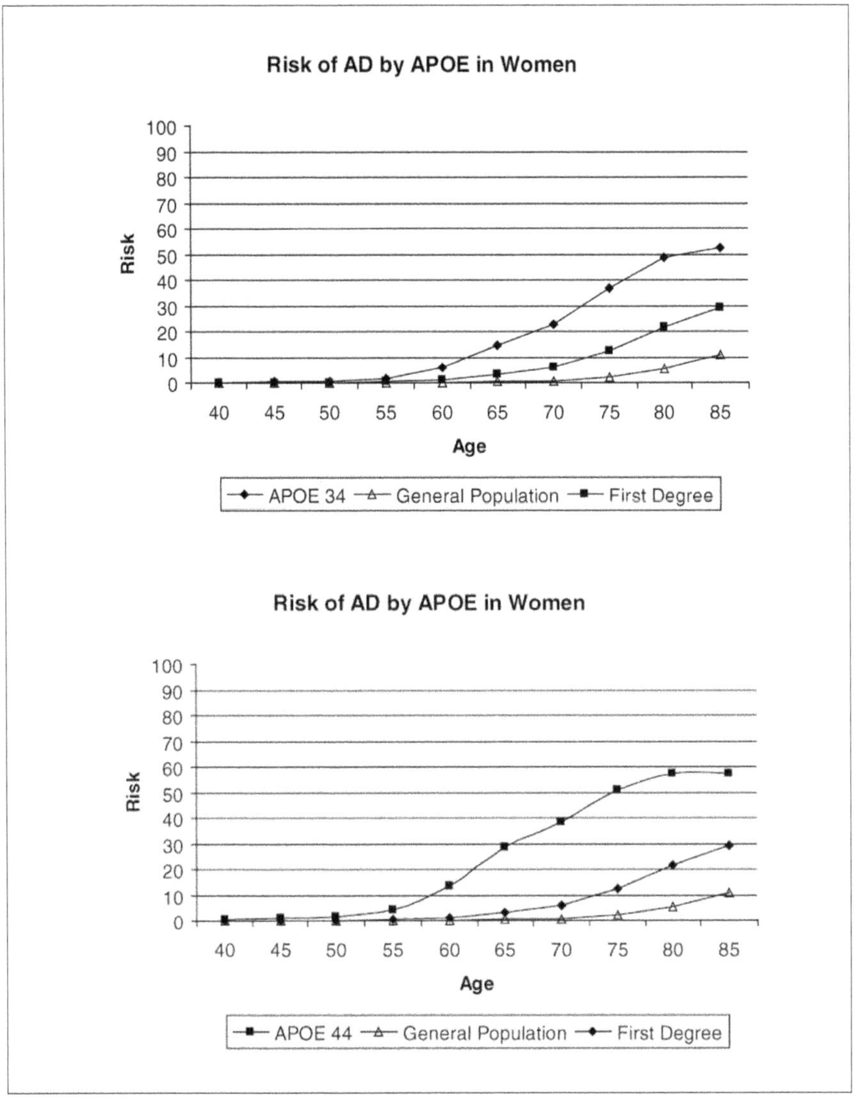

Figure 6.1 Lifetime risk curves for use in the education and counselling protocol for women with genotypes ε3/ε4 and ε4/ε4, for the individual concerned and their first-degree relatives, compared with the general population

Source: Reproduced with permission by the publishers of the journal from J. Scott Roberts, et al., 'Genetic Risk Assessment for Adult Children of People With Alzheimer's Disease: The Risk Evaluation and Education for Alzheimer's Disease (REVEAL) Study', *Journal of Geriatric Psychiatry and Neurology* 18(2005), 250–255.

In order to carry out the 'risk disclosure' portion of the study all subjects are shown a 'risk curve' (Figure 6.1). These curves were developed by drawing on gender- and age-specific incidence curves for first degree relatives of persons with AD that had already been calculated on the basis of a meta-analysis of studies involving very large samples of Caucasian subjects (Green et al. 1997) (a modified curve is used with the African American sample at Howard University). In addition, the curves were further subdivided by incorporating APOE genotype-specific odds ratio estimates for gender and age, reported in a second pooled analysis of 50 studies worldwide (Farrer et al. 1997). This gives a total of 12 curves based on the six possible combinations of APOE alleles for both males and females. Risk curves for the control group in REVEAL I were based on gender, age and family history alone. Genetic counsellors and clinicians (in the case of half of the REVEAL II participants) show the risk curve appropriate to each trial participant, and explain their individual estimated increased risk for AD into old age.

The graph for subjects who were assigned to the control group has two curves on it: one shows the curve for the 'normal' population and the second, slightly steeper curve, represents increased risk by age for individuals who are first degree relatives of AD patients. Those people who have undergone genotyping are shown three curves on the graphs they view; the third curve represents increased risk on the basis of genotype. For individuals who are e2/3 or e3/3, their risk is increased only a small amount, on the basis of their affected relative alone. For those individuals who are ε3/4, and especially ε4/4, risk is clearly increased, but to a maximum for the 4/4's of 52 per cent by age 85. Creating these risk curves entails exceedingly complex mathematical formulations (Cupples et al. 2004).

One justification for this research is that testing for susceptibility genes, it is argued, is likely to become increasingly common, especially in the private sector, and therefore knowledge about how people deal with risk information when it is impossible to make predictions with a high degree of confidence is urgently needed. A second justification is that to withhold information about their bodies from people is patronizing. A third justification is that in many families where someone has died of AD some members of the next generation may well believe that they have a virtually 100 per cent chance of contracting the disease. If individuals can be taught that, even if they are homozygous for APOEε4, their lifetime risk for getting AD is never more than approximately 52 per cent for men and 58 per cent for women, then anxiety levels may well be lowered. The fourth explicit justification for the research is to create a pool of APOEε4 individuals whose bloods can be used at any time to 'enrich clinical trials'. The majority of people who participated in the NIH study stated that they did so primarily to assist with research, rather than to learn about their own APOE status, although this information was also of considerable interest.

Interpretation of Risk Estimates

Results from the follow-up questionnaires indicate that people do not experience increased anxiety levels that extends much beyond the time of actually receiving their result (LaRusse 2005). By the time the open-ended interviews were carried out, more than 12 months after being told of their estimated risk, the majority of participants had transformed the estimates they had been given into accounts that 'fit' with their experience of being related to someone with AD, personal assessments of their own family history and the accumulated knowledge about the disease that they had gathered from a variety of sources. In other words, risk estimates provided in the REVEAL study rarely displace 'lay knowledge' that participants bring with them to the project about who in their family is particularly at risk. Rather, this 'scientific' information is either nested into pre-existing knowledge, simply forgotten or even actively rejected.

Carolyn, a 52-year-old psychiatric nurse from the Boston area, in contrast to most of the other subjects, clearly remembers the risk assessment she was given as part of the study. She expresses her major motivation for participating in the project as supporting her sister, who also took part in REVEAL. Carolyn is married but has no children, whereas her sister has two children, and Carolyn perceives an enormous difference in the significance of testing for the two of them: 'If Alzheimer's happens to me, it happens to me. But I would be much more concerned if I had children … I would want to know every single thing out there. She has two kids, you know … So when my sister learned that the testing was in Boston, I really came along for her, not so much for myself … I mean, it's good knowledge to have for myself, but I wanted to be there for her … To do it together as sisters.'

Carolyn and her sister were both in the randomized group that received their APOE status. Carolyn learned she has a 3/3 genotype, whereas her sister has a 3/4 status. Carolyn's experience as a caregiver contributed to her response to her sister's results: 'In all honesty, I try not to think about it, because when I think about it I think about what I went through with my dad. I really don't want to think about going through it with her, you know.'

When asked specifically about her reaction to her own results, Carolyn responded: 'I didn't think one way or the other when I found out my risk factor.' But she adds: 'Knowledge is power. I really believe that. I mean, I don't think you can necessarily change your destiny, but certainly to go through life with your eyes only half open doesn't help you at all.'

However Carolyn remains unsure of what kinds of actions such power might motivate: 'I think (REVEAL) provides useful information … Just don't ask me how I would use it … I honestly don't know.'

Perhaps this response by Caroline is a partial answer as to why, a year after testing, nearly 75 per cent of the participants had forgotten, mixed up or were confused about their risk estimates. This is particularly noteworthy when 91 per cent of the informants stated that 'wanting to know' their genotype was a major motivation for participation in the REVEAL study. And they would recommend that their friends and relatives also go through such testing.

Although most could not recall their risk estimates accurately, nearly half had retained the gist of the information – usually they were able to recall if they have a 'good' or 'bad' gene. Among the four people who were given the highest risk estimates, the homozygous ε4s, three were able to recall their genotype, and the fourth remembered that she has the 'bad genes'. She said, when interviewed: 'I'm still totally confused, although I know I have two of them, whatever those bad things are.' Another individual, also a homozygous ε4, although she remembers that her increased lifetime risk is not quite 60 per cent (some of which she has lived through), nevertheless remains convinced that she will without a doubt get the disease, as she already believed before she entered the study. This individual has seven affected relatives, and no doubt this contributes to her certainty about her future, despite what she has been taught about AD risk in REVEAL.

The single African American who is homozygous for ε4 has only one affected relative, her mother. Pearl is able to recall her genotype, and has a rough idea of her increased risk over the coming years; however she says that she knew about this risk anyway because of her 'blood' (meaning her family history) and adds: 'Really, it's all up to God, you know.' She is pleased she was tested and angry with her sisters because they simply 'brushed off' her result, as she puts it. Pearl was hoping REVEAL would 'prove' that she wouldn't get AD, but now she is back in God's hands. She says she was anxious while going through the study, but that this anxiety let up quite quickly once she had completed all the interviews. As a result of the project she has reduced the fats in her diet and is thinking about changing her health insurance, but cannot really afford to do this. Other than her immediate family, Pearl has not told anyone about her result, not even her family doctor. She believes that what counts more than anything else is a positive attitude coupled with faith.

Other informants very clearly express their confusion about the test results: 'I would come in – from one meeting to the next, I would come in and I couldn't remember what my risk was. And to this day, I'm not 100 per cent sure. But I know that it's elevated.'

Another responded: 'I don't remember much … to be truthful, not much. I'm sure I have (my risk estimate) somewhere, but I don't remember where.'

A third person demanded of us: 'Is it the 3/4 that's the least likely to get it? I don't even remember. But it was good news. Whatever it was.'

And another stated emphatically: 'Well, I know where I am at, where I stand. I can let my kids know where we stand. You know, I mean, maybe get it, maybe not.'

One woman, when asked to explain more about the 'bad things' replied: 'I don't know. I don't know what gene it is … It's not the BRCA [a gene associated with breast cancer].'

Several people found that the information provided by REVEAL conflicted with their own understanding about the future. Rebecca, 48, who learnt that she has 3/3 genotype has four affected relatives. She insists: 'According to that [AD test], I don't have the risk, okay? So, technically I should feel better. But I don't believe it, given my family.'

Subjective experiences about memory loss appear to raise anxiety levels more so than does genotyping: 'I can say that I've always felt all my life that I've had some memory issues … so, I have that little question, whether it's something that you actually had in some way even when you were very young … Do people wind up getting Alzheimer's who were aware of some memory problem when they were younger, and the connection hasn't been researched yet?'

The concept of 'blended inheritance' put forward some years ago by Martin Richards refers to a prevalent understanding among the public involving a 'mixing or blending of influences from each parent', rather than one entailing a Mendelian transmission of genes (Richards 1996, 222). Such ideas stem from a long tradition of such reasoning evident as early as classical times (Turney 1995, 12). Richards suggested, in connection with single gene disorders, that the notion of blended inheritance not only conflicts with professional explanations about genetics, but also works to reduce acceptance of those same explanations, both in the classroom and the clinic (1996).

The REVEAL qualitative findings make clear that blended inheritance is, not surprisingly, also drawn on by families when confronted with inconclusive risk estimates for a complex disease such as Alzheimer's. In other words, there is a consistent tendency to identify a family member who in some way resembles the afflicted person as the individual most likely to be at risk for developing the disorder, whether individual genotypes are known or not. Anne Kerr and colleagues commented some years ago that, in effect, individuals act as their own authority about the interpretation of genomic information and this is what we also found (1998).

For example, Jane, who was given a 3/3 typing and has one affected relative comments: 'My risk before 85 was just minimally more than others. After 85, like 15 per cent more. To me, that made no sense … I really believe I don't have much chance of missing it just by my genealogy. I mean … when I look at both sides of my family, my mother's family is all – there's nothing else, just Alzheimer's. My father's side, there's no Alzheimer's. It's heart trouble and high cholesterol and high triglycerides. Well, I take after my mother.'

Similarly, Laura said: 'I've shown you the picture of me and my dad. We look like clones, practically, physically. And nobody's really said – I don't know whether the information is out there because I haven't read it – whether or not that makes a difference, a person's physical appearance. But I have a suspicion that it does.'

When Katherine is asked if she worries about AD, she says: 'Worry is a big word; does it ever cross my mind? Yes. Do I worry about it? My brother worries, and my mother worries more about my brother than me. She thinks his personality is more likely to be similar to hers than mine.'

A middle aged man, Robert, commented: 'Do I think I have a higher than normal chance? Yes. Heredity. And also I'm so much like my mother, who had Alzheimer's. There's a very high likelihood that one or more of her children will have a predisposition toward it. And I would say I'm front-runner because of so many other characteristics that are very much like my mother's.'

When the REVEAL interviewees discussed theories of causation, multi-causal explanations were common and, despite the emphasis given to genetics throughout the project, this did not dominate the exchanges. When asked what caused her father's illness Carolyn responded: 'I can't pinpoint any one thing.' Another 74-year-old participant, when asked in what way she believes genetics is involved in Alzheimer disease causation replied: 'I think it plays a part, but I don't think that's all. I'm sure that a lot of the diet, and the health, and the exercise that we do today will prolong life and mental acuity.'

And a 52-year-old woman noted: 'It's a Russian roulette kind of thing. Everything's got to be working against you, whatever those factors may be. And I don't even know what. Aluminum in your teeth? You hear some of those things. I don't know.'

Every one of the REVEAL participants seemed particularly receptive to what they had been taught about the uncertainty of how exactly genetics contributes to AD. The education sessions that REVEAL participants were required to attend in all probability worked to reinforce the concept of blended inheritance already in the minds of the majority of participants prior to the study. No doubt because it was repeatedly emphasized that the APOEε4 allele does *not* determine disease occurrence but only puts individuals at increased risk, participants were not reassured about what the future has in store for them, even after testing.

The genetic counsellors are experienced and empathetic, and they spent a great deal of time with each subject at their test site. As noted above, in addition to the education session, and the disclosure session, counsellors had three follow up interviews with subjects over the course of a year. It was evident from the qualitative interviews that REVEAL participants were comfortable with the counsellors and two were described as 'treasures', or the equivalent. However, the uncertainty associated with the information that they had to impart made counsellors and participants feel frustrated. One counsellor communicated to me that it was not so much the 'fuzziness' of the information that that concerned her (she already had experience in discussing results of breast and colon cancer testing with patients), but the standardized method used by REVEAL to impart the probability data. This counsellor believes that many of the REVEAL subjects did not grasp the import of the graphic data, even when it was explained to them. In my opinion, the relatively low estimates of increased lifetime risk, late onset of the disease, and the number of affected family members that above all accounts for the reactions of trial subjects.

In summary, genetic testing for APOE status did not apparently cause increased anxiety, or only temporarily so, in part, I believe, because genomic or 'science-based' explanations do not displace common sense explanations. It is also evident that many individuals who believed they are at 100 per cent risk for AD because of their family history were reassured that this is not the case – this reassurance was welcomed most keenly by those individuals (the majority of participants) who were told that they do not have an ε4 allele.[3] There is, of course, a possibility that some of these people now believe they will *not* get AD, but the education session was designed to avoid this misunderstanding. Given that this project took place in the US, some people were motivated to improve their health care insurance coverage on the basis of their test results.

Subjectivity and Susceptibility Genes

The APOE gene is an effective research tool, and continued use of it by both basic scientists and population geneticists may well unravel some of the impasses with which they are currently confronted. However, it seems unlikely that much progress will be made unless serious attention is paid to epigenetics and how APOE functions in cellular contexts, that are in turn influenced by larger macro-environments (Jablonka and Lamb 2005; Lock 2005; Oyama et al. 2001; Rose 2005; Weiss and Buchanan 2003). It is highly likely that the findings from such research will show that future risk for AD can never be accurately predicted on the basis of APOE testing alone, and that other environmental and/or developmental variables may prove to have greater predictive power. Given the state of current knowledge, as noted above, APOE test results are not considered valuable for use in the clinic, except on occasion to give added weight to a diagnosis of probable AD. Unless clinical trials with genotypically specific medication prove successful, this situation is unlikely to change.

I believe that the validity of the individualized risk curves and increased risk estimates that people are being given as part of the REVEAL project have to be questioned, given the complexity of APOE functioning. But responses of REVEAL participants suggest that in any case few if any significant changes take place with respect to their sense of identity or subjectivity as a result of the testing. Individuals do not apparently adopt 'genetic identities,' nor believe their futures to be profoundly changed from what they had already envisioned. Rather they hold firm to ideas already internalized about hereditary and the power of phenotypic resemblances, AD multi-causality and the impossibility of ever being sure about the future when a stubborn disease such as AD is at issue. By far the majority of people in the REVEAL study were not, it seems, vulnerable to media hype, nor had they been fed a false optimism by taking part in the project. Quite the contrary. Although some people had come into the study seeking out definitive information, only to be thwarted and disappointed.

3 Results from the REVEAL quantitative interviews show that 80 per cent of a subgroup of people who tested 3/3 were very positive about the study, and 67 per cent had lower anxiety levels about AD than they did prior to the study (LaRusse et al. 2005).

However, given how often articles appear in the newspaper these days about clinics offering genetic testing (see, for example, Abraham 2005), there may well be members of the public, believing they would be acting prudently, who want to learn about their APOE status. But few, if any, would get the counselling that the REVEAL participants were given, and for them the odds of misunderstanding the probabilistic results, if indeed they are given this type of information at all, are very high indeed, especially so since it is clear that, even with extensive counselling, people often come away confused. Research shows that family doctors, AD societies, the media and Internet chat rooms (Lock et al. 2007) do not lead people to believe that one specific gene determines late-onset AD. And testing is not actively encouraged by of them. It seems unlikely therefore that many people will seek out such testing, even should it become more widely available, although direct to consumer advertising may in part counter this cautionary approach.

Even when people learn about their APOE status, there is no way of knowing who among those who test positive for ε4 are likely to become demented, even within any one family. And, equally, there is no way of knowing who among the ε3s and ε2s will become demented. An acquaintance of mine, herself a researcher, decided to find out the APOE status of several of her family members because two of the older generation had AD. She was stunned to learn that these two family members are homozygous for ε2, the allele that is supposedly protective. Translation from population databases to individual cases is an insurmountable difficulty. Given the present state of our knowledge, family history rather than APOE status continues to be a better predictor of the future for both clinicians and the public, although it is by not means fool proof given that sporadic cases, regardless of genotype, are common. This situation of uncertainty may well persist unchanged for some time to come making routine testing highly questionable.

References

Abraham, C. (2005), 'Would You Gaze into a Genetic Crystal Ball', in *The Globe and Mail* (Quebec edition), 1, 9, 10.

Bertram, L. and Tanzi R.E. (2004), 'Alzheimer's disease: One disorder, too many genes?', *Human Molecular Genetics* 13, R135–R141.

Condit, C.M. (1999), 'How the public understands genetics: Non-deterministic and non-discriminatory interpretations of the "blueprint" metaphor', *Public Understanding of Science* 8, 169–180.

Corbo, R.M. and Scacchi, R. (1999), 'Apolipoprotein E (APOE) allele distribution in the world: Is APOE*4 a "thrifty" allele?', *Annals of Human Genetics* 63, 301–310.

Corder, E.H. et al. (1993), 'Gene dose of apolipoprotein E type 4 allele and the risk of Alzheimer's disease in late onset families', *Science* 261, 921–3.

Cox, S. and McKellin, W. (1999), '"There's this Thing in our Family": Predictive Testing and the Construction of Risk for Huntington Disease', in P. Conrad and J. Gabe (eds), *Sociological Perspectives on the New Genetics* (London: Blackwell Publishers), 121–148.

Cupples, L.A. et al. (2004), 'Estimating risk curves for first degree relatives of patients with Alzheimer's disease: The REVEAL study', *Genetics in Medicine* 6, 192–196.

Draper, E. (1991), *Risky Business: Genetic Testing and Exclusionary Practices in the Hazardous Workplace* (Cambridge: Cambridge University Press).

Duster, T. (1990), *Backdoor to Eugenics* (2nd edition) (New York and London: Routledge).

Farlow, M.R. et al. (2004), 'Impact of APOE in mild cognitive impairment', *Neurology* 63, 1898–901.

Farrer, L.A. et al. (1997), 'Effects of age, sex, and ethnicity on the association between apolipoprotein E genotype and Alzheimer's disease: A meta-analysis', *Journal of the American Medical Association* 278, 1349–1356.

Farrer, L.A. et al. (2000), 'Association between angiotensin-converting enzyme and Alzheimer disease', *Arch Neurol* 57, 210–214.

Franklin, S. (1995), 'Science as culture, cultures of science', *Annual Review of Anthropology* 24:163–184.

Green, R.C. et al. (1997), 'Early detection of Alzheimer's disease: Methods, markers, and misgivings', *Alzheimer Disease and Associated Disorders* 11, S1–S5.

Growdon, J.H. (1998), 'Apolipoprotein E and Alzheimer's disease', *Archives of Neurology* 55, 1053–1054.

Hallowell, N. (1999), 'Doing the right thing: Genetics risk and responsibility', *Sociology of Health and Illness* 5, 597–621.

Halpern, S. (2005), 'The Gene Hunters: Closing in on the Origins of Alzheimer's Disease', in *The New Yorker*, 84–93.

Hardy, J. (1997), 'The Alzheimer family of diseases: Many etiologies, one pathogenesis?', *Proceedings of the National Academy of Science USA* 94, 2095–7.

Heath, D. et al. (2004), 'Genetic Citizenship', in D. Nugent and J. Vincent (eds), *A Companion to the Anthropology of Politics* (London: Blackwell), 152–167.

Hyman, B.T. et al. (1996), 'Apolipoprotein E and cognitive change in an elderly population', *Annals of Neurology* 40, 55–66.

Jablonka, E. and Lamb, M.J. (2005), *Evolution in Four Dimensions: Genetic, Epigenetic, Behavioral, and Symbolic Variation in the History of Life. Life and Mind* (Cambridge, MA: MIT Press).

Kerr, A. et al. (1998), 'The new human genetics and health: Mobilizing lay expertise', *Public Understanding of Science* 7, 41–60.

Khachaturian, Z.S. (1997), 'Plundered memories', *The Sciences* 37, 21–25.

Kier, F.J. and Molinari, V. (2003), '"Do-it-yourself" dementia testing: Issues regarding an Alzheimer's home screening test', *Gerontologist* 43, 295–301.

Kitcher, P. (1996), *The Lives to Come: The Genetic Revolution and Human Possibilities* (New York: Simon & Schuster).

Korovaitseva, G.I. et al. (2001), 'Genetic association between the apolipoprotein E (APOE) gene and different forms of Alzheimer's disease', *Human Genetics* 37, 422–427.

LaRusse, S. et al. (2005), 'Genetic susceptibility testing versus family history-based risk assessment: Impact on perceived risk of Alzheimer's disease', *Genetic Medicine* 7, 48–53.

Lippman, A. (1992), 'Led (astray) by genetic maps: The cartography of the human genome and human care', *Social Science and Medicine* 35, 1469–1496.

Lock, M. (2005), 'Eclipse of the gene and the return of divination', *Current Anthroplogy* 46, S47–S70.

Lock, M. et al. (2006), 'Genetic Susceptibility and Alzheimer's Disease: The Penetrance and Uptake of Genetic Knowledge', in A. Leibing and L. Cohen (eds), *Thinking about Dementia: Culture, Loss, and the Anthropology of Senility* (New Jersey: Rutgers University Press), 123–156.

Lock, M. et al. (2007), 'Susceptibility Genes and the Question of Embodied Identity', *Medical Anthropology Quarterly* 21, 256–276.

Michie, S. et al. (1995), 'A comparison of public and professionals' attitudes towards genetic developments', *Public Understanding of Science* 4, 243–253.

Moss, L. (2004), *What Genes Can't Do* (Cambridge, MA: MIT Press).

Myers, R.H. et al. (1996), 'Apolipoprotein E epsilon4 association with dementia in a population-based study: The framingham study', *Neurology* 46, 673–7.

Nijhout, H. (2001), 'Cycles of Contingency: Developmental Systems and Evolution', in S. Oyama, P.E. Griffiths and R.D. Gray (eds), *Cycles of Contingency: Developmental Systems and Evolution. Life and Mind* (Cambridge, MA: MIT Press), 129–140.

Novas, C. and Rose, N. (2000), 'Genetic risk and the birth of the somatic individual', *Economy and Society* 29, 485–513.

Oyama, S. (2001), 'Cycles of Contingency: Developmental Systems and Evolution', in S. Oyama, P.E. Griffiths, and R.D. Gray (eds), *Cycles of Contingency: Developmental Systems and Evolution. Life and Mind* (Cambridge, MA: MIT Press), 177–193.

Oyama, S. et al. (2001), *Cycles of Contingency: Developmental Systems and Evolution. Life and Mind* (Cambridge, MA: MIT Press).

Parens, E. and Asch, A. (1999), 'The disability rights critique of prenatal genetic testing: Reflections and recommendations', *Hastings Center Report* 229, S1–S22.

Paul, D.B. and Spencer, H.G. (1995), 'The hidden science of eugenics', *Nature* 374, 302–304.

Rapp, R. (2003), 'Cell Life and Death, Child Life and Death: Genomic Horizons, Genetic Diseases, Family Stories', in S. Franklin and M. Lock (eds), *Remaking Life and Death: Toward and Anthropology of the Biosciences* (Santa Fe: School of American Research), 129–164.

Richards, M. (1996), 'Lay and professional knowledge of genetics and inheritance', *Public Understanding of Science* 5, 217–230.

Risner, M.E. et al. (2006), 'Efficacy of rosiglitazone in a genetically defined population with mild-to-moderate Alzheimer's disease', *Pharmacogenomics Journal* 6, 246–254.

Rose, S.P.R. (1997), *The Future of the Brain: The Promise and Perils of Tomorrow's Neuroscience* (Oxford and New York: Oxford University Press).

Roses, A.D. (1998), 'Apolipoprotein E and Alzheimer's disease: The tip of the susceptibility iceberg', *Annals of the New York Academy of Sciences* 8, 738–743.

Saunders, A.M. (2000), 'Apolipoprotein E and Alzheimer disease: An update on genetic and functional analyses', *Journal of Neuropathology and Experimental Neurology* 59, 751–8.

Selkoe, D.J. (2002), 'The Pathophysiology of Alzheimer's Disease', in L.F.M. Scinto and K.R. Daffner (eds), *Early Diagnosis of Alzheimer's Disease* (Totawa, New Jersey: Humana Press).

Silverman, J.M. (2003), 'Familial patterns of risk in very late-onset Alzheimer's disease', *Archives of General Pyschiatry* 60, 190–197.

St. George-Hyslop, P. (2000), 'Molecular genetics of Alzheimer's disease', *Biological Psychiatry* 47, 183–199.

Templeton, A.R. (1998), 'The complexity of the genotype-phenotype relationship and the limitations of using genetic "markers" at the individual level', *Science in Context* 11, 373–89.

Tilley, L. et al. (1998), 'Genetic risk factors in Alzheimer's disease', *Journal of Clinical Pathology: Molecular Pathology* 51, 293–304.

Turney, J. (1995), 'The public understanding of genetics – where next?', *European Journal of Genetics and Society* 1, 5–22.

Weiss, K. and Buchanan, A.V. (2003), 'Evolution by phenotype: A biomedical perspective', *Perspectives in Biology and Medicine* 46, 159–182.

Yoxen, E.J. (1982), 'Constructing Genetic Diseases', in P. Wright and A. Treacher (eds), *The Problem of Medical Knowledge: Examining the Social Construction of Medicine* (Edinburgh: University of Edinburgh), 144–161.

Chapter 7
'If Only I Had (Not) Known That': About Risk-Individualization, Chance-Specification and the Loss of Certainty of Not-Knowing

Tjeerd Tymstra

Introduction

There is an explosive increase of knowledge within the scientific field. Thousands of new 'discoveries' are being made daily and subsequently published in one of approximately 400,000 scientific journals. A considerable number of these concern health issues. The possibilities offered by the new information technology have led to a vast amount of research into the risks of illness and chances of health. Over time, this has, for example, resulted in the enumeration of hundreds of risk factors connected to cardiovascular disease. This quest for risk factors takes place at a time when there is a great increase in insight into the social origins of illness. Working with a population-orientated approach, one quickly arrives at the lifestyle of the population, for it is well known that an unhealthy lifestyle is the cause of many of the 'premature deaths' and 'avoidable illnesses' which occur in society today. Meta-analytical research has provided a good insight into the magnitude of the damage to health caused by such lifestyle variables as smoking, excessive use of alcohol, overeating and physical inactivity. That optimal use is not made of the preventative possibilities already in existence is, of course, common knowledge.

Early Detection

Although, in the field of medicine, much can be achieved with regard to health improvement through lifestyle prevention, attention is paid, above all, to the technical forms of prevention, such as screening. The main characteristic of screening is that diagnostic procedures are offered to people without health complaints. The premise is that early diagnosis of a disorder increases the chances of a cure, whereby life can be prolonged. In addition, early detection can also lead to a better quality of life as less drastic measures have to be taken. This information formed the basis for the public screenings which have been set up in many countries during the last 20 years. There are, however, also disadvantages and objections connected to early detection. Drawbacks of early detection are:

false positive results (false alarm), false negative results (false reassurance) and the certificate of health effect (whereby people declared 'healthy' can continue their unhealthy lifestyle). Critics also point out the anxiety inducing character of public screening and the fact that it can lead to an unhealthy obsession with health. Screening means that the diagnosis takes place earlier, but this does not necessarily lead to the prolongation of life. Many women who received an early diagnosis of breast cancer did not live longer, but were patients for longer. Early detection, in fact, means the sacrifice of carefree years for the chance of a longer life. Public screenings are about collective benefit. Whereas some profit from the procedure, others are disadvantaged.

The public sets great store by the benefit of early detection. Research was done into this in the Netherlands. It showed that three-quarters of (the random sample of) the population endorses the view that 'almost all illnesses are curable if detected at an early stage'. (Only 18 per cent of Dutch GPs agree with them.) The drawbacks of screening would also appear to be accepted without problem: 87 per cent of the Dutch population agrees with the statement: 'It is better to examine 1,000 people for nothing than to miss something in 1' (10 per cent of GPs agree (van der Voort et al. 1995)). Screening participants faced with a false positive test result will rarely complain about the 'unnecessary' damage caused to them. More often, there is a 'feeling of relief' and those involved state that they are 'happy that it has been sorted out'. Several questions about public screening for breast cancer were put to American women. False positive results are a great problem in this research (follow-up tests, biopsies, anxiety 'for nothing'). Respondents were asked how many cases of 'false alarm' they considered acceptable in order to save the life of one woman. More than one-third of the respondents considered that 10,000 or more was acceptable. Notably, an almost identical answer pattern was given by those women who had themselves received a false positive test result (Schwartz et al. 2000).

As diagnostic procedures are refined and disorders brought to light earlier and earlier, the question arises as to where the boundaries lie. As far as the public is concerned, they hardly seem to exist. Worth looking at in this connection is recent research carried out among the American public. From this, it would appear that two-thirds of those questioned would allow themselves to be tested for cancer 'even when nothing could be done about it'. Another of the questions put was: 'Would you allow tests to be done for forms of cancer which grow so slowly that they would never be a problem during your lifetime?' This question was answered with in the affirmative by 56 per cent of the respondents (Schwartz et al. 2004).

Risk-individualizing Diagnostics

Where screening programmes are set up with the aim of finding abnormalities at an early stage, in fact, it is more often related to charting the risk of becoming ill. In the world of medicine, more and more diagnostic procedures are being developed with which the relevant risk of approaching disaster (illness, death, congenital defect) can be determined and quantified for a specific person. With such diagnostics, the collectively relevant general risk is made explicit for one specific person and 'individualized'. The result makes it possible to make predictions about the course of the relevant person's health, but can also lead to considerable changes in their living circumstances.

Important developments are taking place in the area of image-making technology (ultrasound, MRI, PET-scans, and so on). 'Visual techniques' are of value when treating people with health problems, but the question arises as to in what degree they should also be applied to those without complaints. This question is, for example, topical with regard to the early detection of an increase in size of the abdominal artery (aneurism), a disorder found mostly in older men. If an aneurism is found, then preventive surgery is possible. Determining the risk of the artery bursting and, as a result of this, ensuing death, can be weighed against the – not to be neglected – risk of death that an operation brings with it. In the long run, there are advantages to be gained and that is, for some people, reason enough to advocate large scale screening (Mass 2002).

Even people with no complaints, who feel healthy, can benefit from this ultrasound technology. A while ago, the cover story of the much read *Time* magazine was that of Michael Fackelmann, a sporty and healthy feeling 49-year-old American (*Time* September 5, 2005). When a cardiologist friend of his wanted to test a new scan machine, he asked Fackelmann to act as guinea-pig. Totally unexpectedly, the scan showed up a serious cardiovascular abnormality and the – until that moment perfectly healthy – man had to undergo emergency surgery. The headline on the front page of *Time* read: 'How new heart scan technology can save your life.' What happened to Fackelmann can happen to any one of us. Does that mean that all healthy people should be examined? What would be the benefit of such a screening program, how much harm would it do and what would be the financial consequences?

Biochemical research also offers no end of possibilities to procure quantified information about a person's risk of illness. One well known example is the determination of the serum cholesterol level. In many countries, the application of this knowledge has led to a widespread quest for individuals with 'cholesterol abnormalities'. It is often a question of solving a behavioural disorder with collectively paid for medication, when much benefit could be obtained from a healthier lifestyle. There are more irrational situations in this area. For example, it is possible that a person leading a very healthy lifestyle, but with a slightly raised serum cholesterol level, will be prescribed cholesterol reducing medication, whereas their neighbour, who smokes, is overweight and lacks exercise, but has a normal cholesterol level 'goes unpunished', but statistically has a much greater chance of cardiovascular problems. Also, the person 'declared healthy' may seize the test result as an excuse to continue his unhealthy lifestyle (the 'certificate of health effect'). At this point in time, scientists are desperately searching for new biochemical variables with which predictions about the progress of a person's health can be made (prostate-specific anti genes, homocysteine, microalbuminuria, and so on). This is a quest that is heavily subsidized by the pharmaceutical industry because it opens up the possibility for the development of new – and lucrative – 'risk reducing medicines'.

The DNA Technology

At the beginning of the third millennium, the mapping of the human genome has confronted mankind with a true biotechnological revolution. It is an auspicious revolution because it brings with it the promise of an improvement in people's welfare, but one which, at the same time, arouses anxiety because it confronts us with the very basis of our existence. The expectation that genetic knowledge and technology could be of great therapeutic value to people with serious (inherited) illnesses has not yet been fulfilled. The progress being made is, above all, within the field of diagnostics.

Families affected by such diseases as Huntington, myotone dystrophie and breast cancer are, on the whole, aware of the hereditary character of these (monogenetic) disorders. The discovery of the genetic basis of these illnesses brought with it the possibility of identifying a carrier through pre-symptomatic diagnostics. Those related to the patients can use the results of this research to plan how they will lead the rest of their lives. In the field of hereditary breast cancer, clinical geneticists in many countries have laid down criteria to which a patient must comply before DNA diagnostics are carried out (there must be more than one member of the family with breast cancer, particularly at a young age). In the US, where healthcare is less collectively organized and where commerce plays a far greater role, women have much quicker access to DNA diagnostics. There is a move to track down women at risk via 'direct to consumer' advertisements and Internet websites (for example <www.dnadirect.com>).

Approximately 1 in 500 to 1,000 women is a carrier of the breast cancer mutation. How long will it be before every woman will have the chance to be tested to find out whether or not she is one of them?

As the insight into the genetic background of illnesses grows, so does the number of disorders in which heredity plays a role. At the moment, if a 50-year-old man is diagnosed with intestinal cancer, then the question soon arises as to in what degree 'there are more cases within the family'. If there are any, then heredity tests can be considered for the patient's relatives, because, as of that moment, they are at 'increased risk'. Because there are worthwhile preventative (screening) options in existence for intestinal cancer, this can lead to a significant gain in terms of health. One of the outcomes of the genetic technical developments is that this 'hereditary approach' will be in evidence in a growing number of illnesses, because an increasing number of 'families at risk' is being mapped out. The sons of a prostate cancer patient have twice as much chance of developing the disease as men from a family where the disease does not occur. For the brothers of the patient, the risk is three times as great. Even the brothers' sons – the nephews – are at greater risk of what nowadays is referred to as 'familial prostate cancer'. In this way, an ever increasing number of people will be confronted with the fact that 'there can be something wrong in the family'.

Everyone 'At Risk'?

Geneticists will confront people more and more often with the possibility of gaining insight into the hereditary risks which they may be exposed to. Modern DNA chips make it possible to measure the activity of thousands of genes at the same time. DNA chips can provide an enormous amount of information about 'polygenetic disorders', whereby a role is played by multiple factors relating to predisposition. This information can be coupled to all sorts of lifestyle and environmental variables pertaining to those involved and, in this way, provides an interesting area of research for scientists. At the moment, there are no end of research projects being carried out in which factors relating to predisposition and lifestyle data are being collected and analyzed at group level. It is leading to an enormous production of scientific knowledge about genetic predisposition and multifactor illnesses.

Scientists have opened a major genetic-epidemiological quest which will confront society with an avalanche of information about risks of illness and chances of health. It will often involve different options regarding the choice of medication, lifestyle regulation and medical checkups. It will not be limited to physical health alone; research is also being done into all sorts of predispositional, lifestyle and environmental factors in relation to psychological health. By carrying out longitudinal research, whereby information from parents is coupled to that from children and analyzed, 'vulnerable personalities' can be tracked down. In this way, a range of information will become available which can be used to map out people's 'genetic sensitivity to illness', and upon which recommendations for 'risk-avoiding behaviour' can be based. In this context, the developments in the area of 'functional foods' play a role: foodstuffs which make claims on grounds of health. Enormous amounts of money are invested in this sector and commercial interests play an important role. Some people expect that it will lead to 'individual health management': people will use their genetic profile to plan out their lifestyle. In the future, there would be special areas within shops where people whose genotype predisposes them to rheumatism or cardiovascular illnesses would be able to find suitable foodstuffs. Should guests be coming to dinner, then it would no longer suffice merely to ask whether they liked meat or fish or whether they were a vegetarian, but complete DNA patterns would be 'mailed on ahead'. In England, the Body Shop offers people the opportunity – for a large sum of money – to have mucus from their cheek genetically tested in a laboratory (see, for example <www.sciona.com>). Several weeks later, the participant receives a wad of paper in which recommendations are given for a 'gene-conforming' lifestyle. A vision looms large of a population suffering from increasing hypochondria and of people who believe that without constant screening and health controls the human body will fall apart and disintegrate.

Procreation: Turning Pregnancy into a Problem

Women who wish to become pregnant – and their partners – have access to vast amounts of information whereby they can maximize the chance of bringing a healthy child into the world. No smoking, no consumption of alcohol, raw meat or unwashed vegetables, avoiding the cat litter: these are lifestyle factors which are important for pregnant women to take into consideration. But even in this field of health care, optimal use is still not being made of the preventive measures available. By no means all pregnant women succeed in their efforts to give up smoking or alcohol drinking and it is a known fact that this is a threat to the health of their baby.

Medical science is developing ever more technology whereby information can be obtained as to – the risk of – congenital deformities. Even before conception, DNA tests can provide information about the risks of certain fetal deformities. One example of this is cystic fibrosis (CF). In CF, tacky mucus piles up in the lungs and pancreas causing infection of the bronchial tubes and digestive problems. Approximately half of all CF patients die before the age of 40. In the western world, many people are CF carriers. In the Netherlands, for example, that figure is 1 in 30. In 1 in 900 couples, both partners are carriers and with each pregnancy there is a 25 per cent chance that their child will be born with CF. In other words, 1 in 3,600 is born with the disease. Modern DNA technology makes it possible to test people wanting children and to find out whether or not they are carriers. Those couples found to be carrying the gene have several options: to take the risk, to refrain from having (their own) children, sperm donation and prenatal diagnostics. In the Netherlands, research has been done into the question of whether it is worthwhile offering preconceptional DNA diagnostics to future parents on a large scale (Henneman 2002). It is obvious that such screening would raise many questions, for example what does screening mean for such aspects as: the self image of the gene carrier, the partner and/or relations – brothers and sisters of gene carriers have a 50 per cent chance of being carriers themselves – and is this diagnostic the beginning of the 'gene passport' feared by so many?

In the area of pregnancy, more and more screening possibilities are being developed. It has long been known that the chance of chromosomal abnormality in the fetus is related to the age of the mother. It is, therefore, mainly older women who make use of the opportunities provided for prenatal diagnostics (amniotic fluid puncture, chorionic villi sampling). Most Down Syndrome children are, however, born to young mothers as this is far and away the largest group. In the last 10 years, technology has been developed whereby a pregnant woman can have a simple blood test which then gives her insight into the degree of risk of her having a Down Syndrome child (the maternal serum screening or 'triple test'). If there is an increased risk of Down Syndrome, she can still decide to have an amniotic fluid puncture. A (young) pregnant woman of 28 whose age-related risk is approximately 1 in 1,000 can, for example, have an individualized risk of 1 in 2,245, 1 in 480 or 1 in 155. In the last case, the risk is just as great for her as for a woman of 38 and this could be a reason for having an amniotic fluid puncture in order to obtain a definite answer. More recently, it has been shown that this biochemical determination can be 'supplemented' by an ultrasound examination in which the thickness of the neck fold is measured (nuchal translucency test). Blood tests in combination with neck fold measurements are better able to calculate the chances for each individual woman of a Down Syndrome baby than blood tests alone. It is apparent that, for a pregnant woman, the image of her child with an increased amount of fluid in the neck at the time of screening means much more than receiving only a figure as an abnormal serum screening result. Therefore the visualizing of an increasing risk can cause a higher level of anxiety (Weinans et al. 2004).

Large-scale application of blood tests and neck fold measurements would lead to the detection of far more cases of Down Syndrome than is at present the case. These are not the final developments, however, as, undoubtedly, in the future, new methods will be developed enabling the detection of other fetal abnormalities. The expectation is that, in several years time, it will be possible to remove DNA/RNA material from floating fetal cells in the mother's serum which can then be used for prenatal testing. A simple blood test done early in pregnancy can provide a considerable amount of information about the fetus (sex, chromosomal abnormalities, carriership for breast cancer, CF and so on). Application of this new technology will drastically change the state of prenatal diagnostics: it will become very difficult for pregnant women to say 'no' to the offer of such a test.

Obviously, there are numerous social and psychosocial consequences attached to prenatal screening. Opponents cite the medicalizing character of the diagnostic tests, which result in more and more pregnant women being placed under medical supervision. What is more, they take away the spontaneity of being pregnant and interfere with the feeling of 'joyful anticipation' associated with pregnancy. A woman making use of the tests has to wait until she receives the (favourable) test result before allowing herself to believe that she's pregnant and before telling the rest of the world ('the tentative pregnancy'; Katz Rothman 1986).

Possibly an even more drastic consequence of screening is that the ever-increasing diagnostic possibilities may lead to a situation in which eventually not one single child will come into the world spontaneously and in which every birth is subject to conditions ('I really wanted you, but I checked first to see if everything was in working order'). In this way, screening technology generates 'the conditional child'.

Chance and Risk Information Management: 'At Least We Tried Everything'

The above makes it clear that developments within the medical technical field will make chance and risk information management an increasingly important aspect of our society. The psychology of decision making has taught us that thinking about chances and risks is both difficult and complicated, especially where sickness and health are concerned. The information available often refers to relative risks ('You have an increased chance of …'; 'You have three times as much chance of …') and people are often susceptible to this, even in cases where the absolute risk is minimal. Research has shown that the perception of risk is greatly influenced by such factors as ignorance of the consequences, the degree to which it can be verified and the catastrophic potential of the threat (Slovic 1987). Remarkably, the statistical probability – the objective risk – plays only a very small role.

Decisions about sickness and health are always made in the context of feelings and emotions. It would appear that the human being is not a homo economicus who can consider the pros and cons of a situation according to the laws of logic before making a decision. If one were to offer young mothers the (imaginary) option of bringing their child to a screening clinic for 24 hours in order to preclude a serious illness of which the chance is 1 in 90,000, then many of them would accept. If one were then to explain that the chance of their child having the illness was almost the same as the chance of their being involved in a traffic accident on the way to the clinic, then this information would, in the majority of cases, in no way influence their decision. When confronted with information such as this, people are inclined towards 'binary thinking': whether the risk of 'having something serious' is 1 in 100 or 1 in 100,000, they will argue that 'a risk is still a risk', and even if the possibility is slight, they will say 'suppose that one person is me' (Tymstra 1995). The desire to avoid feelings of regret is also an important motivational factor. Women on a waiting list for IVF explicitly say that that wishing to prevent feelings of regret is important in the decision they make. Many of them would willingly undergo IVF treatment even if the chance of success were no greater than 2 per cent. 'I don't want to look back and say, if only I'd …', they say (De Zoeten et al. 1987). This 'anticipated decision regret' forms the basis of what is called 'the technological imperative' (Tymstra 1989). These are mechanisms well known in the world of marketing which can lead to forms of 'commercialized exploitation of anxiety' and which can be used by profit-oriented organizations. Aggressive marketing methods reminiscent of these are being used more and more often within the field of health care.

The above raises the question of the degree to which such medical technical options should be offered. This is a question which, considering the ever increasing possibilities for making health-related predictions, will only increase in relevance. Not everyone wants to know about the health risks which may affect them, and some people adopt an information avoidance attitude. They realize that knowledge brings responsibility, a responsibility which can then no longer be avoided because one cannot unlearn that which one already knows. Take, for example, prenatal diagnostics. Women who had their children 40 years ago will often say that they are 'glad that they didn't have to take all those difficult decisions'. But the pregnant women of today live in a culture ruled by technology and numerics and cannot avoid these decisions. Today's women are confronted with the two faces of technology: it can offer them certainty and spare them from suffering, but often not until they have endured a period of uncertainty. Many pregnant women wrestle with the probabilities associated with the prenatal tests. Some of the pregnant women underestimate the chance of having a Down Syndrome child. Does this mean that steps should be taken to 'make them aware' of this underestimation? How far do we accept that people subconsciously wish to protect themselves from threatening information and choose instead the security of ignorance?

The Future

In the Western world, the accruing of knowledge is greatly valued. Knowledge and the resulting technologies have not only increased life expectancy, but also made life more agreeable. This is certainly true when it comes to sickness and health. The explosive growth of knowledge with regard to risks and threats to health made possible by modern information and biotechnologies also poses problems for society. Physical, biochemical and, above all, genetic research offer an increasing number of possibilities for the detection of abnormalities and the determining of the risk of future abnormalities. The consequences of this development are difficult to predict. What is certain is that there is a high degree of acceptance among the population of these diagnostics, but the disadvantages are seldom acknowledged. In other words, this technology encounters a culture which invites unlimited application. A further complication is the existence of a strong and widely held belief, based on eighteenth century rationalism, in the ability of humans to act logically. Social scientists are increasingly sceptical as to the existence of this 'rational calculating citizen'.

In western society, the School of Enlightenment has led to great store being set by the right to self-determination. It was not so long ago that the medical professionals determined – and were allowed to determine – what was good for the patient. In modern day society, it is the 'autonomous patient' who is paramount. The starting point for medical procedures is that people must be adequately informed about the treatments they will receive. The emphasis on this right of self-determination becomes problematical when it comes to offering diagnostic procedures to people who have no complaints and where there is no question of their requesting help. Where are the limits of what may be offered with regard to early detection and risk determination?

From the above, it would appear that people find it difficult to say 'no' to offers of screening. This places particular responsibility on policy makers and politicians; it is their job to see that people are not offered screening which is of little intrinsic value. Developments in the field of market orientation, privatization and internationalization – the Internet – make it increasingly difficult for policy workers to provide guidance. It is, therefore, important that the population is made aware of the true facts concerning the advantages and disadvantages of the ever-increasing medical interference with people who have no complaints. People need to realize that sustaining a state of good health is, in the first place, their own responsibility and that there are many ways in which to do it. A very sober lifestyle is not a prerequisite as, contrary to the impression given nowadays, we do not come into this world with a brittle and vulnerable body which needs to be constantly examined, checked and monitored. The surprising fact about an unhealthy habit such as smoking is not so much that it leads to premature death in so many people, but that the human body is capable of enduring such a physical onslaught for so many decades.

In the future, people's lives will increasingly be determined and regulated by technology. In this 'technological culture', a technical approach will be taken to health problems. Sickness and death will no longer be seen as a personal challenge, but will become problems for which the world of medical science will be expected to provide solutions. The medical profession has contributed to this idea by making the fight against death one of the fundamental laws of medical science. With the ever increasing attention paid to threats to life and prevention of illness, an image is being created wherein the pursuit of good health is without question considered to be the ultimate goal. But no matter how healthy a life people lead, each and every one of them will at some time be confronted with sickness, suffering and death. Because there is so much focus on the avoidance of setbacks, there is a danger that people will lose their ability to cope with pain, illness and death. In other words, modern technology creates the illusion of invulnerability whereas, in fact, it makes us vulnerable. This process was described by Ivan Illich thirty years ago (Illich 1974). It is now even more topical than then.

References

Henneman, L. (2002), *Preconceptional Cystic Fibrosis Carrier Screening. Desirability and Feasibility in the Netherlands*, PhD (Amsterdam: Free University).

Illich, I. (1974), *Medical Nemesis. The Expropriation of Health* (London: Calder and Boyars).

Katz Rothman, B. (1986), *The Tentative Pregnancy. Prenatal Diagnosis and the Future of Motherhood* (New York: Viking Press).

MASS (2002), 'The multicentre aneurysm screening study (MASS) into the effect of abdominal aortic aneurysm screening on mortality in men: A randomised controlled trial', *The Lancet* 360, 1531–39.

Schwartz, L.M. et al. (2000), 'US women's attitudes to false positive mammography results and detection of ductal carcinoma in situ. Cross sectional survey', *British Medical Journal* 320, 1635–40.

Schwartz, L.M. et al. (2004), 'Enthusiasm for cancer screening in the United States', *Journal of the American Medical Association* 291, 71–8.

Slovic, P. (1987), 'Perception of risk', *Science* 236, 280–5.

Tymstra, T. (1989), 'The imperative character of medical technology and the meaning of "anticipated decision regret"', *International Journal of Technology Assessment in Health Care* 5, 207–13.

Tymstra, T. (1995), 'Prenatal diagnosis, prenatal screening, and the rise of the tentative pregnancy', *International Journal of Technology Assessment in Health Care* 7, 509–516.

Van der Voort, H.P.M. et al. (1995), NHG-NIPO-enquête 'Huisarts en zinvol handelen' [General Practitioners and worthwhile practices], *Huisarts en Wetenschap* 38, 351–4 [in Dutch].

Weinans, M.J. et al. (2004), 'A comparison of the impact of screen-positive results obtained from ultrasound and biochemical screening for down syndrome in the first trimester. A pilot study', *Prenatal Diagnosis* 24, 347–51.

De Zoeten, M.J. et al. (1987), 'The waiting-list for IVF. The motivations and expectations of women waiting for IVF treatment', *Human Reproduction* 2, 623–6.

Chapter 8
The Symbolic Fallout of Gene Talk: Replacing the Person with Manageable Constructs

Silja Samerski

Introduction

The past hundred years have been called 'the century of the gene' (Keller 2000). For decades, the idea of genes as biological building blocks, as material determinants transmitted from one generation to the next has ruled the minds of geneticists, eugenicists and psychiatrists. At the beginning of the twenty-first century, the search for this 'quasi-mythical entity' (Keller 2000, 143) has come to a stuttering end. By now, research on the complexity of the genome rebuts the hypothesis of genes as stable, functionally definable, discrete and causal hereditary factors. Today many geneticists publicly admit what the geneticist Johannsen, who coined the term gene, clarified as early as 1913: the idea of material factors which determine characters and traits, 'must be dismissed not only as naïve, but also as totally misguided' (Johannsen 1913, 144).[1] From the point of view of contemporary genetics it has become obvious that announcements of the identification of the 'gene for' boozing, stupidity, a fat belly or going gaga have been nothing more than a series of sensational fictions.

Despite this paradigm shift in genetics, 'gene' is a powerful neologism in colloquial language. Released from the laboratory, it has spread into parliamentary debates, medical practice and the living room. Imbued with powerful connotations, it is attributed to patients, used to justify grant applications, occurs as a heatedly debated key word in talk shows, academic conferences and newspaper articles. Irrespective of its status in technical discussions and laboratory practices, the word 'gene' has become a loaded term in everyday speech.

This colloquial 'gene' merits an investigation. What does 'gene' say, suggest and demand when it mutates into an everyday reality? What happens when people are asked to think of themselves as gene carriers? In order to analyze the symbolic function of gene talk, I analyze genetic counselling. The session with a geneticist exemplifies the passage of genetic terminology into everyday language.

---

1 Author's translation. The German wording is: Diese Vorstellung 'muß nicht nur als naiv, sondern auch als ganz und gar irrig aufgegeben werden'.

The expert directly informs a lay person about inheritance, DNA-mutations, genes and genetic risks. As an analysis of my ethnographic observations show, when crossing over from the laboratory to colloquial speech, gene talk has the effect of fundamentally redefining the person. When the counsellor addresses a vis-à-vis in genetic terminology and claims to say something meaningful about them, the term 'gene' acquires an extraordinary transformative power: it imputes subjectivity to probabilistic reasoning and self-management. It supplies clients with a kind of self-understanding which presupposes the abandonment of the personal 'I'. The most concrete and intimate, namely the present person, dissolves into risk calculations and probabilistic predictions. The 'gene' redefines the client as a statistical construct.

The 'Gene' as a Fading Scientific Fact

The 'gene for' is not the first scientific fact that has passed away. Scientific ideas have come and gone. At the end of the nineteenth century, a flood of new and contradictory observations and the short shelf life of scientific theories made scientists like the French mathematician and physicist Henri Poincaré dizzy (Daston 2001, 213). A few decades later, the physician and philosopher Ludwik Fleck published his pioneering work in which he analyzed the 'genesis and development of scientific facts' (Fleck 1979) as the results of social activities. Scientific facts, at the time considered purely objective, are not discoveries made in the crucible of calculations and measurements, Fleck says, but are instead deeply rooted in what is most human: prejudices, ignorance, styles of thought and practice.

What was almost scandalous for Fleck's contemporaries is commonplace today. Belief in the permanence and cumulative progress of scientific knowledge has crumbled. Thus the growing consensus that the idea of the gene as a hereditary causal factor is obsolete should not create a great stir. In Fleck's terms, the gene grew into a 'thought pressure' and finally into a seemingly unquestionable scientific fact at the beginning of the twentieth century. For several generations it ruled the minds of biologists, physicians, psychiatrists and psychologists. At the beginning of the twenty-first century, however, in the age of dynamic networks, multifactorial causality and irreducible complexity, determining hereditary factors are antiquated. According to the geneticist Falk, molecular biology turned the gene back into what it had been from the outset: a useful working hypothesis, a conceptual crutch. 'With each new development in molecular genetics, it became obvious that the gene was nothing more than an intellectual device helpful in the organization of data' (Falk 1984, 196). What the word used in a lab conversation refers to depends solely on who uses it in what context: whether the speaker is a population geneticist calculating the frequency of alleles in the population, a molecular biologist conducting a biochemical analysis of DNA and referring to certain base sequences as 'genes', a computational molecular biologist projecting 'signal-to-noise' ratios, or finally, a doctor tracing the hereditary patterns of diseases and basing them on Mendelian hereditary characteristics. 'Gene' does not mean the same things in the cases cited here. The philosopher of science Philip Kitcher thus suggests the following definition of a gene: 'A gene is anything a competent biologist chooses to call a gene' (Kitcher 1992, 131).

Thus in the laboratory, 'gene' refers to something arbitrary. It has no univocal denotation or stable empirical referents – 'gene' stands neither for a mathematical function, such as the 'information' in cybernetics, nor for an observable phenomenon, such as the 'chromosome' in biology. Yet while the 'gene' as a seemingly objective, definable scientific concept has started to vanish, gene talk prevails. Paradoxically, just at the time when biologists began to forgo the hypothesis of discrete, localizable and functionally definable entities, the term 'gene' emigrated into biology classes, political debates, talk shows and medical consultations. Evelyn Fox Keller has characterized this curious career of the word 'gene' as follows: 'Most efforts to define the gene broke down at that very moment, when the belief in the causal power of genes reached its cultural and scientific zenith' (Keller 1998, 77).[2] In the public domain, the gene has become a 'cultural icon' (Nelkin and Lindee 1995), a symbol for the biologically determined human, for the predictability of health and disease and for the possibility of reshaping the human condition. It raises hopes, stokes fears and is used as an incantation to explain the mysteries of human existence. What makes the idea of the gene so attractive and the belief in it so persistent?

Genetic Counselling as Lessons in Decision Making

The power of the 'gene' in colloquial speech reveals itself most clearly when gene talk directly confronts everyday life. Thus, there is hardly a better instance to explore the symbolic function of the gene than genetic counselling. The educational session with a geneticist is an paradigmatic exemplar of the release of genetic terminology into the everyday world. First, experts directly talk to lay people. They have to spell out their arcane knowledge in a manner comprehensible to ordinary people. To do so, the expert has to find common sense explanations for such scientific constructs as chromosomal aberrations, DNA-mutation and probability model. Second, the counsellors' genetic lessons aim at empowering people to act: The aim of genetic counselling is not only to enlighten clients about genetics but also to prime them for action. Geneticists see it as their task to give 'individual assistance in reaching a decision',[3] namely the choice between taking

2 Author's translation. The German wording is: 'Anders ausgedrückt brachen die meisten Versuche, das "Gen" zu definieren, fast immer genau in dem Augenblick in sich zusammen, in dem der Glaube an die ursächlichen Fähigkeiten der Gene seinen kulturellen und wissenschaftlichen Zenit erreicht hatte'.

3 Author's translation. The German wording is: 'medizinisch kompetente, individuelle Entscheidungshilfe' (Kommission für Öffentlichkeitsarbeit und ethische Fragen der Gesellschaft für Humangenetik 1996, 129).

a genetic test or not. Thus, facing the counsellors' gene talk, clients rightly expect experts to say something concrete and tangible about them. Urged to make a decision, they inevitably ask themselves: What does all this say about me? What does all this mean to me? What should I do?

In order to bring about their client's 'informed choice', genetic counsellors lecture on genes, risks and test options. Clients have to learn that being 'autonomous' and 'informed' means having to make decisions under the shadow of risk. For the most time during the session, geneticists specify the probabilities that a client or a client's offspring will contract certain diseases in the future. Based on the family history and, where available, genetic test results, geneticists engage in future-telling supported by probability figures derived from statistical tables and formulas. Clients learn to anticipate their future in terms of a distribution of possible outcomes and to follow the rationale of decision theory for reducing risks and making the optimal choice. In prenatal counselling, geneticists lecture on different genetic diseases, the probabilities of birth defects, the pregnant woman's location in various risk diagrams and announce their ominous prognostications about the unborn's future. Every pregnant client receives a so-called 'basic risk' of 5 per cent indicating that something might be wrong with the child and is informed of everything that could happen to her and her coming child. Then the counsellor ascribes to the pregnant woman her 'personal risk' (for example, 1:435 or 1:100) of producing a child with Down Syndrome and offers the option of a chromosomal checkup. Lastly, counsellors insist on a modern woman's obligation to feel responsible for decision making.[4] This decision is historically unique: since there is no therapy, an abnormal genetic test result will inevitably and, only, put into question the continuation of her pregnancy. Thus, many women are in a quandary when they are confronted with abnormal test results. They agonize over the decision they are expected to make. Prenatal tests fabricate the profile of a patient that cannot be helped but only be aborted.

Genetic counselling for cancer patients is not significantly different: geneticists derive a 'high risk' for breast or colon cancer from their clients' family tree. A genetic test, counsellors explain, could either confirm this high risk status or, if the test is negative, reduce the risk to that enjoyed by the average population. No matter how high or low the risk figures, counsellors have to concede, they cannot predict if this one client sitting in front of them will get the disease or not. Again counsellors stress the client's sole responsibility in making the decision to take the test or not.[5]

In fact, the counsellors' instructions make a decision practically inevitable. No matter if a lump in the breast or a fetus in the belly: By lecturing on the probable

4 On the meaning and function of 'risk' in prenatal genetic counselling (see Samerski 2002).

5 For details on the structure and content on genetic counselling sessions in Germany, see Samerski (2002) and Samerski (2006) for prenatal genetic counselling; Duden and Samerski (2007) for cancer genetic counselling.

outcomes of both taking a test and abstaining from it, counsellors manoeuvre their clients into a situation where they can only choose between different risks. From the point of view of the expert, there is no way out: They frame their client's future as a menu of risk-laden options from which one has to be chosen. Even the refusal to make such a decision is considered as choosing the 'no test' option with its associated risks.[6] Thus, genetic counselling sets clients a trap: The 'decision trap' (Samerski 2007). In the name of 'autonomy', clients are urged to root a personal decision in statistically constructed 'ifs' and 'mights'. They are asked to submit personal deliberation to the calculation of potential genes and risks. Therefore, genetic counselling is a privileged instance to investigate how the gene reshapes self-perception and deliberation.[7]

For my analysis, I draw on a study on the 'pop-gene', the 'gene' in popular parlance, in which I analyzed the strategic function of the words 'gene' and 'genetic' in genetic counselling sessions (Duden and Samerski 2007).[8] For that study I observed and recorded four cancer genetic counselling sessions and transcribed 14 other sessions, some of them prenatal genetic counselling, which I had observed and recorded for a previous study.[9] Rather than investigating the content of the information, I focused on its symbolic effects: What does the geneticist explaining the so-called genetic causes for diseases and handicaps tell their client about themself and, in case of a pregnant woman, about her unborn child? When they foretell their clients' future by attributing to them a risk for breast or colon cancer, to what kind of self-perception and reasoning do they invite them? And, finally, when they ask them to base a personal decision on genetic test results and statistical risks, what do they tell them to do?

6 For further analysis of this 'decision trap' laid out in professional counselling sessions see Samerski (2007).

7 From Berlin to San Francisco, the goal and principles of genetic counselling are the same: See Wertz and Fletcher (1989). For genetic counselling in the US, see the anthropological study of Rapp (1999). What differs is the counsellor's professional background: In North America, a master's degree programme has turned genetic counselling into a growing profession almost completely dominated by women. By contrast, German genetic counsellors are men and women with an MD and a 5-year advanced training in molecular biology, genetic epidemiology, chromosome preparation and counselling techniques.

8 A special thank you goes to the BMBF (German Federal Ministry for Education and Research) for funding the research project on which this article is based.

9 All quotations are taken directly from my transcripts. Translations by Nancy Joyce.

Epistemic Misunderstandings: Risks as Personal Threats and Statistical Correlations as 'Genes For'

In the nineteenth century, when anything from horse kicks to the size of behinds was counted and statistically registered,[10] the sociologist and statistician Adolphe Quételet pointed out that the statistical laws that govern society and the masses cannot be applied to the individual. 'These laws have, depending on how they have been determined, nothing personal about them, which is why they can only be applied to individuals with certain restrictions. Applying them to an individual would be as erroneous as using a mortality table to determine the day when a certain person will die' (Ewald 1993, 196). More than 100 years later, however, we have grown used to regarding probabilities as personal predictions. Every consultation with a doctor today is potentially loaded with frightening risks. Doctors frame statistical probabilities as a diagnosis or a personal danger, giving the appearance of concreteness to an abstract frequency.

Gene talk aggravates this epistemic misunderstanding of statistical probabilities as personal threats. The gene evokes a future which is determined in one's bodily make-up. Week after week, newspapers announce such 'genes for' – there is hardly a vice or virtue which has not yet been foisted on some alleged genetic cause. These blown up news stories report nothing but the fact that somewhere a geneticist has made up a correlation between a genetic marker and some human peculiarity. From a snowballing mass of genetic data, geneticists calculate probabilities which allow them to predict the frequency with which an event will occur in the artificial population from which the sample has been drawn. As soon as they find their way into clinical practice, however, these frequencies become a threatening 'genetic disposition' or 'genetic risk'.[11] For the epidemiologist, the correlation between a genetic variation and the frequency of diseases is a statistical tool to construct risk populations. They know that the probabilistic 'gene for' and its corresponding 'risk of' does not say anything about a single patient. By definition a probability does not refer to a concrete person but to a constructed case; never to the 'I' or 'you' in a colloquial statement, but always to a case of a statistical population. However, when insurers and doctors transfer these statistical constructs into medical practice,

10 About the history of probability and statistics, see Gigerenzer et al. (1989), Hacking (1990).

11 Patricia Kaufert and John O'Neil have analyzed how risk mutated from a statistical frequency to a concrete threat when Canadian physicians tried to convince the Inuit to give up births at home. Taking a seemingly objective mortality rate, the doctor declares that traditional midwifery is too risky. But taken out of its original epidemiological context, this rate becomes an empty 'pseudo rate.' And for the Inuit, this risk is meaningless anyway: 'For the woman, risk is the occasional threat of danger in childbirth accepted as part of a natural process' (Kaufert and O'Neil 1993, 50). But a 'risk' which seems to objectify a threat to health and life allows no objection: 'The physician dismisses her claims as irrelevant for a definition of risk which is objective, scientific, expressible in numbers' (Kaufert and O'Neil 1993, 50).

they mutate into something the patient 'can have'. Doctors attribute genes and risks to their patients and thereby conjure up a personal threat. Patients rightly expect their doctor to say something concrete and tangible about them. Thus, at the patient's bedside or in the office, statistical prognostications turn into a diagnosis which then hang over their present-day lives like a Damoclean sword.[12]

Gene Lessons

Genetic counselling is a professional service nurturing the epidemic misunderstanding of probabilities as personal threats. During the session, clients learn to make personal decisions in the shadow of risk.[13] The counsellor lists the client's options – which basically boil down to having the test or not – and spells out the chances and risks associated with each option. After the counselling session, clients have not heard anything about themselves or their coming children, but have been saddled with risks. Anything that might happen has been turned into a risk which they either have to accept or 'clarify' by testing.[14] But tests such as an amniocentesis include new risks: counsellors warn their pregnant clients that the puncture might induce an abortion, and furthermore, the test result might put the coming of the child into question.

In such lessons for decision making under the shadow of risk, the 'gene' exerts a crucial symbolic function: 'genes' seem to bridge the gap between the abstract risk and the concrete person. Gene talk supplies clients with a conception of body and self that makes them compatible with frequencies and populations. It seems as if the statistical calculations directly reflect their physical and mental constitution. In the counselling sessions, the gene appears as a material thing, as a causal agent, as something that can be 'defective', as something that has been from the beginning and is 'everywhere', as a 'building plan' for the organism and as a carrier of information. These diverse notions cement the figment of a latent and predictable future that may be embodied. What might happen tomorrow, it is alleged, is latently present in the DNA.

12 Taking the example of benign lumps in the breasts, Sandra Gifford describes how physicians treat risk factors as 'objective clinical signs of disease' (Gifford 1986, 222). According to Lorna Weir: '"clinical risk", that is, risk at the bedside or in the doctor's office, is a chimera: it puts together heterogeneous concepts such as clinical diagnosis and treatment with statistical frequencies. It "acts upon individual bodies"' (Weir 1996, 374) but is generated through epidemiological knowledge.

13 On genetic counselling as lessons in managerial decision making, see Samerski (2002) and Samerski (2009).

14 Counsellors suggest that risks can be 'clarified' (in German: das Risiko 'abklären').

Genes as Things and Causes

In genetic counselling, genes are taken for granted. Most counsellors do not even explain how clients should imagine such a gene. They simply talk about the 'gene' as if it were a natural matter of fact. Univocally, they equate genes with the antiquated term 'hereditary factors' (German: *Erbanlagen*), invoking common sense connotations for the sake of plausibility.

Genetic counsellors bespeak genes as things which exist, as do cells and tissue in cytology, hearts and lungs in anatomy lessons and cooking pots in a kitchen. The geneticist's illustrations and pictures, for example, the genes 'packed' in the chromosomes or threaded on them as pearls strung on a necklace, suggests that genes are tangible and localizable. One counsellor puts a diagram on the table that shows a chromosome with a series of discrete definable entities:

> G(eneticist): Here is a simple diagram. This is what a chromosome looks like, and here are the various bands, and here are the genes like a row of pearls …

By invoking those simplified pictures, geneticists confers thinginess to an abstract technical notion. One genetic counsellor attributes the fact that they cannot be seen to the size ratio: they are simply too small, the geneticist claims, to be seen under a microscope.

> G: The chromosomes, which are the carriers, the packaging for our genes, we have perhaps 70,000 of them, and they are so much smaller, our genetic factors, that we cannot see them under the microscope …

The geneticists give genes an unquestionable, material reality which is accessible to experts, but invisible to lay people. The irreality of genes, the fact that they cannot be smelled, touched, seen or perceived otherwise, is transformed into a problem of the finiteness of human faculties. According to the geneticist, it is the human condition that is too deficient to perceive the ultimate reality of the gene. When the same counsellor talks about chromosomes, they explain genes as their immaterial content, a hidden message or text which again can not be perceived but only analyzed by experts. The hidden information, they suggest, can be read and assessed by technical means:

> G: Chromosomes … can be compared with an audiotape. A cassette is a storage medium, and I cannot read what's on it without a device. If genes are in the chromosomes, we need a device, a different kind of device.

Humans are carriers of invisible things and immaterial information that can be revealed by geneticists. And this hidden reality has, according to geneticists, enormous effects: The genetic make-up of a person is not only decipherable, but it also acts. Verbs linked to genes such as 'trigger', 'cause' or 'are responsible for' evoke notions of unilinear causality and the capacity to do something. Genes appear as active causative agents. In the following excerpt the counsellor declares that people become ill 'when they have a certain gene … ' They are establishing an if-then relation that assumes that genetic testing can predict a disease

> G: We can test for the gene of some diseases that are caused by a few altered hereditary factors when we know, when they have a hereditary factor once or twice, they'll get the disease. And we can, of the more than 7,000 hereditary diseases known today, test for several hundred of them.

This depiction justifies the assumption that testing these 'genes' will enable a prognosis of the future. The myth of the causal power of genes is reinforced by formulations such as 'gene defect' and 'gene for'. These catchy notions intimate causal factors whereas they are only shorthand for the correlation between a DNA sequence and appearance, between genotype and phenotype (Lewontin 1992; Hubbard and Wald 1993). Except for a few cases such as Huntington's Chorea where the genetic variation correlates almost 100 per cent with the disease in question, the geneticist can only deduce a probability from a genetic test result.[15]

In the genetic counselling sessions I have recorded, genetic counsellors confronted their clients with outdated genetic textbook knowledge. In molecular biology, the hypothesis of 'genes' as distinct determining building blocks of all life is outdated. 'Among (molecular) geneticists,' says the geneticist Burian, 'there is a fact of the matter about the structure of the DNA, but there is no single fact of the matter about what a gene is' (Burian 1986). In genetic counselling, clients are asked to believe in a 'gene' that has disappeared from scientific discourse several decades ago. According to the expert enlightening a client, genes are discrete physical entities which determine the organism. Here, genes are still the 'quasi mythical entity' (Keller 2000, 143) which had occupied the minds of geneticists during the first half of the twentieth century. What makes these 'genes for' so useful and plausible that they survive in genetic counselling sessions? What is their symbolic function in an educational ritual teaching clients to make decisions in the shadow of risk?

The Threat from Within

As counsellors explain, 'genes' are not only the causes for a person's physical make-up, but also carry future possibilities. It is an obligatory lesson in prenatal genetic counselling to inform the client about the various risks she accepted by

15 In their article on the pitfalls of genetic testing, the geneticists Ruth Hubbard and Richard Lewontin give the example of 'Retinis pigmentosa', a so-called hereditary disease which affects the retina: Two siblings share the alleged 'gene for' – one is almost blind, another is a truck driver working at night. See Hubbard and Lewontin (1996).

becoming pregnant. Everything that can be wrong with a newborn makes up a so called 'basic risk', which is attributed to the mother-to-be as something she has to face. Geneticists make sure that clients become aware of what might be wrong with their offspring: They list various inborn diseases, many of which their listeners have never heard of: harelip, congenital heart defect, spina bifida, Cystic Fibrosis. Then experts explain to the woman that genetic diseases not only run in the family, but can also pop up unexpectedly.

> G: Of course, although it is estimated that we all have one to ten genes in us that are recessive, we can't test for all of them. Something could happen to any of us one day.

The mother-to-be learns that she has little agents inside her which might cause suffering and affliction to her offspring. Her child's potential disease might already be preprogrammed inside her. But in fact, just like attesting a 'risk', attributing a 'gene for' means nothing else than placing the testee into a statistical cohort in which the frequency of certain events is higher than average. Even two of the so called 'severe mutations', once considered the definite cause for Cystic Fibrosis, do not necessarily lead to the disease (The Cystic Fibrosis Genotype-Phenotype Consortium 1993).

When counsellors move from explaining genetic models in general to making statements about a specific case, they shift linguistic registers. As soon as they say something about the person in front of them, their statements are no longer definitive, but only speculative. The 'modus irrealis' becomes dominant: They speak to their clients mainly in terms of what *could* be and what *could* happen – this *could* is couched in statistical terms. And they concede that even the 'gene for Cystic Fibrosis' does not predict that the 'gene carrier' will ever become ill. But popular scientific gene talk about 'genes which cause diseases' and 'genes for' foster the myth that a genetic test reveals a bodily predisposition or even a preprogrammed fate. 'Genetically caused' seems to be a statement about something which already exists, whereas it is only a shorthand for a probabilistic relation.

Risk transforms a probabilistic future into a present threat that must be guarded against. It mobilizes people to act today based on a fictitious tomorrow created by experts. The fullness of the present atrophies under the shadow of a made-up future. The possible disasters evoked by the geneticists' talk about risk, however, do not threaten the clients from somewhere outside them, but from within themself. In contrast to environmental or lifestyle risks which are understood as hazards from outside, genetic risks indicate a bodily disposition, a present disorder. One's own body becomes the major threat to one's own health.

I Am My Genes

The 'gene', however, not only blurs the distinction between what is and what might be, but also conflates scientific objects and bodily essence. The most personal and intimate, namely the being-as-it-is, is equated with 'genetic defects' and 'genetic information.' As Kavanagh and Broom (1998) have shown with the example of the PAP smear test, doctor-attributed risks invite the patient to imagine a threat that is already present within herself. 'Embodied' or 'corporeal risks' (Kavanagh and Broom 1998) transform a healthy person into an ailing patient who considers herself on the verge of a threatening disease. One of the women interviewed after having been told she has an increased risk of cancer says that she would prefer to have everything cut out of her body that she does not really need in order to live: 'Because the tiniest bit can go wrong, and if that's not there, well, you can't have a problem with it' (Kavanagh and Broom 1998, 440). This pathogenic effect of doctor-attested risk is even more powerful when it comes to genetics. As the counsellors explain it, humans have tiny little things inside them that have powerful effects. And these causal agents are everywhere in the body; there is no distance between the somatic self and our genes. In contrast to a diseased organ or body part, genes cannot be treated or excised. In the following excerpt, a man in his forties who worries about the many cancer patients among his relatives asks if he cannot just get rid of 'it'. The counsellor has to explain to him that talking about genes as something 'defective' does not mean that they can be localized and treated.

> M(an): This gene that's, uh, somehow responsible or is defect, can it be identified and removed, or is that not possible?
>
> G: (loud) No, no, we can identify it, test it, that's possible …
>
> M: But it's not so easy to get rid of?
>
> G: But we don't know all of them, we can't treat or manipulate them, it's not possible.
>
> M: They can or they can't.
>
> G: No, no, at this level it's not possible.
>
> M: Mm, and this all's in the blood, it's detected in the blood, right?
>
> G: Mm, in the blood, yes.
>
> M: In the blood?

> G: Because the hereditary carrier substance is practically in every cell.
>
> M: Yeah, yeah, otherwise it'd be easy, if they could see what was wrong and could simply take it out.
>
> G: Exactly, it's in every cell, so we can't do that, that's the problem.

One not only 'has' a genetic defect, the counsellor explains, but one 'is' this defect: it is congenital, it is present in every single body cell. People cannot distance themselves from their genes. They are their genes. The idea of 'genetic information' intensifes this equation between genes and flesh, between an objectifiable something and the personal 'I'. In the following quote, a pregnant woman learns that she is the execution of a hidden plan:

> G: And *how* the person develops, that is, how her growth progresses, and how the person fulfils her functions after that, this is all recorded in a genetic blueprint, which in our genes is called … DNA.

The 'gene' as the carrier of authorless instructions transmutes the person into the fulfilment of a plan. The building plan which makes up the human being is located in every cell, as the counsellor continues:

> G: Every cell contains all the information that makes up a person. This means that if I take *one* cell from someone's body, I have representative genetic information about that whole person.

In this last quotation, the transformative power of gene talk becomes glaringly apparent. The 'genetic information' transforms the embodied ego into the product of a hidden text, of authorless commands. The genes and related notions have a somatic *deixis* (Duden and Samerski 2007), they point to something corporeal, something substantial in the person. But they also denote something that can be objectified, localized in cells and read by experts. At the same time, gene refers to what is most concrete, personal and intimate – the bodily presence of the addressed – while also referring to scientific constructs such as 'information' and 'risk'.

Conclusion: Gene Carriers as Faceless Constructs

In genetic counselling, a hypothetical construct which is – if at all – defined by experimental settings and calculations, migrates into the domain of speech. Genes become subjects of utterances that claim to be meaningful. Thus, in the light of the genetic counselling sessions the symbolic effect of gene talk becomes visible. References to 'genes' implant a determining agency, readable information and a preprogrammed future in the corporeal makeup of the person. Thus, it conflates what, by definition, is incompatible: It merges the calculable and the unique, the abstract and the concrete, present and future, statistical constructs and the uniquely embodied 'I'.

The session with a geneticist does not add an iota to a client's knowledge about themself and their future, nor does it make them more familiar with scientific thinking. But clients learn something else: they are taught that genes matter, and that these genes can pose a serious threat to their health and to their future. And this belief in the existence and power of genes paves the way for a fundamental transformation of the client's self-understanding. Thinking of themself as a gene carrier, they are prepared to take statistical calculations and probability curves as meaningful statements about themself and their family. Believing that they are some kind of executed program, the phenotype of a genotype, they cannot trust their senses anymore, and are trained to rely on nothing but a collection of data whose only significance is statistical.

Genetic counselling is a paradigmatic example for an educational ritual which prepares citizens for a new kind of responsibility: they learn to manage themselves according to professional imputations; they are told to make personal decisions by weighing benefits and risks. This new task of self-management requires a fundamental confusion: It demands replacing the unique and personal 'I' and 'you' with manageable constructs. In their lectures on probabilities, counsellors seem to address their vis-á-vis, but in fact make statements about fictive populations. In their gene talk, the counsellors talk at but not to or about the woman facing them. Here, the everyday gene exercises a crucial symbolic function: Genes obscure the gulf between the person to whom the counsellor speaks and the referent of what they say.[16] Addressing someone as a gene carrier transforms the person into a statistical critter, into a faceless risk profile.

References

Burian, R.M. (1986), 'On Conceptual Change in Biology: The Case of the Gene', in D.J. Depew and B.H. Weber (eds), *Evolution at a Crossroads: The New Biology and the New Philosophy of Science* (Cambridge, MA: MIT Press), 21–42.

Daston, L. (2001), 'The Historicity of Science', in W.M. Glenn (ed.), *Historicization – Historisierung* (Göttingen: Vandenhoeck and Ruprecht), 201–221.

Duden, B. (2002), 'Meine Gene und ich', in *Die Gene im Kopf – der Fötus im Bauch* (Hannover: Offizin), 253–264.

Duden, B. and Samerski, S. (2007), '"Pop-genes": An Investigation of "the Gene" in Popular Parlance', in R.V. Burri and J. Dumit (eds), *Biomedicine as Culture:*

16 About the fundamental heterogeneity between the somatic referent of the pronoun 'I' and the reference of the word 'gene' see Duden (2002).

Instrumental Practices, Technoscientific Knowledge, and New Modes of Life (New York and London: Routledge), 167–189.

Ewald, F. (1993), *Der Vorsorgestaat* (Frankfurt am Main: Suhrkamp).

Falk, R. (1984), 'The gene in search of an identity', *Human Genetics* 68, 195–204.

Fleck, L. (1979), *Genesis and Development of a Scientific Fact* (Chicago: Chicago University Press).

Gifford, S. (1986), 'The Meaning of Lumps: A Case Study of the Ambiguities of Risk', in C.R. Janes et al. (eds), *Anthropology and Epidemiology: Interdisciplinary Approaches to the Study of Health and Disease* (Dodrecht: Reidel), 213–246.

Gigerenzer, G. et al. (1989), *The Empire of Chance. How Probability Changed Science and Everyday Life* (New York: Cambridge University Press).

Hacking, I. (1990), *The Taming of Chance* (Cambridge: Cambridge University Press).

Hubbard, R. and Lewontin, R.C. (1996), 'Pitfalls of genetic testing', *New England Journal of Medicine* 334, 1192–1194.

Hubbard, R. and Wald, E. (1993), *Exploding the Gene Myth. How Genetic Information is Produced and Manipulated by Scientists, Physicians, Employers, Insurance Companies, Educators, and Law Enforcers* (Boston, MA: Beacon Press).

Johannsen, W. (1913), *Elemente der Exakten Erblichkeitslehre* (Jena: Fischer).

Kaufert, P. and O'Neil, J. (1993), 'Analysis of a Dialogue on Risks in Childbirth. Clinicians, Epidemiologists, and Inuit Women', in M. Lock and S. Lindenbaum (eds), *Knowledge, Power and Practice: The Anthropology of Medicine and Everyday Life* (Berkeley: University Press), 32–54.

Kavanagh, A.M. and Broom, D.H. (1998), 'Embodied risk: My body, myself?', *Social Science and Medicine* 46, 437–444.

Keller, E.F. (1998), 'Das Gen und das Humangenomprojekt – zehn Jahre danach' in *Gen-Welten. Katalogbuch* edited by Kunst und Ausstellungshalle der Bundesrepublik Deutschland GmbH. Bonn, 77–81.

Keller, E.F. (2000), *The Century of the Gene* (Cambridge, MA: Harvard University Press).

Kitcher, P. (1992), 'Genes', in E.F. Keller and E.A. Lloyd (eds), *Keywords in Evolutionary Biology* (Cambridge, MA: Harvard University Press), 128–131.

Lewontin, R. (1992), 'Genotype and Phenotype', in E.A. Lloyd and E.F. Keller (eds), *Keywords in Evolutionary Biology* (Cambridge, MA: Havard University Press), 137–144.

Nelkin, D. and Lindee, M.S. (1995), *The DNA-mystique: The Gene as a Cultural Icon* (New York: W.H. Freeman).

Rapp, R. (1999), *Testing Women, Testing the Fetus. The Social Impact of Amniocentesis in America* (New York: Routledge).

Samerski, S. (2002), *Die verrechnete Hoffnung. Von der selbstbestimmten Entscheidung durch genetische Beratung* (Münster: Westfälisches Dampfboot).

Samerski, S. (2006), 'The unleashing of genetic terminology. How genetic counselling mobilizes for risk management', *New Genetics and Society* 25, 197–208.

Samerski, S. (2007), 'The "Decision Trap": How Genetic Counseling Transforms Pregnant Women into Managers of Fetal Risk Profiles', in P. O'Malley and K. Hannah-Moffat (eds), *Gendered Risks* (London: Routledge Cavendish), 55–74.

Samerski, S. (2009), 'Genetic Counseling and the Fiction of Choice: Taught Self-Determination as a New Technique of Social Engineering', *Signs: Journal of Women in Culture and Society* 34, forthcoming.

The Cystic Fibrosis Genotype-Phenotype Consortium (1993), 'Correlation between genotype and phenotype in patients with cystic fibrosis', *The New England Journal of Medicine* 329, 1308–1313.

Weir, L. (1996), 'Recent developments in the government of pregnancy', *Economy and Society* 25, 372–392.

Wertz, D.C. and Fletcher, J.C. (1989), *Ethics and Human Genetics. A Cross-Cultural Perspective* (Berlin: Springer-Verlag).

Chapter 9
Predictive Genetic Testing of Adolescents at Risk of Inherited Arrhythmic Death

Jane Kaye, Michael Parker and Edward Blair

A number of inherited cardiac diseases, such as Long QT syndrome (LQT) and hypertrophic cardiomyopathy (HCM), confer an increased risk of sudden arrhythmicdeath (or sudden cardiac death, also known as SCD). In many cases this increased risk is life long, although often peaking in the adolescent and young adult years. It is anticipated that HCM affects one in 500 of the population. LQT syndrome is less common than HCM, affecting one in 5,000 to 10,000 adolescents. A greater understanding of the molecular basis of these conditions has allowed the development of predictive genetic tests. Establishing an individual's genetic status can have a number of benefits, such as early treatment if they are a gene carrier, or discharge from further follow-up, if found not to carry the mutant gene. However deciding whether to have a genetic test is not always a straightforward decision, for a number of reasons and this can lead to disagreement between different family members about the best way to proceed Such situations are further complicated when the children are adolescents who are not emerged fully from childhood and yet have not attained the adult status that allows them to make decisions on their own behalf. Disagreement between parent and child questions the scope of a parent's responsibility and obligations and how these relate to the rights of a child, both legally and ethically. It also raises issues for practice as to whether a genetic test is indicated and where the duty of the clinician or genetic counsellor should lie when there is disagreement in the family.

The purpose of this article is to present a case study of in the form of two scenarios and to analyze them from a clinical, ethical and legal perspective. The primary focus of the legal analysis will be on the UK and in particular, the law that applies in England, Northern Ireland and Wales.[1] This comparative analysis will demonstrate the complexity of the issues involved in decision making in practice.

Why Test Adolescents for SCD?

The purpose of in this setting make an early diagnosis of the institution of treatments that reduce the risk of disease-related complications. Clinical diagnosis of these

1 An analysis of Scottish law is beyond the scope of this chapter.

conditions is not straightforward and can involve a series of clinical tests such as an electrocardiogram (ECG), and monitoring the heart rhythm over an extended period for arrhythmias. A great deal of clinical expertise is required to correctly interpret the data generated. A detailed family history can enable clinicians to determine the natural history of the disease in family and with the data from clinical tests, the risk of SCD for individual members of a family. A molecular genetic test is newer diagnostic tool that is becoming available to clinicians In many instances molecular data can clarify with some certainty whether or not an individual has inherited the disease causing mutation and hence whether or not they require further medical evaluation; individuals who have not inherited the disease-causing gene can be excused from further cardiological risk stratification and treatment. Furthermore, many research groups around the world are working to develop disease or even gene-specific therapies for these conditions. If this dream is realized then knowledge of the precise genetic mutation within a family may dictate which therapeutic options are available.

Although SCD affects adolescents, the use of redictive genetic testing for children is controversial. The report of a working party of the Clinical Genetics Society on the Genetic Testing of Children recommended that genetic testing of children is clearly appropriate where onset of the condition regularly occurs in childhood or there are useful medical interventions that can be offered.[2] However the working party made it clear that predictive testing for an adult-onset disorder should generally not be undertaken. The complicated picture of inherited cardiac disease means that there are not always proven medical interventions that can be offered and it is not always clear what level of risk any individual child may face. In the case of HCM and LQT, predictive testing can be useful in order to decrease the risk of complications and could result in lifestyle modifications, drugs or even the implantation of a cardioverter-defibrillator. However the decision of whether predictive genetic testing is useful in any given situation is complex and depends on the balancing of a number of different factors. In order to elucidate this complexity, we will discuss two case scenarios, one for HCM and the other for LQT.

The Child Wants to be Tested

Rachel is 13 years old. Her mother, Diane, was diagnosed with HCM in her teens. In Diane's family there is a strong history of the condition. On Diane's father's side of the family the gene mutation for HCM has been identified. Diane's older brother Joe was also found to be affected with the condition and an older sister who was a sprinter, died suddenly at the age of 19, after a race. Diane has remained asymptomatic but feels her quality of life has been reduced, as after she was tested

2 Working Party of the Clinical Genetics Society 'The Genetic Testing of Children' March 1994.

and found to have the gene mutation for HCM, she was advised to discontinue her training to be a competitive rower. Rachel asks her GP to refer her for genetic counselling as she would like a predictive test for HCM. Her mother refuses to discuss this and will not consent to her having a genetic test. Rachel wants to know whether she is affected as, like her mother before her, as she has been given the opportunity to join the National Rowing Team.

Should Rachel be Allowed to Have the Test Against Her Mother's Wishes?

The Clinical Perspective

Clinical geneticists often regard their patients not as isolated individuals but as members of a family. It is clear that when dealing with genetic disease that the consequences of a consultation for an individual can ripple through the family with potentially damaging effects.

Rachel's family situation and request is complex. The risk of SCD for an individual such as Rachel is higher than many patients at risk of having inherited HCM. Her family history shows us that the disease causing mutation in this family can cause SCD (her aunt died at 19 years of age); this is a predictor of increased risk in this family. Rachel is an elite athlete and a diagnosis of HCM would have significant implications for her sporting ambitions, especially as the SCD in her aunt may have been precipitated by sudden exercise.

As the mutation causing HCM in this family is known, predictive genetic tests in this setting are likely to be close to 100 per cent accurate. Rachel has a risk of 50 per cent of having inherited the mutant gene. In stark terms Rachel has 3 options: 1) do nothing; 2) molecular genetic testing with appropriate follow-up; or 3) repeated clinical screening and appropriate management.

A molecular genetic test in this setting will show that an individual either has, or has not, inherited the disease-causing mutation. If they have not inherited the disease gene, they are not at increased risk of HCM and can be safely discharged from follow-up. If they have inherited the disease gene appropriate follow-up should be instituted. In the case of HCM this will require regular cardiac ultrasound (echocardiogram) and ECG recording, with further clinical tests required for full risk stratification and drug and device treatment when indicated. Lifestyle modification including the avoidance of competitive sport is a further cornerstone of risk reduction. Follow-up tests are performed at intervals determined individually for each patient, but these are often at 6 monthly or yearly intervals.

Although not wanting molecular genetic testing for her daughter, Diane, in all likelihood, will still wish that Rachel have clinical screening. This is something which would routinely be offered to a 13-year-old at risk of HCM. The option of doing nothing is rarely an attractive one. As Diane also has HCM she will require clinical follow-up. It is important for her own future care that the relationship between Diane and her doctor is not damaged and it would be unwise to make decisions about her children with which she did not agree. Clinical screening by ECG and echocardiogram is a medically acceptable strategy for managing Rachel.

In this setting, with a prior risk of Rachel having inherited the mutant allele of 50 per cent it is interesting to consider clinical tests almost as surrogate molecular genetic tests. This is because clinical results consistent with HCM would be a very strong indication that Rachel had inherited the mutant gene.

Clinical screening may be an option that might be acceptable to Rachel and her mother. It is possible that this 'half way' measure could be more palatable for Diane. Normal results would mean that Rachel had not inherited the mutation from her mother and Rachel may gain some of the reassurance she needs. This path may buy the time in which one could have further discussions with Diane about the implications of the molecular genetic test for Rachel and why she may want to make this choice. However one must also strike a small word of caution. A subset of HCM patients are at high risk of SCD with only very subtle changes on the routine screening tests, the molecular genetic test would remove such uncertainty if Rachel had not inherited the mutant allele from her mother. It is with these considerations in mind as well as the legal and ethical position detailed below that one must asses the merits of any course of action for Rachel's family.

The Ethical Concerns

The primary ethical concern in a case of this type will be to support Diane, Rachel and the other members of the family and to help them to find ways of reaching agreement about a way forward through mutually respectful discussion, facilitated perhaps by the genetic counsellor. Working with families in this way can take time but it is important to recognize the tremendous importance for a child's well-being, as well as for that of the rest of the family, of the long-term supportive care of those around them. Geneticists and genetic counsellors are highly skilled and experienced in working with families in this way and this work is of tremendous ethical importance. It is important to begin with considerations arising out of support and communication because these highlight the fact that in many cases the key ethical issues do not concern genetic information or genetic testing per se but are more concerned with encouraging good communication, support and understanding between family members. This may or may not lead in the end to a genetic test but is nevertheless a key feature of good clinical and ethical care.

The difficulties in the case above arise out of a tension between the wishes of the parent, in this case Diane, on the one hand and those of the child, Rachel, on the other. Where agreement is not possible through something like the process described above, this raises the question for health professionals of how their duty of care to each of these patients should be met. It is important to remember however that in relation to the particular choice at hand it is Rachel who is the patient and Diane who is, despite being a patient in her own right, involved in this instance in her role as Rachel's mother.

It is a fundamental principle of patient-centred medicine that patients should be treated in ways that respect them as people in their own right with interests in living and making medical choices that accord with their own values. Arising out of this ethical concern is a commitment to the belief that medical treatment ought to be carried out in accordance with the informed, voluntary and competent wishes of those being treated (or not treated). In the case described above the patient, Rachel, wishes to have a genetic test to see whether she is at risk of being affected by HCM. She has a family history of the disease and good reason to be anxious about her own health. She is also missing out on important lifestyle choices and opportunities because of uncertainty about her health uncertainties that have a 50 per cent chance of being removed in a positive direction by a genetic test. And were it to prove that Rachel did in fact carry the mutation, appropriate treatment and care could be provided.

If Rachel were an adult all of these considerations would mean that her wishes to be tested would be respected. Rachel is not an adult however but a 13-year-old living at home with her family and in such cases, and more so the younger the child, it is usually felt that the parents ought to have a significant role to play in assessing and deciding upon, with the involvement of the child herself, the child's best interests. Whilst it might be that Diane's refusal is in fact motivated by other more personal concerns, if we assume for the time being that her concern is for Rachel's well-being and that she genuinely feels, despite Rachel's wishes, that it would not be in her best interests to have the test (perhaps because Diane feels that Rachel would be unable to cope with 'bad news') these concerns should be taken seriously. Diane is likely to know Rachel well. She might also believe that Rachel is unable to fully understand the implications of the test and would not be able to grasp the important uncertainties, both informational and clinical, arising out of any test result. If this is the case, these concerns too will need to be taken seriously.

Whilst many even very young children will be capable of understanding and making medical decisions there will also be many adults too, who will not be able to understand the key features of the decision at hand. In such situations it will still be important to involve the child as much as is possible in their own care, but some decisions may need to be made by others in their best interests. A key consideration in the above case and others like it therefore will be an assessment of the extent to which the child or young person understands the nature of the choice at hand. Age and ability to understand do not always go hand in hand, some very young children, because of their experiences and perhaps the educational efforts of others, for example, health professionals, are capable of understanding and making such decisions. This is often the case with children who have grown up in families where genetic disease and inheritance have been discussed openly. Perhaps Rachel is, because of her experience, able to understand the nature of the decision at hand, or could be with some support. Where this is the case, it will not simply be that the test should be given immediately however. We suggested earlier that in any assessment of how best to proceed in the treatment of young people it will be important to maintain as far as is possible good relationships and a network of support for their future, long-term care. This would also of course be true in the care of adults. What this suggests is that the decision to test Rachel will need to be built into a package of care to ensure that Rachel and her family are, where this is possible, mutually supportive. This will require in some cases a rather extensive process of counselling and other support and compromise on both sides. For example, it may involve reaching agreement that a decision about testing be delayed for several months to enable support to be put in place and for all those concerned to come to terms with the approach adopted. This is an approach that will require maturity of all those involved including Rachel but ought, in our view, ultimately to lead to the testing of Rachel if this is what she wishes.

The key ethical considerations in this case will therefore include:

- Finding ways to work together with the family to good relationships and to establish and maintain a network of support for their care.
- An assessment of the young person's competence and understanding and an assessment of what might be done to enhance these.
- Getting clear about the child's wishes and her reasons for wanting the test.
- An assessment of the ways in which communication and agreement about a way forward might be achieved within the family.
- A consideration of possible clinical interventions and support, with or without the test.

The Legal Position

The law in this area is the same in England, Northern Ireland and Wales but is different in Scotland. The basic principle in Scotland is that a competent child may consent to treatment irrespective of age under the Age of Legal Capacity (Scotland) Act 1991, s.2(4) if they are considered competent by a medical practitioner. Therefore, a person may make decisions on a young person's behalf only if the young person lacks the capacity to do so. In contrast, in England, Northern Ireland and Wales, the starting point is that a child cannot give consent, and that a doctor cannot lawfully operate on, or treat someone, under the age of 18 years unless someone who has authority has given consent. Normally this will be the parents of the child, or in some cases, the courts. However, there are a number of exceptions to this basic principle which allows a child to make a decision and to consent to treatment for themselves. These exceptions in the law are largely determined by age and maturity. The *Gillick* case[3] established that children under 16 years can give consent to advice, treatment or physical examination, if they have 'sufficient understanding and intelligence to enable him or her to understand fully what is proposed.'[4] This judgment is made by the clinician when the child is less than 16 years of age. If children are between 16–18 years of age, then they can give consent to 'a surgical, medical or dental treatment', as if they were an adult, under s.8 of the Family Law Reform Act 1969. This does not require a judgment by the

3 *Gillick* v. *West Norfolk and Wisbeck Area Health Authority* [1986] AC 112, HL, 188.

4 *Lord Scarman Gillick* v. *West Norfolk and Wisbeck Area Health Authority* [1986] AC 112, HL, 188.

clinician but the child's consent must be respected. In both cases if the necessary conditions are satisfied, the consent of the parent is not required.

According to the *Gillick* decision, the proper course will be for the doctor to try and persuade the adolescent to bring the parents to the consultation. If this fails, it will be up to a doctor to determine whether a person under 16 years would have the sufficient understanding and intelligence to make a decision whether to have the treatment or physical examination. According to Lord Fraser, 'A doctor would be justified in providing contraception to a girl under 16 without the parents' consent or knowledge if he was satisfied that:

- the girl despite her age, would understand his advice;
- he could not persuade her to inform her parents, or allow him to inform them;
- she was very likely to have sexual intercourse with or without contraception;
- her physical or mental health were likely to suffer unless she received contraception; and
- it was in her best interests.'[5]

Is a Genetic Test 'Treatment or Advice'?

From the recent case of *R (on the application of Axon)* v. *Secretary of State for Health* that reaffirmed the *Gillick* case as good law, it seems as if the *Gillick* test is not restricted to contraceptive advice, but could be applied to medical 'advice and treatment' more generally. As Justice Silber said, 'There does not appear to be any reason why that approach should not also apply to other proposed treatment and advice as the litmus test for determining if any such treatment and advice can be given without parental knowledge'.[6]

However, it is not clear that a genetic test would come under the ambit of treatment and advice. If Rachel has a genetic test it could lead to further treatment options and advice but is not of itself 'treatment or advice'. In legal terms the taking of blood for a genetic test would be a trespass to the person unless it was accompanied by consent. However the courts seem to be prepared to take a broad view of what constitutes 'treatment and advice'. In *R (on the application of Axon)* v. *Secretary of State for Health,* Justice Silber went on to say that abortion could come under contraceptive advice, and therefore did not make a distinction between a trespass to the person (such as the taking of blood for a genetic test) and other types of treatment and advice. This would suggest that a genetic test would also be considered 'treatment or advice' and so the *Gillick* principle would apply, if the child were under 16 years of age.

The statutory provisions under the Family Law Reform Act 1969, apply specifically to minors that are aged 16–18 years. Under s.20(2) of the Act, a child who has attained the age of 16 years can consent to the taking of a bodily

5 Ibid., 413.

6 [2006] All ER (D) 148 (Jan), para 87.

sample as if they were an adult. Under s.23 of the Act, a 'bodily sample[s]' means a sample of bodily fluid or bodily tissue taken for the purpose of scientific tests. It has not been decided by the courts whether a blood sample that is needed for a genetic test would come under the definition of 'bodily fluid'. In common sense terms it could be argued that it could. Within the Act there is also a more general provision, that only applies to a minor aged 16–18 years, that means that, 'A minor can give consent to any surgical, medical or dental treatment which, in the absence of consent, would constitute a trespass to his person.'[7] Genetic testing could conceivably come within the kind of treatment that is referred to in the Act, as a genetic test involves the taking of blood and is a trespass to the person unless carried out with consent.[8] Therefore it would appear that any adolescent under 18 years would be able to consent to a genetic test, and depending upon their age, their capacity to consent would be assessed either under the *Gillick* principles or the statutory provisions.

Does Rachel have Sufficient Understanding and Intelligence?

As Rachel is 13 years old, it is the *Gillick* principles that would have to be applied rather than the provisions of the Family Law Reform Act 1969. According to Lord Scarman delivering his judgement in the *Gillick* case, 'It is not enough that she should understand the nature of the advice that is being given: she must also have a sufficient maturity to understand what is involved.'[9] In the case of contraception, this would involve the moral and family issues involved in becoming pregnant but also the issues of being sexually active without the knowledge of her parents. In *R (on the application of Axon)* v. *Secretary of State for Health* Justice Silber extended this to include, 'All relevant matters and it is not limited to family and moral aspects as well as all possible adverse consequences which might follow from the advice.'[10] In the case of Rachel, the clinician would have to establish that Rachel were aware of the significant issues involved in having the genetic test for HCM, as well as the implications of not having the test, but still pursuing her rowing career.

Taking the test stated by Lord Fraser in *Gillick* and applying it to genetic testing, a clinician should respect an adolescent's request to have a genetic test if they can be satisfied that:

7 S.(1) Family Law Reform Act 1969.

8 In Re W (a minor) (medical treatment) [1992] 4 All ER 627, at 663, it was held by Lord Donaldson that, 'This section does not apply to the donation of organs or blood since, as far as the donor is concerned, these do not constitute either treatment or diagnosis.'

9 Lord Scarman *Gillick* v. *West Norfolk and Wisbeck Area Health Authority* [1985] 3 All ER 402, 424.

10 *R (on the application of Axon)* v. *Secretary of State for Health* [2006] All ER (D) 148 (Jan), para 154.

- the adolescent despite their age, would understand the clinician's advice;
- the clinician could not persuade the adolescent to inform their parents, or allow the clinician to inform them;
- the adolescent's physical or mental health were likely to suffer unless they received the treatment; and
- it was in their best interests (Kaye 2007).

Rachel is only 13 years old, but despite this, would understand the implications of the clinician's advice because her family history has given her first-hand knowledge of the life and death consequences of having the condition. Like the rest of her family she has had to deal with the fact that her older sister died after over-exertion after a race, and that both her mother and her brother have had to make lifestyle changes after being tested positive for HCM. She would also know of her mother's dissatisfaction with the decision not to pursue a rowing career and the effect that this has had on her mother's life. Therefore it would be reasonable to suggest that Rachel would understand the nature of thc advice being given, and the moral and family issues of having the test and being tested positive or negative for the HCM mutation.

In order to fulfil the further requirements of the test, the clinician would have to decide whether Rachel is determined to have the test without telling her parents, even though her mother has explicitly stated that she does not want Rachel to have the test. The clinician would be justified in allowing Rachel to have the genetic test without her parents' consent or knowledge if he was satisfied that he could not persuade her to inform her parents, or allow him to inform them. Rachel may decide not to tell her parents because of her mother's resistance to the idea.

It could be argued that Rachel's mental and physical health is likely to suffer if she does not have the test as she will not know how she should manage her condition. The clinician would have to make a decision about whether having the test would be in Rachel's best interests, considering her family history and the treatment or lifestyle modifications that were available. This would largely be a clinical assessment, and in this case it would appear that a molecular test would be a definitive indicator of whether Rachel was at risk of HCM, but that this could also be discerned by having an ECG and echocardiogram. Therefore, having the test could greatly assist Rachel to make significant decisions about her life choices such as whether to join the National Rowing Team, but she may be able to determine this through other clinical tests. Therefore, it would be up to the clinician to decide whether to offer the genetic test, even though it would appear that Rachel would be considered as having 'sufficient understanding and intelligence' as required by Lord Fraser. In the situation where a genetic test would be considered clinically sound, a clinician could be justified in respecting Rachel's wishes even though they were contrary to those of her mother. The decision by the clinician and the child's decision to consent to treatment can be overridden by the court, but not by the parents.

The Parents Want the Child to be Tested

John and his brother Tim are in their early thirties and both have been diagnosed with LQT. John has had mild symptoms of the condition. In clinical tests his blood pressure failed to rise after exercise and he has heart arrhythmias. Tim has had two children that had died early. Their sister Anne does not have LQT. Although both of their parents are deceased, neither was known to have a diagnosis of LQT when they were alive, but it is highly probable that John and Tim inherited the tendency from one or other of their parents. Genetic analysis reveals that they do in fact both carry the same LQT gene mutation. John and his wife Daisy have two sons: Ben, 14 and Tom, 2. They have had two other children, one that died of cot death and another that died as a result of drowning. Ben has been under annual follow-up for 2 years and clinical tests have shown normal results. Ben's parents want Ben to have a genetic test to establish whether he has inherited the LQT gene from his father. Ben does not want to have the test.

Should Ben be Tested?

The Clinical Perspective
This tragic family history highlights many of the difficulties in the diagnosis and management of LQT syndrome. It is not uncommon to see families where the initial presentation of this illness is with a sudden death. It is also not uncommon to find that after the diagnosis has been made, that other tragic events which have occurred in the past, such as cot deaths and drowning need to be viewed in a new light. There is the possibility is that these events could also be due to LQT.

This family history highlights the diagnostic difficulties faced by cardiologists in managing at risk individuals within pedigrees. Ben had a 50 per cent chance of inheriting the gene that causes LQT from his father. If a positive diagnosis of LQT was made, as has been the case for his father and his uncle, he would undoubtedly be a candidate for lifestyle modification and treatment to reduce his risk of arrhythmia and SCD. The main diagnostic test for an individual such as Ben is the ECG. If his ECG shows a prolonged QT interval (the time between the onset of cardiac depolarization and repolarization as measured on a standard 12-lead ECG) his physician would be confident that he had inherited LQT and appropriate treatment would be started. However the converse is not true. A normal QT interval is a relatively common finding in individuals who have inherited the disease gene and thus does not indicate individuals at low risk of SCD. What is the cardiologist to do? Further invasive provocation tests can be used, that involve pharmacological manipulation of the QT interval in at risk individuals. These tests involving injection of drugs such as adrenaline to unmask a covert 'prolonged' QT interval are generally safe and accurate, but do involve short stays in hospital. They will not detect 100 per cent of gene mutation carriers.

In contrast to the clinical tests that are available, a genetic test in Ben will provide a clear indication whether he is or is not at risk of LQT. A result showing he had not inherited the mutation could relieve his family and cardiologist of a great deal of anxiety. However whether the clinician can 'force' Ben to take this test is a complex matter which will be discussed below. However on purely diagnostic grounds, a genetic test for LQT could give the certainty that the parents desire.

The Ethical Concerns

The concept of 'consent' only has any meaning where it brings with it the possibility of refusal. How can one be said to have consented to a treatment, for example, when there was no possibility of one doing otherwise? Patient-centred medicine, medicine that is, based in the belief that people's wishes and values ought to be respected places for this reason great weight on the right of competent patients to refuse treatment even if that treatment has the potential to be of great benefit to them and even to save their life. The concept of competence has an important role here because the justification for allowing someone to come to harm as a result of a decision to refuse treatment depends upon the fact that the patient is in fact capable of bringing their beliefs, values and so on to bear on the decision at hand and this depends in turn upon a certain degree of understanding of what the decision and its consequences involve. Without competence it cannot legitimately be claimed that the health professionals are respecting a patient's values when they respect their 'consent' or 'refusal'.

The degree of understanding and competence required for a patient's refusal of treatment to be respected will depend to some extent upon an assessment of both the seriousness of the consequences of non-treatment and the consequences of imposing treatment on someone against their wishes, even where they are not competent. The second of these is not a trivial matter. Failing to respect the bodily integrity of a patient, perhaps especially that of a developing child, is a significant harm and can have, in addition to the immediate distress, important implications for future trust, for example, that between the child (Ben) and his parents or between the child and health professionals. Imposing treatment on a 12-year-old is, in addition, not a trivial matter practically.

Nevertheless, the consequences of respecting a refusal of treatment can be serious. In the case of, for example, refusal of a blood transfusion this could lead to the death of the patient. Key considerations therefore in any decision about imposing treatment on a child or young person will, in addition to an assessment of their understanding and competence, involve an assessment of the size of the risk and the seriousness of the harms associated with failure to treat. Assessment of the size of the risk will of necessity include an assessment of the availability and effectiveness of interventions. In relation to LQT such considerations will include the extent to which interventions (or a degree of certainty about risk), not available on the basis of clinical tests such as ECG alone, might be made available on the basis of a genetic test and the effectiveness of these interventions at mediating risk.

What these considerations suggest is that priority ought to be given to working with families, in ways that are inclusive and respectful of children, to help them to reach agreement about a way forward. Respect for the wishes of children and young people means that the imposition of treatment on them against their competent wishes should be very much the exception and can only be justified on the basis of the avoidance of a high risk of a very serious harm. It is unlikely that genetic testing for LQT per se is ever going to meet such criteria. It is also an implication of the above arguments however that even where a child is not competent, or where there are concerns about competence, treatment should not be imposed without very serious consideration both of the clinical need for such treatment and of the medical and non-medical harms of such imposition, for example, for trust.

The Legal Position

Although the courts are prepared to recognize that a child can consent to treatment if they have sufficient maturity and understanding, it appears that they are less willing to regard children as having the capacity to refuse treatment. The decision of the parents are given priority when the child refuses to consent to treatment, and the courts have been prepared to exercise their jurisdictional powers to override both parental and children's decisions to refuse treatment, [11] particularly in life-threatening situations. The case of refusal to have a genetic test or clinical tests, such as ECGs, has not been addressed by the courts and so only general principles apply in regard to treatment. For the purposes of this discussion, genetic testing and ECGs will be considered as 'treatment'.

Can Ben's Parents Force Him to have the Test?

The case law suggests that if Ben's parents want him to have the genetic test or a ECG, then it is very difficult for a minor to refuse treatment when his parents think that he should have the treatment. In the situation where there is a difference of opinion between the child and the parents, as to refusal of treatment, then the opinion of the child who is under 16 years has influence but it can still be overridden. In *Re W (A Minor) (Medical Treatment: Court's Jurisdiction)*[12] Lord Donaldson stated that:

> No minor of whatever age has power by refusing consent to treatment to override a consent to treatment by someone who has parental responsibility for the minor and a fortiori a consent by the court. Nevertheless such a refusal is a very important consideration in making clinical judgments and for parents and the court in deciding whether themselves to give consent. Its importance increases with the age and maturity of the minor.

This means that it is very difficult for a child, such as Ben, to refuse treatment, and while the child's decision will be considered, ultimately it can be overridden by the consent of someone having parental authority, or the court. However the court

11 *Re E (A Minor) (Wardship: Medical Treatment)* [1992] 2 FCR 219 per Ward, J.

12 [1992] 4 All ER 627, 637.

would be bound to consider the child's 'best interests' and therefore may decide that the genetic test or EGC would not be appropriate. However, Lord Donaldson, in *Re R (A Minor) (Wardship: Consent to Treatment)*[13] did acknowledge that 'the failure or refusal of the "*Gillick* competent" child is a very important factor in the doctor's decision whether or not to treat, but does not prevent the necessary consent being obtained from another competent source'.

Would it Make a Difference if Ben were 16 Years Old?

If an adolescent is aged between 16 and 18 years, s.8 of the Family Law Reform Act 1969 comes into effect. The interpretation of the statutory provisions by the courts means that an adolescent does not have the right to refuse treatment. *Re W (a minor) (medical treatment)*,[14] was the case of a 16-year-old girl suffering from anorexia nervosa, who had refused to move hospitals in order to get treatment for her condition. The court held that s.8 only gave a right to consent to treatment, and it did not confer a right to refuse treatment. Therefore the fact that Ben was 16 years or older, would still not give him the right to refuse treatment.

Could the Clinician Refuse to Provide the Genetic Test?

In the situation where the opinion of the clinician differs with the parents or the child as to whether treatment should be given, it is the professional opinion that will be most important. As Lord Donaldson concluded his judgment in *Re R (A Minor) (Wardship:Consent to Treatment)*:[15]

> 1. No doctor can be required to treat a child, whether by the court in the exercise of its wardship jurisdiction, by the parents, by the child, or anyone else. The decision whether to treat is dependent upon an exercise of his own professional judgment, subject only to the threshold requirement that, save that in exceptional cases usually of emergency, he has the consent of someone who has authority to give that consent. In forming that judgment the views and wishes of the child are a factor whose importance increases with the increase in the child's intelligence and understanding.

Therefore the clinician could take into account Ben's views and refuse to offer the genetic test. This would force Ben's parents to reconsider their original insistence, or go to another clinic. However due to the small number of genetics clinics in the UK offering a genetic test for LQT, it would be difficult for them to get treatment elsewhere.

13 [1992] 4 All ER 627.
14 [1992] 4 All ER 627.
15 [1992] 2 FCR 229, at 246F.

Can the Court Order Ben to have the Test?

Foremost in the mind of the court in making any decision as to whether allow the treatment of a child without consent, is whether the course of action contributes to the welfare of the child. According to Lord Justice Nolan in *Re W (a minor) (medical treatment)*[16] this is fulfilled if the court takes into account the requirements of the Children Act. Under s.1(3) of the Children Act the court must have regard to: (a) the ascertainable wishes and feelings of the child concerned (considered in the light of their age and understanding); (b) their physical, emotional and educational needs; (c) the likely effect on them of any change in their circumstances; (d) their age, sex, background and any characteristics of theirs which the court considers relevant; (e) any harm which they have suffered or is at risk of suffering; (f) how capable each of thier parents, and any other person in relation to whom the court considers the question to be relevant, is of meeting thier needs; and (g) the range of powers available to the court.

In doing so the court must consider the wishes of the child. According to Lord Justice Balcombe, 'The Judge should approach the exercise of the discretion with a predilection to give effect to the child's wishes on the basis that prima facie that will be in his or her best interests.'[17] The weight that the court gives to the child's wishes will increase depending on the age the child. In *BRB* v. *JB*,[18] in which the court authorized the performance of a blood test upon a child of 4 years of age, Lord Denning MR said:

> A question was asked as to the extent to which the child should be consulted. If the child is of tender years – say under 7 years, and thus unable to give consent, one way or the other – then the High Court judge can order a blood test without consulting the child. If the child is older, say 14 or 15 years of age, then the views of the child should be taken into consideration; but the child's views are never decisive. Even if the child is difficult, the court can order a blood test if it is clearly in the interests of the child, just as it can order an operation in the case of a ward of court.

It would be very difficult for the court to ignore the wishes of Ben, a 14-year-old, if it has been established that he is *Gillick* competent and if the genetic test or ECG did not have any benefit for him. However if the court decided that to have the genetic test would benefit Ben and contribute to his welfare, then it could order him to have the test.

However even with a statutory right to refuse treatment or examination the courts have tended to override the adolescent's right to object to treatment. Under the Children Act 1989, a child 'of sufficient age and understanding to make an

16 [1992] 4 All ER 627, 645.

17 *Re W (a minor) (medical treatment) [1992] 4 All ER 627 at 642 per Balcombe J.*

18 [1968] 2 All ER 1023 at 1025.

informed decision', can refuse to submit to medical or psychiatric treatment or examination when it is required for interim care or supervision order (s.38); child assessment order (s.43); an emergency protection order (s.44); and for a supervision order (para 3, Sch 3). The case of *South Glamorgan County Council* v. *W and B*,[19] is a good example of where the court overrode a refusal of consent to a psychiatric assessment by a 15-year-old girl. The young woman was entitled to refuse the assessment under the Children Act 1989, s38(6) and had been deemed by the court to be Gillick competent, but her refusal was still overridden by the court. This was also followed in the cases of *Re K, W and H (Minors) (Medical Treatment)*;[20] *Re C (Detention: Medical Treatment)*;[21] and *Re L (Medical Treatment: Gillick Competency)*.[22] It is not clear how the courts would approach Ben's case, which concerns genetic testing for LQT and does not rest on a statutory right to refuse a genetic test. However the current case law suggests that the courts would be unlikely to support an application to refuse treatment from an adolescent.

In conclusion, the refusal of treatment by an adolescent can be overridden by the parent and the court. The cases that have come before the courts are largely involving life-threatening situations, but in cases, such as Ben's, that do not require an immediate decision, the courts have still been reluctant to give voice to the adolescent's wishes. This has been the case even when there has been a statutory right for the child to refuse treatment or examination under the Children Act. Whilst there have been no cases involving genetic testing, and because of current practice, it's unlikely that such a case will make it to the courts. However this analysis suggests that there is the scope for further development of the law in order to reflect the change in social attitudes which increasing gives adolescents the power to make decisions regarding their treatment and care.

Conclusion

The decision whether to have a genetic test can have grave implications for the lifestyle and future life choices for the person being tested for life-threatening conditions such as LQT and HCM. In the case of HCM, clinical tests can be as predictive as having a genetic test, whereas in the case of LQT, a genetic test will provide conclusive evidence whether the individual is affected. In the case of adolescents, where parent and child may disagree over whether to have a genetic or clinical test, conflicts are bound to arise. It is ultimately up to the professionals within the genetics clinic to help the family come to some resolution which will not result in the severing or impairment of family relationships. The focus of this article has been on the two situations of when the parents wish their child to have

19 [1993] 1 FLR 574.
20 [1993] 1 FLR 854.
21 [1997] 2 FLR 180.
22 [1998] 2 FLR 810.

a predictive test, or they refuse to give consent to allow their child to have a test, even though the child would like to do so. By giving the perspectives of a clinician, an ethicist and a lawyer we have attempted to illustrate how these three different approaches analyze the same case study. What is clear from all of these approaches is the importance of the clinician's judgement, not just clinically, but as a negotiator of relationships and as a person whose opinion the court will give overriding consideration to. The focus of the professionals working in a genetics clinic is to respect the wishes of the family as a whole and to work to some common ground within the family. In contrast the law offers a solution and statement of principle that has been developed in extreme situations, when a decision must be reached. The legal approach offers a clear answer to a specific problem but this may not lead to a harmonious situation and enable family relationships to be sustained over time. In this chapter we have dissected each of these approaches, but in the reality of clinical decision making, all of these approaches will be considered and employed at different times, and with varying degrees of emphasis, to reach an outcome that offers the best possible resolution for the adolescent and their family.

References

Alderson, P. (1993), *Children's Consent to Surgery* (London: Open University Press).

Borry, P. et al. (2006), 'Carrier testing in minors: A systematic review of guidelines and position papers', *European Journal of Human Genetics* 14, 133–138.

Clarke, A. (ed.) (1998), *Genetic Testing of Children* (Oxford: Bios).

Gaff, C.L. et al. (2005), 'Facilitating family communication about genetic testing: Probands' perceptions', *Journal of Genetic Counselling* 14:2, 133–140.

Hendriks, K.S.W.H. et al. (2005), 'High distress in parents whose children undergo predictive testing for Long QT community', *Genetics* 8, 103–113.

Kaye, J. (2007), 'Testing times: What is the legal situation when an adolescent wants a genetic test?', *Clinical Ethics* 2.

Malpas, P. (2005), 'Predictive genetic testing in children and respect for autonomy', *International Journal of Children's Rights* 13, 251–263.

Maron, B.J. et al. (2004), 'Proposal for contemporary screening strategies in families with hypertrophic cardiomyopathy', *Journal of the American College of Cardiology* 44:11, 2125–2132.

Maron, B.J. et. al. (2004), 'Recommendations for Physical Activity and Recreational Sports Participation for Young Patients with Genetic Cardiovascular Diseases', June 8, *Statement of the American Heart Association.*

PART 3
Responsibilities

There is an ambiguity in the distinction between obligations that arise from a perceived moral responsibility in certain types of situations regarding those persons who will be affected by a decision, and obligations that are created by formal legal or moral accountabilities. The latter can shape the decision-making rationale in a way that may not always be ethically unproblematic. Some of the perceived moral responsibilities demand clarification from an ethical perspective. What is their meaning, and what impacts do they have on the good organization of decision-making practice? This third part of the book focuses on the diversity of legal, moral and ethical responsibilities in communicating predictive genetic information, in professional settings of genetic counselling and beyond.

The first two chapters are written by legal experts. *Daniel Wied*, *Susanne Listl* and *Maximilian Seibl* give a detailed overview of how legal frameworks in different countries construct patterns of liability in genetic counselling. Ethics needs to consider this because legal liabilities cannot easily be overridden by good moral arguments in singular cases. *Michael Steel* analyzes the question of whether and how clinical geneticists have legal and moral responsibilities towards relatives of an 'index' patient. He stresses that the potential benefits of knowing relevant genetic information depend on the practical options that are open to the individual at risk, and he calls for a balanced view, each case on it merits.

Two following chapters import experience from oncology. Delicate communication is not confined to genetics but is needed in other fields as well, and ethics of genetics can learn from them. *Wolf A. Langewitz*, a specialist in psychosocial medicine, reports from his experience with cancer diagnoses. 'Breaking bad news' in oncology was a focus of research in medical ethics that can inform the discussions of disclosure dilemmas in genetics. Langewitz develops a model of 'individualized information giving' that takes into account the objective, subjective and relational aspects and social context together with environmental variables. Oncologist *Thomas Cerny* then reflects about genetic testing for hereditary cancer and starts with a, perhaps surprising, comparison with the Delphic Oracle. He presents an ethics of truth-telling: truth-tellers have particular ethical obligations. They must be 'Socratic', which means that they should carefully clarify the usually exaggerated expectations attached to 'truth'; they also must engage in a 'humbling, ongoing process' that goes much further than the explanation and interpretation of some results of a test.

Decision making in prenatal risk assessment is investigated by social scientists *Nete Schwennesen, Lene Koch* and *Mette Nordahl Svendsen*. The introduction of risk assessment by ultrasound is combined with the provision of a normative cut-off point. In Denmark, an invasive test is only offered when the risk of abnormality is 1:250 or higher. The authors indicate how the process of translation of knowledge about risk is not a value-neutral process. It constructs situations in which responsibilities for injustice and justice are allocated. Their conclusion is that it is ethically questionable to locate responsibility for the outcome of the choice solely with the pregnant woman and her partner while society has contributed to establishing the offer systematically. *Jackie Leach Scully*, a former molecular biologist, now bioethicist and sociologist, focuses on the mutuality of making sense of genetic information in the counselling process. She demonstrates that making sense of genetic information is a joint enterprise, an essentially intersubjective process with interpretation on both sides of a genetic dialogue. Medical geneticist *Peter Miny* stresses the point that the autonomous decision of the patient necessarily requires clarity about facts and figures. Disclosure of all relevant information, in his account, is an ethical obligation grounded in respect for the autonomy of the patient. But he also sees the principle of beneficence as important for providing adequate support to the patients in the process of informed consent. The final chapter by bioethicist *Christoph Rehmann-Sutter* sums up and integrates the different strands of evidence and reflection in this book in an ethical model for communicating personal genetic information. His idea is that the principle of non-directiveness in genetic counselling should be replaced with a more integrative model of good communication that keeps the useful elements of non-directiveness (respect) and avoids the unhelpful elements (pre-emptive individualism). He proposes that the goal of communicating personal genetic information to others, in clinical situations and beyond, can be described as allowing the person concerned agency. 'Agency' is explained as an ethically demanding concept.

In a concluding chapter, the editors present their afterthoughts, and ask the question: what has been clarified and which ethical questions remain open?

Chapter 10

How Legal Frameworks Construct Patterns of Liability in Genetic Counselling: An International Perspective

Daniel Wied, Susanne Listl and Maximilian Seibl[1]

Introduction

The development of various methods of detecting genetic diseases in a fetus, or even predicting genetic diseases before conception, can be looked at from various angles. This chapter intentionally leaves aside the rather moral considerations and confines itself to providing a broad international overview of the law as it stands in relation to genetic counselling. Admittedly, this approach is not and cannot be an absolute one. It is a commonplace that the law reflects moral concepts of societies. While acknowledging this function of the law, this chapter does not attempt to give an account of the moral considerations behind each legal aspect. Hence, moral considerations will be part of the legal analysis only where they directly influence the legal outcome of a claim.

The issue will be tackled as follows. In a first step, an overview of the available options to detect genetic diseases will be given. In a second step, the basics of the relevant grounds upon which claims can be founded in the examined jurisdictions will be set out. Before entering the main part, which deals with the requirements of liability, it is crucial to mark out the factual settings that will be subjected to legal analysis in the next sections. The next two sections will carve out the exact content of the duty to counsel adequately and the relevant legal actions. Finally, the very controversial issue of identifying the possible heads of damages will be addressed.

Options for Genetic Counselling

The methods of detecting genetic diseases divide into options that are available prior to conception (Pre-implantation Genetic Diagnosis, PGD) and options that are available during pregnancy (Prenatal Diagnosis, PND).

---

1 The authors are assistants to Professor Dr Andreas Spickhoff, Chair for Civil Law, International Private Law, Comparative Law and Procedural Law, University of Regensburg.

Prior to Conception (PGD)

PGD stands for a series of genetic screenings whose common feature is that they are applied to the fertilized human egg outside the womb. The examination methods are the Polymerase Chain Reaction (PCR) and the Fluorescence DNA *In Situ* Hybridization (FISH). The examination object, a fertilized human egg, is either withdrawn from the womb or created by *In Vitro* Fertilization (IVF). The legitimacy of the PGD is the subject of a hot-tempered international debate, for the embryo is doomed to decay either as a direct consequence of the examination itself or, in case of a negative outcome, of the screening. The 'Convention for the Protection of Human Rights and Dignity of the Human Being with Regard to the Application of Biology and Medicine: Convention on Human Rights and Medicine' by the Council of Europe has not yet been signed by all European member states and deals neither with PGD nor PND. PGD is currently considered legal in Belgium, Denmark, Finland, France, Greece, UK, Italy, Holland, Norway, Sweden, Spain and in many states of the USA. By contrast, it is considered illegal in Germany, Austria, Ireland and Canada (Schlussbericht der Enquête-Kommission 'Recht und Ethik der modernen Medizin', 2002, BT-Drs. 14/9020, 92 seq.; Genetische Diagnostik vor und während der Schwangerschaft-Stellungnahme des nationalen Ethikrates, 2003, 53). Switzerland adopted a statute on genetic research on the human being on October 8, 2004 (GUMG). The statute only covers methods for prenatal diagnosis resulting in PGD remaining illegal according to article 5 section (3) of the Swiss Fortpflanzungsmedizingesetz. However, the Swiss Federal Council has been asked to propose a rule allowing PGD by the second half of 2008.[2]

During Pregnancy (PND)

During pregnancy it is essential to obtain fetal cells as examination material in order to guarantee the most accurate diagnosis of fetopathies. Depending on the gestational age several invasive techniques are available, chief among them amniocentesis and choronic villus sampling (CVS), but also fetal blood withdrawal and fetoscopic biopsy.

Amniocentesis is performed most frequently around the 14th to the 16th week of the pregnancy to determine the fetal karyotype, later to determine the bilirubin concentration in the amniotic fluid in order to detect a possible blood group incompatibility or to obtain material for a later DNA analysis. Backed up by ultrasound control, amniotic fluid is extracted by trans-abdominal puncture of the amniotic sac. The complication rate is approximately between 0.4 per cent and 1 per cent. Complications include premature miscarriage and amniorrhexis, and more rarely infections and haemorrhage.

---

2 <http:/www.bag.admin.ch/themen/medizin/03878/03879/index.html?lang=de>, accessed on March 1, 2008.

CVS is available around the 10th to the 12th week of pregnancy. Accordingly, it presents a diagnostic method operating earlier than amniocentesis. CVS serves mainly as an alternative to amniocentesis for the diagnosis of chromosomal anomalies and metabolic diseases. Compared to amniocentesis, CVS allows for an abortion 5 weeks earlier, which is considered less traumatic for the mother, as she will not have experienced movements of the child at that time (Soler et al. 2008, 127).

From a medical point of view all invasive methods of prenatal diagnosis carry an inherent procedure-related risk leading to the strong necessity to identify risk patients in order to avoid unnecessary invasive diagnosis (Saller and Canick 2008, 24). Non-invasive techniques of prenatal diagnosis, mainly ultrasound diagnosis and tests involving the search for maternal blood markers, serve as risk assessment methods for aneuploidy, triggering further invasive diagnosis as the case may be (Saller and Canick 2008, 26). For example, ultrasound diagnosis permits the detection of neck transparency as a soft marker for trisomy 21 (Down Syndrome), 18 or 13, as well as for developmental disabilities and abnormal head shapes (for example, 'lemon sign'). The determination of alpha-foeto-protein (AFP) in the maternal serum serves as evidence for open neural tube defects which occur in cases of anencephaly and open spina bifida. Further frequently tested blood markers pointing to deformities of the child are non-conjugated estriol (uE3), ß-hCG and pregnancy-associated plasma protein-A (PAPP-A), which, for instance, find application in the course of the so-called triple test (ß-hCG, AFP, uE3) around the 16th to the 20th week of pregnancy (β-hCG, AFP, uE3).

The most common application of prenatal diagnostics is – especially influenced by advanced maternal age – Down Syndrome, as the most common genetic cause for mental retardation. Therefore, it is suggested that prenatal diagnosis in relation to Down Syndrome should be performed as screening, that is, no matter whether individually indicated or not (Saller and Canick 2008, 25). However, prenatal diagnosis, particularly in the first and second trimester, is subjected to criticism even amongst gynaecologists, for its results might lead to abortion of the fetus (Szymańska and Knapp 2007, 183).

It is still open as to whether the briefly usable technique of detecting cell-free fetal DNA and fetal cells as a source of fetal DNA respectively in the serum of the mother, which hitherto has only allowed fetal sex identification and rhesus D blood typing of the fetus, will be able to serve as an additional screening marker, or will even evolve into a non-invasive diagnosis of fetal aneuploidies (South et al. 2008, 69; Sekizawa et al. 2007, 750–764; Saller and Canick 2008, 35).

The Basic Grounds Upon Which Liability Can be Based

If patients believe that the treatment they received was not appropriate, they can found a claim on two main grounds, and a breach of contract and delict/tort.

Germany

Under German law a patient and a physician establish a contractual relationship. The prevailing opinion characterizes the underlying contract as a contract to render services according to § 611 Bürgerliches Gesetzbuch (BGB), but it might be better characterized as a contract *sui generis* (Deutsch and Spickhoff 2008, Rn 113). Whichever classification is adopted it is agreed that the physician does not guarantee the success of their treatment. Generally, success-orientated and service-orientated obligations mix depending on the purpose of the respective treatment. In the context of supervising a pregnancy the physician might be expected to render medically indicated genetic counselling, and advise as to the available diagnostic and therapeutic methods, as well as to describe content, risks and possible consequences. If the physician advises inaccurately or neglects to provide the legally required counselling on available methods at all, the fault will amount to a breach of contract which makes them liable to pay damages caused by their breach in accordance with § 280 section (1) Bürgerliches Gesetzbuch. It might be interesting to note that the father can avail himself of the same contractual action as the mother of the child, even if he is not a party to the contract between the mother and the physician. That is because German law construes the contract as having protective effect on the people who are liable for maintenance of the child (BGHZ 86, 240, 249 seq.; BGHZ 89, 95, 98). The rule does not only apply to the father who is married to the mother but also to the unmarried father (Palandt/Heinrichs (2008) vor § 249, Rn 48).

The claimant can also found their action on delict in accordance with § 823 section (1) BGB. To bring a claim in delict, the claimant must be able to prove an infringement of their health or physical integrity caused by an intentional or negligent action which led to proximate damage. It is well established that the omission to act despite a duty to act is considered equally wrong. It is worth noting that each therapy, even when conducted in order to heal the patient, is considered an injury and has to be accompanied by informed consent of the patient to be legally justified (BGH NJW 2005, 1716, 1717; Deutsch and Spickhoff 2008, Rn 341). In the context of unwanted pregnancy due to inadequate counselling, the unwanted pregnancy and birth itself are regarded as the relevant violation of physical integrity (BGH NJW 1980, 1452, 1453). A claim founded on the general right to self-determination ('allgemeines Persönlichkeitsrecht') is denied by the German Federal Court of Justice in the context of genetic counselling (BGH NJW 1994, 788, 792), although academic writers advocate such a claim (Mörsdorf-Schulte 2007, 968).

Following traditional doctrine, claims in tort and contract do not rule each other out and can be brought simultaneously. However, there is a discernible tendency by German courts to analyze the action in contract terms. In fact, claims in tort have been only considered by the courts when damages for pain and suffering were claimed, since such an action could only succeed in tort up to the year 2000. Due to a legislative reform, damages for pain and suffering can now be claimed in an action for breach of contract as well, § 253 section (2) BGB. The requirements for damages for pain and suffering remain the same, however. Nevertheless, this is likely to result in an even greater dominance of contract analysis.

Austria

Austrian law adopts a similar solution to German law. The patient can bring actions on both a contractual and a delictual basis. The contract between physician and patient is characterized as a 'free service contract' involving both a service element and a warranty as to the success of the treatment (Juen 2005, 57). Depending on the circumstances the contract might entail an obligation to provide the patient with appropriate counselling and to conduct the medically indicated prenatal diagnosis (OGH, JBl. 1999, 311, 314). The claim in tort rests on § 1325 Allgemeines Bürgerliches Gesetzbuch and has similar requirements for liability as German law.

Switzerland

Swiss law clearly prefers to found the claim on the breach of contract. The contract between patient and physician is characterized as a non-gratuitous mandate contract which also entails duties to disclose (Kuhn 1999, 248). The claim in contract is based on article 97 section 1 and 398 section (1) Obligationenrecht (OR). Apart from that, a delictual claim can be brought in accordance with article 41 section (1) OR.

France

Although French law provides for contractual and tortious claims, it is thanks to the famous French doctrine of '*non-cumul des responsabilité*' that claims in tort are entirely blocked if a contractual relationship is established between the parties (Cour de Cassation Civile, May 20, 1936, Dalloz 1936.1.88). As a result, the claim of the patient is bound to be founded on a breach of contract in the majority of cases. The liability of a physician largely depends on the requirement of '*faute*', which in the context of a contractual liability equals the breach of a contractual duty. Both civil and administrative courts – in France medical welfare is provided on public and private level – have assumed '*faute*' if a flawed prenatal diagnosis led to damage suffered by the other party to the contract (Conseil d'État, February 14, 1997, Jurisclasseur périodique 1997 II, 22828, Cour de Cassation Civile, March 26, 1996, Dalloz 1997, 35).

Anglo-American Legal Systems

The laws of the US and the UK (including Scottish law) differ from continental civil law systems in that they show a preference for the tort of negligence or the more refined variant of medical malpractice (*Jackson* v. *Bumgardner* 318 N.C. 172, 347 S.E. 2d 743). The requirements for both actions are the same. The claimant has to prove a duty of care, a breach of that duty and damages resulting from that breach. There is also tortious cause of action for lack of informed consent, which is the equivalent to the continental European doctrine that a physician can avoid liability only if they have duly explained the procedure and revealed the material risks prior to the medical therapy in order for the patient's consent to be effective (*Reed* v. *Campagnolo* 332 Md. at 226–241, 630 A.2d at 1145–1152, Md., 1993). In the context of medical liability, claims that are founded on a breach of contract are rarely advanced in Common Law courts (for example, *Jackson* v. *Bumgardner* 318 N.C. at 172–184, 347 S.E. 2d at 743–750; *Emeh* v. *Kensington and Chelsea and Westminster Area Health* [1985] Q.B. 1012, 1023, CA; for a Scottish case see *Sciuriaga* v. *Powell* (1979) 123 S.J. 406). One might ask oneself why this is so. One reason might be that there is some reluctance to award certain heads of damages in contractual actions (that is, damages for pain and suffering see *McFarlane* v. *Tayside Health Board* [2000] 2 A.C. 59, 69, HL with reference to *Thake* v. *Maurice* [1986] Q.B. 644.). In contrast to that proposition, English authority usually does not differentiate between claims in contract and delict with respect to the availability of damages for medical liability, unless the contract involves something more than an obligation to render services like a warranty of an outcome (*McFarlane* v. *Tayside Health Board* [2000] 2 A.C. 59, 76, HL; *Howe* v. *David Brown Tractors (Retail) Ltd.* [1991] 4 All E.R. 30, 40–41). There seem to be two factors that explain the tort preference of the Common Law. First, the standard of care owed under negligence principles and contractual principles are the same, as far as a contract for services is concerned. When rendering the service, reasonable skill and care have to be used (*Walkin* v. *South Manchester Health Authority* [1995] 1 W.L.R. 1543, 1551, CA). Consequently, a contract claim has one more requirement than a claim in tort, that is, the contract itself, without providing any advantage to a claim in tort. Secondly, Common Law judges do not set about examining all possible grounds of the claim and ignore grounds upon which the claim could be based but are not pleaded (*McFarlane* v. *Tayside Health Board* [2000] 2 A.C. 59, 76, HL).

Situational Distinctions in Genetic Counselling

It is important to clarify what kinds of factual situations will be analyzed in the next section. The questions that one has to ask to be able to answer the question of liability depend entirely on the given factual situation. In the framework of genetic counselling two scenarios commonly arise. A patient might come to see a physician to clarify whether she and her partner can have a child that is free from genetic diseases. In the absence of a warning by the physician, the patient becomes pregnant and gives birth to a child suffering from a genetic disease. In the other group of cases a pregnancy is supervised by a physician. Despite the counselling a disabled child is born and the patient claims she would have aborted had she known about the genetic diseases.

These two groups of cases are to be distinguished from cases that involve failed vasectomies or sterilization procedure and in which mostly healthy children are born (for a case combining a failed sterilization and a handicapped child, *Parkinson* v. *St. James and Seacroft University Hospital NHS Trust* [2002] Q.B. 266, CA). The latter category is not within the scope of our appraisal as the birth of a healthy child is the objective of adequate genetic counselling. Nevertheless, it is worth mentioning that it is highly disputed whether the costs of rearing a healthy child can be regarded as recoverable damage. The House of Lords, some American courts and the Austrian Federal Court of Justice have declined to award damages (*McFarlane* v. *Tayside Health Board* [2000] 2 A.C. 59, HL; *Johnson* v. *University Hospitals of Cleveland 44* Ohio St. 3d 49, 540 N.E. 2d 1370; OGH JBl 1999, 953; but see *University of Arizona Health Sciences Center* v. *Superior Court* (1983), 136 Ariz. 579, 667 P. 2d 1294), whereas the German Federal Court of Justice takes a different view (BGH 76, 259). It should be noted that the decision of the House of Lords in *McFarlane*, a case which was decided on appeal of a decision of the Scottish Court of Session, is far from being universally accepted in the Common Law world. The decision overturned both a Scottish (*Anderson* v. *Forth Valley Health Board* 1998 S.L.T 588; *McFarlane* v. *Tayside Health Board* 1998 S.L.T. 307) and an English (*Emeh* v. *Kensington and Chelsea and Westminster Area Health* [1985] Q.B. 1012 CA; *Allen* v. *Bloomsbury Health Authority* [1993] 1 All E.R. 651) line of cases. It is not very surprising that both English and Scottish courts had previously taken a different view on this issue, since it is admitted that the reasoning in *McFarlane* deviates from traditional tort analysis (*Rees* v. *Darlington Memorial Hospital NHS Trust* [2004] 1 A.C. 309 at 314 per Lord Bingham, HL; Bernat 2004, 316). The arguments advanced in support of the achieved result are quite diverse, which is shown best by the different reasons the five Law Lords invoked to arrive at the same result in *McFarlane* (just see *Parkinson* v. *St. James and Seacroft University Hospital NHS Trust* [2002] Q.B. 266, at 277 per Brooke LJ 'five voices', at 289 per Hale LJ, CA). However, the shared ratio of all decisions that decline to award damages for the upkeep of a healthy child seems to be that a healthy child is to be regarded as a blessing and cannot be seen as damage. Also, the benefits of having a child are considered impossible to set-off against the costs, as such an operation would be either entirely speculative (*Gallagher* v. *Duke University* 852 F. 2d 773 at 777) or simply distasteful (*McFarlane* v. *Tayside Health Board* 2000 S.C. (HL) 1 at 42 per Lord Millet). Essentially, the decision not to award damages for the costs of bringing up a healthy child is based on policy reasons (in favour of public policy: *Johnson* v. *University Hospitals of Cleveland 44* Ohio St. 3d 59, 540 N.E. 2d 1378; in favour of legal policy, while refusing the public policy argument: *McFarlane* v. *Tayside Health Board* 2000 S.C. (HL) 1 at 32 per Lord Clyde, at 39 per Lord Millet). The decision not to award damages for the costs of rearing a healthy child is highly criticized both in result and reasoning (Thomson 2000, 45) and has been recently, albeit by a bare 4/3 majority, rejected by the High Court of Australia in *Cattanach* v. *Melchior* (2003) 77 A.L.J.R. 1312.

Furthermore, we are not concerned with cases in which an undetected infection of rubella or other pathogens lead to the birth of a disabled child. While the failure to detect the infection and to counsel on the impacts of the infection on the child has given rise to extensive case law (for example, BGHZ 86, 240; *Hardman* v. *Amin* [2001] P.N.L.R. 11, QBD; Cass. ass. pl. 17. 11. 2000; Dalloz 2001, 332 with comment Mazeaud), those cases are not within the scope of this chapter, as the condition of the fetus was not genetically determined. Nevertheless, the case law which has been produced in this context is sometimes useful for analyzing the cases under consideration.

Finally, the chapter does not address the question of liability for an inaccurate surgery that had to be undertaken, for example, to obtain material for genetic testing. Obviously, such surgeries can lead to injuries to the patient. In such cases the focus will be on the accuracy of the therapy and the disclosure of material risks inherent in the therapy. Without proper disclosure the necessary informed consent cannot be obtained (see above). Interesting as these issues are, they are not typical features of genetic counselling and will remain undiscussed for this reason.

The Litmus Test for Liability: The Duty to Provide Adequate Counselling

No matter whether a claim is pursued in contract or tort, the claim is founded on a breach of duty. More specifically the success of a claim turns on the duty to counsel adequately with respect to potential genetic diseases of the fetus. The realization of the nature of the relevant duty is not only of theoretical importance. In contrast to the existence of informed consent, the burden of proof that the duty to counsel correctly with respect to genetic diseases has been breached rests on the patient, not the physician (OLG München VersR 1988, 523, 524; Kern 2002, 24; *Al Hamwi* v. *Dr Johnston, The North West London Hospitals NHS Trust* [2005] Lloyd's Rep. Med. 309, QB). The definition of the standards and limits of the duty to counsel lies at the heart of the liability issue. It is quite plain that not all possible genetic tests have to be applied to each patient. Such a proposition would be unreasonable considering the limitation of resources and the potential risk associated with genetic tests. It appears to be a sensible approach to define the standard of care in genetic counselling by reviewing the relevant case law. Starting from there we will categorize distinguishable obligations and critical criteria that determine the intensity of the duty required.

Incorrect Interpretation of Test Results

In a case which came to be know as the 'Tübinger case', a couple who were already parents of a disabled daughter asked a hospital with a department for human genetics to perform a genetic screening, since they wanted to rule out the possibility of passing on a genetic disease before trying to have a second child. The couple underwent several tests. A physician concluded that the probability of a genetic anomaly would be very low. Believing in the correctness of this statement the couple decided to have another baby which was born as disabled as the first child. Relying on expert evidence, the German Federal Court of Justice held that the physician had failed to counsel properly, for they did not sufficiently factor in the cause of the disability of the first child (BGHZ 124, 128). The incorrect advice amounted to a breach of contract on which liability was founded.

In the US, the United Court of Appeals in *Gallagher* v. *Duke University* (852 F. 2d 773) decided a similar case. The parents of a newborn child who had died after 3 weeks due to several birth defects had a chromosome analysis performed on a sample of the child's blood. The hospital informed the couple that their chances of having a normal child were the same as the general population. The staff advised the couple that there was no reason for either of them to be tested. Relying on this advice the couple conceived a second child. The child was born suffering from birth defects similar to those that afflicted the first child. Tests later conducted revealed that the father carried a genetic abnormality which he had passed on to both children. The couple succeeded in an action based on medical malpractice.

A Case for Comprehensive Counselling: Amniocentesis

On several occasions courts were concerned with deficient counselling in relation to amniocentesis. In the leading German case a pregnant woman asked a gynaecologist whether an amniocentesis should be carried out in view of her age of almost 39 and the risk inherent in giving birth to a child with Down Syndrome. The gynaecologist answered that he considered a test unnecessary and left out all further medical details. The woman gave birth to a child with Down Syndrome. The Federal Court of Justice did not blame the gynaecologist for not having recommended an amniocentesis. Neither did the court criticize the conclusions the gynaecologist had drawn, as the risk of a miscarriage due to amniocentesis was around 1 per cent in 1977 and, therefore, on par with the risk of giving birth to a child with Down Syndrome (BGHZ 89, 95, 100, explicitly followed by OLG Stuttgart VersR 1991, 229, 230). However, the court held that he owed the woman comprehensive disclosure about the risk of bearing a child with Down Syndrome at her age and the risk involved in the testing procedure. On the basis of his advice the woman must be in a position to be able to make a self-determined choice whether or not to undergo the test. Neither religious nor ethical beliefs of the physician are allowed to influence the advice. As the gynaecologist's counselling did not live up to these standards, he was in breach of a contractual duty. It was explicitly left undecided whether such a comprehensive duty to provide information on the available tests according to the medical knowledge of the time was to be imposed on a gynaecologist who had not been asked a particular question in relation to genetic defects.

Later, two Higher Regional Courts clarified the content of the obligation to counsel with respect to amniocentesis tests. In 1986 the Higher Regional Court of Munich decided that a physician was under the obligation to counsel a 39 and a half-year-old woman on the risks and dreadful consequences of giving birth to a child with Down Syndrome, regardless of the fact that the patient had not asked the physician to counsel on the risks and available tests (OLG München VersR 1988, 523). The court also pointed out that the physician had failed to make sure that the patient had understood his counselling properly. Thereby the intellectual abilities and the state of mind of the patient have to be taken into account. Finally, the court held that the physician's failure to recommend an amniocentesis did not meet the standard of care of the time and amounted to a breach of his duty to counsel comprehensively.

The Higher Regional Court of Düsseldorf shared this view in a very similar case (OLG Düsseldorf NJW 1989, 1548). A 43-year-old woman who had given birth to a child with Down Syndrome sued her gynaecologist. Interestingly the court made clear that short phrases and technical terminology do not meet the standard envisaged by the law. Again the age of the patient played an important role. The reasoning of the court fostered the view that the counselling has to be communicated understandably and be tuned to the educational and intellectual ability of the patient. Eventually, the court mentioned that the information is supposed to be presented in a balanced and objective way, omitting any ethical or moral suggestions, to enable the patient to make an informed and free decision.

It is worth noting that the Higher Regional Court of Munich has held adversely in slightly different circumstances. A 32-year-old pregnant woman asked for an amniocentesis because she had a sister with Down Syndrome and wanted to rule out any possibility of her child suffering from the disease. The result of an invasive prenatal diagnosis technique, which used the blood of the mother to analyze the chromosomes, was negative. The hospital suggested no further testing for want of medical indication. The child was born with Down Syndrome. Nevertheless, liability was denied because an amniocentesis was neither indicated by the family record nor by the age of the patient (OLG München VersR 1988, 194, 195).

Finally, a last German case should be mentioned. A rubella infection remained undetected by a general practitioner. While being treated for eczema, the woman had mentioned a possible pregnancy. The court ruled that the contract to find out about the reason for the eczema did not contemplate the supervision of a pregnancy (BGH NJW 2005, 891). It said that the purpose of the contract did not cover the avoidance of the birth. Therefore, the costs flowing from a failed treatment could not be recovered. The restrictive flavour of this reasoning does not fit in the general line of the Federal Court of Justice, which usually construes the extent of protection of duties arising from a medical contract quite extensively (Deutsch/Spickhoff 2008, Rn 447). Anyhow, the ratio of this case is not likely to influence claims in the context of genetic counselling as the general supervision of the pregnancy will be regularly the purpose of the treatment.

In 2003 the Austrian Federal Court of Justice disposed of a rather tricky case by using doubtful arguments. A pregnant patient who had already given birth to two healthy children had a family history of the rare Morbus Niemann-Pick. She asked an ambulance physician in a regular hospital whether it would be possible to check on the disease by amniocentesis. The physician denied the possibility, which was the local state-of-the-art answer, although a special institute in Austria could have conducted the check in collaboration with foreign institutes. It was established that the state-of-the-art treatment would have been to refer the patient to the relevant Institute where the disease would have been detected. Nevertheless, the court denied liability for questionable reasons. The Court argued that the parents should have found out about their genetic dispositions before making the decision to have another child. Furthermore, they were to be blamed for not telling the physician about their determination to abort the child if it suffered from the disease. Based on these arguments the court concluded that the negligence of the ambulance clinician was eclipsed by the gross negligence of the parents. The reasoning of the court has been harshly criticized for being unsystematic and simplistic (for example, Bernat 2004, 317). Also, the result has been frowned upon (Deutsch/Spickhoff, 2008, Rn 448).

The list of decisions dealing with amniocentesis is completed by three rather straightforward cases from the UK. In a Scottish case an amniocentesis was not carried out, although the hospital was aware that the patient's brother was affected by Down Syndrome (*McLelland* v. *Greater Glasgow Health Board* 2001 S.L.T. 446, Ex Div.). It was agreed that non-diagnostic screening tests which resulted in no pathological findings were not sufficient to meet the standards of reasonable skill and care under the given circumstances. In an English case a 37-year-old pregnant woman had not been given counselling at all in relation to screening tests and amniocentesis. The court held that this amounted to negligence (*Ann Enright* v. *Dr Tse Sak Kwun* [2003] EWHC 1000, QB). In another case, a breach of a duty of care was admitted by a general practitioner who failed to promptly refer the claimant with a family record of children born with mental and physical impairment to an obstetrician after diagnosis of pregnancy. However, the court laid down the standards for genetic counselling in relation to the second defendant, a hospital. The court proceeded on the basis that a clinician must take reasonable care to give a warning which is adequate in scope, content and presentation, and take steps to see that the warning is understood. In relation to the last requirement a subjective standard was considered too onerous a burden on the physician and an objective approach prevailed. The plaintiffs claimed that the warning was exaggerated, so that the woman could not make the informed choice not to undergo amniocentesis. The court stated that the counselling must be balanced and non-directive. The claim against the hospital failed for want of proof of a breach of duty, whereas the claim against the practitioner failed because causation could not be proved (*Rana Al Hamwi* v. *Dr Johnston* [2005] EWHC 206, QB).

Triple Test

In 1999 the Higher Regional Court of Munich was concerned with the standards of care with regard to the so-called triple test (OLG München MedR 1999, 466). The court held that a gynaecologist in private practice who had failed to counsel a pregnant woman on the triple test did not breach his duty. The background was that the common opinion in 1991 considered the results of the test useless for want of certainty. The medical assessment of the triple test might have changed over the years, so that counselling on the availability of the triple test, if medically indicated, might be the safer option.

Ultrasound Diagnosis

In the same decision the court also decided that the lemon-sign of the fetus was not something a gynecologist in private practice in 1991 could have known. Although there had been articles on this distinctive feature in foreign technical literature, the German medical standards of the relevant time did not pay attention to such features. The court held that a gynaecologist in private practice was not obliged to read foreign technical literature, but pointed out that this might be different for physicians in a university hospital. However, the court mainly based its decision on the character of these scientific publications as food for thought rather than solid knowledge. In doing so it fostered the position of physicians who rely on the medical standard as it is represented in the national standard literature and national congresses.

In another case, a gynaecologist in private practice did not diagnose a hydrocephalus by using ultrasound in the 22nd week of the pregnancy. He did not disclose the availability of more extensive diagnostic options in more specialized institutes. Neither the course of the pregnancy nor the anamnesis (<http://dict.leo.org/ende?lp=ende&lang=de&searchLoc=0&cmpType=relaxed&sectHdr=on&spellToler=on&chinese=both&pinyin=diacritic&search=anamnese&relink=on>) was regarded as demanding any further counselling on genetic diseases. The Higher Regional Court of Karlsruhe held that a physician in private practice is not obliged to disclose these options without being asked about the general scope of prenatal diagnosis or without them being medically indicated. The court even pointed out that there was an obligation not to address the general potential of deformities without medical indication or being asked (OLG Karlsruhe VersR 1993, 705, 706). The argument put forward by the court was that the duty to counsel would otherwise include a substantial risk of bothering the parents unnecessarily. Notably, the court was determined to avoid overstretching the duties to counsel and disclose as to the available options.

Distinguishing Relevant Obligations

On a very general level one may conclude that the physician is under a duty to apply reasonable skill and care according to the common standards of the time. More specifically, several distinct obligations can be distinguished. The following list is derived from the case law just analyzed and should not be regarded as exclusive.

Obligations in Relation to Test Results

If tests have been conducted, the results have to be interpreted accurately according to the medical standard of the time. If previous tests are not conclusive, further testing may be required.

Counselling on Available Options

The obligations associated with counselling on available options for genetic testing are manifold. Of course, answers to particular questions must be accurate. Depending on the question and the facts, this may include a duty to refer the patient to specialized institutions. If the physician is not confronted with a certain question, he is under an obligation to provide the patient with information and counselling on medically indicated tests. On the other hand, references to the general probability of having a handicapped child and the available tests are not required, if not forbidden.

Giving Balanced Counselling

Collateral to the obligation to inform the patient about the medically indicated tests is the duty to give balanced counselling. It is one thing to tell the patient all the relevant facts and another to present those facts in an impartial, non-directive way. Under no circumstances should the religious or ethical beliefs of the physician influence their advice. It is paramount to present the benefits and risks of a particular test in a manner that keeps all aspects in perspective. Moreover, each case requires the physician to strike a balance between the disclosure of risks and the avoidance of fear-mongering. At the end of the day, the counselling is supposed to put the patient in a position that enables them to make an informed, uninfluenced choice.

Avoidance of Misunderstandings

Obviously the choice is impaired if the patient has not understood the counselling. However, the courts struck a balance between the interests of the physician and the patient by adopting an objective standard. The physician is, therefore, only obliged to take reasonable steps to satisfy themself that the patient has understood the information which has been provided. However, they are obliged to take the patient's intellectual abilities and educational background into account when giving the advice.

Defining Criteria

As we have concluded, the content of the duty to counsel adequately is highly dependent on the facts of each case. This applies particularly to the obligation to inform and counsel on available tests. Nevertheless, we have seen that certain criteria do trigger and define obligations to disclose and counsel. The age and the family anamnesis especially are of crucial importance. The need for a genetically indicated amniocentesis appears to be wholly dependent on those criteria. The intellectual abilities and educational background of the patient come into play when the physician communicates their counselling. It is important to note that the required standard may depend on the exact position of the physician (private practice or university hospital). This will be of significance whenever new theories and therapies are on the edge of turning into consolidated findings. It has to be said in all fairness that a judge will hardly rely on any case law when they set about determining the content of obligations in this context. Neither are they allowed to substitute the findings of an expert witness for their own judgment when scientific findings have to be made (OLG Stuttgart VersR 1991, 229, 230). That is why expert evidence forms a necessary tool for judicial reasoning in cases concerning medical malpractice in genetic counselling.

Illegal Genetic Practices

The next point is derived from a general legal principle. As we have seen PGD is considered illegal in some countries. As a result, there cannot be a duty to counsel on PGD. If a legal system disregards a method which is technically possible, the consistency of this legal system cannot penalize an omission, the non-counselling, by admitting a duty to counsel with respect to this method. Of course, the physician would act in the realms of legality by giving a hint as to the availability of PGD in other countries. Nevertheless, the law cannot prohibit a certain method on the one hand and construe duties with respect to this method on the other. A legal system should avoid such contrariness for the sake of its own reputation. It is convenient to give an extreme example to put the above reasoning to the test. A couple turns up at a hospital and asks about the general availability of PGD. According to the above analysis a physician could not be held liable for negligently giving the incorrect advice that PGD is universally prohibited. At first sight, it appears hard to argue that a physician is not liable for giving an incorrect answer. However, this is a perfectly sound result given that the legal system objects to PGD. Apart from this rather construed example, which may well be put to an opposite analysis, it seems compelling that there cannot be a duty to counsel on PGD without being asked in the first place.

Distinguishing the Relevant Actions

It is necessary to discriminate three constellations which are commonly separated into 'wrongful life', 'wrongful birth' and 'wrongful conception' claims. However, these labels are not very instructive when it comes down to making legal judgments. Any wrongfulness lies not in the life, the birth, the conception or the pregnancy, but in the negligence of the physician. The harm, if any, is not the birth itself but the effect of the defendant's negligence on the parents, resulting from the denial to the parents of their right, as the case may be, to decide whether to bear a child or whether to bear a child with a genetic or other defect (*Reed* v. *Campagnolo* 332 Md. at 226–237, 630 A. 2d at 1145–1150 Md., 1993). Nevertheless, the terminology is adopted for practical reasons.

Wrongful Life

The action that parents bring on bchalf of a disabled child against the physician and/or the hospital is called a 'wrongful life' claim. Such claims cannot be brought successfully in most countries. In Germany, an action by the child is discussed controversially. While some academics advocate a direct claim by the child (Deutsch 1983, 451; Spickhoff 2002, 391), the courts and the rest of the academic literature refuse to entertain any claim by the child (BGHZ 86, 240; Schünemann 1981, 577). Equally, English courts deny any claims by the child (*McKay* v. *Essex Area Health Authority* [1982] QB 1166, CA). Meanwhile legislation has explicitly ruled out the possibility of a 'wrongful life' claim by the child (see section 4 (5) of the Congenital Disabilities (Civil Liability) Act 1976). The great majority of US courts have adopted the same rule (*Becker* v. *Schwartz* (1978) 413 N.Y.S. 2d 895; *Phillips* v. *United States of America* (1980) 508 F. Supp. 537). California seems to be the odd one out (*Turpin* v. *Sortini*, 31 Cal. 3d 220, 643 P. 2d 954 Cal., 1982; *Curlender* v. *Bio-Science Laboratories* ((1980) App., 165 Cal.Rptr. 477). The main argument advanced by the courts is that a child has no right to be born as a whole, functional being without defects. Therefore, there cannot be a right not to be born. Furthermore, it is impossible to measure the damages for being born with defects because it is impossible to compare the life of a child born with defects and non-existence as a human being.

By contrast, French courts accepted a delictual claim by the child according to Art. 1382 Code civil in *Perruche* (Cour de cassation, March 26, 1996; Recueil Dalloz 1997, 35; Deutsch, NJW 2002, 26, 27; affirmed by Arrêt de l'Assemblée plénière de la Cour de Cassation, November 17, 2000, Jurisclasseur périodique 2000 II, 10438). In *Perruche* and the following line of cases (Arrêt de l'Assemblée plénière de la Cour de Cassation, July 13, 2001, Jurisclasseur périodique 2001 II, 10601; Arrêt de l'Assemblée plénière de la Cour de Cassation, November 28, 2001, Jurisclasseur périodique 2002 I, 10018) the courts regarded the suffering flowing from the genetic impairment as relevant damage. When this jurisprudence was subjected to criticism due to a lack of causation and ethical concerns, the legislator stepped in and made clear that nobody can bring a claim based on the sole ground that a failure has caused his birth (*Loi numéro 2002–303 relative aux droits des malades et à la qualité du système de santé*, last change by *Loi numéro 2005–102*). Claims by the child are only admitted on the basis of an error in treatment which has directly caused the handicap. Hence, there is no claim in a constellation of erroneous prenatal genetic counselling because the failure has not brought about the handicap itself. In an attempt to compensate this legislation, the handicapped child is referred to a public social fund (Deutsch and Spickhoff 2008, Rn 447).

Whether it is the right approach to deny a cause of action to the one who actually suffers from the breach of contract or the negligent behaviour, cannot be subjected to a detailed analysis for lack of space. One point should be made however; a direct claim by the child would help the disabled child to live a more dignified life when the parental maintenance obligation ceases to exist (for example, upon death of the parents). Ultimately, it appears grotesque that the same moral considerations that are advanced to defend the child's worthiness, serve to impede an otherwise justified claim. However, the international survey has shown that a claim for 'wrongful life' is almost universally rejected.

Claims by the Parents

The parents of a handicapped child might be able to recover damages on their own behalf in two distinct situations.

Wrongful Birth

'Wrongful birth' refers to a cause of action whereby parents allege that a failure to diagnose or discover a genetic defect through prenatal testing or counselling deprived them of the choice of terminating pregnancy by abortion. It is crucial to understand that the claim can only be successful if the abortion could have been undergone legally (BGHZ 86, 240, 244; *Sally Margaret Rand, Peter Frederick Rand* v. *East Dorset Health*, 2000 WL 774894). A change in the German Abortion Law which entered into effect on October 1, 1995 has the effect of lowering the chances of success of wrongful birth claims in Germany. The former embryophatic indication has been excluded. More importantly, the German Federal Court of Justice interpreted the medical-social indication according to § 218a section (2) Strafgesetzbuch as requiring a significant danger for the mental health of the mother by the expectation of having and raising a disabled child (BGHZ 151, 133). This jurisprudence focuses strongly on the impact on the mother, whose mental toughness will ultimately determine the legality of the abortion. Indirectly, the degree of the impairment of the child will also be an important aspect. All in all, German decisions strongly suggest that 'wrongful birth' claims cannot succeed on the sole basis that the child will be born heavily handicapped (for Down Syndrome OLG Düsseldorf, VersR 2003, 1543; for other handicaps OLG Hamm, NJW 2002, 2649).

Wrongful Conception

'Wrongful conception' involves a situation in which the parents allege that they would have prevented pregnancy but for the negligent counselling of the physician. An unwanted pregnancy can either arise in cases of failed sterilization/vasectomy or of failed genetic counselling prior to conception. We are only concerned with the latter case. Unlike 'wrongful birth' actions, 'wrongful conception' claims do not require that an abortion of the disabled child would have been legal (*Parkinson* v. *St. James and Seacroft University Hospital NHS Trust* [2002] Q.B. 266, CA where the mother even refused to abort; BGHZ 124, 128). Furthermore, it seems very clear that the parents are not required to abort the fetus in order to mitigate the loss (*Parkinson* v. *St. James and Seacroft University Hospital NHS Trust* [2002] Q.B. 266, 286, CA). Since the success of both 'wrongful birth' and 'wrongful conception' claims mainly turns on the question of whether the claimants can formulate recoverable damages, it seems more appropriate to give the full account of the international legal practice in the next section.[3]

Heads of Damages

Costs of Rearing a Disabled Child

Whenever parents bring a claim for 'wrongful birth' or 'wrongful conception' the main point of argument is whether they can claim damages for rearing the disabled child.

In Germany, there has been a large controversy about whether the maintenance expenses are recoverable. In 1980 the Federal Court of Justice decided for the first time that the parents can recover the costs for rearing the disabled child (BGHZ 76, 259). The decision of the court was subjected to criticism for regarding the existence of a child as a source of damage. This controversy has been wrongly labelled as the '*Kind als Schaden*' issue. The dispute reached its peak when the second chamber of the Federal Constitutional Court mentioned obiter that the existence of a child cannot be construed as legal damage (BVerfG NJW 1993, 1751, 1754). In response to this obiter dictum the Federal Court of Justice defended its approach by pointing to the economic impact of having a child (BGHZ 124, 128, 140). In the opinion of the Court, granting damages for the expenses of rearing the child was the result of a neutral numeric operation, wholly different from devaluing the child in its existence. Subsequently, this reasoning has been accepted by the first chamber of the Federal Constitutional Court (BVerfG NJW 1998, 519). In the meantime the

3 The ratio of *McFarlane* is predominantly seen as a limitation on the damages rather than on liability for example, *Parkinson* v. *St. James and Seacroft University Hospital NHS Trust* [2002] Q.B. 266, 293, CA. In *McFarlane* the Lords were divided on this point (*McFarlane* v. *Tayside Health Board* 2000 S.C. (H.L) 1, at 10 (liability) per Lord Slynn, at 38 (limitation on damages) per Lord Millet.

approach taken by the Federal Court of Justice has been applied in numerous cases and is, despite some criticism (for example, OLG Koblenz NJW-RR 2006, 967), established practice (for example, BGH NJW 2002, 2636; OLG Düsseldorf NJW 1989, 1548). Furthermore, the Federal Court of Justice has established that the parents can claim the full expenses of rearing the disabled child as opposed to the additional expenses caused by supporting a handicapped child (BGHZ 124, 128, 146). According to the Federal Court of Justice it would be unconstitutional to split the expenses in money needed for rearing a 'normal' child and money needed for the special care relating to the disability (not followed by LG Köln MedR 1999, 323, 327; Deutsch/Spickhoff 2008, Rn 447). The bottom line is that under German law full compensation in both 'wrongful birth' and 'wrongful conception' actions is available. The Austrian Supreme Court for Civil Justice follows suit (OGH, 5 Ob 165/05h=EF-Z 2006/27, 53), whereas most Austrian academic writers take a different view (Memmer 2007, 195 seq.).

In England the parents are entitled to recover compensation for the cost of providing for the child's special needs and care relating to the disability, but not for the basic cost of maintenance (*Parkinson* v. *St. James and Seacroft University Hospital NHS Trust* [2002] Q.B. 266, CA). The same is true for Scotland (*McLelland* v. *Greater Glasgow Health Board* 2001 S.L.T. 446, Ex Div.). Apparently both English and Scottish Courts consider themselves bound by *McFarlane* and do not see themselves in a position to award damages for the basic cost of maintenance. However, not all UK judges seem to believe in the correctness of the decision, since the ratio of *McFarlane* might be curtailed to 'healthy child' cases (for example, *Hardman* v. *Amin* [2001] P.N.L.R. 11, 318; *McLelland* v. *Greater Glasgow Health Board* 2001 S.L.T. 446 at 458 per Lord Morison in his dissenting speech). To confuse the situation completely, it is not so clear whether the House of Lords does appreciate the judgment in *Parkinson*, since two Law Lords have implicitly overruled it in *Rees* v. *Darlington Memorial Hospital NHS Trust* (Cane 2004, 189). This would mean not allowing compensation of the extraordinary costs of rearing a disabled child. As far as one can see, the decision in *Parkinson* was not the last word in this debate. However, the situation is less complicated than in the US because 'wrongful life' and 'wrongful conception' claims are treated alike in the UK (for example, *Anderson* v. *Forth Valley Health Board* 1998 S.L.T. 588, 603).

In the US all courts recognize claims for 'wrongful conception' (cf. the overview in *Jackson* v. *Bumgardner* 318 N.C. 172, 347 S.E. 2d 743), whereas some state courts refuse to accept claims for 'wrongful birth' (*Azzelino* v. *Dingfelder*, 315 N.C. 102, 337 S.E. 2d 528, 1985). The main argument run against a 'wrongful birth' claim is that the existence of a human life, even a life with severe defects, cannot constitute an injury cognizable at law. 'Wrongful conception' claims are distinguished by regarding the pregnancy as a medical condition as cognizable injury (*Jackson* v. *Bumgardner* 318 N.C. 172–180, 347 S.E. 2d 743–748). Even in the US this reasoning is being rejected, for it ignores the economic impact on the parents altogether (*Reed* v. *Campagnolo* 332 Md. at 226–238, 630 A.2d at 1145–1151, Md., 1993). Also, the continuation of the pregnancy itself might be regarded as legal injury (*Hardman* v. *Amin* [2001] P.N.L.R. 11, 308; but see *Reed* v. *Campagnolo* 332 Md. at 226–238, 630 A.2d at 1145–1152, Md., 1993). Moreover, one wonders whether the court in *Azzelino* would have arrived at the same conclusion in an action in contract. The language of the court in *Azzelino* ('legal injury') gives the impression that the court was concerned with the question of whether the plaintiffs have completed a cause of action and not whether cognizable damage was inflicted upon the plaintiffs. The distinguishing feature in *Jackson* supports this view. Anyway, those courts recognizing 'wrongful birth' claims seem to award damages on the basis of the extraordinary costs of supporting a disabled child, but do not award damages for the basic maintenance (*Gallagher* v. *Duke University* 852 F. 2d 773 at 777–778).

Drawing on the purpose of the duty of care that has caused the birth of the disabled child, it would be convincing to differentiate between 'wrongful birth' and 'wrongful conception' cases. Such a differentiation would not, however, be carried out along the lines of all or nothing, for in both situations the physician's negligence caused economic loss. It would rather place importance on the factual situation that conception has already taken place in 'wrongful birth' cases, whereas the avoidance of conception under certain circumstances was the very reason for obtaining counselling in 'wrongful conception' cases. Consequently, damages for the basic maintenance plus extraordinary costs of rearing a disabled child should be awarded in 'wrongful conception' cases, whereas only the extraordinary costs should be recoverable in 'wrongful birth' cases (Schünemann 1981, 575).

Damages for Pain and Suffering

As far as damages for pain and suffering related to the pregnancy and the delivery of the child are concerned the international survey shows more unanimity. Damages are awarded in all jurisdictions. Noteworthy is the German practice to award full compensation only in 'wrongful conception' cases. In those cases the physical integrity is harmed by the unwanted pregnancy, so the pain and suffering related to the pregnancy and birth is to be fully compensated (BGH NJW 1980, 1452, 1453, then in tort; Hofmann 1999, 133). In 'wrongful birth' cases the pregnancy itself is not caused by the negligence of the physician, which has to be taken into account when assessing the damages for pain and suffering. Thus, the Federal Court of Justice awards damages for pain and suffering only for the trouble that goes beyond a normal pregnancy and is caused by the disability of the child, for instance, pain and suffering that is inflicted upon the woman by having a C-section which has become necessary due to the handicaps of the child (BGHZ 86, 240, 248). Here, the inconsistency of awarding full compensation for the costs of maintenance while taking a restricted approach in relation to damages for pain and suffering becomes obvious.

Damages for Emotional Distress/Loss of Amenity

Lastly, we need to deal with damages for emotional distress caused by having and raising a disabled child. In the Common Law world damages for emotional distress are frequently granted. The courts do not seem to have trouble in regarding a handicapped child as source of emotional distress or loss of amenity (*Sally Margaret Rand, Peter Frederick Rand* v. *East Dorset Health* 2000 WL 774894; *McLelland* v. *Greater Glasgow Health Board* 2001 S.L.T. 446, 449, Ex Div.; *Gallagher* v. *Duke University* 852 F. 2d 773 at 779). Even the male parent is entitled to claim damages for emotional distress short of illness (*McLelland* v. *Greater Glasgow Health Board* 2001 S.L.T. 446, 449, Ex Div.). In accordance with § 823 section (1) BGB the German Federal Court of Justice requires a physical injury in the first place (BGHZ 86, 240, 249). As a result, damages for emotional distress as understood by Common Law standards are not recognized in Germany.

Conclusion

The analysis has proved that the law cannot be described as clear-cut when it comes down to defining negligence in genetic counselling. The duty to counsel on the available options of genetic screening is particularly hard to define without examining the facts of each case. Consequently, it is hard to formulate a rule of thumb. The standard of reasonable care appears to be nothing more than a flowery phrase which is not very helpful in deciding what the law exactly requires in a particular situation. Two main conclusions should be drawn from this analysis. Firstly, each practitioner is advised to assess his/her duties on the facts of each individual case. Secondly, the judge depends heavily on expert witnesses to be able to narrow down which, if any, methods of genetic counselling were to be explained and recommended in the given circumstances. Undoubtedly such dependence on individual circumstances is liable to create a discernible amount of legal uncertainty. Yet one may be reminded of the often repeated mantra that the outcome of a claim always depends on the facts. Insofar the law concerned with genetic counselling is not a world of its own and follows the same rules as other areas of the law.

Furthermore, we have seen that the legal consequences national laws place upon a breach of duty of care are very different. It does not seem unfair to conclude that the law of remedies, when looked at from an international perspective, can be described as slightly inconsistent, which might be attributed to the difficult socio-legal issues at stake. As a consequence, the question of the applicable law will often determine the outcome of law suits involving a foreign element.

Finally, there is an inherent tension between ethical and legal interests that deserves to be noted. Interestingly the issue only arises in wrongful birth cases. Statistics say that a fetus diagnosed with a genetic disease will be aborted in 90 per cent of all cases (Kern 2002, 21). Based on this figure the fulfilment of obligations that the law under certain circumstances imposes does ultimately lead to the abortion of the disabled fetus. As long as the dilemma of knowing and not being able to cure due to the lack of fetal therapy for most genetic diseases continues to exist, the discrepancy between the ethically demanded preservation of disabled life and the legal obligation to counsel on prenatal diagnosis will remain. However, this assessment does not add anything to the legal analysis as set out above. Nevertheless, it remains an important facet of the grander scheme of disclosure dilemmas associated with genetic counselling.

References

Bernat, E. (2004), 'Comment on OGH, 6 Ob 303/02f', *Juristische Blätter* 316–317.

Cane, P. (2004), 'Another failed sterilisation', *Law Quarterly Review* 189–193.

Deutsch, E. (1983), 'Anmerkung zu BGHZ 86, 240', *Juristenzeitung* 451–452.

Deutsch, E. and Spickhoff, A. (2008), *Medizinrecht* (Berlin: Springer Verlag).

Hofmann, K. (1999), *Rechtsfragen der Genomanalyse* (Frankfurt am Main: Peter Lang Verlag).

Juen, T. (2005), *Arzthaftungsrecht – die zivilrechtliche Haftung des Arztes für den Behandlungsfehler; der Arzthaftungsprozess in Österreich* (Wien: Manz Verlag).

Kern, B.-R. (2002), 'Zivilrechtliche Aspekte der Humangenetik', in T. Hillenkamp, (ed.), *Medizinrechtliche Probleme der Humangenetik* (Berlin: Springer Verlag), 17–33.

Kuhn, M. (1999), 'Die Arzthaftung in der Schweiz', *Zeitung für Medizinrecht*, 248–254.

Mörsdorf-Schulte, J. (2007), 'Vermögensschutz beim One-Night-Stand?', *Neue Juristische Woche*, 965–969.

Memmer, M. (2007), 'Die Entscheidungen des Obersten Gerichtshofes zum Familienplanungsschaden', *Imago Hominis* 14:3, 195–211.

Palandt, O. (2008), *Bürgerliches Gesetzbuch* (München: Beck Verlag).

Saller, D.N. and Canick, J.A. (2008), 'Current methods of prenatal screening for down syndrome and other fetal abnormalities', *Clinical Obstetrics and Gynaecology* 51:1, 24–36.

Schünemann, H. (1981), 'Schadensersatz für Mißgebildete Kinder bei Fehlerhafter Genetischer Beratung Schwangerer?', *Juristenzeitung* 574–577.

Sekizawa, A. et al. (2007), 'Recent advantages in non-invasive prenatal DNA diagnosis through analysis of maternal blood', *The Journal of Obstetrics and Gynecology Research* 33:6, 747–64.

Soler, A. et al. (2008), 'A retrospective and theoretical evaluation of rapid methods for detecting chromosome abnormalities and their implications on genetic counseling based on a series of 3868 CVS diagnoses', *Fetal Diagnosis and Therapy* 23, 126–31.

South, S.T. et al. (2008), 'Genomic medicine in prenatal diagnosis', *Clinical Obstetrics and Gynecology* 51:1, 62–73.

Spickhoff, A. (2002), 'Comment on BGH FamRZ 2002, 386', *Zeitung für das gesamte Familienrecht* 389–391.

Szymańska, M. and Knapp, P. (2007), 'Opinions of gynecologists on prenatal diagnostics in first/second trimester and abortion – ethical aspects', *Advances in Medical Sciences* 52, 182–5.

Thomson, J. (2000), 'Abandoning the law of delict', *Scots Law Times* 43–45.

Chapter 11
Responsibility Towards Relatives

Michael Steel

Background

Clinical geneticists become involved with individual patients either because several instances of the same disorder have been noted among close relatives – breast cancer or haemochromatosis are good examples – or because a single case of a well-recognized genetic disorder, such as Cystic Fibrosis or Duchenne muscular dystrophy, has been diagnosed. In both situations, the initial consultation normally involves only the immediate family of the 'index' patient but it is standard practice to take a family history that extends at least to grandparents and as many members as possible of subsequent generations. That history may require further extension and verification work on the part of the family members and the geneticist, but ultimately becomes integral to an understanding of the heritability of the disorder in question which, in turn, will allow the distribution of prior risk (that is, the risk derived from position in the family tree, before individual specific tests have been applied) to be mapped throughout the wider family.

The question then arises: 'What is the responsibility of the geneticist towards relatives, including those not known to them and possibly not in contact with the family member (the 'index case') who has sought professional advice?' The issues raised are ethical, legal and practical. No two situations are identical and therefore it is not easy to set out simple, universal applicable, recommendations. As the UK Human Genetics Commission (2002) puts it: 'We do not feel that all personal genetic information (need) be treated in the same way in every set of circumstances. Requirements for consent and confidentiality, for example, may be expected to differ according to the specific circumstances.' Yet problems in this area are encountered quite frequently; therefore an airing of views is necessary and may even prove helpful.

Good Samaritan or 'Officious Intermeddler'?

There is no general 'Good Samaritan' principle in European Law, nor in most North American codes. That is to say, the law places no explicit obligation on the citizen to offer practical help to another individual and there is no legal sanction against someone who withholds such help (Kortmann 2005).

There are some qualifications to this general stance. A member of the police, fire or rescue services, for example, has a professional duty to render assistance in such circumstances and failure to perform that duty could have serious consequences. Parents have legal obligations towards their children, employers towards their employees, airline pilots, bus, train and taxi drivers towards their passengers and shopkeepers, publicans and hoteliers towards their customers. These relationships, of course, involve some degree of dependency, recognized by law, and hence differ from my relationship (or lack of it) with the unknown family in a house I may happen to be passing, in a strange town, when I notice smoke issuing from an upstairs window. It requires no great display of altruism to ring the doorbell, or telephone the emergency services, but perhaps I am hurrying to catch a train or my mobile phone is not working or I assume that the people inside the house are dealing with the problem. If, for whatever reason, I take no positive action, the house goes up in flames and lives are lost as a result – and let us assume that a CCTV camera in the street had recorded my presence at the scene and my reaction on noticing the smoke – could I be found guilty in law of any crime or misdemeanour? Could the relatives of those who died claim compensation from me for negligence? Perhaps surprisingly, under most legal codes, the answer on both counts appears to be 'no'.

On the other hand, if I do try to alert the occupants but, failing to raise a response, I force entry by breaking through the door, then find the source of the smoke to be innocuous, can the homeowner sue me for damage to their property? The answer, in at least some countries and states may well be 'yes'.

Scenarios of both types, real and theoretical, have exercised legal brains in many countries so that subtle variations in 'Private Law' have evolved (and continue to evolve) across Europe, in Canada and among the States of the US. Their relevance to disclosure or non-disclosure of medical – and specifically genetic – information is obvious but the degree to which 'Good Samaritan' motivation ought to determine or justify the actions of geneticists has yet to be tested in any legal system. Indeed it is debatable whether the question is capable of satisfactory resolution by statute, as distinct from an agreed ethical framework.

For those who wish to pursue these issues in greater depth, I commend Professor Jan Smits' Inaugural lecture at Maastricht University (2000) 'The Good Samaritan in European Private Law; On the Perils of Principles without a Programme and a Programme for the Future'.

The Obligation of Health Care Professionals

The doctor (or nurse, clinical psychologist or other health care professional) is, of course, not a stranger to their patients and has very obvious duties towards them. These responsibilities stem first from the Hippocratic Oath, or its modern equivalent, to which virtually all health care professionals subscribe explicitly or implicitly (Nathanson 2003). The three common elements of every form of that oath are 1) to place the interests of our patients above all other priorities; 2) to abjure any harmful use of our professional knowledge or skills; and 3) to respect the confidentiality of our patients.

There are, however, additional elements that can be added and which have tended to assume greater importance in recent years. These include an undertaking to keep our professional knowledge and skills up to date and to contribute to the public good. For example, the current version of 'Good Medical Practice', the guidance on duties of a doctor, issued by the UK General Medical Council (2006), lists as its second item 'Protect and promote the health of patients and the public'. The third item includes the instruction to 'Keep your professional knowledge and skills up to date', while 'Respecting patients' rights to confidentiality' appears only in item four. The order of listing does not necessarily reflect the relative weight attached to each of these precepts but there is, perhaps, an inference that problems of competing obligations may arise and that the ethically correct path may not be clear.

For example, it has been recognized for many decades that the duty of confidentiality to one's patients is not absolute (Reilly et al. 1997; Vandenbroucke 1998; Moodie and Wright 2000). A patient with a notifiable infectious disease is subject to restrictions in order to limit its spread and if they refuse to comply with these restrictions it is accepted that their doctor must alert the public health authorities. Similarly, the patient whose ability to drive safely is impaired for health reasons should be persuaded by their doctor to desist from doing so. If they refuse, the doctor is entitled to share their concerns, first with the next-of-kin or other responsible adult member of the family and then, if necessary, with the authorities who issue driving licences and who have the power to withdraw them. These breaches of patient confidentiality are sanctioned in the interests of public safety and recognize the concept that we all (patients and doctors alike) have a responsibility not to harm our fellow citizens. Laurie (2002) refers to 'the tension at the interface between the public and private areas of life' and observes 'paradoxically, it is the development of a public interest in the welfare of individuals that has proved to be one of the greatest threats to individual privacy in the last century'. Yet matters become still more complicated when we have to consider our duties not simply towards 'society' or 'the public' in general but to specific individuals and in relation to incompletely quantified risks.

Who Owns Genetic Information?

Although genetic information is usually acquired in the first instance from one individual, by its very nature it is a 'property' shared (actually or potentially) with other family members. Hence the definition of 'confidentiality' can become blurred and the duties associated with it may be uncertain. Take the case of Mr M, diagnosed by a geneticist as having Marfan's syndrome, a condition of very variable severity, characterized by a tall, thin physique, long limbs, long fingers and toes, a liability to lens dislocation and, most significantly, to potentially fatal cardiovascular problems, including aortic aneurism (Pyeritz 2000). The condition is inherited as an autosomal dominant so that first degree relatives of an affected individual are at 50 per cent risk. Mr M has a brother, from whom he is estranged but whom he describes as 'tall and thin like me'. Despite an explanation that screening for aortic dilatation is indicated in asymptomatic Marfan's syndrome, he refuses to allow any information about his condition to be passed to his brother. Is the geneticist obliged to respect this prohibition on the grounds of patient confidentiality?

To pursue the question further: the geneticist reports the findings (and the refusal to pass information to the brother) to Mr M's GP (family doctor), as is standard practice in the UK. It happens that Mr M's brother is a patient of the same GP. How does that doctor now discharge their responsibilities to the two brothers? The simplest way out of the dilemma would be for the GP to advise the second brother, ideally in the course of a consultation for some other reason, that screening for aortic aneurism should be arranged in view of his physical characteristics which suggest the possibility of Marfan's. They need not make any reference to Mr M's diagnosis. Of course the true sequence of events may emerge in due course but it is unlikely that a complaint of breach of confidence, against either the geneticist or the GP, would be upheld. The real issue is whether the GP had 'done the right thing' and most reasonable people would probably say 'yes'. The underlying logic here is that, while Mr M may be entitled to withhold information about his own condition, he does not 'own' the genetic knowledge relevant to other family members. It must be admitted that separating the two can be difficult and commentators differ in the degree to which they accept the view that genetic information belongs to the whole family (Nuffield Council on Bioethics 1993; Richards and Green 1995; Pembrey and Anionwu 1996).

Since this is central to the whole question of duty to relatives, let us examine another set of circumstances. A 35-year-old woman, Mrs C, seeks advice because her mother had developed breast cancer at age 50, while her mother's sister had also suffered from breast cancer and had died from epithelial ovarian cancer at 46. Mrs C has read that breast and ovarian cancer occurring together in the same family may indicate a genetic predisposition and is concerned both on her own account and for her two daughters. She is advised that this family history is quite strongly suggestive of a mutation in BRCA1 or BRCA2, affecting her mother and aunt. In that event, she herself will be at 50 per cent risk of carrying the same mutation. Her options include regular screening and/or prophylactic surgery, the most extreme form involving total removal of both breasts, both ovaries and fallopian tubes (Steel 2007). Clearly she would not wish to contemplate such major surgery if she herself is not carrying the mutation and the information on her own carrier status will be important to her daughters in the future. Unfortunately, BRCA1 and BRCA2 are both large genes and many different mutations are responsible for breast/ovarian cancer risk. Finding a causal mutation in any given family is a difficult, time-consuming and expensive exercise, requiring DNA for analysis from at least one cancer-affected member. Testing an unaffected individual at 50 per cent risk is unsatisfactory, since a negative result can mean either that they do not carry the mutation or that a mutation has been missed by the test. In Mrs C's case, her mother is alive and has had early-onset breast cancer. She is therefore a suitable candidate for mutation-testing in this family. If a mutation is identified, then testing other family members for that precise DNA change only is technically simple and inexpensive. Unfortunately, Mrs C's mother can not be persuaded to provide a blood sample for mutation-screening. She does not wish to contemplate the possibility that she carries (and may have passed on) a serious genetic 'defect'. This, and similar attitudes, though unusual, are by no means unknown. The geneticist is bound to respect the mother's refusal. They cannot force her to give a blood sample against her will and presumably it would be unlawful, or at least unethical to obtain DNA from her (say from a buccal scrape or a hair root) by subterfuge. That position might be tested if the daughter were to make application to the courts on the grounds that her mother owed her a duty of care and therefore should be ordered to provide a DNA sample but, to my knowledge, no exactly comparable case has yet been determined.

There is, however, a possible way round the difficulty. The aunt, who died from cancer, was equally likely to be a carrier of a BRCA1 or BRCA2 mutation – arguably even more likely since she suffered two cancers and at an even earlier age than Mrs C's mother. Fixed tumour tissue – particularly from an ovarian cancer, which tends to be highly cellular – can be used to extract DNA from which BRCA1 and BRCA2 can be sequenced. This has been undertaken many times on a research basis and, while it is not routinely available as a diagnostic service, it would be possible in circumstances where a result is important to living family members and cannot be obtained by other means. In the UK, tumour tissue removed for diagnostic purposes or as part of treatment from a patient who has since died, can be used in this way without requiring consent from the next of kin, though the law in this regard may vary from country to country. The UK Human Genetics Commission (2002) states: 'The approach we favour is that a presumption should be made that the dead person would have consented in his or her lifetime to such testing and that this justifies post-mortem testing.' Now, does the geneticist have an obligation to Mrs C to explore the alternative route to identifying a mutation in the family? If they do so and a mutation is found, then Mrs C can be tested to establish her own genetic status and cancer risk and hence can make informed decisions about her own management. However, if Mrs C does prove to be mutation-positive, then her mother's mutation status can be inferred with certainty, which would be against her expressed wishes.

As in the previous example, most reasonable people would probably agree that, while, in accordance with the Universal Declaration on the Human Genome and Human Rights (1997) Mrs C's mother has the right 'not to know' (and indeed the right not to participate actively in obtaining genetic knowledge) she does not have the right to deny other family members access to that knowledge by other routes.

Mrs C and the geneticist may very well agree that her mother should not be told about the finding. This will obviously be easier if Mrs C proves not to be a mutation-carrier so that no subsequent surgery takes place. However let us suppose that a cousin of Mrs C (a daughter of her mother's brother) now comes forward independently enquiring about her own cancer risk. The geneticist has information about the family mutation but has agreed with Mrs C that this will remain confidential. Does the geneticist now go through a charade with Mrs C's cousin pretending that the whole exercise – testing tissue extracted DNA from her aunt – must be undertaken to establish whether a mutation can be identified, or do they breach their previous agreement and tell the cousin that the mutation is known and that a simple test is available to determine her own status? In practice the geneticist would probably consult Mrs C and seek her consent for the information to be shared, but would Mrs C have the right to refuse? She might be very anxious that the more family members who know about the mutation, the greater the risk that her mother will find out and suffer distress. Nevertheless, Mrs C was not herself the source of the DNA in which the mutation was detected and it is questionable whether her role in finding it gives her 'ownership' of the information in any legal or ethical sense. The geneticist's duty of confidentiality to Mrs C and her mother surely does not take precedence over their duty of care to the cousin.

Would this still apply, however, if the cousin had not come to the geneticist's own clinic but had sought advice in some distant town or even another country? This is commonplace in genetic practice and when a family history has been taken in any centre, it is normal to contact whatever clinic has provided care for other family members. In that setting, the cousin is not a patient of Mrs C's geneticist. Does that alter the balance of their duty of care towards Mrs C and her mother on the one hand and towards Mrs C's cousin on the other? Probably not, but again the argument rests partly on the tenuous nature of any claim that Mrs C and her mother may have to 'ownership' of the genetic information. It might be harder to resolve the dilemma if Mrs C's mother had indeed agreed to give a blood sample but on condition that the result be shared with her daughter alone. This will be explored further in later sections.

Why Withhold Genetic Information?

People not directly involved in clinical genetics or family counselling may be surprised that the sharing of genetic information among relatives should present any problem at all. However several studies, particularly in the field of inherited cancer risk, have shown that transmission of relevant information to other family members is often selective. For example, first degree relatives (parents, siblings, children) are much more likely to be told of mutation test results than nieces, nephews or cousins. In the case of familial breast/ovarian cancer, even among first degree relatives, females are more likely to be told than males (Patenaude et al. 2006a, b; Gadzicki et al. 2006). Not all of the withholding of information is deliberate concealment. For understandable reasons, many people do not appreciate that a disease affecting only women can nevertheless be transmitted via male carriers so male relatives may not be told because the news is thought to be of no relevance to them. Similarly, cousins and other more distant relatives may not be informed because no one member of the family feels it is their responsibility – they assume 'someone else will do it'. However a survey of genetic counsellors in the US (Dugan et al. 2003) revealed that almost half were aware of instances where an individual affected by a genetic disease (or their next of kin) had specifically refused to allow the information to be passed on to a relative at risk. The commonest reason was a breakdown in family cohesion – a feud. Other reasons included concern about insurance or employment discrimination or the prospect that the information would damage fragile relationships. To this may be added misplaced feelings of guilt or shame on the part of the individual in whom the mutation has been discovered.

In compiling a family history, many genetics centres make use of a standardized form seeking information (dates of birth and death and any relevant illnesses) about siblings, children, parents, grandparents and, if possible, cousins, nephews, nieces, aunts, uncles, great aunts and great uncles. The form is sent or given to the 'index' patient with a request to consult widely within the family to achieve maximum accuracy. In a few cases, the request cannot be met because the patient is an only child; their parents are dead and they have no contact with more distant relatives. However, much more commonly, the exercise is highly productive. In most families there is at least one member who likes nothing better than tracing their ancestry and finding out more about their living relatives. Equally important, the effort expended in completing the family history form brings the family together and ensures that they are all aware of the genetic issues that have arisen. It is then much less likely that problems will arise in the sharing of any information that may subsequently emerge. If such problems are going to arise, then at least the geneticist and the index patient are alerted to them at an early stage, which reduces the risk of making matters worse by blundering into an unforeseen situation.

Genetic information acquired in the course of research, rather than through a clinical service, is particularly liable to cause difficulties because the motivation – to discover something new in the field – may undervalue the need for detailed consideration of the implications for family members. Thus, for example, if an affected family member is tested, in the setting of a genetics service, for a mutation that may cause familial polycystic kidney disease (PKD), at-risk relatives should already have been identified and the patient's attitude to sharing relevant information should have been established. However if they are screened as part of an epidemiological research programme to determine the frequency of mutations among people with PKD, there may have been no prior consideration of the implications for their family and, despite the information provided to obtain informed consent for the study, the patient may be unprepared for the ensuing ramifications.

In the immediate aftermath of the identification of BRCA1 (Miki et al. 1994), many families were enrolled in research projects to establish the frequency and nature of mutations in particular populations. The extent of clinical support offered to participating families was sometimes less than ideal and this resulted, on some occasions, in the detection of mutation-carriers (particularly men) who felt no obligation to pass that information on to other family members and indeed refused to do so.

It is obvious that communication among family members should be encouraged before proceeding very far down the road of genetic investigation and that thorough explanation of the nature of inheritance, the implications of any likely test results for all relatives and the management options for those at risk, should be discussed widely within the family. Genetics nurse specialists or genetic counsellors have an invaluable role in ensuring that this is the case. Problems of information sharing are thereby greatly reduced, and the occasions when a geneticist has to wrestle with their conscience over a conflict between the duty of confidentiality to one patient and the duty of care to relatives ought to be few and far between.

Obligations to Breach Patient Confidentiality

Case law, particularly in the US, has established that there are circumstances in which a doctor owes a duty of care to a specific third party, who is not their patient and that this duty of care may override their duty of confidentiality towards their patient. The classic precedent is the 'Tarasoff' case in which a mentally disturbed patient told their psychiatrist that they intended to assault a named individual. The patient would not allow their doctor to warn the intended victim and the psychiatrist felt bound by patient confidentiality. The pyschiatrist hoped, of course, that the threat would not be carried into practice but when it was, the court subsequently ruled against the psychiatrist and made it clear that physicians ought to warn third parties of immediate potential danger even at the cost of breaching patient confidentiality (*Tarasoff* v. *Regents of the University of California* 1976, 17. Cal.3d 425). Subsequent rulings by state supreme courts have addressed specifically the duty to warn relatives of a genetic cancer risk but the decisions have not been entirely consistent (see discussion in Dugan et al. 2003).

The American Society for Human Genetics (1988) has issued a statement in the following terms:

> Genetic information, like all medical information, should be protected by the legal and ethical principle of confidentiality. Disclosure should be permissible where attempts to encourage disclosure on the part of the patient have failed; where the harm is highly likely to occur and is serious and foreseeable; where the at-risk relative(s) is identifiable; and where either the disease is preventable, treatable, or medically accepted standards indicate that early monitoring will reduce the genetic risk. The harm that may result from failure to disclose should

> outweigh the harm that may result from disclosure. At a minimum, health-care professionals should be obliged to inform patients about the implications of their genetic test results and about the potential risks to their family member.

The UK Human Genetics Commission (2002), after extensive consultation, reached a similar conclusion:

> Bearing in mind the principle of genetic solidarity and altruism, we take the view that disclosure of sensitive personal genetic information for the benefit of family members in certain circumstances may occasionally be justified. This would arise where a patient refuses to consent to such disclosure and the benefit of disclosure substantially outweighs the patient's claim to confidentiality.

The 'Cousin in Australia'

Quite apart from the unusual circumstance in which there is refusal to share genetic information, the geneticist is more commonly faced with the dilemma of being able to identify individuals on the extended family tree who may be at risk but who have no contact with the branch of the family known personally to them. This is often referred to as the 'Cousin in Australia' problem (Bobrow et al. 1992). It is a problem on two counts. First, the 'cousin' may be difficult to trace and, second, the 'cousin' may not wish to be told that they could be at risk of some genetic disorder.

This poses a dilemma of a different order from the above. There is not usually any issue of refusal to share information but the question arises: 'When is it right to seek out someone, who has not come to you for advice, and thrust upon them information which they may not welcome?' Alternatively: 'Am I at fault (legally or ethically) if I make little or no effort to reach someone at risk and that individual subsequently suffers through ignorance?'

Several legal and ethical principles seem to apply (Marta 1999). First, in law, there is no absolute right 'not to know'. To paraphrase Professor John Harris (1992) we may not wish to know we are an 'ugly so-and-so' but we have no right of redress if someone tells us we are and it is true. The Universal Declaration on the Human Genome and Human Rights (1997) does go some way towards treating genetic test data as a special category, specifying the individual's right not to be informed of the results of such tests. That has yet to be incorporated into common law but is unlikely to be challenged. The 'Cousin in Australia' may not wish to know that she is at risk of Huntington's disease or Retinitis pigmentosa, on the basis of genetic investigations in their wider family but if this is the case, and only that information is given to them, they have no legal grounds for complaint. However a second principle that applies is that of autonomy – the freedom to make and act upon one's own personal choices. There would be no question of forcing the cousin to take any action – for example, undergoing medical examination or

DNA testing – as a consequence of their familial risk status. 'There are limits to how far we should seek the welfare of others. In particular, if our concern for the welfare of others prevents their making autonomous decisions, then the concern may go too far. Paternalistic interventions in the lives of others may be prompted by a desire to protect their welfare, but may be indefensible in terms of personal autonomy' (Human Genetics Commission 2002). Of course, it is likely that a cautious and sensitive initial approach would be made, sounding out the cousin's likely attitude before specifying even what kind of genetic information is actually available. Nevertheless, it is difficult to see how the news coming 'out of the blue' could be anything other than disturbing and the decision to make contact cannot be taken lightly.

The third principle is that of beneficence or non-malfeasance – that is doing good or avoiding doing harm. It is self-evident that in attempting to resolve any ethical dilemma in clinical practice, the doctor, nurse or other health care worker will seek to maximize the good and minimize the harm that is likely to ensue. Good intentions, however, may not be sufficient if the actions are subsequently examined in a court of law or a professional tribunal. Some effort must therefore be made to balance the harms and benefits likely to follow each of the possible courses of action. The principal subject of these benefits or harms is the distant relative who may or may not receive genetic information but some attention should be given to the other family members, to the health care professional who takes the decision and to the wider community.

Dealing with these in reverse order, it must be recognized that the public (and, of course, the profession) would lose something real, though intangible, if confidence in the absolute privacy of communication between doctor and patient were diminished. That being granted, exceptions to the primacy of medical confidentiality are already recognized, as noted earlier, and provided further encroachment is rare and the reasons clearly explained, they will probably prove acceptable. Nevertheless, as medicine advances, the balance between beneficence and malfeasance in any given situation can shift subtly or suddenly and we enter ever more dangerous waters in relation to public perception. This is particularly true of genetics, in which the popular press and the public take a keen interest. It is therefore essential that society is fully engaged in framing and updating the ethical framework in which medical research is undertaken and applied.

The health care professional who takes responsibility for informing, or not informing the 'Cousin in Australia' is wise to seek the opinion of colleagues and to consult authoritative guidelines, such as those quoted above from the American Society for Human Genetics and the UK Human Genetics Commission, before acting. These rarely have the force of holy writ, let alone of law, and they may be equivocal in their conclusions. Nevertheless they represent considered views and should afford the best protection available against subsequent legal or professional criticism.

The family found to carry a mutation (or perhaps simply a genetic disorder without known molecular basis) will normally also have provided the information on family structure through which it has been possible to identify geographically and/or socially distant relatives at risk. They may therefore feel uneasy about any approach to the latter. Will there be repercussions, recriminations, blame, hostility? Unreasonable and unlikely though such outcomes may be, they should be discussed with the family and an assurance of moral support given. If they, individually or collectively decide that, on balance, they would prefer not to have information released to far-flung cousins, then that reluctance must be taken into account in weighing the balance of benefits and harms.

Ultimately, however, the crux of the argument rests on what good or harm is likely to come to the 'Cousin in Australia' a) if they are told that there is relevant genetic information available; and b) if they are not told. The possible harm has already been considered – they may not want to know and may be distressed by any approach. On the other hand, they will not be obliged to take up the option of finding out what the genetic information entails nor need they take any action on their own account if they do decide to access the information. Many patients at risk of Huntington's disease choose not to undergo predictive testing (Meiser and Dunn 2000) and, perhaps surprisingly, at least one patient with a BRCA2 mutation reported that, having informed all of her at-risk relatives, none opted to be tested (Muller et al. 2000). The potential benefits of knowing there is relevant genetic information will depend on what options are open to the individual at risk. At present, Huntington's disease is not amenable to treatment, so many people at risk may feel there is no point in knowing their precise status. Some, however, wish to make decisions about their future – having, or not having children, for example, while others may simply find uncertainty intolerable and so will choose to be tested. In Marfan's syndrome or familial breast cancer and many other conditions, pre-symptomatic identification of risk offers prospects of screening that can improve the outcome of treatment. As time goes on, better treatments and perhaps even correction of genetic defects will become more readily available for many genetic disorders. Hence the balance of advantage or disadvantage from knowing personal risk status will shift and the geneticist must be prepared to change their practice in relation to contacting other family members in the light of changing clinical realities.

In purely practical terms, there are questions of how far the duty of care extends and how much effort can be expected on the part of the doctor – for example, does the duty apply to first cousins but not second? If the family cannot supply a name and current address is the geneticist absolved from any obligation to pursue the matter further? These really are issues for debate and for determination initially on a case-by-case basis but it might seem sensible to link the duty of care to the level of estimated risk rather than closeness of kinship with the index patient. It can be argued that any relative identified as being at 50 per cent prior risk from a serious genetic disorder, for which effective screening and/or therapy depends on recognition of that risk, should be contacted if practicable. Whether this should extend to lower levels of estimated prior risk – say 25 per cent – is bound to be controversial.

Where full details – name, address, date of birth – are available for the 'Cousin in Australia', then difficulty in communication is not a justification for inaction. At the other extreme, the geneticist cannot be expected to mount a full scale 'search and rescue' expedition for someone whose details are vague. In between will be many cases where some traceable information is provided. Exchange of information between genetics centres about dispersed members of the same family is already routinely undertaken on an international scale. Contacts therefore exist that can require little additional effort at least to establish whether there is a reasonable prospect of tracing a 'lost' relative.

Ultimately, as in so many complex dilemmas of human existence, we come down to a need for balance. Nobody expects medicine to be easy and genetics is no exception. Individually and collectively we can only do our best.

References

American Society for Human Genetics (1998), 'ASHG statement: Professional disclosure of familial genetic information', *American Journal of Human Genetics* 62, 474–83.

Bobrow, M. et al. (1992), 'Panel discussion', *Disease Markers* 10, 211–18.

Dugan, R.B. et al. (2003), 'Duty to warn at-risk relatives for genetic disease: Genetic counselors' clinical experience', *American Journal of Medical Genetics* 119C, 27–34.

Gadzicki, D. et al. (2006), 'Communicating BRCA1 and BRCA2 genetic test results', *Journal of Clinical Oncology* 24, 2969–70.

General Medical Council (UK) (2006), *Good Medical Practice. The Duties of a Doctor Registered with the General Medical Council* (London).

Harris, J. (1992), 'The use of information (autonomy and confidentiality)', *Disease Markers* 10, 195–8.

Human Genetics Commission (UK) (2002), *Inside Information: Balancing Interests in the Use of Personal Genetic Data*, Dept of Health, London.

Kortmann, J. (2005), *Altruism in Private Law: Liability for Nonfeasance and Negotiorium Gestio* (Oxford: University Press).

Laurie, G. (2002), *Genetic Privacy: A Challenge to Medico-legal Norms* (Cambridge: Cambridge University Press).

Marta, M.R. (1999), 'Genetic testing: Do health care professionals have a duty to tell a patient's family members that they may be at risk?', *Journal or Health Risk Management* 19, 26–38.

Meiser, B. and Dunn, S. (2000), 'Psychological impact of genetic testing for Huntington's disease: An update of the literature', *Journal of Neurology, Neurosurgery and Psychiatry* 69, 574–8.

Miki, Y. et al. (1994), 'A strong candidate for the breast and ovarian cancer susceptibility gene BRCA1', *Science* 266, 66–71.

Moodie, P. and Wright, M. (2000), 'Confidentiality, codes and courts: An examination of the significance of professional guidelines on medical ethics in determining the legal limits of confidentiality', *Anglo-American Law Review* 29, 39–66.

Muller, H. et al. (2000), 'Genetic testing for cancer predisposition – an ongoing debate', *Lancet Oncology* 1, 118–24.

Nathanson, V. (2003), 'Why we need a new Hippocratic oath', *Medical Education* 37, 1123–4.

Nuffield Council on Bioethics (1993), *Genetic Screening; Ethical Issues* (London).

Patenaude, A.F. et al. (2006a), 'Sharing BRCA1/2 test results with first-degree relatives: Factors predicting who women tell', *Journal of Clinical Oncology* 24, 700–06.

Patenaude, A.F. et al. (2006b), 'Communicating BRCA1/2 test results' (authors' reply), *Journal of Clinical Oncology* 24, 2697–71.

Pembrey, M. and Anionwu, E. (1996), 'Ethical Aspects of Genetic Screening and Diagnosis', in D.L. Rimoin et al. (eds), *Emery and Rimoin's Principles and Practice of Medical Genetics* (New York: Churchill Livingstone).

Pyeritz, R.E. (2000), 'The Marfan syndrome', *Annual Review of Medicine* 51, 481–510.

Reilly, P.R. et al. (1997), 'Ethical issues in genetic research: Disclosure and informed consent', *Nature Genetics* 15, 16–20.

Richards, M. and Green, J.M. (1995), 'Genetic Screening, Conselling, Consent and Family Life', in *Proceedings of a Symposium on Genetic Screening*, Centre for Medical law and Ethics, Nuffield Foundation (London).

Smits, J. (2000), 'The good samaritan principle in European private law: On the perils of principles without a programme and a programme for the future', Inaugural lecture, Maastricht University (available on Internet).

Steel, C.M. (2007), 'Cancer of the Breast and Female Genital Tract', in D.L. Rimoin et al. (eds), *Emery and Rimoin's Principles and Practice of Medical Genetics* (5th edition) (New York: Churchill Livingstone), 2093–2121.

Tarasoff vs Regents of the University of California (1976) Cal.3d 425.

United Nations Universal Declaration on the Human Genome and Human Rights (1997), UN New York.

Vandenbroucke, J.P. (1998), 'Maintaining privacy and the health of the public', *British Medical Journal* 316, 1331–1332.

Chapter 12
Careful Communication of 'Bad News': The Cancer Experience

Wolf Langewitz

The term 'careful' applies to three different objects or areas of interest within the context of the communication of 'bad news': being careful with the content of what is said, being careful with the person to whom the information is delivered, and finally being careful with oneself when having delivered bad news. The first two aspects will be dealt with in this chapter, with the hope that the experience gathered in the delivery of bad news in cancer care might extend to the delivery of genetic information.

Taking care, first of all, means avoiding harm (*primum nil nocere*). Therefore, the question is whether there is anything potentially 'delicate' or even harmful in giving information about a cancer diagnosis or about the hopeless condition of a patient. Every physician has had the experience that no matter how carefully they have picked their words, the effect of the news they have delivered seems to be disastrous: patients – and relatives – reacting with intense negative emotions, claiming that this news has destroyed all their hope, may leave one doubting whether telling the truth should be as high a goal as avoiding harm. One might say the major risk that lies in knowledge of the 'truth', that is, the statistically most likely course of a disease, is its potential to destroy illusions. This can, indeed, be viewed as a risk when illusions are to some extent supportive, for example, when they keep an individual going in the hope (perhaps illusory) that an improvement can be achieved. Arguing in this way means accepting that the degree of individual freedom that is based upon the knowledge of one's own condition is given a lower priority than the integrity of unrealistic hopes. In clinical practice, however, such an argument is not well supported: even though an immediate negative reaction to bad news sometimes occurs, it often transforms to an active, information-seeking position, even within the first session. Patients – often faster than relatives – regain their composure and start asking for concrete details, like whether they will experience pain or shortness of breath, or how long is it going to take. As the 'truth' in a given clinical situation is usually complex and laden with insecurity, it is necessary to communicate the most relevant information appropriate to the moment. Especially in a situation when there is little realistic chance that the patient is going to recover, or when it seems likely that they are going to die within a few weeks, one of the most difficult issues still remains to achieve a balance between telling the truth (being honest) and leaving room for hope (Surbone 2006, 56 ff.).

On the other hand, leaving illusions in place by not providing information is, in itself, harmful because illusions are often misleading, and may lead to consequences that prevent an individual from making an appropriate choice that matches their actual situation. It can easily be seen from these few remarks that patients with conditions difficult or impossible to treat represent a group of individuals for whom it may be extremely challenging to define general rules about the risks and benefits of telling the truth or maintaining 'protective' illusions. This is all the more complicated by the fact that patients have no prior experience of receiving a diagnosis of their own fatal disorder and are confronted by a very threatening and unfamiliar situation. Thus, both the health care professional providing the information and the receiver of this information constantly have to work on the best way to process this sensitive information. Despite the formidable complexities, there are some data in the literature that – though not defining definite rules – characterize the range of professional behaviours and common patient responses and needs.

The first section of this chapter will quote some landmark studies reporting on common experiences of patients and professionals in breaking bad news, the second section will develop and discuss suggestions for professional behaviour, and the third section will propose some additional suggestions, based upon contributions from Neo-Phenomenology, as developed by the German philosopher Hermann Schmitz. In my view Schmitz's thinking has the potential to broaden our perspectives on appropriate communication in difficult clinical situations (for an overview see Langewitz 2007). Schmitz coined a different definition of the term 'situation', referring to a certain mode of being in which meaningfulness cannot be ascribed to particular observations but is dissolved in variety (Schmitz 2005a, 56 ff.). Situations are opposed to constellations – an arrangement of facts in time and space that, although possibly very complex, can be deduced to single observable and countable units. Furthermore, he describes personal feelings as similar to weather phenomena, for example, the tense and heavy climate inside a room when there is trouble brewing. In this way, feelings are no longer the exclusive affair of an individual shielded from the environment, but open out into the environment, taking on the quality of an atmosphere poured into a rimless room (Schmitz 2007, 23 ff.). If this holds true, two individuals may jointly partake of a specific situation not only by the exchange of factual information, but also by sharing a common atmosphere. As physicians, we have been trained to convert a situation into a constellation as quickly as possible, protecting us from the invasiveness of feelings as atmospheres and 'sticking to the facts'. According to Schmitz, the receptive organ responsive to atmosphere is the felt body (Leib), as opposed to the corporeal body (Körper). Whereas the surface of the corporeal body can be touched and seen, the felt body can only be perceived in the region of the corporeal body without the use of the senses. If we would allow ourselves as professionals to immerse in mutual embodiment within a 'situation', we might be better able to adjust our behaviour to the present status of our patients.

What is Already Known

Instead of yet another literature review (a recent review can be found in Surbone 2006), a selection of papers will be referred to below that represent the most recent developments in communication research in cancer care. There have been a number of recent studies that investigate the opinion of patients and relatives concerning the communication of bad news in cancer care. Even though this is certainly to be preferred to statements from experts who are not victims of bad news themselves, this approach is not free of methodological problems, which will be alluded to later in this chapter.

In a large study by Kaplowitz et al. (2002) 352 out of 1,576 cancer patients responded to a questionnaire sent by mail; 83 per cent were female, 63 per cent of all respondents suffered from breast cancer, and over 90 per cent were white. The results showed that 80 per cent of the patients wanted qualitative or more general information (for example, a response to the question, is the patient probably going to die from their case of cancer?); 66 per cent indicated that they had actively asked for it, and 89 per cent actually received qualitative information of this kind. Concerning quantitative or specific prognostic information (for example, how long the patient is expected to live), results were different: only 53 per cent indicated that they wanted this information, 35 per cent reported having directly asked for it, and 30 per cent said that they had actually received quantitative information.

Another interview study examined how parents of children suffering from cancer wished to be informed (Mack et al. 2006). Results showed that the majority of parents desired as much information about prognosis as possible (87 per cent), and wanted it expressed numerically (85 per cent). More than a third of parents found information about their children's prognosis very upsetting (36 per cent), yet they still wanted this information to be given – even more so than parents who felt less upset by the information they had received. Furthermore, parents who found information upsetting were no less likely to say that knowing prognosis was important, that knowing prognosis helped in decision making, or that hope for a cure kept them going. Thus, it does not seem wise to accept avoidance of upsetting the receiver of information as the ultimate goal of providing information; the upsetting nature of prognostic information does not diminish parents' desire for such information, its importance to decision making or parents' sense of hope.

If we accept that telling the truth has the potential to destroy illusions, the most important illusion in this context is the hope that an untreatable disorder (from a professional standpoint) might still be cured – if not by the remedies of medicine, then by the effects of a miracle.

Therefore, a questionnaire study from Australia merits a closer look. It tries to define physician behaviour that is linked to the provision of hope (Hagerty et al. 2005). A major advantage of this study is that patients were able to give their personal definition of hope in addition to choosing among four pre-defined definitions that read: hope is a feeling or expectation:

- that things can go well (19 per cent);
- that because one thing has gone wrong, it doesn't mean that other things will not go well (14 per cent);
- that you have just as good chances (if not better) as the next person of having the best outcome (3 per cent);
- that you can still enjoy a good quality of life, even if life expectancy is uncertain (3 per cent).

Many participants chose different definitions that could be grouped according to: quality of life and fulfilment of goals (23 per cent), receiving treatment that would provide the best cancer and symptom control (8 per cent), and hope for cure and remission (8 per cent). Answers to the question, what in general helped them to be hopeful, put the professional's role into a more modest perspective: the vast majority named family (87 per cent), religious beliefs or spirituality (28 per cent), or friends (24 per cent), with scientific advances in cancer care in only 9 per cent of cases.

Physician behaviour that was perceived as increasing hopefulness could be attributed to three factors that were labelled expert/positive/collaborative (28 per cent of total variance explained), avoidant (14 per cent of total variance explained), and empathic (12 per cent of total variance explained). Typical descriptors of the first factor included such aspects as: 'appeared to know all there was to know about my cancer', 'said my pain will be controlled' or 'suggested we work together on this as a team'. The factor 'avoidant' was characterized by statements like: 'used euphemisms like growth and did not use the word cancer' and 'appeared nervous or uncomfortable'. The factor that contributed the least was the factor that is often stressed the most in communication training for oncologists: be empathic! Typical items on this factor were: 'physician expressed their own feelings', 'asked about my reaction to my prognosis' or 'offered to answer all my questions'.

In the light of expert recommendations concerning breaking bad news and giving prognostic information, one finding needs special attention: the most powerful factor in maintaining or building up hope contains items that pertain to physician's competence as an expert in oncology. A similar finding has been reported by Parker et al. with a similar methodology (Parker et al. 2001). The most powerful factor was related to the content of what the physician was saying, explaining 33 per cent of total variance. The second factor could be named supportive behaviour, accounting for 11 per cent of total variance. This factor included items like: 'doctor telling me where I could find resources in the neighbourhood or community' or 'telling me it's okay if I am becoming upset'. The third factor was named facilitation by the authors; it contained those physician behaviours that most communication skills programs, including our own (Kiss 1999), focus upon: 'doctor giving full attention', 'being told in person' or 'keeping eye contact'. This factor explained only 6 per cent of total variance!

Suggestions for Professionals Breaking Bad News

On the Importance of Individualized Information Giving

Few characteristics of a patient predict their need for information (Kutner et al. 1999). Therefore, an individualized assessment of needs and expectations is recommended. Requirements change over the course of the disease, as does the way patients and relatives cope with the burden of their suffering. A good summary can be found in a recent study (Kirk et al. 2004), in which data were generated from 1-hour interviews with patients or relatives. Subjects were terminally ill cancer patients in palliative care.

Kirk et al. differentiate between two different aspects of communication: content and process characteristics. Their findings are summarized in the following section. Concerning process characteristics, patients and relatives stress the importance of health care providers being honest and direct. Patients, for example, would have preferred the physician to be straightforward in naming the disease as cancer. While patients want a clear message in layman terms, they also expect the health care professional to give information in a compassionate and empathetic manner. To the recipients of information it is clear that the process of providing information requires time, they appreciate it when the health care professional 'actually sits down and really talks to them'. When providing information, health care professionals must take into account patients' and relatives' ability to assimilate information. Patients and relatives felt reassured when health care professionals told them of their willingness to continue to provide care and not to forget about them, even when specialists become involved.

Important elements with regard to content of information delivered included health care providers assuming the role of an expert who is willing to provide specific prognostic information, and who can respectfully provide the level of detailed information desired by the patient or their family. Many patients seem to interpret prognostic information as a means of increasing control over the remaining period of life; they use such information as a guide to getting their affairs in order and talking with their family. Still, the provision of prognostic information should be sensitive to possible resistance, on the part of patients and their family, to processing this difficult and threatening news.

A final aspect of these interviews also related to the provision of hope. It seemed that patients and family members were able to live in parallel worlds, on the one hand, recognizing the strong odds against an extended period of life, and on the other, wanting to believe in a miracle – and they often seemed to hope that their doctor might also entertain the possibility of a miracle. Furthermore, patients were well aware that any one physician is unlikely to know everything about the disease, its treatment or all about palliative care. They also realised that the need for information varies substantially during the different phases of approaching death, as does interaction with family members. Health care providers should acknowledge these transitions and be sure to adapt the manner and content of the communication to the changing needs of their patients and their families.

Another additional important issue emerged: if trust was not established during the initial encounter, either when the diagnosis was first provided or the change from a curative to a palliative approach was explained, the lack of trust remained a topic during many follow-up visits. Thus, the busy surgeon or oncologist has to pay attention to the way they first break bad news. Thus the physician should be aware of their paramount importance for the course of the interaction between patient and health care professionals – that, in fact, they are laying the ground for all consecutive health care providers.

If we define hope as a confident desire that something positive is going to happen, sources of hope (circumstances or the person most likely to offer what is hoped for) and likelihood of achievement will depend on the circumstances under which someone is experiencing hope. Summarizing the above quoted questionnaire and interview studies, it might seem that in the face of cancer, hope depends to a large extent on factual information, which should be given almost irrespective of its impact upon the receiver.

According to Kaplowitz et al. (2002), patients want factual information, preferably as concrete numbers. The problem again is whether or not patients (or any sample of two persons) understand numerical information correctly, or at least in the way the information provider wants them to understand them. As Thorne et al. have shown (2006), this is not easy to achieve: they present findings related to various uses and abuses of numbers within cancer care communication. Giving numbers in various ways produces different and often unpredictable results with regard to understanding, interpretation and whether or not numerical information produces hope or despair. Drawing upon the literature on risk communication, Thorn et al. propose examining the specific challenge of providing numbers in cancer communication in two interrelated areas. The first aspect relates to the provision of information about the probability of a negative event and about the timeframe within which it is most likely to occur. The authors state: 'Accounts of the role and meaning of numbers within patients' communications with professional health care providers revealed that numerical information played a prominent role in their subjective experience and in the way they coped with the challenge of cancer.' In some instances, especially when the clinical situation was not complex, patients simply went away with the message: 'He mentioned that the success rate with these operations was 90 per cent which made me extremely happy.' If the news were less favourable some patients expressed their tendency to beat the odds: 'If they tell you that you have a 1 per cent, I'll be in that one rather than the one that's – you know – doomed.'

Patients were also rather creative in reframing their understanding of numerical information. This ranged from emphasizing the less probable positive outcome, as above, to a frank neglect of the importance of numerical information: 'Well, in the end, it's just numbers.'

This second type of issue focuses on the receiver of information and highlights various sources of ambiguity or frank misunderstanding. Looking at the provider of information makes the picture even more complex: physicians have been shown to have problems in interpreting numerical data on their own. In the paper by Gigerenzer and Edwards (2003), physicians highly overestimated the probability of breast cancer in women with a positive result on mammography when they were given conditional or relative probabilities (that is, information given in per cent terms as opposed to absolute numbers). The problem in using per cent terms lies in the switch between the class of individuals these figures refer to, specifically whether the class of reference is a population-based figure or whether it is an individual risk. The authors conclude: 'The switch of reference class can confuse the minds of physicians and patients alike.' Yet, this is the type of information patients often receive when they ask for prognostic information!

Some Critical Remarks Concerning the Apparently Low Support for Empathy as a Central Quality of Caring

Based upon the results from questionnaire and interview studies in cancer patients and their relatives, one is tempted to conclude that empathy has a very limited role in providing bad news. Results seem to indicate that professionals must provide more and better information if they wish to improve the quality of breaking bad news. However, one could argue that the data generated from questionnaire studies do not show a correct picture of the problem. There are two main reasons why results should be interpreted cautiously. The first is a methodological problem: when asked to list desired physician behaviour in breaking bad news, patients refer to the instance when they were first given the diagnosis of cancer or when they were informed that a switch from a curative to a palliative approach was necessary. Many patients describe this moment as if they were in an outer state of consciousness, some feeling completely numb, almost locked in and not in contact with the environment. On the other hand, others talk about an almost lucid state of consciousness. I wonder whether the task of filling in a questionnaire with pre-selected physician behaviours accurately reflects the patients' immediate experience at that very traumatic moment, or rather a retrospective reconstruction of what this interaction could have been like.

The second reason for caution is linked to the first: if patients express their desire for clear and even upsetting information, they seem to disentangle content aspects from the way the information was provided. I do not think that this is possible at all. I assume that even upsetting information – whether from an insensitive or sensitive physician – is inevitably given within an embedded context of two persons interacting. This probably holds true for any kind of information giving. Even talking about the vacation last summer takes a certain degree of sensitivity, to realize whether the recipient is still willing or able to take in yet more information. If this task is achieved successfully, a 'sense' of STOP or CONTINUE signals emerges, which governs the quantity and type of information provided. The question of what this 'sense' might constitute will be alluded to in the last section.

How Could Individualized Information Giving be Achieved?

Summing up the literature it becomes clear that individualized care is needed, but the question remains: how is this achieved? In an ideal conversation, health care provider and patient or relative interact like experienced carpenters, operating a two-handed saw: before one can even think of a different mode of action – least of all communicate about it – they instantaneously adjust speed and pressure to changes in the structure of the wood.

Much of the literature takes a different position. Instead of investigating how this type of 'understanding without (non-verbal or verbal) explication' is created, it circles around the question of which single cues or signals patients use to influence the amount of prognostic information that they wish to hear. In other words how do they convey the orders STOP or CONTINUE (providing information)? Why should this be interesting? A basic assumption underlying the research in this area is that physicians or other health care providers can, in fact, be trained to identify these signals, and thus adapt their information style to an individual patient's needs: The relevant research findings are employed to enable practitioners to accurately identify the transitions between phases in which the patient can cope with the situation and times when the emotional suffering becomes substantial or overwhelming. The focus is upon complex interrelated behavioural indices of facial expressions and verbal utterances that communicate the patient's state of mental competence and emotional reactivity (Morse et al. 2003).

To start from simple assumptions, one might first consider the explicit exchange of the above mentioned stop and go commands. Typical examples are the patient's explicit requests like: 'Could you please tell me more about the prognosis of my cancer – with and without chemotherapy?', or simply something like: 'Ok and what next?' In order to make such an open exchange of 'regulatory phrases' easier, health care providers have to offer space to the patient; the patient needs time to decide whether they want more information or not. Providing space is a typical goal of patient-centred communication, which assumes that patients do not automatically and immediately fully share in the conversation but may need assistance and encouragement to do so. Typical techniques that can successfully be taught include the use of pauses, echoing, mirroring or summarizing (Langewitz et al. 1998; Smith et al. 1995).

However, some patients may not be able to use the space offered by the health care provider. They may not be accustomed to having it, or they may be in such a state of shock that real participation in the conversation is difficult to achieve. In such moments the literature suggests that professionals would do well to pay attention to more subtle signals. Beach et al., for example (Beach et al. 2005), showed how contradictory verbal and non-verbal cues – from both patients and physicians – may serve to blur the intentions of certain utterances. When a physician asks a seemingly open question (in the sense that the patient could answer with a positive or a negative response) and, at the same time, shakes their head, they makes clear that only a negative response would meet their expectations.

A good indicator of the patient's attention is gaze: the first patient in Beach et al. gazes away from the physician several times while reconstructing her cancer experience from memory, and then looks back into his direction when she has completed her sentence. Physicians in this study use gaze aversion to mark a shift away from the patient to 'the facts' laid down in the chart. Hence, both partners demonstrate that they may lose contact with one another when they interrupt eye contact. Similar findings have been observed by Morse et al. (Morse et al. 2003) who investigated those verbal and non-verbal signs that indicate a shift from being able to cope with a difficult situation (one's own disease or disease and death of a close one), as opposed to attempting to maintain control of oneself in order to avert strong emotional reactions. When subjects in the interview regained control over their emotions, they redirected gaze to the interviewer, thus demonstrating a shift from being immersed in their feelings to returning to the ongoing verbal interaction.

The metaphor of carpenters operating a two-handed saw and the meticulous analyses of researchers like Beach or Morse imply that a 'shift' during a conversation could be prompted by subtle stimuli extremely difficult to identify by an observer – all the more so by an observer who is not intimately involved in the dyadic interaction. Many researchers argue that signals of non-verbal communication enable people to regulate an intimate communication. Regulation in this sense refers, for example, to the timing of turn-taking or the length of pauses, that is, the time they look at each other without perceiving a long gaze as transgressing or hostile (see Schmid Mast et al. 2007 for a recent overview).

However, there are instances when it is hard to imagine that even subtle non-verbal cues are governing the interaction. Alternatives to the meticulous search for subtle single observable signals or cues will be discussed in relation to Schmitz's phenomenological formulations.

Communication as the Formation of a Common Felt Body (Leib) – Possible Contributions Of Hermann Schmitz's New Phenomenology

Think of a person entering by chance a room where two people are talking to each other. There are instances – we all know them – when the visitor instantaneously draws back, silently closing the door without further comment. If the visitor doesn't know the interlocutors, it is very unlikely, for example, that they precisely registered the facial expressions of the two persons in the room, or interpreted them correctly based upon prior experience. It is also quite possible they may not catch a single word or be able to rely even on the tone of voice, since the example also functions when both persons in the room are silent. Still, if there is no speech, they may, nevertheless, immediately, intuitively feel and know that this is a type of silence that is loaded with intensity and intimacy. This knowledge of the appropriate reaction – to close the door and to leave the two persons alone – comes very fast. It must rely on something other than contemplated inferences derived from the identification of particular verbal or non-verbal cues. The German philosopher and founder of New Phenomenology, Hermann Schmitz, uses the term 'multifaceted impression' to describe this phenomenon. Feelings can form part of such an impressive situation when they, for example, affect the climate inside a room by creating a particular atmosphere (Schmitz 2005a, 106–111; 2005b, 91–133). He argues that something similar occurs when a landscape is perceived as 'breath taking'; it is the felt body (der Leib) that reacts in those moments when we are deeply impressed. This does not refer to the height, for example, of oak trees or the width of their crown, but to the specific, sometimes termed 'holy' atmosphere of such a place. Another good example of the phenomenon under discussion is the sense one may have that a specific action is highly appropriate for a certain situation. When we visit a person in hospital, there may come a moment when the visitor feels an urgent need to leave, sometimes immediately followed by a quick glimpse at their wristwatch. However, it is not the precise time elapsed that matters, it is the sudden realization that the time has come to end the visit that makes the visitor turn their eyes away from the patient and glance at their watch. In accordance with Hermann Schmitz (Schmitz 1997, 67–90), I propose that something quite similar happens when two or more people communicate with each other. Specifically when a patient and a health care professional jointly confront bad news, the situation is loaded with meaning, distinct from everything else that has ever happened before, as well as what might happen after this moment. The powerful existential novelty of this moment contains many elements that cannot be disentangled during the conversation. Three characteristics have been posited as the core elements of a situation in the terminology of Hermann Schmitz (Schmitz 1995, 65–79).

Situations are characterized by:

- a unified entity (Gestalt) that stands out from the environment;
- meaningfulness, consisting of facts, programmes, and problems; situations 'have something to say';
- diffusion within the situation: not everything contained can be listed as single items; meaningfulness is dissolved in variety.

Reading patients' descriptions of the moment when they were given bad news or going back to our own experience in the face of unexpected news, it becomes very clear that physiological processes are deeply involved. Expressions like 'being hit in the stomach', point to the sometimes abrupt and painful nature of these experiences; others describe a vague light-headedness and an impression of lost orientation that isolated them from the environment. In Schmitz's terms, these are phenomena that can be attributed to the felt body (Leib) and not to the 'corporeal body' (Körper); they have a certain vague or metaphorical quality to them, they cannot be localized precisely. The axis along which phenomena of the felt body can be arranged is the 'vital drive'. It is antagonistic in nature, being composed of the antagonistic forces of narrowing and widening (Engung und Weitung). Normally widening and narrowing exist together, entwined in a mutual antagonism. Each of these characteristics can at times become dominant. When widening prevails Schmitz calls this status 'swelling' (like the ship that left the harbour with wind-swollen sails). When narrowing prevails, he employs the term 'tightness'. When two or more persons meet, variations of these tendencies have the potential to exude from each individual, joining all the individuals into a kind of communal embodiment, characterized by either antagonism (as in wrestling) or solidarity (like singing in a choir or operating a two-handed saw).

I suggest that this common felt body provides the evidence – as in the example above – of the necessary and appropriate moment to leave the room; it is a 'felt' certainty that cannot be located anywhere within the corporeal body (Körper), and yet is clearly and unquestionably there. The health care professional and patient are embedded in a common situation suffused with an atmosphere. In the case of breaking bad news in oncology, this atmosphere 'tastes of' despair, impending death, being lost and loneliness, while at the very same time, there may also be the hope of escaping death and being cured, a sense of clear orientation, and an underlying tone of concern, care and empathy. It may be important for health care professionals to accept that 'any illness has objective, subjective, and relational aspects (that is, interactions between the affected individual, the doctor and family, as well as social context and environmental variables during the course of the disease). Together, these aspects contribute to the shared and dynamic nature of the truth of the patient's illness (quotation from Surbone 2006). In this way, patients and professionals can then embark upon a delicate balancing act of exchanging different aspects of truth. Perhaps, the movement within the swinging elements of a mobile could serve as a metaphor to describe what it takes to weigh the diverse elements within this situation against each other, among them, the information needs of the patient, truthful disclosure and, without destroying hope, the physician maintaining the position of a factual expert while at the same time clearly demonstrating care, concern and compassion. Instead of constantly checking and interpreting each other's more or less subtle cues, two individuals might focus more on impressions from the felt body. Perhaps, learning to trust these vague and intuitive sensations of appropriateness may have a unique potential for governing an interaction; they might establish the basis for the above-mentioned STOP and CONTINUE signals that form within the common situation, cues that are not necessarily merely emitted by one person and received by the other.

A recent review by Epstein comes to similar conclusions when he combines his own experience as a patient and the relevant literature on physician patient communication. He lists 'some clinical habits of physicians that promote good communication', which include attentiveness, curiosity, flexibility and presence. Informed flexibility and the ability to see a situation with new eyes can enhance communication and diagnostic accuracy (Epstein 2006). He and his colleague advocate heightened self-awareness to prevent errors in clinical practice, without specifically referring to the concepts of New Phenomenology (Borrell-Carrio and Epstein 2004). The question is, however, how heightened awareness might be achieved.

Mindfulness-based approaches represent well-defined and practical phenomenological methods that may offer physicians an avenue for enhanced awareness and sensitivity during consultations with patients. Mindfulness-based interventions derive from ancient, but well-described and systematic meditation practices aimed at cultivating the ability to sustain attention to moment-to-moment experience of both inner states and external input within an affective mindset characterized by kindness, openness, patience, tolerance, generosity and curiosity (Grossman 2008). These latter affective qualities are seen to be fundamental to the capacity to pay attention to experiences without getting caught up in critical judgements, discursive thought or rumination about what is happening. They are also thought to be strengthened by extended mindfulness training and to generalize to feelings toward others (for example, empathy). Thus, central elements of mindfulness-based stress reduction training (MBSR – for an overview see Grossman 2004) might provide a practical framework for the New Phenomenology within which 'atmosphere' and 'situation' can coalesce in physician-patient encounters. Assuming that occupational stress and lack of moment-to-moment awareness keep professionals from behaving in an empathic way, interventions that both promote non-judgmental awareness and reduce stress would seem promising. Indeed, recent MBSR studies in medical students have shown that just eight 2-hour sessions, plus home work, reduced work-related stress and anxiety, and increased empathy scores (Rosenzweig et al. 2003; Shapiro et al. 2005).

An alternative approach also relates to the distinction between situation and constellation as outlined above. This distinction could be used during Balint groups (Balint et al. 1993). It may be argued that the setting of Balint groups provides an excellent opportunity for physicians to realize the extent to which they rely on single facts within the realm of a constellation. The Balint method consists of regular case discussion in small groups under the guidance of a qualified group leader (quotation from <www.balint.co.uk>). As soon as a case history has been presented, participants typically start asking questions like: 'Is the patient married? Does he have a sibling?' They rarely reflect on their immediate multi-facetted impression that could result from mutual embodiment with the physician presenting a problem case. In layman's terms, one might say physicians respond with their head and not with their heart. One way to avoid an immediate switch to rational reasoning is the recommendation to begin Balint group sessions with a short trance induction. The presenting physician talks about their patient while a trance helps the other group members 'to listen with their hearts' or in Schmitz's terms, to pay attention to the atmosphere that 'tints' the perception of their felt body.

Generally, physicians should learn to appropriately alternate between working within a situation and within a constellation, depending on the task in a given clinical encounter. For example, if the goal of the consultation is to decide whether an invasive procedure is appropriate, the constellation of individual items must be taken into account; this calls for thinking inside constellations – the arrangement of particular facts in space and time. Focusing on a task renders it difficult to focus on oneself, and vice versa – as we all know too well. Most people will have developed techniques to avoid too deep an emotional involvement or expression ('Don't start to cry at your daughter's wedding!'). Often, these techniques consist of ways to concentrate on particular sensations like squeezing the skin of the forearm, counting the number of pink roses in a flower arrangement or counting the number of words starting with an 'e'. When this approach works, the effect is not a smooth transition from one state of being into the other, but rather a sudden jump from emotional reactivity, to neutral observation. In order to improve awareness in a clinical encounter, a transition from a constellation mode into a common situation need not be complicated or take a long time. In training seminars on physician-patient communication, I propose to practise 'dipping' for just a few seconds, during which a physician might try, for just a few moments, to establish contact with the receptive organ of the atmosphere that characterizes a particular situation – their Leib. Even such a brief interlude might be sufficient to listen with the whole body – and not just with ears and eyes – before verbally or nonverbally responding to the circumstances.

Acknowledgements

Writing this chapter would not have been possible without the generous and meticulous help of Paul Grossman, PhD, who translated my 'German Englisch' into readable English! His sensitivity to phenomenological questions alluded to in this chapter was of great help in finding appropriate terms for Schmitz's not so easily comprehensible terminology.

The first version of this chapter was written in a precious and calm environment, a seventeenth century house in Ftan Pitschen, Lower Engiadina, kindly offered by Maja and Hans Dahler.

References

Balint, M. et al. (1993), *The Doctor, the Patient and the Group: Balint Revisited* (London and New York: Routledge).

Beach, W.A. et al. (2005), 'Disclosing and responding to cancer "fears" during oncology interviews', *Social Science & Medicine* 60:4, 893–910.

Borrell-Carrio, F. and Epstein, R.M. (2004), 'Preventing errors in clinical practice: A call for self-awareness', *Annals of Family Medicine* 2:4, 310–316.

Epstein, R.M. (2006), 'Making communication research matter: What do patients notice, what do patients want, and what do patients need?', *Patient Education and Counseling* 60:3, 272–278.

Gigerenzer, G. and Edwards, A. (2003), 'Simple tools for understanding risks: From innumeracy to insight', *British Medical Journal* 327:7417, 741–744.

Grossman, P. (2004), 'What's enough criticism in MBSR research? A response', *Focus on Alternative and Complementary Therapies* 9, 5–7.

Grossman, P. (2008), 'On measuring mindfulness in psychosomatic and psychological research', *Journal of Psychosomatic Research* 64, 405–408.

Hagerty, R.G. et al. (2005), 'Communicating with realism and hope: Incurable cancer patients' views on the disclosure of prognosis', *Journal of Clinical Oncology* 23:6, 1278–1288.

Kaplowitz, S.A. et al. (2002), 'Cancer patients' desires for communication of prognosis information', *Journal of Health Communication* 14:2, 221–241.

Kirk, P. et al. (2004), 'What do patients receiving palliative care for cancer and their families want to be told? A Canadian and Australian qualitative study', *British Medical Journal* 328:7452, 1343.

Kiss, A. (1999), 'Communication skills training in oncology: A position paper', *Annals of Oncology* 10:8, 899–901.

Kutner, J.S. et al. (1999), 'Information needs in terminal illness', *Social Science & Medicine* 48:10, 1341–1352.

Langewitz, W. (2007), 'Beyond content analysis and non-verbal behaviour – what about atmosphere? A phenomenological approach', *Patient Education and Counseling* 67:3, 319–323.

Langewitz, W.A. et al. (1998), 'Improving communication skills – a randomized controlled behaviorally oriented intervention study for residents in internal medicine', *Psychosomatic Medicine* 60:3, 268–276.

Mack, J.W. et al. (2006), 'Communication about prognosis between parents and physicians of children with cancer: Parent preferences and the impact of prognostic information', *Journal of Clinical Oncology* 24:33, 5265–5270.

Morse, J.M. et al. (2003), 'Identifying signals of suffering by linking verbal and facial cues', *Qualitative Health Research* 13:8, 1063–1077.

Parker, P.A. et al. (2001), 'Breaking bad news about cancer: Patients' preferences for communication', *Journal of Clinical Oncology* 19:7, 2049–2056.

Rosenzweig, S. et al. (2003), 'Mindfulness-based stress reduction lowers psychological distress in medical students', *Teaching and Learning in Medicine* 15:2, 88–92.

Schmid Mast, M. et al. (2007), 'Disentangling physician sex and physician communication style: Their effects on patient satisfaction in a virtual medical visit', *Patient Education and Counseling* 68:1, 16–22.

Schmitz, H. (1995), *Der unerschöpfliche Gegenstand – Grundzüge der Philosophie* (2nd edition) (Bonn: Bouvier-Verlag).

Schmitz, H. (1997), *Höhlengänge. Über die gegenwärtige Aufgabe der Philosophie* (Berlin: Akademie-Verlag).

Schmitz, H. (2005a), *Situationen und Konstellationen: wider die Ideologie totaler Vernetzung* (München: Alber).

Schmitz, H. (2005b), *System der Philosophie. Studienausgabe* (2nd edition, vol. III, 2) (Bonn: Bouvier Verlag).

Schmitz, H. (2007), *Der Leib, der Raum und die Gefühle* (Bielefeld: Edition Sirius).

Shapiro, S.L. (2005), 'Mindfulness-based stress reduction for health care professionals: Results from a randomized trial', *International Journal of Stress Management* 12:2, 164–176.

Smith, R.C. et al. (1995), 'Improving residents' confidence in using psychosocial skills', *Journal of General Internal Medicine* 10:6, 315–320.

Surbone, A. (2006), 'Telling the truth to patients with cancer: What is the truth?', *Lancet Oncology* 7:11, 944–950.

Thorne, S. et al. (2006), 'Hope and probability: Patient perspectives of the meaning of numerical information in cancer communication', *Qualitative Health Research* 16:3, 318–336.

Chapter 13
The Responsibility of the Truth-Teller

Thomas Cerny

'Responsibility starts precisely where certainty ends.'

Jacques Derrida (1930–2004)

Over 2,000 years ago, the oracle of Delphi demonstrated the fundamental problems of truth telling. The dilemma and the often tragic outcome of interpreting potentially predictive information are well documented and have many parallels with prediction in medicine. To be a counsellor in modern genetic counselling means to be an expert with many talents. Not only is expertise in medical genetics very important, but so too is a real understanding and meeting of the very complex individual needs of the counsellee and their family. Furthermore, nowadays genetic counselling has important implications regarding ethical, political and legal aspects. The risks taken by the counsellor as well as the counsellee are manifold. In general, the occurrence of the disease at risk is remote and the accuracy of predicting the 'truth' is usually very low. Many competing risks, mostly unknown, will arise over time and interfere with today's interpretation. The responsibility of the truth-teller is to lead the well-informed counsellee to a shared decision and thus avoid unnecessary harm. In this chapter some of these duties of the 'truth-teller' will be explained and discussed.

In many cultures 'truth telling' is regarded as an old tradition. In ancient Greece, truth telling at Delphi was disguised in the form of enigmatic divine oracles. Humans trying to escape the consequences of their own oracle usually got deeper and deeper into trouble, but ingenious heroes with an indomitable fighting spirit and pure cleverness could – after many sufferings – eventually earn a better end. We have to remember that only this spirit of fighting against the boundaries of nature or the gods eventually led to the development of human skills, technology and culture.

But at the same time we lost our natural innocence – now we have to make choices and we have to take responsibility. This eventually forced mankind to create normative systems, moral codes based on ethical considerations for each culture and generation.

Genetic testing for hereditary cancer certainly touches such hitherto divine fields and again brings us into deep trouble. In the context of this chapter, the Delphic oracle is like a genetic test with a clear message but uncertain meaning. The priest or priestess is a genetic counsellor and the hero is a counsellee forced to decide what to do with all this information.

Genetic counselling in oncology has multiple difficulties, such as the identification of a deleterious genetic mutation with a high probability of developing cancer, and the implementation of preventive measures or strategies of early detection. The consequences range from close surveillance to the decision to perform mutilating prophylactic surgery, and mostly include communicating disturbing information to the patient and other family members.

In this chapter we have to reflect the Delphic standpoint, this means the responsibility and the ethical considerations of the truth-teller and especially the responsibility of being a modern type of truth-teller. This is far from a unidirectional transfer of information and should lead to a patient-centred process of informing and facilitating shared decision-making.

The Dilemma of Wanting to Know, and its Justification

In genetic counselling the dilemma starts with trying to know about the future. Not knowing, at a certain point in time, might also be an appropriate option to avoid the tortures of a dilemma. The first step for the counsellor will be to make an informed choice, with someone at risk, about whether genetic testing is the appropriate way to go. In a modern society where every individual has the right to all kinds of information, and where we as individuals take responsibility for the conduct of our lives, genetic counselling should enable us to make best use of this information for our lives. To my knowledge, there is no right or duty in any Western society to withhold information that is potentially useful to any individual at risk. Only the contrary is true, namely the right for the individual to know and to refuse as a human right. According to the sociologist Peter Gross, we live in a rapidly expanding multi-optional society and have the burden of making choices over and over again, or to refuse to do so (Gross 1994). But the choice not to be part of this world does not exist.

The need for genetic counselling generally derives from the following facts:

- the existence of a significant number of patients at risk of a hereditary cancer;
- the possibility of taking effective preventive measures and/or making an early detection of cancer with the option of improving outcome or cure;
- the possibility of reliably testing for some well-defined cancer genes;
- the existence of individuals at risk who have a desire to avoid premature suffering and death.

Therefore to counsel per se is a reasonable, necessary and ethically justifiable process.

Does the Genome Contain the Whole Truth, and What are the Questions?

And what kind of 'truth' are we talking about? In general, the genome is regarded as containing highly conserved, stable and deterministic information for an individual, valid for their whole lifetime. But the more we know about molecular genetics, the less we can defend this position. This information is not as stable as we originally postulated. It can and will be changed during one's lifetime through acquired mutations, and can be further modified in its functioning by epigenetic changes, and influenced by mechanisms like RNA-interference (Jones and Laird 1999; Toyota and Issa 2005; Galm 2006).

Today, we still do not know enough about the interplay of the gene products. In the future, newly discovered protective genes or gene silencers could be detected which would neutralize a well-defined cancer linked gene. The same holds true for future therapeutic possibilities, where a potentially useful manipulation of the genetic information is likely to happen. At any point in time later in life the possibility to therapeutically modify epigenetic changes or RNA-interference might influence and change our interpretation and the consequences (Esteller 2005; Paul 2006).

Despite all these considerations, is our genome the treasure-trove of information we are looking for? Does a genetic test result contain the true biological destiny regarding a specific cancer risk? Yes and no. *Yes* since a test result is true as far as the test is precise, reliable, correctly performed and valid for our purpose; and *no* since it does not reflect the whole prognostic truth. Therefore it only adds some important pieces of information relevant to the whole puzzle of our lives, but not the entire relevant truth.

Because of this imperfection in genetic testing and counselling, we have to ask ourselves if this will be helpful to a counsellee. Therefore we have to answer three questions:

1. What is the qualitative and quantitative meaning of a genetic test?
2. What is the benefit a counsellee can derive from testing and counselling?
3. What is the potential harm for the counsellee?

What does a test result say and what does it not say? What is the probability that this test result will influence the life of the counsellee? When is the occurrence of cancer to be expected? Can it be avoided and, if yes, how and when? What are the alternatives and their risks?

The qualitative aspect of a genetic test refers to the respective disease entity, where different mutations or epigenetic changes might result in a different expression of the phenotype, and where the quantitative aspects, in terms of probability of or time until occurrence of a disease, might be influenced further by the test result. To tackle all these very individualized problems of a counsellee as an expert, necessitates not only a broad personal experience but also the capability to act in a multiprofessional and multidisciplinary fashion with all other professionals involved. The counsellee must be approached with their language, according to their comprehension, in order to gain trust. This will enable them to ask all the relevant questions and to use all the time that is needed to be ready to take over responsibility for their own firm decision on how to proceed. Also, to retract from further counselling might be a reasonable result, or to involve other members of the family according to their needs.

After discussing these questions extensively and appropriately with the counsellee, a clear shared decision should be the goal. To answer all these questions with the best possible knowledge means that a counsellor must be perfectly up to date in his field, and remain so (ASCO guidelines 2003 and Ackermann 2004). They are the reliable, trustworthy expert for the counsellee, and takes over full responsibility for all that they say, and what they withhold. They must be able to explain the kind of doubt that still exists and how this will be tackled in the future (Sass 1998). This should be done in a clearly understandable and emotionally empathic fashion. It will usually take enough time for reflection and discussions, and might well involve other specialists or family members. Therefore counselling should always be regarded as a multidimensional process. This also means that all relevant new aspects to come in the future have to be considered and weighed again, and this makes genetic counselling an ongoing long-term process (Cummings 2000; Patterson 2005). In fact, the best possible result in reducing harm in the long run will rarely result in a once and for all decision, but calls for regular updates with the counsellee. It is also important for the counsellor themself to understand the true outcome and the possible burdens put on the counsellee, and to learn as much as possible from the whole follow-up. This attitude also reflects the will on both sides to take responsibility, in a broad sense, for making the whole process a mutual success.

Bearing all this in mind we will be very modest in our initial counselling. As medical doctors we are in fact the companion and teacher of the counsellee, which is also underscored by the Latin origin of the word 'doctor', which meant teacher. In short, truth telling *sensu strictu* is not possible, but fair and helpful interpretation and discussion of a genetic risk is.

What We do Not Know or Cannot Yet Know

Many competing lifetime risks will interfere with discrete genetic testing, and add further to the complexity of the truth telling. So far we have only talked about one particular risk, that of developing a specific malignant disease. What if a different competing risk turns out to be more important?

At a given time we might not know if the risk we are considering now will be the dominant one in someone's lifetime because:

- there are competing risks, which cannot be known;
- there are competing risks, which we do not know;

- there are competing risks that will be known soon;
- there are competing positive (that is, protective) factors, which have been overlooked or are not yet known;
- there will be fundamentally new techniques available in the future to prevent cancer, diagnose very early with a high curative potential, or treat a specific disease to make it non-fatal and compatible with a good quality of life, and possibly a normal or close to normal life span.

In summary what we call 'the truth' is only a reflection of the moment, that is, the best information available now. The occurrence of the disease in many instances is far away, and the greater the gap between counselling and occurrence of disease, the more we have to accept the above-mentioned dangers of being wrong. The more a disease is likely to lead to premature death or severe disability, the better we will be prepared to accept this fact if we at least have the chance to take measures to avoid unnecessary damage in the future. If there is no immediate possibility at all to reduce possible future damage or to change life in one way or another to gain at least some benefit from the counselling process, there might still be a window of hope that the future will change that for the better by offering new and effective therapeutic options.

Genetic counselling mostly addresses the young, or younger, healthy population at risk. The time lag of the occurrence of an event can easily extend to the far future of 30 or 40 years or more from now. The accuracy of a prediction will rapidly decrease the more an expected event lies in the long-term future. But even for the near future, we might be terribly wrong in predicting, even if we apply all the available knowledge in the best possible way, because of the paucity of our specific knowledge so far for many situations.

Risk and Responsibility

To learn more about the risks entailed in genetic counselling we can look into the field of non-medical 'ethics of risk' and 'ethics of prevention'. This is top on the political agenda in the worldwide discussion of global warming and protection of our environment. Do we know enough now to take firm measures that will hurt, and which might seem costly? Can we wait longer and collect more information and experience? Who sets the standards, who is responsible and what is the ethical justification for acting or waiting? Who will benefit most from certain measures, and who pays for them?

Taking risks in general has led to many important developments of humankind, and will continue to do so. But for this progress, we implicitly have an important price to pay. If we could have progress without risks and consequential harm we certainly would seize it. But this is unfortunately not the case. It has been accepted that progress is necessary for the good of society, that growing knowledge leads to more new possibilities which then have to be explored further. The 'no risk society' is a term that brings the dilemma into focus. Do we really have a choice to have no risk? Being free to choose always includes the risk of being wrong. In my mind we only have a choice to restrict the risks to a point where the balance between benefit and risk seems to be favourable. This process is a difficult and permanent one.

To take responsibility requires one to have a choice and also to be free to choose (Nida-Rümelin 2005). To choose relies on having all necessary information, in a clearly understandable form, to make a firm and helpful individual decision. The information has to be tailored to the counsellee's needs and comprehension. To come to a decision also requires enough time to mature through the process of intellectual and emotional weighing of all relevant aspects. For the individual decision there is no right or wrong, and the decision might even change over time. Even if a decision is apparently against rational thinking, we have to accept it. We all have learned during our lives that non-rational or more intuitive decisions might turn out to be as useful as more rational ones. Society has to protect the individual from being harmed or punished for the decision, and if necessary the counsellor has to also fight for this protection in the political arena.

As long as the need for giving information to a counsellee is met, and as long as the information is correctly given, adequately transmitted according to the legal needs, the responsibility of the counsellor is met as well. Furthermore there is no imperative of truth telling, and a true choice always includes the right to refuse to know more. Also, relatives should not feel pressure to be involved in this process, but they should have a chance to decide to be involved.

Here He Is: The Truth-teller

We all know from many courtroom dramas the sentence: ' I swear to tell the truth, the whole truth and nothing but the truth …', and legally we have a broad consent in our society to have the right to know the truth about ourselves. To know as much as possible of the truth requires the expertise of many persons constantly working and communicating in a specific field. In genetic counselling the responsibility of the truth-teller lies primarily in providing all relevant and necessary information to an individual, usually in a situation of above average risk for a dangerous disease, which can lead to disability, debilitating chronic disease or severe disease with premature death.

One of the first obligations of the truth-teller is to be 'Socratic': this means to carefully clarify the usually overestimated expectation of 'truth', and essentially to say how much at the moment we don't know about the mid- and long-term future of a given counsellee. Probability in a medical context is far from being a precise quantity, and the likelihood of something happening in the future might often be smaller than the likelihood of it not happening.

Therefore, truth telling is a humbling, ongoing process, which has to be adapted again and again over time. Because of the complexity of life, it is expected that many new insights in molecular biology will arise and show that in a given disease many more mechanisms are involved than we had thought, even a few years ago. Therefore, positive and negative new information is likely to accumulate in the future, and this can lead to quite dramatic changes in the understanding of a disease with a known genetic background. The responsibility of the truth-teller will not only be to provide this new information to their clients, but also to make it understandable to each individual and their relatives. A good number of the clients will become more and more expert themselves, and it will be important to give them a chance to discuss new findings gathered from the media which might, for the right or the wrong reasons, influence their expectations and decisions. They should have assurance that they will receive information from the counsellor whenever they need it.

A crucial responsibility of the truth-teller is absolute confidentiality in order to protect the counsellee and to avoid any further damage to them and their relatives. Obviously, no one can or will be forced to be tested in a specific risk situation as a general rule. In certain situations, this might be a heavy burden for the truth-telling clinician, if they feel that the decisions taken by the individual and the relatives are not the best for their future. A Socratic attitude will help to overcome such a dilemma. If we accept that knowledge, as well as the tools in diagnosis and therapy, will steadily improve over time, we should never try to enforce a conviction on someone. The hope for a better decision in the future when our background knowledge has increased might soften our anxiety.

Such an expert attitude has the potential to create an atmosphere of competence, trust, confidentiality and durability. If an individual at risk can stay within a counselling network as long as it is helpful for them, as long as they are at risk, and as long as unsolved problems are pertinent, then the chance will be high that the best possible counselling effect can be achieved.

Lastly, in contrast to the priests and priestesses of the ancient oracle of Delphi, who spoke the truth in trance, and were only transmitters of the words of the gods, the modern counsellor has to take responsibility for what they say and how they say it. This is much more difficult, but also much more human, and if done in the right way the counsellee will understand and accept a remnant of uncertainty in the so-called truth.

References

Ackermann, T.F. (2004), 'Ethical Issues in Genetic Testing for Cancer Susceptibility', in C. Neal Ellis (ed.), *Inherited Cancer Syndromes: Current Clinical Management* (Springer), 61–82.

Asco Special Articles (2003), 'American society of clinical oncology policy statement update: Genetic testing for cancer susceptibility', *Journal of Clinical Oncology* 21, 2397–2406.

Cummings, S. (2000), 'The genetic testing process: How much counseling is needed?', *Journal of Clinical Oncology* 18, 60–64.

Esteller, M. (2005), 'Dormant hypermethylated tumour suppressor genes: Questions and answers', *American Journal of Pathology* 205, 172–80.

Galm, O. et al. (2006), 'The fundamental role of epigenetics in hematopoietic malignancies', *Blood Rev* 20, 1–13.

Gross, P. (1994), *Die Multioptionsgesellschaft* (Frankfurt am Main: Suhrkamp Verlag).

Jones, P.A. and Laird, P.W. (1999), 'Cancer epigenetics comes of age', *Nature Genetics* 21, 163–7.

Nida-Rümelin, J. (2005), 'Warum es keine Verantwortung ohne Freiheit gibt', in J. Nida-Rümelin (ed.), *Ueber menschliche Freiheit* (Stuttgart: Philipp Reclam jun.).

Patterson, A.R. et al. (2005), 'Custodianship of genetic information: Clinical challenges and professional responsibility', *Journal of Clinical Oncology* 23, 2100–2104.

Paul, N.W. (2006), 'Humangenetik und Medizin: Geschichte, Theorie, Ethik', in S. Schulz et al. (eds), *Geschichte, Theorie und Ethik der Medizin* (Frankfurt am Main: Suhrkamp Verlag).

Sass, H.-M. (1998), 'Medizinethik', in A. Pieper and U. Thurnherr (eds), *Angewandte Ethik: eine Einführung* (München: Beck), 80–109.

Toyota, M. and Issa, J.P. (2005), 'Epigenetic changes in solid and hematopoietic tumors', *Seminars in Oncology* 32, 521–30.

Chapter 14

Practising Informed Choice: Decision Making and Prenatal Risk Assessment – The Danish Experience

Nete Schwennesen, Lene Koch and Mette Nordahl Svendsen

Introduction

Since 1978 the organization of prenatal testing in Denmark has been structured around an age limit, offering pregnant women of 35 years of age or above invasive tests such as CVS or amniocentesis. In this regime, age – as associated with high risk – served as the main predictive selection criteria on the basis of which women were offered prenatal testing. In 2004, The Danish Board of Health decided that the organization of prenatal testing should be changed, and instead be organized on the basis of informed choice. Following this principle, the Board suggested that a first trimester risk assessment consisting of a blood test, the so-called double test and an ultrasound scan, the so-called nuchal translucency scan, should be offered to all pregnant women – regardless of age – on the basis of 'objective information' (Danish Board of Health 2004a). This, the Board suggested, would allow women and their partners to decide for themselves whether or not they want to undergo the risk assessment and, on the basis of the provided risk knowledge, whether they want to undergo an invasive diagnostic test.

In suggesting a reorganization of prenatal testing in Denmark, the Board of Health wanted to signal an overall health political criticism of the previous practice of prenatal testing. This system, they argued, represented a paternalistic prevention-oriented paradigm, since it was grounded on particular screening criteria such as age. The older regime was now presented as unethical and incompatible with recent legislation on patients' rights (Act on Patient's Legal Rights and Entitlement in Denmark 1998). According to the Board of Health, the new guidelines represented a move away from this paradigm towards what they called a self-determination-oriented paradigm, more compatible with current neo-liberal legal trends. The guidelines described the shift of paradigm in this way: 'The purpose of prenatal risk assessment is – within the framework of Danish legislation – to assist a pregnant woman who wants such assistance to make her own choices. Neutral and complete information is the basis for this … The objective of prenatal diagnosis is not to prevent the birth of children with hereditary disease or handicap' (Danish Board of Health 2004a). This statement echoes a quotation from the first governmental report on prenatal diagnosis from 1977, which formulated the then official state policy and objective of prenatal screening as a way to 'prevent the birth of handicapped children' (Ministry of the Interior 1977) – a statement which has been quoted again and again in the public debate proceeding the new guidelines (Parliamentary Proposal 2003). Distancing itself from the objective of disease prevention, the new paradigm of informed choice served as a solution to the problem of what the Danish Parliament and The Danish Board of Health described as the paternalistic past of antenatal care in Denmark (Danish Board of Health 2003). Rhetorically the ideal of informed choice demarcated a past practice of prenatal testing – said to be based on the norm of prevention – from future practice of prenatal diagnosis – said to be based on the norm of choice.

These guidelines have now been implemented in the Danish health care system and have replaced previous practices. Today, every pregnant woman is offered the chance to undergo the risk assessment. According to the Danish professor in fetal medicine, Ann Tabor, at least 90 per cent of all pregnant women – regardless of age – accept the offer (Tabor 2006).

Denmark is one of the first European countries to introduce the method of first trimester risk assessment as a routine offer to all pregnant women. Under the banner of informed choice, the method is already practised at a huge number of clinics throughout Europe.[1]

From Disease Prevention to Informed Choice

The new guidelines are based on the values of rights, choice and autonomy. The underlying logic of this paradigm is that individuals have a right to be appropriately informed about their genetic risks so that they become able to act rationally on the basis of this knowledge.

The norm of non-directiveness forms a key aspect of the embracing of informed choice in prenatal testing and counselling. As Emery explains: 'Genetic counselling aims to be non-directive, simply providing patients with information regarding their risk of a genetic disorder and options for managing that risk … such a non-directive approach … demonstrate[s] its primary role in offering patients informed choice' (Emery 2001, 81). This view is echoed by most textbooks on genetic counselling. Thus Harper points out that: '[I]t is not the duty of a doctor to dictate the lives of others, but to ensure that individuals have the facts to enable them to make their own decisions …' (Harper 2004, 81). In this regime,

1 The Fetal Medicine Foundation (FMF), based in London, has set up a process for standardizing the risk assessment. Clinics in Britain and internationally are certified after attending training courses and a continuous submission of nuchal translucency images to the foundation for assessment. See <http://www.fetalmedicine.com/fmf/training-certification/certificates-of-competence/>.

genetic counselling is seen as a straightforward process, where the production and communication of facts are viewed as the means through which non-directiveness is performed. It carries the ideal of risk information as a factual object that can be produced, transmitted and received in a value-free transaction; it presupposes that knowledge enhances autonomy and empowers citizens, who, on the basis of objective risk knowledge, are able to make their own autonomous choices, and it pictures the pregnant woman and her partner as an autonomous decision-making unit.

This chapter wants to challenge this model of information transfer as well as the premises on which this model is based. It does so by taking a relational and processual approach to the analysis of processes of fact production and decision making in the context of first trimester prenatal risk assessment.

This chapter is based on an ethnographic study of the implementation of first trimester prenatal risk assessment at a large ultrasound clinic in Denmark in 2005. Our empirical material includes interviews with pregnant women and their partners, health professionals in the clinic, observations at the ultrasound clinic and printed information material for pregnant women, as well as official documents such as the guidelines.

Processes of Translation

The implementation of the risk assessment method as a routine practice of antenatal care in the Danish health care sector has reshaped and reconfigured the regime of antenatal care in Denmark. With this new method every pregnancy is made an object for surveillance. Although this shift has rendered every pregnancy 'tentative' as Rothman has argued (Rothman 1986), it has also created new spaces of possible action for pregnant women and their partners. Faced with the option of undergoing prenatal risk assessment they now need to relate to a range of questions: whether to acquire risk knowledge about the status of their fetus, how to act on the basis of risk knowledge, whether or not they would like to proceed with further investigations and thereby run the risk of aborting a healthy child, as well as a number of other questions. This new space of possible action, we argue, is situated in what American anthropologist Rayna Rapp and others (Rapp 2000; Franklin 2003; Svendsen 2006) have called 'the gap' between epidemiological data, clinical practices and individual experiences. As Rapp argues: 'There is a gap between epidemiological description, clinical services and individual understandings of affliction which is continuously open to speculation and practical intervention. Technologies of diagnosis, therapies of intervention, and systems of support are all enacted and interpreted within that gap' (Rapp 2000, 185). Rapp here points to the important difference between scientific epidemiological data and pregnant womens' subjective experiences of such data. For the epidemiologist and medical expert the concept of risk expresses a statistical measure of the degree of association between a specific characteristic and a disease within a defined population. For the individual, however, risk is experienced as a state of being (Gifford 1986) and leaves open a space for agency and meaning-making in which to have one's own interpretations (Svendsen 2006).

Using this theoretical understanding as our starting point, the analytical focus of this chapter is on 'processes of translation' (Latour 1986) of prenatal risk information as it travels from the epidemiological context via the clinical encounter and into the social lives of pregnant women and their partners, who need to relate to the question of how to act on the basis of this knowledge. As we trace these processes of translation, the above mentioned 'gaps' gradually become visible as spaces for pregnant womens' decision making. In our analysis of these processes we want to problematize three presumptions in the political ideals surrounding the risk assessment regime: information as facts; non-directiveness as the relational ideal between health professionals and patients; and choice as a decision made by autonomous individuals.

The Cut-off Point

In the risk assessment method a cut-off point is introduced as the threshold value that demarcates a negative from a positive result. The Danish Board of Health recommends that an invasive test is only offered when the risk assessment is higher than or equals 1:250. In establishing a cut-off point, The Danish Board of Health distinguishes between what is a normal pregnancy and what is a problematic pregnancy. A risk number that is higher than 1:250 represents a high risk, and thus a reason to proceed with further tests. Conversely, a number that is lower than 1:250 represents a low risk, and thus a reason not to proceed with further tests. In establishing the cut-off point, The Danish Board of Health creates a boundary around what constitutes a dangerous future (a fetus at high risk of having Down Syndrome) and what constitutes a less dangerous future (a fetus at low risk of having Down Syndrome). In this sense, the cut-off point operates as a statistical standard or norm against which individual difference is measured. The cut-off point is thus a normative measure, which categorizes certain future events as threats.

The definition of the cut-off point is of great economic importance, and determines the preventive benefits of a screening programme. If it is high, only a few women are given access to an invasive test and the socio-economic costs will be high (a greater number of children with Down Syndrome will be born, and require care). If the cut-off point is lowered, more women are given access to an invasive test and the social costs will decrease. In this way the choice of cut-off point represents a political decision balancing a number of interests – most importantly the wish to have a high detection rate versus the wish to reduce the number of invasive tests and, as a consequence, to reduce the number of involuntary miscarriages. Until 2003 the prenatal diagnostic regime was criticized for an unfavourable relationship between detection rate, invasive tests and abortions, and the new regime has been presented as a means of creating a more efficient prenatal screening system, lowering the number of invasive tests and involuntary miscarriages of healthy fetuses per detected Down fetus. Yet, as amniocentesis always implies a risk of aborting a healthy fetus, the very practice of amniocentesis signals that the number of invasive tests and miscarriages of healthy fetuses are costs necessary to obtain the benefits of a low birth rate of Down children. Such cost-benefit considerations were highly visible in the older guidelines based on the above-mentioned 1977 report, but are no longer considered in conformity with the norm of informed choice. Thus they are no longer directly expressed in the Danish guidelines, or in other ways made accessible to a larger public. The level of the cut-off point remains contested among Danish hospitals, and ranges between 1:250 and 1:400 (Tabor 2006). To make matters more complicated, some hospitals only use the cut-off point as a guideline when deciding which pregnancies are allowed invasive testing.

Summing up, the risk figure is presented as a neutral fact to the pregnant woman and her partner, and as such cleansed of any normative assumptions. Yet, the cut-off point establishes a normative framework within which pregnancies are categorized as high risk or low risk.

Three Obligatory Passage Points

In the following text, we will turn to a description of the route through which prenatal risk knowledge is translated from epidemiological data on a population level into risk knowledge about a particular fetus in the form of a proportional risk figure. We shall focus on three obligatory passage points that the woman and her partner have to go through when faced with the option of undergoing prenatal risk assessment. First we will briefly describe the decision about whether or not to undergo prenatal risk assessment; second we will analyze the performance of a scan, and third we will go into more depth about the interpretation of a risk figure, as it is made sense of in the context of a lived life.

Entering Prenatal Risk Assessment – A Routine Act

In Denmark, the general practitioner (GP) is responsible for offering the woman and her partner information about prenatal examination possibilities when she presents for her first pregnancy check-up. If the woman accepts the offer, the GP is responsible for providing her with basic information about the different possibilities and technologies. In addition to personal information and a conversation about possible family dispositions, the pregnant woman and her partner will receive a pamphlet which informs them about the different possibilities. Under the heading 'Information gives you the possibility of choice', the purpose of the folder is explained: 'This information will give you knowledge about different prenatal examination possibilities. The purpose is not to persuade you to undergo the examinations, but to make sure that you yourself will be able to decide whether you want to avail yourself of the different offers' (Danish Board of Health 2004b).[2] The risk assessment is presented as the first step in the prenatal examination trajectory.

While the guidelines and the information pamphlet emphasize that the decision to undergo prenatal risk assessment should be taken on the basis of an act of choice, in interviews most women emphasized that they had not really thought that much about whether or not to undergo the risk assessment. Metaphors such as 'routine act' and 'security check' were used to describe their motivations for doing so. One woman explained: 'To me it is a routine act. It is not something extraordinary. I see it as a check-up, as another check out of the many check-ups you undergo during pregnancy.' In a similar vein another woman pointed out: 'I did not think that much about whether it was a choice or not. I was just like, "yes please, we accept that, just as we accept the midwife and antenatal classes … we accept the whole thing, the whole package"'. The interviews indicate how prenatal risk assessment is experienced as a natural part of the whole system of professional support and prenatal care in Denmark. In our conversations with pregnant women and their partners they emphasized that the ultrasound scan of the fetus was a very positive element of the risk assessment and an element which played an important role in the sense of how the risk assessment came to symbolize security and control. As one woman said: 'We have also used it as a proof that there is something in there … you want to confirm that something is actually going on.' Such statements indicate that the decision to undergo prenatal risk assessment was experienced as a routine part of a 'normal' pregnancy trajectory rather than a discrete choice. We might even say that the couples experienced no choice but to choose.

The Image of the Scan

Undergoing an ultrasound scan between the 11th and 13th week of pregnancy represents the second obligatory point of passage for women and their partners who have decided to undergo prenatal risk assessment. During the scan the health professional measures the width of the nuchal translucency and the crown-rump length, by marking out specific points on the scan. These data are then used in the calculation of the risk assessment. The pregnant women and their partners all emphasized how seeing the fetus through the scan was a very emotional experience. One woman put it this way: 'We saw how it moved around and bent one of its legs and it waved … well, it didn't wave [laughing] but it did something with one of its arms. It was such a great experience.' And another woman said: 'You could see both arms and legs and head with the jaw and everything. It seemed like a human being. It made me feel warm all over. And then it was like, then it became real, you could really see, that this was, well, it became a real child.'

2 Additional information is available at the hospital's Internet site. There is also an information office, where it is possible to sign up for telephone and personal consultations with midwifes.

Through the visual image of the scan, the fetus was ascribed a temporal and social life of its own – it became a real child. In this sense the scan translated the young fetus into a concrete social actor. Technically speaking, an ultrasound picture can be described as 'a beam of very brief pulses of high-frequency sound, generated by a transducer placed in contact with her [the pregnant woman's] skin. [These are] … directed through her body and partly reflected by soft tissues and follicular, embryonic and fetal structures. The echoes from the reflections are visualized as an image on a screen for the operator to interpret. The developing fetus thus becomes observable' (Price 1990, 124–125). While the scan visualizes interpretations of the echoes as images, further interpretation in the clinical setting is required for the scan to be translated into an image of a child. It is through the interpretation of the scan in the clinical setting that the image emerges as a child. This translational process is created in the interaction between the image on the screen, the health professional and the woman and her partner in the clinical setting of the scan. The health professionals participated in this process by giving a detailed description of the anatomy of the fetus during the scan. They described the fetus by characterizing it as having human qualities: 'it is photogenic'; 'it is active'; 'this is a stubborn one'; 'this one is lazy, it is asleep'; 'Look! It's waving to us'. Moreover, the metaphor of a 'window to the life of the child' was often used to characterize the scan, which was described as if there were a direct referential relationship between the image and the child. The women and their partners participated in this interpretative process, by claiming that the scan made the fetus more real, as shown above. To them this process created a sense of predictability and control, and a sense that they bonded with the fetus. As such, interpretative links of association were made between the image of the scan, the pregnant women and their partners, and the health professionals, which gave shape to a feeling of parenthood. Several partners emphasized that this was the first time they really had to face up to the fact that they were going to be fathers. As such the translational process constituted the partners as fathers-to-be.

Figures and Futures

The interpretation of the risk figure represents the third obligatory passage point. Right after the scan has been carried out, the health professional goes to a separate room, and enters the obtained data into a software program.[3] The machine produces a sheet of paper stating gestational age and risk figure, which is expressed as a proportional figure on an infinite scale, for example, 1:200 or 1:5000.

The risk assessment regime is organized so that the decision about whether or not to proceed with prenatal invasive tests such as CVS or amniocentesis is to be

3 These data are: the size of the nuchal translucency, the distance between the crown and the rump of the image of the fetus, maternal age, and the result of the blood sample. The software to calculate the risk assessment is delivered by the FMF.

made on the basis of the size of the risk figure. In the pamphlet, these methods are presented as technologies which 'can give a definitive answer about whether or not the fetus is affected' (Danish Board of Health 2004b). Moreover, it is emphasized that a disadvantage of these examinations is that '1 in 100 examinations causes a miscarriage because of bleeding or leaking of amniotic fluid' (Danish Board of Health 2004b).

While the interpretation of the scan constitutes the fetus as a child-to-be, the risk figure constitutes this child as at-risk for having Down Syndrome. As such the scan and the risk figure represent two possible futures; one which is hoped for – a healthy child – and one which is feared – a child with Down Syndrome. After the scan has been carried out the women and their partners have the opportunity to buy a sonogram-photo for the family album, which most couples accept with thrill and excitement. One woman we interviewed, however, refused, and she explained why: 'To me it seems very brutal to pay kr.20 to buy a picture of a human being who you consider getting rid off. To me it is extremely brutal.' This woman expressed the contradictory nature of the scan, constituting the fetus as a child-to-be, and the actual aim of prenatal risk assessment: to find the fetuses with Down Syndrome and possibly decide to abort. By refusing to buy the photo she resisted or postponed the engagement in the creation of the fetus as a child.

The majority of women who undergo risk assessment receive a risk figure lower than the cut-off point at 1:300 and accept this figure as insurance that everything is OK.[4] They will walk happily away from the ultrasound clinic with a picture of the fetus for the family album. For them, the outcome of the risk assessment was not a threatening future but confirmed their hope of security and control. A small number of pregnant women, however, receive a risk assessment figure which is either higher than the cut-off point at 1:300 or articulated as higher than they expected or hoped for. For these women the risk figure comes to symbolize a threat and a sense that they face an ambiguous future. The women who were faced with a risk figure which they articulated as higher than they expected, explained how they felt unprepared to deal with this knowledge: 'When you accept to undergo all these tests, then you feel like, as everybody probably does, there is nothing wrong, right? I also felt like that, it was just something obligatory. When I started this, I did not expect that my child would be ill. I think most women feel like that, right? Otherwise, you could do nothing but worry all the time. So, I was really worried when I received the risk figure, I was like, really shocked when I got the message, I must admit, totally knocked out.'

Couples who receive a risk figure which they articulate as high now face another option, the option of undergoing an invasive diagnostic test that provides more certain knowledge, but which also involves a risk of inducing a miscarriage of a healthy child. The other option, however, not to undergo invasive diagnostic technologies, involves uncertainty about the condition of the fetus and possibly

4 Around 5 per cent will receive a risk higher than the cut-off point at 1:300 and around 80 per cent will receive a risk lower than 1:1000 (Tabor 2006).

giving birth to a child with Down Syndrome. This space of action and decision making constitutes an existential dilemma for the pregnant woman and her partner who now have to make decisions in the context of uncertain knowledge and uncertain consequences of diagnostic technology, on behalf of what they consider as a child-to-be at-risk for having Down Syndrome.

Interpreting Risk Figures

Through the practice of informed choice the women and their partners are subjectivized as autonomous choosers (Helén 2005). The primary means through which to make their choice is, according to the guidelines, 'objective and non-directive information' given in the form of a risk figure. Indeed, The Danish Board of Health emphasizes that the strength of presenting the risk assessment as a risk figure is 'that they are objective and value free' and therefore 'suitable as basis for providing neutral (non-directive) information for the pregnant woman' (Danish Board of Health 2003, 57).

However, in interviews, the pregnant women and their partners expressed how they had difficulties relating to – and thus acting on the basis of – the risk figure. Many couples reacted – almost as by reflex – by asking the health professional what they would do if they were in their situation. One woman who received a risk figure at 1:636 – technically below the cut-off point, but stressed by worries – expressed the following: 'I felt immediately that I needed something to compare with. A figure is just a figure, right? I work with figures all day, and I know that you can perceive a figure from 1,000 different views, and it will mean something different every time.' Another woman expressed the same sense of powerlessness and loss of control: 'If she could just tell me, well, the last twenty couples I have seen they have had a risk between 1:2 and 1:2000 and there were this many couples in every category, then I think I could use this figure. Yet, I do not think that I can use a figure which is 1:661 at all. I know that she says that it is in relation to the population as such, and so on. But actually I cannot use that figure at all, because I have nothing to compare with.'

Ironically, risk information in the form of a risk figure – the means through which the norm of non-directiveness is being practiced – was not experienced as meaningful in itself by these women. Instead the couples faced a new challenge: how to render the risk figure meaningful in the context of their entire life and pregnancy. Their statements convey how they are situated in the gap between epidemiological knowledge and the experience of making decisions about the future of the fetus. How do they, in this situation, create boundaries of high risk and low risk? What notions of normality emerged in this process? In the following section we discuss these issues.

Negotiating Risk

When the women and their partners are presented with the result of the risk assessment, they are told that they have an age-related risk. This risk figure is described as 'background risk' and as 'the risk you have when you step into the clinic'. It refers to the statistical risk of having a child with Down Syndrome, pertaining to a particular age group. In our conversations with pregnant women and their partners they would use their age-related risk figure as a resource through which their specific risk figure was classified as being either high or low. One woman at 42 explained: 'When I entered the clinic I had an age risk at 1:31. The figure I received after the risk assessment had been carried out was 1:173. I compared that figure with the age risk. In that case my figure was low, and I think that was positive … I also compared with a friend of mine, who is 40-years-old, 2 years younger than me. Two weeks ago she went through this risk assessment. She received a risk which was 1:153, which was a higher risk than my risk at 1:173. That gave me peace of mind, because I had a lower risk and she was actually 2 years younger than me, right? So I think that was pretty cool. I know it is stupid to compare these figures like that. But you cannot help it, right?' By making connections between her own risk figure, her age-related risk figure and the risk figure of her girlfriend this woman considered that her own risk figure was not dramatic.

Another woman gives voice to the complicated process of making sense of the risk figure she received and acting on that basis. The woman is 40-years-old and pregnant with her first child, conceived after undergoing IVF. She described her pregnancy as her 'last chance' of getting pregnant. She said: 'I received a risk figure at 1:164, which is a tremendous improvement from my age risk. So, in that case it was a positive risk figure. However, there is still a long way to the cut-off point at 300. So, I still thought that it was a big risk. At first I was like, well I do not want to run the risk of undergoing an amniocentesis, now when I have seen the little prodigy in there. I just did not want anything to happen to it. It was this maternal feeling, I think, which came to me. I was thinking a lot about it, that if this is my last chance and if it fails, then I would never be able to forgive my self for wasting this opportunity before even knowing whether something is wrong with this child. At the same time I continuously had this risk explained in detail. In my head it was something like, when you are so far from the boundary [the cut-off point], well, maybe it is OK to be far from the boundary, but I had actually expected that I would receive a risk closer to 300, definitely around 200 or so.' This woman negotiated her decision by connecting her risk figure to her age-related risk figure, the cut-off point and the visualisation of a real baby, as well as to the knowledge that her fetus is at risk of having Down Syndrome. After one week of doubt and uncertainty, she decided to undergo amniocentesis. Her story illustrates how co-existing notions of the fetus as a healthy child-to-be and as a possible abortion emerged and how the cut-off point played a decisive role in creating knowledge about her fetus as 'high risk'. As such both this case and the previous case point to a strong experience during our fieldwork that the cut-off point constituted a most powerful figure in the interpretative processes of the couples. In all cases, except one, this figure served as the primary means through which a risk figure was categorized as so high that the couples decided to undergo CVS or amniocentesis and thereby run the risk of a miscarriage.

Letting the Experts Decide

Several women explained to us how they acted on the basis of a fundamental trust in the cut-off point. As one woman explained: 'Our risk figure is 1:415, which is higher than 300, therefore we decide not to have an amniocentesis. If the figure had been lower than 300, we would have decided to undergo an amniocentesis. So, this boundary is important. To me it is something about letting the experts decide, or something like that, right, because you … well, of course you have to listen to yourself, but … you are placed in a field where you don't have any experience, then I think I do it, per definition.' Some couples questioned the cut-off point at 1:300 by contrasting it to the risk of having a miscarriage by undergoing amniocentesis, which is around 1 per cent (1:100). By constituting the cut-off point as higher than the miscarriage rate, The Danish Board of Health indirectly categorizes a future of giving birth to a child with Down Syndrome as more dangerous than a future of aborting a healthy child. This categorization of futures made some women reflect. One woman who decided to undergo amniocentesis on the basis of a risk figure at 1:44 gives the following explanation: 'When I look back, I actually think that a risk at 1:44, it is actually a low risk, right? After the amniocentesis was carried out, we mentioned that I had actually increased my risk of losing this child. With a 1 per cent risk of having a miscarriage by undergoing amniocentesis, then I had actually increased my risk of losing this child. And I did so without batting an eyelid right? But it is this thing, when you are offered a test by a health professional you also expect that it is because there is a big risk, seen in some kind of perspective right? But, well … you trust that they know more about it than you do.' The cut-off point served as a powerful means of regulating action, but importantly also a helpful device in locating and thereby ordering the chaotic and meaningless message of a risk figure. As a third woman explained: 'I think it is nice that at least you have a figure you can relate to. I know that it is also rather arbitrary, but then there is at least something you can relate to.'

Several studies have pointed out how we are today witnessing a new public critique of medicine, which challenges medical scientific authority (Gabe and Bury 1996). It is argued that expert knowledge is increasingly contested and that people's trust in expertise is in decline. However, our study demonstrates how the pregnant women and their partners were unwilling to give up the health professional as the paternalistic expert, and how they placed a high degree of trust in the health professionals as well as in the overall health care sector. This inclination to trust the publicly financed health system may well be a particularly

Scandinavian feature, where the state has a traditional responsibility for the health of the population – but it may equally be seen as a result of the fact that risk-information is basically meaningless unless located in a meaning-giving social context.

With the notion of prenatal counselling as non-directive and the women and their partners as autonomous decision makers, the locus of responsibility in the process of genetic counselling is in the pregnant woman and her partner. Below, a woman expresses her frustrations when she had to make a decision on the basis of risk knowledge, which she did not think she was able to relate to: 'The risk figure was explained to me in a very professional manner, but I was not able to make sense of it. They, of course, have to be very careful about not indicating anything. They emphasized over and over again, that it, well, it is your choice … So I had to take responsibility for this all alone … Normally I do like to take responsibility and make decisions; I like being responsible and being able to influence things. It fits very well with my personality. But in this situation it was not really a good experience, because I felt like, well, the health professionals are the experts and I know nothing and I was like, well, it is their field and they have the professional knowledge, so it should be possible to get more information or advice. I felt like that … at the same time I knew that I could not demand that. So I did not really like the responsibility I had. It was not a decision I felt like facing up to. At the same time I knew that I was the only one who was capable of doing that.' With the principle of informed choice, and the ideal of the pregnant woman as an autonomous individual, the woman and her partner are constituted as responsible for the choice they are making and thereby also for the future which is created through their decision making. But this responsibility may be a burden as much as a wished for independence from a paternalistic medical system. As Kerr points out: 'What is at stake today is a privatisation of responsibilities for preventing disability, or, if a test is declined, facing up to the future living with a disabled child' (Kerr 2004, 82). This is not a value-neutral process. Rather: 'Making individuals responsible for their own health, and for the birth of healthy infants and their continued wellbeing, is the product of a moral discourse, one which, although it may appear entirely reasonable, is in part politically motivated.' (Lock 1998, 11).

Conclusion

Prenatal risk assessment is a method concerned with producing and ascribing meaning to risk figures. This chapter shows that the meaning of risk and what constitutes facts is not self-evident. Through the analytical lens of the Latourian concept of 'processes of translation' we have shown how knowledge about what constitutes a high risk (a dangerous future) and what constitutes a low risk (a non-dangerous future), as well as categories of normality and abnormality are created and interpreted in the process of prenatal risk assessment. This process of fact production emerges as a relational and social process, taking place between actors (doctors, patients), policies (informed choice and autonomous individuals), diagnostic techniques (statistics) and other objects (scanners, blood tests, cut-off values). Through this process links of interpretations were made, and spaces for agency and meaning-making were constituted.

Gaps between statistical facts, cut-off points, the image of the scan and the lived experience of pregnancies create spaces of interpretation in which pregnant women and their partners make their decisions. In these spaces, statistical facts in the form of risk figures were not experienced as immediately meaningful, but became so by being related to the social context in which the risk information was created and framed. By relating the risk figure to other figures, the meaning of the risk figure obtained its value. In other words, whether the risk figure was interpreted as being high or low, and the fetus seen as normal or abnormal was not made evident by the risk figure itself. Rather, in a complex translational process of interpretation, images of the future (as being dangerous or not) were being created. On this basis, our analysis challenges the notion that a risk figure is an objective fact, which can be transmitted and received in a transaction between two independent actors. Moreover, processes of decision making did not emerge as individual and autonomous undertakings, as the notion of informed choice implies. Rather, spaces for action and meaning making were tied to specific socio-material associations through which subjects and objects were connected.

The cut-off point emerged as a powerful figure in the decision-making process, by constituting some fetuses as high risk and others as low risk. The production of facts in the context of prenatal risk assessment, in this sense, is embedded in a political horizon, where the preventive aim of identifying those fetuses which deviate from the statistically derived norm, is the primary aim. As such, the cut-off point serves as a powerful normative framework surrounding the decision-making process of women and their partners – and a framework based on complex decisions and political judgements that are black boxed as indisputable fact.

Prenatal risk assessment is a process during which subjects are constituted as responsible for their child and for the future by the enactment of informed choice. Yet, by locating isolated and individual risk figures at the centre of the risk assessment, and thereby presenting the process of prenatal risk assessment as value-free and non-directive, The Danish Board of Health renders the normative basis of choice invisible. In doing so, responsibility for the outcome of the choice is located solely with the pregnant woman and her partner, in spite of the fact that society has engaged itself intensely in providing and shaping this health offer – and as a consequence shares the responsibility for its use.

References

Act on Patient's Legal Rights and Entitlement in Denmark, Act. No. 482 of July, 1998.

Danish Board of Health (2003), *Prenatal Diagnosis and Risk Assessment* (Copenhagen: Schultz Information).

Danish Board of Health (2004a), *Guidelines for Prenatal Diagnosis* (Copenhagen: Danish Board of Health).

Danish Board of Health (2004b), *Risk Assessment and Prenatal Diagnosis. Information for Pregnant Women* (Copenhagen: Danish Board of Health).

Emery, J. (2001), 'Is informed choice in genetic testing a different breed of informed decision-making? A discussion paper', *Health Expectations* 4, 81–86.

Franklin, S. (2003), 'Re-thinking nature-culture', *Anthropological Theory* 3:1, 65–85.

Gabe, J and M. Bury (1996), 'Halcion nights: A sociological account of medical controversy', *Sociology* 30, 447–469.

Gifford, S. (1986), 'The meaning of lumps: A case study of the ambiguities of risk', in C. Janes et al. (eds), *Anthropology and Epidemiology: Interdisciplinary Approaches to the Study of Health and Disease* (Dordrecht: Reidel Publishing Company), 213–246.

Harper, P.S. (2004), *Practical Genetic Counselling* (London: Arnold).

Helén, I. (2005), 'Risk management and ethics in antenatal care', in R. Bunton and A. Petersen (eds), *Genetic Governance. Health, Risk and Ethics in the Biotech Era* (London: Routledge), 47–63.

Kerr, A. (2004), *Genetics and Society* (London: Routledge).

Latour, B. (1986), 'The Powers of Association', in J. Law, *Power, Action and Belief: A New Sociology of Knowledge* (London: Routledge), 264–280.

Lock, M. (1998), 'Breast cancer. Reading the omens', *Anthropology Today* 14:4, 7–16.

Ministry of the Interior (1977), *Report about Prenatal Genetic Diagnosis* (Copenhagen: The Danish Publish House).

Parliamentary Proposal, *V105, Under Interpellation 61 on Prenatal Diagnosis*, May 15, 2003.

Price, F.V. (1990), 'The Management of Uncertainty in Obstetric Practice: Ultrasonography, In Vivo Fertilisation and Embryo Transfer', in M. McNeil et al. (eds), *The New Reproductive Technologies* (London: Macmillian).

Rapp, R. (2000), 'Extra Chromosomes and Blue Tulips: Medico-Familial Interpretations', in M. Lock et al. (eds), *Living and Working with the New Medical Technologies* (Cambridge: Cambridge University Press), 184–208.

Rothman, B.K. (1986), *The Tentative Pregnancy: Prenatal Diagnosis and the Future of Motherhood* (New York: Viking).

Svendsen, M.N. (2006), 'The social life of genetic knowledge: A case-study of choices and dilemmas in cancer genetic counselling in Denmark', *Medical Anthropology* 25, 139–170.

Tabor, A. (2006), *Personal communication.*

Chapter 15
Receiving and Interpreting Information: A Joint Enterprise

Jackie Leach Scully

Bioethics as a Dialogue

One way of thinking of bioethics is as a dialogic discipline. For one thing, it is primarily involved in regulating the interactions of distinct agents, including doctors and patients, in medicine and the life sciences, and these interactions often involve the exchange of information. For another, bioethics itself has been described as having originated in a dialogue between practitioners of many disciplines (Borry et al. 2005). With such a history, we might expect bioethicists to take a healthy interest in the practices of information exchange in different contexts: not just between physician and patient, but between other agents in health care settings, and between the various types of expert who call themselves bioethicists.

At least in its early days, however, bioethics was mostly concerned with applying ethical theories to the practical problems with which it was confronted and for which it was supposed to provide some guidance. Such a pragmatic orientation meant that bioethics has paid less attention both to metaethical questions, and to the procedural ones of health care delivery. Both medical and bioethical interest in health care communication, for instance, has been largely placed within the framework of operationalizing patient autonomy in the practices of obtaining voluntary informed consent (Manson and O'Neill 2007). And this rather particular and restricted area of concern necessarily shaped the scrutiny that bioethics has given to the ways through which medical information as a whole, including genetic information, is given and disseminated.

An extensive bioethical literature is proof, if any were needed, that genetics and genetic counselling raise complex ethical issues of confidentiality, privacy and responsibility. Other contributions to this book discuss these areas in more detail. The history of bioethics also shows that, as new technical advances come on-stream, they open up unexpected problems, or bring to the fore issues that previously seemed less urgent. So it is with the movement towards large-scale, effective predictive and prognostic genetic diagnosis (Konrad 2005). Among the areas of concern emerging here are epistemological questions about (i) the nature of the genetic knowledge that can be obtained from complexly interacting, ill-defined probabilities, and (ii) the reliability with which genetic sequence information can be linked to a defined future phenotype at all. At the moment, the sequence data with which predictive genetics is concerned can often only be interpreted much more tentatively than the information made available by the familiar kind of genetic diagnosis involving monogenic conditions, where probabilities are more clear-cut. And in addition to these epistemological concerns there are the well-characterized socio-ethical issues of the consequences for everyday life of having and using predictive, probabilistic genetic information.

In this chapter I want to focus on one aspect of the genetic counselling process: the mutual making-sense of genetic information. My claim here is that such sense-making is a joint interpretative and ethical enterprise between those involved. The genetic diagnostic encounter involves multiple actors, and it brings together multiple perspectives on knowledge that differ in important ways. One cluster of differences is essentially *epistemological*: actors vary in the concepts of knowledge they use, and their ideas about where authoritative knowledge can be found, or how genetic knowledge can and should be interpreted in differing real-life contexts. Unsurprisingly, for instance, there are known to be significant differences between lay conceptions of inheritance and scientific understandings of genetics, notably in the comprehension of risk and probabilities (Bates et al. 2003; Walter et al. 2004). Another cluster of differences is *experiential*. These differences are more to do with the fact that those involved may have markedly different individual and social biographies, with the result that they have undergone different experiences, which then impact differentially on their perception and interpretation of what is going on. Clearly, these epistemic and experiential domains are not isolated from each other, since experience plays a part in determining what people consider to be authoritative and relevant information and how it should be interpreted.

Although genetic counselling is a site of encounter between numerous different agents, we tend to focus on only two of them – the patient (sometimes with the family) and the medical professional. In this chapter I continue this bias, because I am concentrating on the most direct processes of genetic information exchange, but I want to note in passing that there is a 'backstage' presence of laboratory technicians, nursing staff, managers of the health care authority, policy makers and so on that should not be forgotten. These people also contribute to the 'sense' that is made of the genes, for example, by specifying which tests are available and which ones not, how accurate they are, and the guidelines and manuals that govern how the test results are delivered to the counselling room.

Flow of Information

In almost all clinical encounters, both physician and patient are involved in an ongoing process of comprehension. In the clinic, the doctor or genetic counsellor receives information about the patient's possible genetic status by clinical observation, then through the narrative of family history, and increasingly through the results of genetic testing by molecular diagnostic technologies. All our current theories in sociology and psychology suggest that information is not exchanged in an unmediated form. What is to be known first passes through the actors' subjective understanding. When one person communicates with another, the subjectivities of both the person giving information and the person receiving it are involved. Furthermore the reception of information is not straightforward: it must then *be made sense of* in two ways. First, it must be integrated in some way into the recipient's conceptualization of causality in the world. Second, genetic information must also be made sense of in terms of its unique meaning for the life of that specific individual.

The Patient's View

The patient in the genetic counselling situation, face to face with the medic or counsellor, has two central questions: *Can I understand what this person is telling me*, and *What does this message mean for my life?* Difficulties can arise in the patient's engagement with either or both of these.

Can I Understand what this Person is Telling Me?

Incoming information is handled and acted upon through neurophysiological and cognitive processes common to everyone (see, for example, Heekeren et al. 2008). However, these processes are also heavily dependent on more localized conceptual frameworks of understanding made available by their culture or personal experience. So the patient may have difficulty with the terminology that is being used, for example, with the description of unfamiliar physiological processes, or with conceptualizing abstract probabilities (Hopwood et al. 2003). Here, it could be argued that the patient can legitimately expect the practitioner's competence to extend to conveying medical information in a way that is both accurate and accessible. A patient would surely be justified in thinking that if practitioners are simply unable to communicate in a clear and accessible way, they are failing in an important part of their job.

But in some cases, of course – and this is a particular problem for predictive genetics of complex, multifactorial conditions – the genetic data are not clear enough for an unqualified clinical statement to be made. This is the difficulty that currently distinguishes novel genetic data from most other kinds of clinical data – the fact that, at the moment, both the predictive value and existential meaning of genetic information is more often than not unclear. Although in principle this can also be true of other kinds of clinical data, in practice we tend to have had longer experience with them and to have a more thorough grasp of the relevant science and its implications for real life. Genetic data can often validly be interpreted to give widely differing outcomes. The 'disclosure dilemma' here is how to communicate the genuine significance of what might be frustratingly ambiguous information (Etchegary and Perrier 2007). For example, there is still debate over the meaning of a positive BRCA1/2 test result, in particular for those patients considering prophylactic mastectomy (Ray et al. 2005).

What Does this Mean for My Life?

Alternatively there may be difficulties with the second question. The patient can struggle to integrate the potential meaning of the results and to cope with the consequences for their life. In a study of patients' genetic testing decisions based in Switzerland, for example, participants spoke about periods of physical and mental alienation following their test result or even while deciding whether or not to take the test (Scully et al. 2007). The practitioner's responsibility is to facilitate this integration to the extent that they can in the course of medical treatment. There are ethical issues here in terms of how far the practitioner can or should go to make integration easier for the patient. In visiting a genetic counsellor, patients generally want advice that is informed by the practitioner's expertise and experience, which they can then use in the process of making their own choices. Non-directive counselling has long been upheld as the gold standard for showing respect for patients' autonomous decision-making capacity, and at the same time reining back any tendency a practitioner might have, even with the best of intentions, to tell the patient what to do (Oduncu 2002). But it must also be borne in mind that, ultimately, *patient autonomy is best fostered* by ensuring that information is given in a way that facilitates their own decision-making processes, and precisely what this requires is not uniform from case to case (Hodgson and Spriggs 2005). This means the practitioner must be able to perceive what the patient needs, what is explicitly or implicitly being asked for, and the limits to what can be provided. It requires considerable skills of self-reflection to ensure that efforts to convey information in an unambiguous way do not result in communications that are undeniably, even if unconsciously, directive. And although this is not the place for a detailed discussion (cf. Rehmann-Sutter, this vol.), I should note the ongoing argument within counselling about whether, when patients must make decisions informed by highly technical and complex information, patient autonomy is always best served by a total abstention from giving direction (Weil et al. 2006).

The point I want to emphasize here is that the processes of interpretation and integration that I have described occur on both sides of the genetic dialogue. Even when more 'dialogic' models of genetic counselling are offered (for example, White 1998) it is tempting for experts to adopt a model of unidirectional flow, in which the physician provides factually correct information, and the patient receives it. If we bear in mind the mediated nature of knowledge and understanding, however, it is clear this model is inadequate. Not only are impressions about the life of the patient inevitably filtered through the physician's personal and professional experience, the *manner* in which physicians in turn convey their professional understanding will often be unconsciously as well as consciously shaped through their comprehension of the patient and what the information means for the patient's life. Hence the physician must inevitably engage in an interpretative venture within the unfamiliar horizon of the patient's world – just as the patient has always had to step a little inside the alien medical framework in order to comprehend clinical information. The genetic encounter, then, involves two or more persons, separate but part of an intersubjective dynamic of speech and conscious interaction, as well as feelings and unconscious processes that are less apparent.

Knowing the Lives of Others

To have the sort of insight into other lives that will permit such interpretative ventures and help the practitioner help the patient involves, at a bare minimum, an adequate grasp of the features of those lives. And one of the difficulties here is that practitioner and patient often do not share the salient features. Because of this, the practitioner may be required to make a considerable imaginative leap, to 'put themselves in x's shoes', that is to try to see things from the point of view of another whose situation and perspective appears very different from their own, or whose actions and judgements they find disturbing or incomprehensible. The idea of 'putting yourself in someone else's position' suggests that each person has a distinctive point of view and that we need to engage imaginatively with that view in order to understand how others see things. A number of moral and political philosophers over the centuries have taken up this idea. For example, Hume claimed that moral judgement requires an agent to counter his natural tendencies towards partiality by trying to find 'a point of view common to him with others' (Hume 1968, 252). In another example from the contemporary philosophy of mind, simulation theorists propose that the task of understanding other people's thought processes involves simulating their mental states in our own minds (see for example Davies and Stone 1995).[1] But when we simulate or imaginatively recreate another person's thought processes, we generally assume that the other person's reasoning processes work along the same lines as ours, and that therefore we have a baseline of knowledge about their beliefs and values that means we ought to be able to follow their thinking, even if we do not agree with them.

One difficulty with the concept of 'putting oneself in another's shoes' in order to understand events from their perspective is that there are several forms of imaginative projection (Mackenzie 2000). In one, we can simply imagine *ourselves* in the other's situation, and draw on our own experience. In the genetic context, for instance, could see ourselves growing up in a family where there is Huntington's disease, or wondering whether we are at risk of familial cancer. Everything else about ourselves (character, interests, relationships, occupation, biases and so on) remains the same: the single change is the presence of specific genetic risk. The success of this version of imagining oneself as other depends on factors such as how well informed we are about the experience, and whether we have other kinds of experience from which it is possible to extrapolate with more or less accuracy. In practice, this kind of imaginative projection may be best suited

1 Note that I am not defending simulation theory as the best model of understanding other people; however it remains influential in the philosophy of mind, and I refer here only to one implication of it.

to visualizing the concrete consequences of a different way of life: what it might mean *financially* to be unable to work because of cancer, for example. By contrast, the emotional responses and demands of such a situation are harder to imagine unless one has already gone through the experience, or something very like it (Mackenzie and Scully 2007).

A second mode of imaginative projection involves going beyond imagining ourselves in the situation, and imaging ourselves *as* that other person. Whether or not we can do this successfully depends on the same sorts of factors as before, and in addition on how much we know and understand about the other person in terms of their character, history, interests and emotional attitudes. An additional requirement here is sensitivity to the salience of differences in gender, age, culture, religion or class between ourselves and the other person that might compromise an ability to extrapolate accurately from one to the other. Often, however, there are simply too many aspects of the other into which we have no insight or which we do not share: we may be unaware of crucial and substantial areas of divergence. As a result, attempts at this kind of imaginative projection will involve a mixing of the other person's perspective with one's own rather than the pure adoption of another life perspective.

Moral Understandings

A person's understanding is constituted by situational particularities – the specifics of real-life moral and social worlds. It is ironic then that what could be called standard ethics has for a good part of its history been ambivalent or actively hostile to the idea that situational particularities may be important for ethical analysis. Certainly since the dominance of Anglo-American analytic philosophy, conventional moral philosophical analysis has tended to downplay the worldly particularities (physical, social, material, emotional) of the people concerned and the settings they inhabit, as data irrelevant to producing the universal action-guiding codes that are the desired end. Crucially, this not only misses the health care practitioner's need for these kinds of data about their patients in order to engage meaningfully with them, but also fails to see the need for awareness that the practitioner's own circumstances and biases also come into play.

Taking seriously the effect of social contexts like this is effectively a shift in focus from classical to social epistemologies. In classical epistemology, attention is given to individuals acquiring and justifying reliable knowledge. In this view, what might be called the epistemic norm is a single subject consciously pursuing the information that they need to make sound decisions. In the genetic counselling setting that would be medical facts, information on actions and outcomes, and so on. Social epistemologies, on the other hand, turn attention away from the individual to the collective (Schmitt 1994). They thereby spotlight an alternative set of concerns about the knowledge held by and about moral agents. It is this analytic perspective that makes social epistemologies especially sensitive to the impact of social position and power differentials on knowledge. Feminist epistemologies, for instance, observe that gendered patterns of social advantage tend to give rise to similarly gendered distributions of epistemic authority (Alcoff and Potter 1993).

The epistemology of social margins is most fully elaborated in standpoint theory. Feminist and other theorists who use standpoint epistemology take note of the epistemic effects of social positioning: the different 'knowledges' that go with particular social categories. Standpoint epistemologies claim that there are cognitive and affective changes in the perception and interpretation of events that follow from being a member of a marginalized social group, and that this results in a privileged insight into the domains of life that are most affected by their subordinate social status (Hartsock 1987; Harding 1993). Social epistemologies can therefore be important tools in identifying the barriers that block one group of people, such as medical professionals, having knowledge of how unfamiliar lives, such as those of their patients, are lived. The claim that the specific historical and social location of individuals limits their knowledge of other people's lives is not particularly contentious. Standpoint epistemology however emphasizes the fact that social organizations manage to give especial power and authority to some perspectives while simultaneously sidelining others. Standpoint epistemology also makes the further claim that, in most hierarchical social structures, people who occupy subordinate positions understand more of the lives of those in power than vice versa: as the saying goes, masters know nothing of servants' lives but servants' know all about their masters'.

The concern of individual epistemology is with how people acquire and justify reliable knowledge; social epistemologies pay more attention to the collective perceptions and interpretations that shape what individuals take to be reliable knowledge and good justification, and how certain perceptions and interpretations acquire authority. An equivalent model of ethical perception can be put forward to parallel this perspectival social epistemology. People come to occupy differing social positions that influence the opportunities made available or the obligations assigned to them, and as a result they are likely to be confronted with different moral issues. More controversial is the suggestion that differently *socially* positioned people experience similar *moral* issues differently, because they have different reserves of economic, social and cultural capital to draw on, and because they will differ in their perception and weighing up of the situation's parameters, and the relative costs and benefits. A socially marginalized person might face barriers to attending a clinic for testing, counselling and treatment that mean they consider the costs (not just the financial costs, but cost of time and energy) not worth the benefit of resolving uncertainty, while another person with more secure social status could come to a different evaluation. Such an understanding is based on differential costs and benefits to which the two are exposed. Since medical professionals are, generally, not socially marginalized, it would be understandable if they found themselves able to 'grasp' intuitively one patient's decision but be puzzled or disturbed by the other.

Margaret Walker's influential *Moral Understandings* (Walker 1998) makes the point that all moral life is socially situated, and suggests that the effect of social location can be seen in all moral interaction, not just those that involve people of obviously unequal status. She shifts the focus of ethical attention from the generation of action guides, for example the guidelines of genetic counselling, and on to the experiences, values and practices that, a long way down the line, give rise to articulated moral principles. Walker contends that moral behaviour takes place against backgrounds of implicit knowledge that 'constrain and make intelligible' the interactions between people within a community. Background moral understandings are conveyed to us by the communities in which we have grown and live. They include notions of good lives, and accounts of precedent that indicate the sorts of practices and choices that the community expects, and so they certainly do guide actions. But beyond that, they also provide the vocabulary for narrating and justifying actions; they instruct on common moral practices such as assigning blame, or accepting or deflecting responsibility; and they indicate the appropriate roles and institutions through which aspects of moral life are expressed. In Walker's view, standard moral philosophy spends a disproportionate amount of time on the activities of judgement and evaluation, neglecting the many other practices (perception, description, interpretation, communication, narration, explaining, defending, response and so on) that constitute the bulk of everyday moral life. In turning from the individual to the collective, then, social epistemologies draw attention to the barriers to intersubjective understanding that are presented by different background moral understandings.

What I referred to earlier as standard moral philosophy – a style of moral thought that privileges the ideals of abstraction and universalization – generally works from the assumption that 'we' (those of us reflecting on a moral problem, or evaluating other people's solutions to it) already know enough about the situation and persons we are reflecting on, or can gain access to them through the exercise of imagination and logical deduction, to make those kinds of moral judgements. That epistemological confidence goes hand in hand with the belief that people do not vary much in terms of the moral terrain they occupy. The chances are therefore high that others will agree with the way I frame a given situation, weigh up morally salient features of it and carry my argument through to a conclusion. But if it isn't the case that moral knowledge is very similar between agents, then bioethical reflection and the practical clinical guidelines it produces must incorporate the systematic study of moral understandings, through analyzing the 'actual moral arrangements' of what people in the situations of interest really do, and what reasons can be found for those acts and choices.

An analysis of the moral understandings of the participants in the genetic encounter clearly differs from the approach of normative ethics. In making normative statements, moral philosophers are looking for generalities (and hoping for universals). But collecting, and then analyzing ethically, individual accounts like these requires an individuated perspective. This perspective assumes that every person making a genetic testing decision has a different story to tell – not because what happens to each person is so very unique, but because their narrative is less about what happened than about the sense they make of it, and this sense is shaped by a unique constellation of many other variables. And to return to the point I made earlier, an individuated moral perspective also implies that every health care professional has their own story, and hence their own framework of understanding and limits to their powers of imaginative projection. These parameters condition first their ability to comprehend and react to the information about other people (patients) coming into their professional lives. Second, and just as important, these parameters also shape how they use this information in attempts at communicating information to others.

Need for Empirical Data

Because of the growing recognition of the salience to ethics of the social-moral positions the involved actors occupy, bioethical research has recently begun to show more interest in the value of empirical input into bioethical reflection. One painfully obvious rationale is a growing track record of serious ethical issues that were simply not predicted ahead of time, or recognized early enough, by traditional forms of ethical analysis. The argument is that these problems might have been predicted or noticed earlier if more attention had been paid to the real-life behaviour, attitudes and opinions of those involved. The classic example here is the relatively low uptake of carrier testing for the autosomal dominant neurodegenerative condition Huntington's disease. After the single locus genetic test became available, uptake was much lower than had been predicted (Binedell and Soldan 1997; Creighton et al. 2003). A more recent example is the unanticipated use by members of the deaf community of prenatal and pre-implantation genetic diagnosis to select for, rather than against, children with heritable hearing impairment (Mundy 2002; Scully 2008). In both cases, it is arguable that closer attention to the sociology of Huntington family members (carriers and non-carriers) or of deaf people, would have given better insight into the ambiguous and nuanced response of these families to predictive and prenatal testing.

In two projects based in Switzerland, I and colleagues at the University of Basel used qualitative empirical methods to investigate decision making in areas of bioethical interest, one of which was genetic testing (Scully et al. 2007; Scully and Rehmann-Sutter 2006; Haimes et al. 2008). In both studies, our aim in acquiring empirical data on 'actual moral and social orders' was not purely sociological, but to help understand the factors that influence people's ethical thinking in these areas. In the genetic testing study, we were particularly interested in the factors that affect decision-making processes, and especially whether time (the passage of time, choice of the right time to test, and so on) plays a role. In both studies, we reached a number of conclusions about the ethical choices of involved agents that would not have been predicted from existing theory, and that, crucially, could not have been reached without the venture into the moral understandings of our participants that the interviews and subsequent analysis required us to make.

Ethics of Encounter

Inherent in this model of the exchange of genetic information is a particular moral stance towards difference. In encounters like these, each person is confronted with another's residual unknowability. For the counsellor, there is a professional requirement to resist the temptation to force the patient's account into pre-existing frameworks of understanding, regardless of whether or not it actually fits. This is also an ethical demand rooted in a fundamental respect for the ontological 'otherness' of the other.

Similar considerations about the ethics of encounter are present in the work of many philosophers. The absolute respect for the residual unknowability of the other is most familiar to us from the writing of the French philosopher Emanuel Levinas (1969, 1981). His most famous assertion, that ethics precedes ontology, is a claim that human identity is never constituted in isolation but rather out of the relationships we form with whatever and whoever is not ourselves. In Levinas's understanding, a metaphysical desire (to breach our own self-limits by reaching towards what is *not* ourselves) finds everyday expression in a particular quality of attention towards the real, embodied other sitting across from us. This does not mean attention without *any* preconceptions about what the other is like – which would be epistemologically impossible – but one which does not expect the other to be immediately, or ultimately, completely accessible to knowledge. Levinas wrote most directly about the ethical relation of the self to the other in terms of the response of one person to someone else's suffering. He was not, however, saying that such a relationship between two people is moral *because* of this benevolent response – an encounter doesn't have to involve the amelioration of suffering in order to be moral. The other person *always* makes an ethical claim on us in the implicit demand that we recognize their radical otherness, whether they are in pain or not. And our ethical response is judged according to whether we respond with that recognition or refuse it.

Levinas's work, then, attempts to explore the ethical implications that follow from the belief that my sense of my own self is *defined* through knowing the other person as not coterminous with me. When Levinas talks about an asymmetry here he is not talking about a power differential, but about the inevitable inequality of ethical call and response. In the genetic encounter as described earlier, the practitioner has to renounce some of her power over the patient, but from a Levinasian perspective it would be inappropriate to talk of gains and losses. Levinas would say this kind of attention to another even in the face of irreducible otherness is precisely the act that confirms the practitioner's own ethical humanity.

Systemic Ethical Issues

The genetic encounter is an asymmetry in terms of the practitioner's greater technical expertise (which is after all what the patient is paying for), but it is fundamentally also reciprocal. This chapter has argued that although biomedicine and bioethics have been sensitive to the knowledge deficit on the part of the patient, there is much less awareness that the practitioner's epistemic standpoint is also constrained, and that this affects their ability to engage with the patient's own understanding. Ideally, then, what we are looking for is a counselling process that is based on an appreciation of the patients' preferences developed within an ongoing dialogue between parties familiar enough with each other to be able to comprehend as fully as possible the others' worldviews, and recognize their own cognitive and imaginative limits.

However desirable all this is, many clinicians would argue such an ideal is currently unattainable. An ongoing, reflective dialogical relationship between doctor and patient presupposes lots of things, not least of which is having enough time and resources. Extended time can be clinically problematic, since babies or tumours do not conveniently stop growing for a few weeks while difficult ethical issues are explored. But there are other, non-biological barriers that arise as a result of present day health care provision. Up to now the bioethical examination of clinical communication has tended to focus on the microlevel of interpersonal ethics, but it is important to recognize that the brute practicalities of how a service (such as genetic testing) is provided is an issue with ethical consequences. I have been arguing that the clinical genetic encounter is always a reciprocal process, and focusing on the (often neglected) knowledge deficit of the practitioner. It seems plausible to argue that some genetic disclosure dilemmas would be eased, and better resolutions found for others, if practitioner and patient have the opportunity to work jointly towards clarifying what the information being disclosed means for the life of the patient. If the testing service is provided in such a way that practitioner and patient are hindered in their collaborative efforts towards finding a good solution, then we need to start considering the existence of a systemic problem in how health care is provided. Insofar as they work against the dialogic understanding I have described, the structural constraints of the health care systems within which genetic counselling is made available may ultimately exacerbate the intensity of the ethical dilemmas that surround the disclosure of genetic information. It is often easier, to concentrate all our efforts on rectifying the microlevel areas of difficulty in bioethics. The bioethics emerging at the start of the twenty-first century is showing a turn towards the consideration of larger-scale systemic and justice issues. In this context, the problem of a health care system which routinely impoverishes the hermeneutic resources of the clinical genetic encounter should be of as much ethical concern as practitioner confidentiality or individual patient autonomy.

References

Alcoff, L. and Potter, E. (eds) (1993), *Feminist Epistemologies* (London: Routledge & Kegan Paul).

Bates, B.R. et al. (2003), 'What does "a gene for heart disease" mean? A focus group study of public understandings of genetic risk factors', *American Journal of Medical Genetics A* 1;119:2, 156–61.

Binedell, J. and Soldan, J.R. (1997), 'Nonparticipation in Huntington's disease predictive testing: Reasons for caution in interpreting findings', *Journal of Genetic Counseling* 6, 419–432.

Borry, J. et al. (2005), 'The birth of the empirical turn in bioethics', *Bioethics* 19, 49–71.

Creighton, S. et al. (2003), 'Predictive, pre-natal and diagnostic genetic testing for Huntington's disease: The experience in Canada from 1987 to 2000', *Clinical Genetics* 63, 462–475.

Davies, M. and Stone, T. (1995), *Mental Simulation* (Oxford: Blackwell).

Etchegary H. and Perrier, C. (2007), 'Information processing in the context of genetic risk: Implications for genetic-risk communication', *Journal of Genetic Counseling* 16:4, 419–32, Epub 2007 May 1, Review.

Haimes, E. et al. (2008), 'So, what is an embryo? A comparative study of the views of those asked to donate embryos for hESC research in the UK and Switzerland', *Special issue of New Genetics and Society*.

Harding, S. (1993), 'Rethinking standpoint epistemology: What is "strong objectivity"?', in L. Alcoff and E. Potter (eds), *Feminist Epistemologies* (London: Routledge), 49–82.

Hartsock, N. (1987), 'The feminist standpoint: Developing the ground for a specifically feminist historical materialism', in S. Harding (ed.), *Feminism and Methodology: Social Science Issues* (Bloomington: Indiana University Press).

Heekeren, H.R. et al. (2008), 'The neural systems that mediate human perceptual decision making', *Nature Reviews Neuroscience*, May 9, Epub pre-print.

Hodgson, J. and Spriggs, M. (2005), 'A practical account of autonomy: Why genetic counseling is especially well suited to the facilitation of informed autonomous decision making', *Journal of Genetic Counseling* 14:2, 89–97.

Hopwood, P. et al. (2003), 'Do women understand the odds? Risk perceptions and recall of risk information in women with a family history of breast cancer', *Community Genetics* 6:4, 214–23.

Hume, D. (1751), *An Enquiry Concerning the Principles of Morals*, section 9. Reprinted in D.H. Aiken (1968), *Hume's Moral and Political Philosophy* (New York: Hafner).

Konrad, M. (2005), *Narrating the New Predictive Genetics* (Cambridge: Cambridge University Press).

Levinas, E. (1969), *Totality and Infinity*, translated by Alphonso Lingis (published in new edition by Duquesne University Press 1999).

Levinas, E. (1981), *Otherwise than Being or Beyond Essence*, translated by Alphonso Lingis (published in new editions by Duquesne University Press 1999).

Mackenzie, C. (2000), 'Imagining Oneself Otherwise', in Mackenzie et al. (eds), *Relational Autonomy* (New York: Oxford University Press), 124–150.

Mackenzie, C. and Leach Scully, J. (2007), 'Moral imagination, disability and embodiment', *Journal of Applied Philosophy* 24, 335–51.

Manson, N. and O'Neill, O. (2007), *Rethinking Informed Consent in Bioethics* (Cambridge: Cambridge University Press).

Mundy, L. (2002), 'A world of their own', *Washington Post Magazine*, March 31.

Oduncu, F.S. (2002), 'The role of non-directiveness in genetic counseling', *Medicine, Health Care and Philosophy* 5:1, 53–63.

Ray, J.A. et al. (2005), 'Risk-reduction surgery decisions in high-risk women seen for genetic counseling', *Journal of Genetic Counseling* 14:6, 473–84.

Schmitt, F.F. (ed.) (1994), *Socializing Epistemology: The Social Dimensions of Knowledge* (Lanham, Maryland: Rowman & Littlefield).

Scully, J.L. et al. (2007), 'You don't make genetic test decisions from one day to the next. Using time to preserve moral space', *Bioethics* 21:4, 208–17.

Scully J.L. (2008), *Disability Bioethics: Moral Bodies, Moral Difference* (Lanham: Rowman & Littlefield).

Scully, J.L and Rehmann-Sutter, C. (2006), 'Creating donors: The 2005 Swiss law on donation of "spare" embryos to hESC research', *Bioethical Inquiry* 3, 81–93.

Walker, M.U. (1998), *Moral Understandings: A Feminist Study in Ethics* (New York and London: Routledge).

Walter, F.M. et al. (2004), 'Lay understanding of familial risk of common chronic diseases: A systematic review and synthesis of qualitative research', *Annals of Family Medicine* 2:6, 583–94.

Weil, J. et al. (2006), 'The relationship of nondirectiveness to genetic counseling: Report of a workshop at the 2003 NSGC Annual Education Conference', *Journal of Genetic Counseling* 15: 85–93.

White, M.T. (1998), 'Decision-making through dialogue: Reconfiguring autonomy in genetic counseling', *Theoretical Medicine and Bioethics* 19:1, 5–19.

Chapter 16
Without Disclosure, No Informed Choice

Peter Miny

Introduction

The prenatal diagnosis of aneuploidy (numerical chromosome anomalies) has evolved into an issue that is addressed during most pregnancies in the developed world. For the moment, the exclusion of aneuploidy is probably the most common practical application of genetic testing. The rapid technical advances and rather complex test approaches, combined with the need to care for individuals from very different cultural, social and educational backgrounds, have created a situation where communication with patients in order to obtain 'informed consent' is a growing challenge. The duty to inform or disclose is, however, an almost universally recognized legal and ethical principle in western democratic societies, and it certainly applies to elective diagnostic procedures. National laws, professional guidelines and statements of ethics boards usually provide a general framework but offer little guidance on practical solutions in daily patient care. Major changes in the way disclosure issues are considered have been induced by court rulings in various countries following charges of negligence. This kind of individual *ex post* definition of how information should have been provided is a burden for patients and their doctors. A preoccupation with legal issues may also draw attention away from fundamental ethical standards in patient care. This chapter contains a brief summary of current evidence-based established options in prenatal risk assessment and diagnosis of aneuploidy. For a complete review and discussion of the scientific evidence the reader should consult the excellent standard reference edited by A. Milunsky (2004), currently available in its 5th edition.

Prenatal Diagnosis at the Beginning of the New Millennium

Due to the rapid advances in our knowledge of the molecular causes of disease, a growing number of different genetic conditions (currently more than 2,000) can be reliably diagnosed in the unborn child or even embryo (GeneReviews <www.genetest.org>; OMIM <www.ncbi.nlm.nih.gov/sites/entrez?db=omim>). In most populations, however, only a small number of pregnancies (probably ±1 per cent) are at increased risk, because these usually monogenic diseases are rare or very rare. This is also true for familial structural chromosome abnormalities (for example, translocations) that carry an increased risk of unbalanced chromosome complements in the offspring. Using new molecular tools in addition to or in lieu of conventional chromosome analysis, cryptic micro-rearrangements have been identified in patients with a normal chromosome count, and may also be an indication for prenatal diagnosis. In contrast to all these rare conditions, aneuploidy is a major cause of pregnancy loss and sufficiently common in newborns, particularly with older mothers, to warrant preventative measures.

Following the successful introduction of chromosome analyses from amniotic fluid cells some 40 years ago, 'advanced' maternal age became the most frequent indication for invasive prenatal diagnosis. A maternal age of 35 years was chosen as the cut-off in most countries and 38 years in others. This took into account the obstetrical risks to the mother and the fetus as well as the age-specific risk for aneuploidy, but nevertheless is rather arbitrary. Forty years ago, approximately 5 per cent of all pregnancies occurred in mothers older than 34 years. The individual risk to a 35-year-old mother of any unbalanced fetal chromosome anomaly is about 0.5 per cent and rises significantly with age. Amniocentesis has also been performed in a rather small number of pregnancies at younger maternal ages on specific parental request.

During the 1980s two important developments introduced alternative options and the need to choose the prenatal diagnosis of aneuploidy. Maternal serum markers, such as human chorionic gonadotropin (hCG), alpha-Fetoprotein (AFP), unconjugated oestriol (E3) and others, measured in the second trimester of pregnancy, offered an improved identification of pregnancies at increased risk for trisomy 21. A multiparameter risk assessment approach including the maternal age, termed risk screening, or second trimester maternal serum screening, was subsequently confirmed by numerous studies to significantly improve the overall detection rate of trisomy 21 against a 5 per cent false positive rate. The concept of risk screening has been and still is difficult to communicate to patients and even to some professionals. Its introduction into clinical practice has been overshadowed by insufficient information on the purpose and limits of the procedure in numerous pregnancies. The evidence base of the concept and its clinical benefits, however, are beyond doubt.

At the same time, chorionic villus sampling (CVS) was introduced as an early alternative to amniocentesis. Large collaborative studies confirmed that the procedure-related obstetrical risks of CVS did not differ significantly from those of amniocentesis in experienced hands. An unexpected rate of mosaicism in the feto-placental unit and its diagnostic sequelae initiated considerable discussion in the early days. Today the issue has been settled and the diagnostic accuracy of chromosome analyses from chorionic villi is considered to be equivalent to chromosome counts from amniotic fluid cells if mosaicism is absent. Around 1 per cent of all tests show mosaicism, confined to the placenta in the majority of cases. Confined placental mosaicism may indicate an increased risk for clinically relevant conditions such as placental insufficiency or uniparental disomy. Today most professionals involved would probably agree that CVS is the method of choice in high-risk situations for cytogenetic as well as molecular genetic testing.

Also during the 1980s, improvements in ultrasound technology started to allow the identification of fetal anomalies and malformations such as nuchal hygroma or heart defects, some of which were highly indicative of aneuploidy. Later, the quantitative assessment of nuchal translucency (NT) between 11 and 14 weeks of gestation became the single most important marker for trisomy 21, as well as for other unbalanced chromosome anomalies, heart defects and a host of additional rare conditions. In a multiparameter first trimester risk screening approach NT, hCG, the pregnancy-associated plasma protein A (PAPP-A) and maternal age, taken together form the current state-of-the-art approach for assessing the risk of trisomy 21 and other aneuploidies. The sensitivity for a given false positive rate is clearly superior to second trimester maternal serum marker testing. A combination of both approaches (integrative risk screening), which has been confirmed to provide an even higher sensitivity (or lower false-positive rate), is advocated by some, and criticized for being impractical for clinical use by others.

On the laboratory side, conventional chromosome analysis has kept its place as the gold standard for the exclusion of aneuploidy and other chromosome anomalies. Major drawbacks at this time (as well as a cost-intensive approach, with little potential for automatization) include the long waiting time for a final result (1 week at minimum, 2 weeks routinely), and a limited resolution requiring a defect size of more than 5–10 mb to be reliably detectable. Advantages are the high reliability and the screening character of this technique. For specific diagnostic questions the method has been successfully complemented by molecular cytogenetic tools such as fluorescence in situ hybridization (FISH). A potential way of reducing the waiting time is opened up by the possibility of direct chromosome preparation from chorionic villi, allowing an overnight chromosome count in high-risk situations, or just for convenience. In contrast to the conventional use of cultured cells this approach has some technical limitations (for example, reduced resolution), and carries a small risk of false-negative results in the presence of mosaicism within the feto-placental unit. When this became obvious the exclusive use of direct preparations was discouraged, and additional analysis of cultured cells was prescribed by international guidelines.

In recent years, alternative approaches to cut down on waiting time after amniocentesis have also been established. These include FISH on uncultured interphase nuclei, or microsatellite analysis after a semi-quantitative polymerase chain reaction (QF-PCR). In contrast to direct chromosome preparation on chorionic villi, both approaches can only detect a limited number of aneuploidies (for example, five chromosomes) and pick up from 70 per cent to 95 per cent of all unbalanced chromosome constitutions, depending on the a priori risk (indication). Both methods are generally considered as add-on options to the conventional chromosome count, but have sometimes replaced the latter, for example in certain parts of the UK, due to budget cutbacks. At present, numerous groups are researching the application of array-based technologies in the prenatal diagnosis of aneuploidy, and it is not hard to guess that the conventional approach will be abandoned for most indications as soon as the costs for arrays come down.

Current Diagnostic Options and the Necessity to Decide

All mothers-to-be, regardless of their age or other known risk factors, are confronted with the need to make choices very early in pregnancy (Figure 16.1). In most health systems this will start with an ultrasound scan late in the first trimester of pregnancy. This scan is not unlikely to provide evidence of an increased risk of chromosome anomalies and be the first step in a chain of events difficult to stop once it has commenced. Given a normal first ultrasound scan, the decision to undergo first trimester risk assessment for aneuploidy is pending. Independently, carrier testing for other genetic conditions has to be addressed if the parents belong to a known risk population or the family history is suspicious. Following the communication of the aneuploidy risk assessment, the important question of invasive testing involving a certain threat to the unborn child will arise. When the decision is made in favour of invasive testing more details may have to be discussed, such as the type of procedure (CVS versus amniocentesis), clinical necessity or parental request for an additional rapid test using FISH or QF-PCR, or other specific requirements. A mid-second trimester ultrasound scan in a specialized centre in order to exclude physical anomalies of the fetus is not part of routine pregnancy care but may be clinically indicated or requested by well-informed parents. The issue of an invasive procedure to exclude aneuploidy may also arise later in pregnancy if sonographic or clinical findings indicate a significant risk increase. For many parents the most difficult and sometimes agonizing decision of all may emerge at any step in this sequence of testing when significant abnormalities are diagnosed.

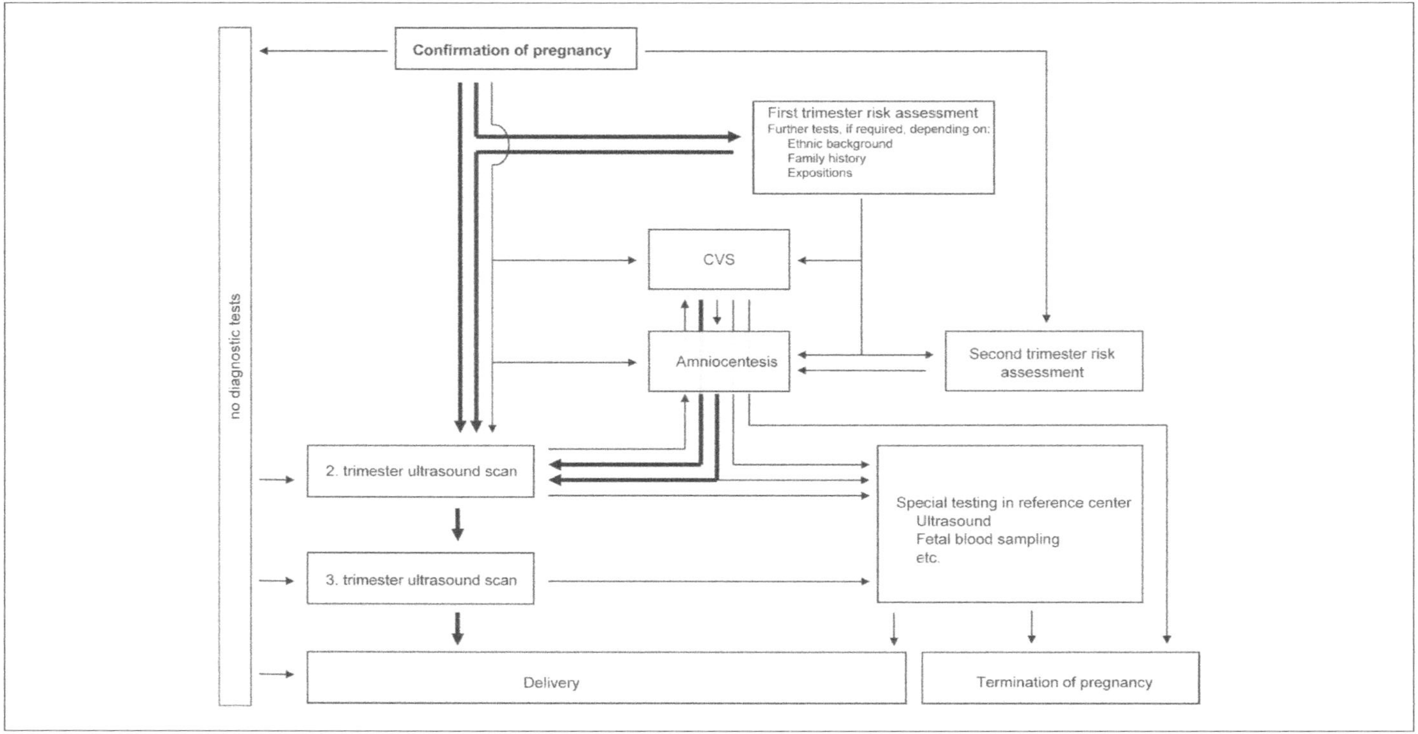

Figure 16.1 Decision options for the prenatal risk assessment and diagnosis of aneuploidy

Note: Decision options for the prenatal risk assessment and diagnosis of aneuploidy; Bold lines indicate the most frequent choices; CVS = chorionic villus sampling or placental biopsy.

The Case for Disclosure

A pointed summary of numerous legal conflicts and ethical disputes over recent decades could read: the non-disclosure of reasonable diagnostic options in pregnancy care is illegal and unethical. Reasonable would be defined as any option with a potential benefit for the patient according to the standards of evidence-based medicine (Nicolaides et al. 2005; Chervenak and McCullough 2004; Sharma et al. 2007).

Legal Aspects

Court rulings in western democratic societies have established the principle of informed consent as a dogma in the relationship of patients and their doctors, replacing earlier more paternalistic approaches that prevailed, at least in parts of the medical community. Recent reviews comment on exemplary court decisions in the US (Pelias 2004) and the UK (Lupton 2005). Regardless of differences in the formal legal treatment of individual cases due to specifics of national jurisdictions, courts elsewhere have also confirmed the obligation of doctors to adequately inform patients on available options prior to obtaining consent. Even in the early days of prenatal diagnosis a German court ruled that a doctor's personal moral or religious beliefs are not acceptable reasons for non-disclosure. A physician had failed to inform a 38-year-old mother of a child with Down Syndrome of the availability of amniocentesis, claiming moral objections against prenatal diagnosis and the subsequent termination of a pregnancy. Two more recent instances from Germany demonstrate that the legal duty to inform may be comprehensive. In a complex litigation case, which became known as the 'Tübinger Fall' and went to the Federal Court, the geneticist involved was held to have a responsibility to inform, during pre-pregnancy counselling, about a paternal chromosomal polymorphism considered to be harmless. The second instance concerns a geneticist/obstetrician who failed to inform about very rare unbalanced cryptic rearrangements leading to Down Syndrome when he performed a chromosome analysis with a normal result on amniotic fluid cells from a mother with an affected brother. He was held responsible to confirm the clinical diagnosis in the affected brother by a chromosome count (1. Zivilsenat, OLG Celle 1 U 63/99). One inevitable consequence of this decision is a significant increase in the number of chromosome analyses that have to be recommended whenever a family member might have Down Syndrome.

From a legal perspective the obligation to inform or disclose is undoubtedly rather absolute and comprehensive (Pelias 2004; Klein and Mahoney 2007). This may, at least in part, be due to the fact that courts usually have to judge an individual situation from the *ex post* perspective and need not be concerned with possible general consequences of their rulings. These circumstances may have significantly contributed to the extension of disclosure requirements criticized by some professionals. Of interest in this context is the occasional exchange of arguments on the disclosure of pre-implantation genetic diagnosis (PGD) information in the German-speaking countries, where this option is illegal. While centres in neighbouring countries are treating increasing numbers of patients from these countries, the disclosure of such information prompted an inquiry in at least one instance in Germany.

Switzerland is one of the first countries in the world to have a law on genetic testing in humans, in effect since April 2007 (<http://www.admin.ch/ch/d/gg/cr/2001/20011087.html>), that codifies internationally recognized standards and provides a framework of regulation with implications for disclosure related to prenatal diagnosis. These include the right to self-determination, the right not to know, the standard of informed consent, and the non-directiveness of counselling. Prenatal testing must be accompanied by pre- and post-test counselling addressing a number of specific topics, which must be documented. Informed consent is also required for laboratory tests or ultrasound scans to assess the risk for genetic conditions.

Ethical Aspects

If legal aspects were the only ones to consider, a multi-page contract designed with the help of a specialized lawyer, to be signed by the patient prior to every procedure would be a fair solution. Decision making in prenatal diagnosis, however, requires a communication process between clinician and patient involving an ethical dimension defined in general terms as the clinician's obligation 'to protect and promote the health-related interests of the patient' (Chervenak and McCullough 2004) within the legal framework. The widely acknowledged ethical principles of beneficence and respect for autonomy apply, and require that the options available as outlined above are addressed, as well as potential benefits or risks, and that the individual decision of the patient is respected. Chervenak and McCullough (2004) introduce the additional ethical concept of the fetus as a patient with relevance for decision making in prenatal diagnosis, and differentiate between the viable and previable fetus. They advocate a balanced directive counselling approach for fetal benefit once viability is reached (usually around 24 weeks of gestation in developed countries) or earlier if the mother 'confers on her fetus the status of being a patient'. Maternal autonomy is considered to be the only authority to confer this status, and counselling, therefore, should be strictly non-directive with a previable fetus.

The principle of beneficence demands not only disclosure of diagnostic options but also an appropriate level of competence, equipment, skill and organization for the application of these options. This has been of concern in the past, when many pregnant women underwent second trimester biochemical risk assessment without proper prior information, consent or with dubious test schemes. Today not all options may be available everywhere. In particular, first trimester risk assessment, currently the best available single approach on which the decision for or against an invasive procedure may be based, is not trivial. The NT measurement, for instance, requires specific skills, a certain case load and participation in quality assessment schemes. If these or other requirements are not met, the principle of beneficence may require the patient to be referred to a specialist centre.

Is There a Case for Non-disclosure?

Patient autonomy clearly includes the rare choice not to be informed about prenatal diagnostic options. In some jurisdictions, including Switzerland, there is a codified right not to know. While non-disclosure is hardly of concern for diagnostic options it may be so for some test results. Communication of fetal sex is one of the controversial issues. Some professionals give highest priority to the patient's autonomy and do disclose, while others, this author among them, decline to communicate non-medical issues that emerge during prenatal diagnosis. This latter policy is clearly covered by the clinician's autonomy not to offer certain services, which in turn has to be disclosed during pretest counselling. In some countries, mainly those with a history of pre- or perinatal sex selection, legal restrictions may apply. The new Swiss law also prohibits prenatal testing for features not directly affecting health, or of fetal sex with the exception of sex-linked disorders. The non-disclosure of test results with no known clinical consequences, such as common chromosomal polymorphisms, is widely accepted. The management of low or very low risk laboratory findings is discussed below.

The question of non-disclosure may come into focus when conventional chromosome analysis is replaced by molecular array-based tools in the future. This technology has the potential to simultaneously detect polymorphisms associated with a risk increase for common conditions such as obesity, diabetes, schizophrenia and perhaps eventually poor school performance.

The growing number of alternative options and the complexity of approaches are certainly not acceptable reasons for non-disclosure. In accordance with central dogmas of western democratic societies, everybody is considered to be capable of and responsible for making the necessary choices for their own life, and as a member of a community, even in most complex matters. This democratic notion of the individual, prevailing in Western societies, necessarily leads to the concept of informed consent when decisions concerning medical care in general or pregnancy care in particular are pending. Difficulties in meeting the requirements of informed consent in routine medical practice do not prove the weakness of the concept, but may rather be due to a lack of time and resources (Green et al. 2004).

Disclosure and Informed Consent: Some Practical Considerations

Disclosure related to the prenatal diagnosis of aneuploidy concerns three main areas and includes information on:

1. The various options for risk assessment as well as invasive procedures required for a definite diagnosis.
2. The obstetric risks of invasive procedures for the mother and the fetus.
3. Laboratory issues such as limitations of tests used, diagnostic errors, failure to obtain a result in time, contamination of cultures with maternal cells and, in particular, test results of doubtful significance.

As outlined above, legal and ethical standards clearly demand that all pregnant women regardless of maternal age are fully informed about current options for assessing the risk of, as well as for diagnosing, fetal aneuploidy. Furthermore, the family history including the ethnic background of both parents and their personal histories must be noted carefully in order to identify additional risk factors and initiate carrier testing if appropriate (Milunsky and Milunsky 2004). The risk of sickle cell anaemia, for instance, may be as high as 1–2 per cent in children of parents from certain parts of Africa. Ideally, these issues should be addressed during preconception counselling in order to avoid decision making and testing under pressure of time. As a side note, an inventive way of premarital non-disclosure carrier testing, popular in some orthodox Jewish communities, involves the individual carrier status remaining undisclosed while the match between two potential partners is tested and disclosed (Prainsack and Siegal 2006).

In experienced hands, ultrasound today is a diagnostic tool with a high potential to detect fetal anomalies indicating a greater or lesser risk of aneuploidy or other genetic conditions. A suspicious scan result may require immediate decisions on further diagnostic procedures and trigger a course of events not originally intended. Mainly for this reason, informed consent prior to ultrasound scans has for some years been required in Switzerland by law. Chervenak and co-workers argued in favour of informed consent for ethical reasons as early as 1989 (Chervenak et al. 1989; prenatal informed consent for sonogram (PICS)), and extended this to NT measurements as part of the first trimester risk assessment for aneuploidy (Chervenak et al. 2005). Bearing in mind the completely different quality of ultrasound scans in routine pregnancy care, as compared to the targeted assessment of specific anomalies in a centre of excellence, which is usually not obvious to the average patient, a detailed discussion of the purpose and limitations of ultrasound in a given situation seems to be highly desirable (Lalor and Devane 2007). Informed consent may help to put unrealistic expectations into perspective and eventually protect the clinician against unfounded accusations (Chervenak and Chervenak 2007).

Not unexpectedly, the disclosure of isolated anomalies or malformations, such as certain heart defects, postaxial polydactyly or others which are of themselves of minor significance but imply an increased risk for a syndromal condition, is one of the most difficult tasks during pregnancy care. One of the most frequent instances is a NT beyond 95 percentiles and a normal chromosome count. Depending on the extent of the NT, a small to moderate unspecific risk increase has to be disclosed, and may be very alarming to the parents when further diagnostic options are unavailable.

Results are normal in the overwhelming majority of all laboratory tests, or show a clear-cut abnormality in most of the remaining cases. Some of the latter may be compatible with a more or less normal development. Classical examples are sex chromosomal aneuploidies such as 47,XXY, 47,XYY, 47,XXX and others. Features to disclose, depending on the individual diagnosis, include infertility, a normal but somewhat lower cognitive performance as compared to siblings, and, occasionally, difficulties with social integration. The rate of pregnancies terminated following the diagnosis of sex chromosome aneuploidy appears to depend on the manner and circumstances in which these features are disclosed (Meschede et al. 1998).

While some of the limitations of conventional chromosome analysis are an integral part of pretest counselling, due to the limited resolution of the microscope or the impossibility of definitely excluding mosaicism, realistically not all rare unexpected findings can and should be disclosed. Many findings, such as abnormalities in a single or two cells, only marginally, if at all, increase the risk of clinically significant mosaicism for this abnormality. Non-disclosure should be considered as an option to prevent unfounded parental anxiety. Given the current court rulings, however, the chances are high that the *ex post* appraisal of the non-disclosure would found to be negligent. It is important to remember that the baseline rate for any anomaly in newborns is significant, and a causal relation between laboratory and clinical findings does not need to be established. In instances like these the court-defined legal obligation to disclose may collide with the ethical principle of beneficence, an example of defensive medicine (Kessler et al. 2006) that unilaterally protects the interests of the clinician. From a population-based perspective, disclosure of very rare events will put immense burdens on hundreds of couples, some of whom will undergo additional testing and accept the risk of losing the pregnancy.

This author's admittedly defensive approach has been to disclose, but also to try hard to put small risks into a realistic perspective in an understandable way, for example by comparison with risks in everyday life, in order to help prevent disproportionate concern and unreasonable decision making. Of crucial importance, in particular when counselling patients with restricted background knowledge, is also to adjust their sometimes unrealistic expectations of the benefits and limitations of prenatal genetic testing, which are often based on oversimplified media reports. It should be made very clear that all options discussed in pretest counselling are intended to assess an increased risk and subsequently exclude the specific condition if necessary. The overall baseline risk of any fetal abnormality will not change significantly after a normal test result.

There is evidence that the benefits of prenatal diagnosis are acknowledged by a large proportion of women and their partners (Green et al. 2004; Dahl et al. 2006a and b), but also that the fundamental requirements of true informed consent are rather frequently not met. Lack of time and resources, as well as inappropriate reimbursement schemes, demand compromises in daily practice. Even if true informed consent is not easily or always achievable (Rehmann-Sutter 2006), it must remain the standard reference governing the relation between clinicians and their patients. Convincing alternative concepts are in any case lacking.

References

Chasen, S.T. et al. (2001), 'Prenatal informed consent for sonogram: The time for first-trimester nuchal translucency has come', *Journal of Ultrasound in Medicine* 20:11, 1147–52.

Chervenak, F.A. et al. (1989), 'Prenatal informed consent for sonogram: An indication for obstetric ultrasonography', *American Journal of Obstetric Gynecology* 161:4, 857–60.

Chervenak, F.A. et al. (2005), 'Clinical implications of the ethics of informed consent for first-trimester risk assessment for trisomy 21', *Seminars in Perinatology* 29:4, 277–9.

Chervenak, F.A. and Chervenak, J.L. (2007), 'Medical legal issues in obstetric ultrasound', *Clinical Perinatology* 34:2, 299–308.

Chervenak, F.A. and McCullough, L.B. (2004), *Ethical Issues in the Diagnosis and Management of Genetic Disorders in the Fetus* (5th edition) (Baltimore and London: The Johns Hopkins University Press).

Dahl, K. et al. (2006a), 'Informed consent: Providing information about prenatal examinations', *Acta Obstetricia et Gynecologica Scandinavica* 85:12, 1420–5.

Dahl, K. et al. (2006b), 'Informed consent: Attitudes, knowledge and information concerning prenatal examinations', *Acta Obstetricia et Gynecologica Scandinavica* 85:12, 1414–9.

Green, J.M. et al. (2004), 'Psychosocial aspects of genetic screening of pregnant women and newborns: A systematic review', *Health Technology Assessment* iii, ix–x, 1–109.

Kessler, D.P. et al. (2006), 'Effects of the medical liability system in Australia, the UK, and the USA', *Lancet* 368:9531, 240–6.

Klein, R.D. and Mahoney, M.J. (2007), 'Medical legal issues in prenatal diagnosis', *Clinical Perinatology* 34:2, 287–97.

Lalor, J.G. and Devane, D. (2007), 'Information, knowledge and expectations of the routine ultrasound scan', *Midwifery* 23:1, 13–22.

Lupton, M. (2005), 'Informed consent: Can a patient ever be fully informed?' *Current Opinion in Obstetrics and Gynecology* 17:6, 601–4.

Meschede, D. et al. (1998), 'Low rates of pregnancy termination for prenatally diagnosed Klinefelter syndrome and other sex chromosome polysomies', *American Journal of Medical Genetics* 80:4, 330–4.

Milunsky, A. (ed.) (2004), *Genetic Disorders and the Fetus* (5th edition) (Baltimore and London: The Johns Hopkins University Press).

Milunsky, A. and Milunsky, J.M. (2004), *Genetic Counseling: Preconception, Prenatal, and Perinatal* (5th edition) (Baltimore and London: The Johns Hopkins University Press).

Nicolaides, K.H. et al. (2005), 'Evidence-based obstetric ethics and informed decision-making by pregnant women about invasive diagnosis after first-trimester assessment of risk for trisomy 21', *American Journal of Obstetrics and Gynecology* 193:2, 322–6.

Pelias, M.Z. (2004), *Medicolegal Aspects of Prenatal Diagnosis* (5th edition) (Baltimore and London: The Johns Hopkins University Press).

Prainsack, B. and Siegal, G. (2006), 'The rise of genetic couplehood? A comparative view of premarital genetic testing', *BioSocieties* 1, 17–36.

Rehmann-Sutter, C. (2006), 'Is informed consent actually possible?', *Therapeutische Umschau* 63:11, 699–702.

Sharma, G. et al. (2007), 'Ethical considerations of early (first vs. second trimester) risk assessment disclosure for trisomy 21 and patient choice in screening versus diagnostic testing', *American Journal of Medical Genetics Part C: Seminars in Medical Genetics* 145:1, 99–104.

Chapter 17
Allowing Agency: An Ethical Model for Communicating Personal Genetic Information

Christoph Rehmann-Sutter

The increasing availability of personal genetic information (a term that we will have to define) creates situations containing challenging, sometimes even morally coercive elements that individuals may experience as difficult to handle. Genetic counselling is supposed to be a measure that allows patients or clients to arrive at self-determined decisions. But genetic counselling can also be a place where new obligations and restrictions are created. From the perspective of bio-politics and bio-governance, genetic counselling can also be seen as a stabilizing element within a preventive regime of 'liberal eugenics' (Habermas 2003), regardless of how nondirective the counselling dialogue is. The ostentatious avoidance of directiveness even assures moral legitimacy and averts the accusation that genetics is a collective and coercive measure at the population or 'gene pool' level. However the liberty provided in these circumstances may be only a reduced form of freedom just strong enough to serve the justificatory needs of a biomedical construction of society. A series of ethical questions have been and need to be raised. I will focus on just a few, which are connected with the communicative acts of exchanging genetic health information with personal impact. My focus is however larger than genetic counselling and includes communication between family members too.

Genetic counselling in professional medical settings is an exemplar of genetic communication, certainly the one most widely investigated and morally reflected upon. There is a vast literature here that has no counterpart on the side of 'lay' genetic dialogues. I will take advantage of the high quality of the available literature and the well-developed professional deontology of genetic counselling, reading it with a critical eye and to uncover lessons for non-professional communicative action. My aim in this chapter is to identify key elements for an ethical model of communication of personal genetic information. Obviously, nondirectiveness does not work outside the professional counselling encounter, because family relationships do not end after a 'session' and require much higher levels of mutual engagement and sharing of responsibility. This responsibility always has both an epistemological and a moral side. Medical, biological and genetic knowledge has to be transformed, interpreted and appropriated ('embodied', as Abby Lippman

1999 has aptly described it) in order to make sense in a particular situation. The moral side comprises the practical dilemmas that may arise: Who should know? How I am going to tell, what and when? Which preventive measures should be taken? Or, in the case of prenatal diagnosis, should a test be taken that might lead to a decision about abortion?

Under the term 'personal genetic information' I understand information that (i) is directly or indirectly produced through genetic diagnostics, genetic tests, sequencing or microarrays (gene-chips) that measure gene activity patterns etc. and (ii) has an impact for an individual. The word 'genetic' has a *pragmatic* component referring to the use of laboratory tools created by molecular and cell biology. But it has also a distinct *meaning*: it provides (or promises to provide) knowledge about the past and future developmental potential of our bodies. It seems to be knowledge about factors that are beyond choice, making us what we are by nature.

I start by reconstructing the discussion about the sense and the limitations of the principle of nondirectiveness in genetic counselling.

What is Nondirectiveness?

There is a striking incoherence between the sociality of genetic knowledge and the individualistic underpinning of the ethics of genetic counselling. For several decades, the criterion of 'nondirectiveness' has been considered to be the gold standard for respecting the autonomy of clients in genetic counselling. One question that will be discussed in this chapter is whether this incoherence is due to the individualistic background of genetic counselling ethics (which could be changed without rejecting a revised version of nondirectiveness and the claims of autonomy), or to the ideals of nondirectiveness and autonomy themselves.

Genetic knowledge is *social* because it is very frequently knowledge about more than one person. It is social in three directions: *backward* because it reveals knowledge about ancestors, *forward* because it anticipates the features of descendants and *lateral* because it has implications for other members of the family. In addition, genetic knowledge is not raw data but is *interpreted* within a social context of symbols, texts, narratives and discourses about genes, embodiment and identities, and as information with a meaning, genetic knowledge is always therefore *mediated.*

In an introductory book to genetic counselling for professionals written about 10 years ago, Ann Platt Walker introduced nondirectiveness as a crucial component of the 'philosophy and ethos of genetics services and counselling'. She notes that adherence to a 'nonprescriptive' approach 'is perhaps the most defining feature of genetic counselling' (1998, 8). Jon Weil (2003), in a more recent critical assessment of nondirectiveness, begins by emphasizing the central role of this principle: 'For thirty years nondirectiveness has been the guiding principle or central ethos of genetic counselling' (199). According to these and many other statements in the literature, nondirectiveness has been the key element of normative self-description of genetic counselling practice: its defining feature, the guiding principle, a central ethos. They leave open whether nondirectiveness is actually practised in reality. But first we need to know more precisely what the *principle* of nondirectiveness is supposed to be.

Walker (1998, 8) gives the following definition: 'Although the counsellor can use clinical judgment in choosing what information is most likely to be important and helpful in a client's adjustment to a diagnosis or decision making, it should be presented fairly and evenhandedly – not with the purpose of encouraging a particular course of action.'

An early outline was given in a workshop of the (US) National Genetics Foundation and reported by F. Clarke Fraser in 1974. Genetic counselling is 'a communication process' that:

> […] involves an attempt by one or more appropriately trained persons to help the individual or family (1) comprehend the medical facts […]; (2) appreciate the way heredity contributes to the disorder, and the risk of recurrence in specified relatives; (3) understand the options for dealing with the risk of recurrence; (4) choose the course of action which seems appropriate to them in view of their risk and their family goals and act in accordance with that decision; and (5) make the best possible adjustment to the disorder in an affected family member and/or to the risk of recurrence of that disorder. (Fraser 1974, 637)

From Fraser's definition it becomes clear that the model situation of genetic testing was prenatal diagnosis, and the course of action (which should not be directed by the counsellor) meant the termination or continuation of the pregnancy. Wertz and Fletcher (2004, 36) quote another definition of a committee of the American Society of Human Genetics in 1974 that differs in relevant ways: '1) helping clients understand their options and the present state of medical knowledge, so they can make informed decisions, 2) helping clients to adjust to and cope with their genetic problems, 3) the removal or lessening of patient guilt and anxiety, 4) helping clients achieve their parenting goals, and 5) the prevention of disease or abnormality.'

Wertz and Fletcher wrongly ascribe this formulation to the quoted 1974 Fraser paper. I don't want to discuss here the consistency of this second version of the five components, which seem questionable to say the least.[1] The real Fraser paper

1 Is prevention of abnormality or the removal of patient guilt about abortion really a step toward a free decision? Elsewhere (Rehmann-Sutter, forthcoming), I have compared the articles on prenatal diagnosis in the three editions of the *Encyclopedia of Bioethics* covering the years 1978–2004, and found that the early texts take a strong population and community perspective on genetics, making the women as individuals and moral agents nearly invisible, whereas the articles in the latest edition regard the situation of the women concerned as central. There was a structural shift of the ethical space.

discusses the question of directive or nondirective counselling and distinguishes three types of counsellors. One minority view is the strictly nondirective approach (believing 'that counselling should stop at the point where an estimation of risk is given and that the parents should make up their own minds what to do', 649). The other extreme is 'the authoritative father-figure type (more often a physician than a genetic counsellor) who tells the parents not to have more children, or to go ahead, as the case may be' (ibid.). But the majority of counsellors in Fraser's account take neither extreme: 'Most counsellors would refrain from directly telling the counsellee what to do, but most would at least talk the matter over and point out the various factors that might be considered' (ibid.). In the current discussions of nondirectiveness, we often hear simpler descriptions such as: genetic counselling 'should not be prescriptive either with regard to testing or non-testing or with regard to the response to a given test result' (Holm 2005, 207). In this description we see one goal. The geneticist should not prescribe what the patient should *do* with the information, or, in pretest counselling, whether a certain test should be taken at all.

One difficulty with defining the nondirectiveness principle arises from the variety of situations of genetic counselling practice *beyond* prenatal testing. The course of action in response to a given test result obviously depends on the situation in which a genetic test is performed. If it is a diagnostic test, the response can be the application of one therapeutic treatment (and not another); if it is a pre-symptomatic genetic test, the response can be a preventive measure; if it is a prenatal test, the response can be termination of the pregnancy; if it is a preimplantation genetic diagnosis (PGD), the response can be the non-implantation of the embryo into the uterus after *in vitro* fertilization (IVF). The degree of required openness of the decision about the response varies, being presumably minimal in the case of a diagnostic test (where the course of action is essentially therapeutic and integrated within general medical treatment) and maximal in the case of a prenatal genetic test (where the course of action may involve abortion). In PGD the conditions under which the embryo should be implanted may be more or less decided before the test is actually done. There, the autonomy of the patient has its proper place at the point of decision making about IVF and in the planning of PGD, but, because of lack of time, is less apparent in the interpretation of the results after embryo biopsy. And in pre-symptomatic testing or cancer risk counselling (at least in cases where high probabilities are detected) the medical advice will also be based on a therapeutic ethos, if it is clear how to avoid risk factors and which preventive measures are appropriate. Nondirectiveness was introduced historically in the context of prenatal diagnosis and has difficulty in acknowledging other situations in which genetic tests are taken.

Another difficulty appears in Walker's quoted statement: the counsellor should not intend to encourage a particular course of action by the counsellee, but on the other hand they cannot avoid using clinical judgment in choosing *which information* is most likely to be important and helpful. Obviously however, much of the client's adjustment to a diagnosis and much of the client's decision making will in fact depend on which information the counsellor finds useful or necessary.

To sum up, nondirectiveness could be defined through clear cut rules:

- providing complete unbiased information; and
- restraining from giving practical advice.

But it is clear that this cannot be realized in a strict way and in practice necessarily involves compromises.

The reason *why* nondirectiveness has gained such central importance in medical genetics can be explained historically. Medical genetics, as it was widely established first in the context of prenatal genetic diagnosis in the late 1960s (after the first successful demonstration of the normal fetal karyotype from cultured amniotic fluid cells in 1965 and the first abnormal karyotypes in 1968; see Milunsky 1978), had a strong anti-eugenic programme. Eugenics was a central element in Nazi ideology and there was a widespread wish to reject eugenics after World War II. Nondirectiveness was a justificatory tool. 'The philosophy stems from a firm belief that genetic counselling should – insofar as possible – be devoid of any eugenic motivation' (Walker 1998, 8).

'Genetic counselling', a term coined by the American Sheldon Reed, in 1947 to replace the earlier 'genetic hygiene' or 'genetic advice,' began in the shadow of the Eugenics Movenment and of World War II. Its founders sought to distinguish it from earlier, more directive forms of interaction in order to avoid accusations of possible coercion' (Wertz and Fletcher 2004, 36).

Individualism was a crucial factor for the establishment of a stable actor network of medical genetics, because it fended off any analogy to eugenics ('the unthinkable, the impossible, the "this must never happen again"', Wieser and Karner 2006, 36) and could provide the basis for a morally acceptable framework: Nobody is forced to anything, everybody can decide for themself. Therefore, the aims of genetic counselling were to provide information that is necessary for an informed decision making, not to influence the decision about the termination of a pregnancy. Information about the future health of our children, if it can be made available by tests, is a positive thing, something we can want and have a right to. Being forced to terminate certain pregnancies, on the other hand, would be an ethical and political nightmare. As Wieser and Karner point out, there were other supporting factors as well: to protect themselves against legal liability, doctors have an interest in informing the patient and not deciding for them (see also Wied et al., this vol.).

If nondirectiveness was mainly a solution formed within a historical perspective, it created new moral problems in the present. In their sociological study of the development of medical genetics in Austria, Bernhard Wieser and Sandra Karner found that the nondirectiveness regime dramatically radicalized the situation of pregnant women. 'Being able to decide for oneself also means being obliged to do so and consequently being obliged to take full responsibility for the decision'

(Wieser and Karner 2006, 39). The individualist appeal in the nondirectiveness rule created a false picture, because actually the responsibility for the practice of prenatal selection is dispersed between many actors. The women slide into it in normal prenatal care. It is a socio-technical system, a regime from which it is very difficult to escape. Individualization of the decision-making process therefore also had ideological components.

For the women concerned, a moral *aporia* is created: a woman is obliged to be autonomous in a decision which calls her identity as a caring mother into question. Wieser and Karner call this a 'conflicting individualization process', when genetic examinations let the woman ask: 'Who am I as a mother if I am calling my unborn child's life in question?' (ibid.). An abortion is not just a decision; it puts many women under serious psychological distress. From the point of view of the woman, the individualist assumption that she alone should also carry the full responsibility for this decision can be worrying, even cynical, given the real societal background.

Choice promises freedom but it is at the same time inescapable. In present prenatal care practice, where women are given risk assessments from nuchal translucency in ultrasound (Schwennesen, this vol.), *not* to decide is no longer an option. The woman is already caught in a regime that governs by posing *inescapable* ethical questions (Wieser and Karner 2006, 43). If there is no counselling prior to screening, no free decision taking all potential consequences into account, talk of decision autonomy has become contradictory. But even with pre-screening counselling, it is difficult to gather all the consequences and give them their proper weight. The decision about screening looks very harmless, just a first step in a course of micro-decisions, leaving everything open. It is a decision that is easy to take, because it is just about getting a better picture of the risks and chances; no invasive procedure and no risk of miscarriage is involved.

Wieser and Karner draw the conclusion that this development has actually led to the fall of the paradigm of decision autonomy in genetic counselling. If the first step is done, it is already too late. The whole decision has become too complicated to grasp, therefore patients disentangle the whole into parts and bits, taking an overwhelming decision in a piecemeal fashion (Scully et al. 2007). While this can be favourably interpreted as a means to safeguard moral agency, it can also be seen as radically questioning individualized responsibility, at least in a framework where a decision is systematically offered in little spoonfuls, each relatively sweet to swallow.

There is currently increasing awareness among medical geneticists and genetic counsellors that nondirectiveness should be either replaced by another guiding principle or integrated into a more differentiated and broader ethos. As Walker points out in the same paragraph from which I have already quoted, the principle of nondirectiveness does not always meet the needs of the patients:

> While this is a time-honored tradition, for the counsellor to avoid expressing *any* opinions in all instances could be at times counterproductive. A client should

> expect a genetics professional to be able to provide guidance in some cases – particularly in the presence of complex genetic and medical issues, conflicting data, or choices that raise problematic moral issues. Being entirely nondirective under such circumstances leaves clients to flounder. (Walker 1998, 8)

This is a serious point and leads to a conceptual contradiction: to ward off eugenics, nondirectiveness should protect the individual against the collective. But if the needs of the individual do *not* demand the counsellor to be 'entirely nondirective', the principle of nondirectiveness cannot do precisely what it is supposed to do, that is, to protect the needs of the individual.

Dorothy Wertz and John Fletcher (2004) have empirically examined geneticists' and genetic counsellors' ethical views in an extended survey covering 37 nations worldwide in 1993–1995 (N = 2906). They asked for participants' attitude to 26 different genetic conditions within a spectrum of gravity (from anencephaly to a predisposition to alcoholism or to severe obesity) and offered a choice of six possible responses (from 'urge parents to carry to term' to 'urge termination', or 'not tell them this particular result'; 'try to be as unbiased as possible' was in the middle) to each condition. They found an overall pattern:

> Geneticists in English-speaking countries would try to present unbiased information about almost all fetal conditions, with the exception of anencephaly. Geneticists in some northern European countries, especially Denmark, Finland, Germany, the Netherlands, Norway and Sweden would be unbiased about some, but not all conditions, and not to the same extent. Belgium and France are less unbiased than other northern European nations. Outside English-speaking nations, most counselling is biased. Most, though not all, of the bias is pessimistic, and most of it occurs by presenting slanted information so that parents will have an abortion without the counsellor suggesting it directly rather than by directly urging abortion. (38 f.)

If we believe these carefully collected data we see that nondirectiveness has been an *ideal*, important for stabilizing the social role of genetic counselling within a broader actor network, but not a common reality in genetic counselling practice. As an ethos for genetic counselling, the principle of nondirectiveness proves idealistic.

In a paper written by six leading American geneticists and summarizing the results of a workshop at the 2003 Annual Education Conference of the National Society of Genetic Counselors, Jon Weil et al. (2006) bring together a whole list of criticisms of the nondirectiveness principle. Among other things they suggest that it inhibits the development of effective counselling approaches; it is itself a value-laden approach; it provides an insufficient basis for a profession that addresses issues such as abortion and quality of life; it fails to address the social and economic context within which individual decision making takes place; and it is inadequate when applied to new areas of genetic counselling such as cancer risk counselling. Weil et al. impressively demonstrate the shortcomings of rationalist individualism and of its correlated ideal of nondirective counselling. An ethic that derives its analysis from the figurations of a rational and autonomous person is cut off from the very interrelatedness which is essential to and inherent in genetic information. The reality of counselling is thicker, deeper, more ambivalent and morally more demanding. The simplifications that are contained in the idea of the patient as a rational decision maker tend to alienate the ethical discourse from the local worlds of those involved, be they counsellors, researchers, patients or other family members.

Re-modelling Genetic Dialogue

But the search for alternatives is not so easy. Nondirectiveness had (and still has) a social reality as a counterfactual defensive description. It works like a myth that stabilizes the network of actors in genetic counselling, especially in the realm of prenatal testing, holding up the image that the medical offer of prenatal testing is 'innocent'. Taken out of context it shows a false consciousness and as an ethical ideal of genetic counselling it is misleading. In the following I want to reconstruct very briefly two strands of recent discussion on ethical ideals, one showing to advantage the full implications of psychosocial counselling, the other triggered by the discovery of distributed responsibility.

Jon Weil (2003) made a new start and suggested that psychosocial counselling should replace nondirectiveness: 'The central ethos of genetic counselling should be to bring the psychosocial component into every aspect of the work' (207). This takes up a strong development going back to early advocates of psychotherapy such as Carl Rogers (1942). His 'person-centred counselling' is still one of the most influential theoretical approaches for addressing psychosocial issues. It is however puzzling to suggest that Rogerian psychosocial counselling should now replace nondirectiveness, because the stance of nondirectiveness belongs to Roger's own central tenets (Marks 1993); it was the term describing his personal approach to psychotherapy, before he renamed his system 'client-centred therapy' (Kessler 1997). But nondirectiveness in the context of psychosocial counselling is a broader model than nondirectiveness as it was applied in a narrow form in genetic counselling. This psychosocial model of nondirectiveness describes the role and task of the genetic counsellor in terms of somebody who does much more than just provide the clients with relevant medical information and genetic facts together with the options open to them. The psychosocial ethos is, as Barbara Bowles Biesecker (2003) explains, opposed to a purely medical model of counselling. And counselling is not teaching. It is a different way of addressing information: 'It is difficult to diverge from the practice of medical genetics sufficiently to exercise our skills as attendees to the loss, hurt, frustration, anger, indecision, and disappointment that our clients experience. Yet it is both the cognitive and the affective meaning of genetic information and their lived experiences that are most relevant to genetic counselling clients' (215).

But Biesecker is also cautious about just promoting a new 'central ethos'. Given that similar proposals were made much earlier by prominent scholars in the US such as Seymour Kessler (1980) and Joan Marks (1993), it would be naïve to believe that the proposal of a new central ethos will now change the practice. Herself a supporter of a psychological/social model for genetic counselling she calls for the definition of the 'specific process and outcome variables that represent a psychosocial ethos'. We need data identifying barriers and proposals for solutions to overcome them. Nondirectiveness cannot be regarded as the obstacle responsible for limiting the establishment of the psychosocial paradigm.

The workshop report on nondirectiveness presented by Weil et al (2006) contains a series of interesting observations made by genetic counsellors that can be read like a focus group analysis. First, it was clearly stated by participants that nondirectiveness has its proper place within a more general goal of promoting the autonomy of patients. Genetic counsellors should 'help' patients in the best possible way. Weil summarizes the discussion by saying that speakers at the workshop supported the idea of 'more proactive counselling from a variety of perspectives: giving more attention to the wants and needs of counsellees, creating a comfortable setting within which counsellees can use as many of their faculties as possible, facilitating active decision-making, implementing meaningful informed consent, and identifying and processing genetic counsellors' personal and professional values' (90). In his commentary Weil clarifies the role of nondirectiveness: 'It may serve as a component of the ethical basis for clinical practice, *insofar* as it supports attention to and respect for client beliefs, values, and personal circumstances; promotes client autonomy, within an appropriate cultural framework and supports effective, knowledgeable decision-making. However, it is not a theory of clinical practice, and thus it cannot serve as a primary theoretical underpinning for the profession' (91, my emphasis). A parallel argument is made by Scully (this vol.) who questions whether the rule of abstaining from giving any direction in the counselling encounter serves patient autonomy. Promotion of autonomy is the underlying ethical rationale, and nondirectiveness is important insofar as it serves it.

A second point in Weil's commentary to the workshop report is relevant, because it explains how autonomy can be understood in this context: The counsellee is involved in a 'psycho-education process that involves two-way interactions between the genetic counsellor and each counsellee, as well as more complex interactions involving three, four, etc., individuals, both present and absent from the counselling session' (91). In this interaction that extends beyond the counselling dyad, medical facts and psychosocial aspects are woven together in order 'to help patients understand their situation and make good health decisions for themselves and their families' (ibid.). I note that autonomy is *not*, as a long tradition of scholarship in bioethics has taken for granted, understood as the capacity of the individual to make a rational decision that takes all relevant facts into consideration. Autonomy is here rather a *relational* capacity of the self: the patient wants to make good health care decisions for themself and the family. And this capacity is to be supported in a two-way communicative setting together with a counsellor, who helps to weave together medical facts, emotional meanings and the implications for others outside the consulting office.

This understanding of the very basic ethos of genetic counselling has no exclusive link to the particular situation of prenatal diagnosis but can be explained in further details of all possible settings, including paediatric, preventive and predictive settings such as cancer risk counselling.

A further step was the publication of the report from a consensus conference among directors of genetic counselling graduate programmes in the US by Patricia McCarthy Veach, Dianne M. Bartels and Bonnie S. LeRoy (2007). They started by defining the structure of a 'model of practice', which in their terminology is different from a 'definition' of that practice or from the 'scope' of that practice. The model of practice 'constitutes a systematic method of problem solving that is applied to clinical situations and is based on scientific process. A model provides: (1) a tentative theoretical framework for organizing interrelated theory, research and practice; (2) a common frame of reference for the systematic assessment of patients and the development of interventions; (3) a common frame for all practitioners in the clinical setting […]; and (4) consistency and continuity of care in the delivery of clinical services' (714). This approach can meet many of the shortcomings of the 'central ethos' approach, which were pointed out by Biesecker (2003) and discussed above. The central ethos is embodied in a model of practice. It is much broader, closer to real experiences and contains many levels that can be implemented practically and monitored.

In the presentation of key elements for a model of practice Veach et al. use a four component approach according to Rieh and Ray (1974) who describe a model of practice as containing '(1) *Tenet* – a principle, doctrine, or belief held in common by members of a group; (2) *Goal* – aim, purpose; content specified as aim for activity; (3) *Strategy* […]; and (4) *Behaviour*' (ibid.). The consensus conference resulted in the formulation of five tenets and their corresponding goals, strategies and behaviours. I cannot go into all in detail but I want to summarize the proposed tenets and goals because they are particularly informative for understanding the ethos incorporated in the model (see Table 17.1).

Table 17.1 Genetic counselling model of practice – postulated tenets and goals

Tenet	Goal
Genetic information is key	Counsellor knows what information to impart. Counsellor presents genetic information. Patient is informed. Patient gains new perspectives.
Relationship is integral to genetic counselling	Genetic counsellor and patient establish a bond. Good genetic counsellor-patient communication. Counsellor characteristics positively influence process.
Patient autonomy must be supported	Establish working contract. Integrate familial and cultural context into counselling relationship and decisions. Patient feels empowered and more in control. Collaborative decisions facilitated.
Patients are resilient	Recognize patient strengths. Adaptation. Empowerment.
Patient emotions make a difference	Counsellor and patient know patient concerns. Patient's family dynamics are understood by counsellor and patient. Patient self-esteem is maintained/increased.

Source: Veach et al. 2007.

The tenet that genetic information is key expresses the presumption that being informed is in general better than being uninformed. Patients who attend genetic counselling desire genetic information and want to have it explained in a way they can understand. They want to understand genetic information in order to be able to draw their conclusions out of it. A second tenet says that relationship between counsellor and patient is key. Genetic counselling is therefore seen as 'a relationally based helping activity whose outcomes are only as good as the connection established between the counsellor and patient' (721). The tenet concerning autonomy suggests that the patient knows best and therefore should be self-directed regarding practical decisions. The individual and their socio-cultural and familial context are valued and respected. Perhaps a surprise is the inclusion of a tenet that patients are resilient. The explanation is that counsellors presume that the typical patient (not each individual patient) is hardy enough to participate as an equal in the genetic counselling process. They can adapt to difficult and painful situations. Given appropriate information and adequate psychological support, patients can draw on their capacity to learn. Assisting clients involves recognizing their strengths in the face of genetic information. Several times the word 'empowerment' is used to express what is at stake.[2]

2 The empowerment perspective has been carefully introduced to the autonomy discussion from a psychological perspective by McConkie-Rosell and Sullivan (1999).

Dialogue in the Context of Other Actors

A second strain of discussion that is relevant for understanding the impacts of genetic communications comes from the sociological and anthropological camps. A common theme is the social construction of the individual decision situation. One can analyze the biomedical construct that creates a desire, even a responsibility to consider genetic testing, counselling and to engage in decision making as a system of 'distributed action'. It is not just 'the test and me' or 'the counsellor and me'. There is a much larger socio-technical system behind it that produces the apparent dyad. The process of individualization of responsibility, for example, for prenatal diagnosis, is morally not neutral because it places the burden of a system of pre-organized decisions on the shoulders of essentially one person – the pregnant woman.

'Actor Network Theory' is a theoretical approach that provides a framework for analyzing socialized action in socio-technical systems. Actions, according to Bruno Latour (1999), can be distributed over many 'actants'. Actants can be persons, institutions or even objects, predominantly human-made (like ultrasound scanners, laboratory tools, DNA test kits or sequencers). This framework allows us to analyze practices as actions performed by hybrid conglomerations of different persons and things, all necessary and co-responsible for the shape and meaning of the action: 'human-technology conjunctions' (Wieser 2006, 124). They realize the action as a collective achievement. And it is clear that behind the technical things involved in such conjunctions stand other human actors who, intentionally or unintentionally, have constructed, produced or purveyed these things that are now used for this purpose and that shape the plans of the users.

For prenatal testing this approach has obvious application. Consider the changes that have happened in the practice of prenatal testing. Increasingly there are risk assessment examinations before invasive testing is carried out. Non-invasive screening methods produce increasingly reliable indicators for the realization of invasive examinations. This means that examination begins in an earlier stage of pregnancy. Non-invasive screening methods are applied to more patients, and to younger women. Ultrasound devices are available in most gynaecological practices. The risk is no longer spread over a group (for instance an age group) but appears as individualized risk estimation. The decision is sequenced and split into a series of subdecisions. One examination leads to the next, one result calls for the next decision. The decision about screening (in contrast to testing) is normally not perceived by the women as such, or it appears as so provisional that it is easy to take (the only outcome is that the next decision can be taken with better information, and it is not invasive). Counselling is offered before and after invasive tests but rarely prior to non-invasive tests. All these elements together (I have taken them from Wieser 2006, 106–108) shape the 'action' of prenatal diagnosis. The woman plays one part in a larger choreography that she has not written herself. Her part, however, essentially implies the adoption of the key responsibility for the whole distributed action, performing an individualistic account of autonomy.

Ethics, after realizing the distributed character of responsibility and the *function* of individualist interpretations of autonomy, can no longer naively play along the preset rules, reinforcing and legitimizing the system by providing the moral background theory for individual decision making. Ethics should rather draw attention to the real patterns of responsibility. They can be revealed when looking beyond the assignment of responsibility to the individual. Recognizing the distributed nature of responsibility in the essentially social practice of prenatal diagnosis must therefore have consequences for the understanding of ethical issues in prenatal diagnosis. 'If action is distributed this can only mean that responsibility is also distributed' (Wieser 2006, 125). In other words, the individualization of action is a kind of false consciousness, functioning to stabilize the actor network as it is, that is, the Foucauldian 'biopower' is working through the network. Individualizing forces must be one type of factor to be recognized by the individual involved, in order to become capable of coping with the demands of the situation.

In another essay, Wieser draws out some consequences for the ethics of counselling and calls for a deepened understanding of empowerment in counselling. The woman is coping with a regime, a form of informal governance. In order to gain moral agency in this situation, she must become capable of understanding what happens, where her options are, how she can participate in reshaping power. This is an important aspect of empowerment and should be further developed in future ethical studies on genetic counselling. Charting responsibilities in a complex network of actors and decoding the hidden programmes in technological arrangements is a crucial step. The individual then can participate more actively. As Margaret Urban Walker pointed out, vulnerability in such networks is socially constructed. And moral philosophy has the task of deconstructing and reconstructing the social patterns of responsibility, in order to create spaces of agency: 'But practices of responsibility are not only ones of assignment. They also include ones of accepting or refusing, deflecting or negotiating, specific assignments of responsibility' (Walker 1998, 94). This may also change the role of ethics, as Wieser (2005) mentions: ethics is not just a communication or a branch of philosophy dealing with rational arguments, but it is also *a place and organization of a process* that allows – more or less efficiently – for clarification and the empowerment of those involved.[3]

---

3 There is an interesting approach from organizational ethics that could be relevant here, as Heller and Dinges (2006) have suggested. The concrete ethical implications however remain unclear. Heller and Dinges suggest that decisions in genetic counselling should be taken in the framework of clinical ethics counselling, involving medical and genetics personnel, as well as a psychologist, an ethicist, even a mother of a handicapped child. I understand the reasons for this proposal: however I think that such a large assembly of experts might be daunting for the pregnant woman who may prefer to keep her privacy and interact only with individuals she knows and trusts personally.

Outside the Counselling Office

Approaching an ethics of genetic communication, we need to be aware that when we speak of 'counselling' we always assume a professional to be there counselling and a client who desires to be informed and supported in some way. The professional setting is however not the only social place where communication of personal genetic information occurs and where ethical questions about disclosure or non-disclosure arise.

Examples are easy to find. In order to know which mutation could be present in a patient, the geneticist frequently needs to know the mutation of another person in the family who is affected by the disease. The patient will frequently be the one to ask this person for a blood sample or for test results. Some genetic knowledge, provided upon request to the consultant, has implications for other biologically related family members. The person who knows about their genetic risk condition turns into a bearer of personal secrets for others within kinship groups, and will frequently even be encouraged by genetic counsellors to disseminate relevant information to at-risk family members (Gaff et al. 2007). Even in the professional counselling encounter the patient (or client) works creatively with the knowledge received. There are various transformative, interpretive and integrative processes in which counsellees are engaged in refashioning received biomedical information: 'Taking ownership of it and weaving it together with their own experiences and understandings and with "inside" information, their feelings and beliefs' (Lippman 1999, 259). Such processes of appropriation and transformation of knowledge into 'embodied knowledge' integrate the dialogue in the counselling room into a vast 'outside' space of lived experiences, relationships and life histories, rather than the other way round. And more recently, there is a growing phenomenon of genetic testing without any (serious) counselling at all: where genetic tests are marketed directly to customers (Human Genetics Commission 2007). In such instances, questions arise about disclosure and non-disclosure, about understanding the knowledge (or the available bits of knowledge), and about identifying the appropriate practical consequences.

That ethics 'lay' people need cannot be just a boiled down version of the professional ethics of clinical geneticists. The preconditions for genetic dialogue within families are different but by no means simple. The actors have roles and virtues to fulfil that relate to the histories of their relationships within the families. It would be misleading to treat them as 'barefoot' geneticists with a semi-professional deontology. But 'lay' gene ethics still resonates with 'professional' gene ethics. I will argue that there is a mutual resonance between the two, and that reflecting about the practices of genetic dialogue within families outside professional settings also contributes to the ethics of professionals. The ethics of genetic counselling improves if the moral perspectives of all those who actively and responsibly deal with ethical issues of genetic communication are considered.

Let us look at a case. Mette Nordahl Svendsen (2006) has studied Danish cancer risk counselling, in particular the experience of the sisters Pia and Rosa.

Both in their 30s, they sought advice because they were concerned about breast cancer in their family. Pia was healthy but her mother and aunt had both been ill with breast cancer and her sister Rosa had recently been diagnosed with breast cancer. Other relatives had also suffered from cancer. In the counselling session, before genetic testing, based only on the drawing of their family tree, Rosa and Pia were told that it was probable that their statistical risk of having the mutated gene was 40 per cent:

> The counsellor listened to their story and told them that their aunt and nieces might also be at risk for hereditary cancer and that, if they were, then prophylaxis was also a possibility for them. She said that in order to make a more precise assessment of their and other family members' risks she would have to obtain their aunt's medical records, along with those of Rosa and her mother. It was up to Rosa and Pia to provide an informed consent form signed by their aunt so that the counsellor would be able to incorporate her medical record into the investigation. Rosa and Pia were a bit hesitant to contact their aunt. They discussed who should do it and, in the end, decided that they would ask their mother (who was not present) to do it. (Svendsen 2006, 145 f.)

The mother, in this case scenario, becomes an accomplice in a preventive regime, others become potential beneficiaries of preventive possibilities that come with genetic knowledge. Within their different parts to play they also adopt commitments and responsibilities. The representation of increased risks, as charted upon a family tree, also indicates a moral commitment to a particular group of people and to particular forms of intervention. Acting responsibly means passing on information that may enable them to initiate preventive measures like further testing, more frequent check-ups, or even prophylactic operations (see a similar case discussed extensively in Ashcroft et al. 2005). The aunt to be contacted, however, lived outside the circle of their mother's close family relations. Mother and aunt 'had very little contact over the last 10 years'. And the aunt herself had three children aged between 27 and 34, the older two daughters being married with children. The commitment to contact the aunt, based on the moral imperative of disease prevention (Koch and Svendsen 2005), leads to a communicative intervention with serious implications for those informed. The hesitation due to the estrangement within the family must (in their own perception) be surmounted in order to pass on the information about further preventive measures, together with the knowledge about the probable existence of a familial genetic risk.

Commenting on this situation, Svendsen speaks of a difference between the biological ties and the social ties: 'a gap between Rosa and Pia's *mapped* and *experienced* kinship' (Svendsen 2006, 150, my emphases). And she points out that the experience of such a gap can constitute 'a *space for agency* in which genetic knowledge of kinship and risks is interpreted and relatedness is created' (157). The existence of such a gap will not undermine responsibility. Genetic ties can appear to prevail over the social. Communicative relationships will have to be initiated, sometimes developed from scratch, grounded on the biological relatedness. Sometimes they are impossible (as in the case discussed in Ashcroft et al. 2005). By this move, the space for agency turns into a challenge with an ethical impact.

Bearers of genetic information do not find the commitment and responsibility that is placed on them as objective facts in their situation. They are not part of an agreed-on system of rules and obligations; there are no rules of professional conduct or good practice. It is rather the result of their personal interpretation of the meaning and of the potential consequences of telling or not telling for those concerned. Such interpretation seems to be foundational and ethical work that configures *local* responsibilities and commitments.

In Svendsen's case study, knowledge about probable genetic risk was sufficient to establish this responsibility and commitment. The reasoning was that a clear confirmation (or refutation) of the genetic risk for Pia was only available from the medical records and later perhaps by a blood sample from the aunt. At the moment of asking, the aunt's medical records were unknown to Rosa and Pia, as well as her genetic situation. But the family tree demonstrated the likelihood that the aunt might have the same mutation and that this mutation was responsible for her own cancer, which she might not yet have recognized as 'hereditary'.

Various conceptions of responsibility could be considered to make sense here. A minimal one is connected to the free will problem and can be formulated along the suggestion of Charles Widmer (1996, 21): 'There is some sort of responsibility when an effect can be attributed to an agent – the agent is then answerable, accountable, for the effect.' But this account would only give a negative understanding of responsibility, as excluding determinism of the action (Kapitan 1995). Widmer goes on to explain what is implied by the notions of 'answerability' or 'accountability': 'Responsibility then supposes the capacity in the agent of being aware of the effect of his, or her, action, whether the action was intentional or not' (loc. cit.). The agent, in order to be responsible, needs to have the capacity for awareness of the consequences of the action upon the person concerned. This is not a simple anticipatory task, because many things beyond medical facts and health prospects may need to be considered. The action itself might be unintentional (disclosing the information by accident) or intentional. In both cases responsibility is there, but with different meanings. The unintentional disclosure would not establish responsibility of a communicative action in the sense that H. Richard Niebuhr (1963, 57) has called 'answer to actions upon us in accordance with our interpretation of such action'.

Niebuhr's account of responsibility however, gives a deeper insight into the possibilities we have in moral relations and might be helpful here. Responsibility is essentially a response, an answer to actions upon us according to our interpretation of these actions and with the expectation of the response to our response. Answering presupposes hearing and understanding. To see (or hear) the relationships and actions that constitute the situation, to interpret them in order to understand, sometimes realizing the tensions and contradictions, identifying the vulnerabilities, leads to local knowledge about the situation and how to act in it.

This aspect of responsibility 'as response' transcends, as Niebuhr explains, the models of ourselves as humans-as-makers who are responsible because they have power, and humans-as-citizens who are responsible to some instance because they are accountable. It depicts ourselves *as answerers* who are responsible actors by responding to the needs of a situation and to the needs of the people in it.

Studies of the experiences of people who disclose genetic information to family members show that informants can experience communication as burdensome or difficult. They feel the dilemma between the desire to protect relatives form potential harm arising from the information, and the wish to provide them with helpful information that may have important health consequences (see the meta-analysis of 29 qualitative studies by Gaff et al. 2007). In weighing conflicting responsibilities, the individual assesses the vulnerability of the addressees of the information as well as their receptivity (Hamilton et al. 2005).

The moral ground for the responsibility and commitment experienced by the informants is the vulnerability of those who will receive information. Vulnerability, in such cases, is established by an intricate constellation of ambivalent knowledge, ambivalent non-knowledge and the relatedness of the knower to those who are affected by the knowledge.

How can we understand vulnerability in this context? It is not vulnerability in general (to someone or other) but concrete, direct *dependency-in-fact*, that is, in Svendsen's case, vulnerability to Rosa and Pia's actions in particular.[4] Vulnerability therefore involves a relation of dependency (due to the circumstances) upon somebody to secure or protect some important need or interest. The dependency emerges here because of the nature of their *biological* relationship (represented by the family tree), not because of some prior agreement or an existing close personal relation between them. This can add to the moral difficulty that is experienced by the informant. The social relationship may not be pre-existing or it may not be prepared to carry *that* load, and therefore not provide a secure platform for dealing with such an additional issue represented by genetic information. If the relationship does not pre-exist, is weak or has a different character than would be needed, there is a morally experienced demand to *develop* the relationship in the course of communication about the genetic issue.

The fact of dependence is obvious, but not its content. Dependence may be a complicated relation, as can be seen again in the case of Rosa and Pia. The cousins, who probably do not know about the genetic risk in their family, are dependent on Rosa and Pia to obtain the information. This is their vulnerability to

4 Here I use the phrase 'dependency-in-fact' that has been introduced by Margaret Urban Walker (1998, 84), in her discussion of Robert Goodin's well-known principle of vulnerability. The notion of vulnerability is explained as follows: 'X is vulnerable to Y in respect to N when X is *actually depending on* or *circumstantially upon* Y to secure or protect N *because* of the nature of their existing relationship, some prior agreement between them or by them, a particular causal history between them, or the fact of Y's unique proximity and capability in light of X's extreme plight' (ibid.).

non-disclosure. But they are also dependent on Rosa and Pia in many more ways, for instance that they do not cause damage through insensitive communication or do not breach confidentiality towards third parties. This is their vulnerability to disclosure. Vulnerability hence arises to disclosure *and* to non-disclosure.

It is interesting to see that the knowledge that will be communicated is not only probabilistic in its form but a twice potential knowledge (here, of cancer). A knows that B *could* have a mutation meaning that she *could* more easily get cancer. If the mutation is detected this would constitute knowledge about a higher-than-average probability of getting cancer. What was known in the case of Rosa and Pia was only that the cancer in the family could be hereditary and that the aunt could have inherited the dangerous mutation. But even twofold potential knowledge can evidently constitute a relation of moral commitment and responsibility.

The ethics of genetic communication therefore relates to professional as well as to non-professional actors. The field of topics is much larger than the counselling office.

Making Sense of Genetic Information: Genetic Hermeneutics

Let us take a closer look at the knowledge involved. There are many different types of knowledge with different kinds of relevance: genealogy and pedigree, family history with the life stories, personal knowledge about the sensibilities and needs of family members, general knowledge about genetics and about its significance for the development of living beings, test results, personalized interpretation of these results constructed and interpreted in interactions with genetic counsellors (and perhaps more).

In the social situations that are generated by predictive genetics there can be no clear separation between scientific knowledge, cultural understandings, personal experience, anticipated individual coping habits and moral concerns. Knowledge often arrives as already intertwined. Scientific information produced in genetic counselling sessions and/or genetic tests is morally relevant because, as we have discussed above, it generates specific vulnerabilities to disclosure, to non-disclosure and to the way of disclosure. The understanding of responsibility and commitment in such situations on the other hand depends on which scientific information is asked for and how it is socio-culturally interpreted.

This has an impact on how we can understand the genetic information that is communicated. The 'genetic information' is not just what is written in the report from the genetics lab. It is not just the correct description of a regular or special sequence of DNA and its accidental mutation at a particular location of the genome. Genetic information is not just what can be quantitatively measured and treated in mathematical information theory as a number of 'bits' or 'bytes'. In the context of medical genetics, counselling and dialogue it is necessary to speak of information as something that is *meaningfully understood* by those seeking information, interpreted in various ways, and sometimes misinterpreted.

Information cannot be treated here as a pattern without reference to meaning, or, as mathematical information theory would suggest, as negative entropy, that is, some order in contrast to randomness (Böhme 1974).

Rob Whithers (2005, 107) asks suggestively: 'Where are the results of the test?' In whose mind are the results of the test to be found? All the participants (counsellor, counsellee, relatives, friends) together can be seen as a 'counselling community' (Ricoeur 1990, 264, uses this term in the much more general context of ethics) who have some common and some non-overlapping understandings of the test, and who struggle to interpret the test results within the context of a particular situation and with reference to life histories that began a long time ago. Genetic information has a considerable *social* life. It requires the participants to become experts in their own cases, to mobilize local knowledge and to put it in relation to the 'facts and figures about chromosomes' learnt from medicine.

Abby Lippman's qualitative interview study with women who were offered amniocentesis gives empirical evidence for this. Women described their negotiations with biomedical information, as they came to claim it, or, as Lippman says, 'embody it', as their own. Four processes seemed pertinent in the interviews: (1) Personalizing the meaning of maternal age: women considered their age not just chronologically and did not take the statistical probability of having a child with Down Syndrome at its face value, 'but also with regard to how they *feel* – how they *are* – their age' (Lippman 1999, 261); (2) Recalculating maternal age in relation to Down Syndrome: probabilistic information is malleable because it does not provide information about the individual case and leaves open space for assessments with reference to personal biographies. Women have a sense of their individual risk and act according to it; (3) Redefining fetal 'health': 'healthy' can mean the absence of genetic disorders. However, many women who rejected being tested seem to hold a different view: 'They tend to emphasize healthy more generally to mean a living baby, one who has no major physical condition that could lead to stillbirth or early infant death' (263); (4) Using genetic counselling to confirm one's own knowledge claims: women told stories about their decision making about being tested or not that suggested 'that genetic counselling actually served to reinforce a decision they had already made' (265). They said that they already had 'a feeling' before having the test or not, and they used the information to reinforce this and to rationalize it as an argument. However we should not underestimate the fact that Lippman's participants told their stories in retrospect. They make present sense of a decision story that already happened in the past. Lippman's study impressively shows (for a particular type of circumstances) how women *actively* make use of the knowledge resources of biomedicine. This must be seen as part of their agency as interpreters in their own cases.

However it is not just the clients who interpret knowledge and embody it. The processes of interpretation and embodiment start on a general level within genetic discourses. The myriad of findings in molecular genetics need to be integrated into an understandable basic picture that says what it is all about. There is a set of powerful metaphors in genetic discourses that perform this role. Genomes, it is said, are 'blueprints' for the organism, they contain a 'code' for life, a 'language' or a 'list of instructions'. Perhaps the most central metaphor for the role of the genome in the organism in twentieth century genetics was the 'genetic programme'. It was generated and brought into circulation around 1960 by eminent biologists such as Jacques Monod, François Jacob and Ernst Mayr (Kay 2000). It contained the hope that by knowing and understanding the 'information content' of the genome, that is, the sequence of DNA, we will be able to predict large portions of the structure and functioning of the whole organism. It was always known that environmental factors also play a more or less significant role. The term 'genetic programme' does not imply a view in which these factors of 'environment' or 'nurture' are insignificant, quite the contrary: the instructions contained in the genome provide a 'norm of reaction', of how the organism should integrate selected environmental factors for actually shaping its development. The idea of the genome as 'genetic programme' ('instruction book', 'script' for development, and so on) is still part of commonly used language and provides powerful interpretative patterns, which are frequently used to 'explain' the significance of genes. Within biology, however, it has become clear that this imagery is misleading. There are real scientific problems with it coming from the vast evidence for the *multi-functionality* of genes. One and the same gene can have different functions and play different roles in the context of metabolic processes, according to time, and the exact place of the cell within the developing multi-cellular organism. There are phenomena like alternative splicing, overlapping genes, alternative reading frames, trans-splicing, anti-sense transcripts, mRNA editing, selective methylation, site-specific multiple function of genes and gene products, which are all at odds with the 'programme' model of the genome (Fogle 2000; Griffiths and Stotz 2006). The basic picture of current genomics and systems biology is not the genome organizing the development of the organism with a series of already written instructions, but rather the cell or the organism (or the organism-within-environment) organizing the actualization of genetic information in the developmental process.

There are alternative views of the genome-organism relationship in discussion (see contributions in Neumann-Held and Rehmann-Sutter 2006) that are better suited to incorporate the evidence of multi-functionality of genes. Elsewhere (Rehmann-Sutter 2008) I have discussed such alternative views and tried to integrate them into a systemic picture of the role of the genome. The key move is not the criticism of genetic determinism, because the programme view of the genome can absorb both epigenetic and environmental factors. The genetic programme view certainly had a history of genetic determinism but it is not necessarily deterministic. The key move is not to discuss *how much* genes determine (this is a purely scientific question to be solved case by case empirically) but *how* they determine and *how* they interact with other factors. This is a question about the role of the genome and it includes the basic theoretical model of genetics. The best way to understand the significance of this question is to start with a fresh reflection on genetic information. The classic contribution is Susan Oyama's 1985 book *The Ontogeny of Information*, where she stresses that the information content of DNA, that is, its sequence, is different from developmentally significant information. DNA does not mean anything before it becomes involved in the processes of regulation or transcription on the level of a phenotypic, somatic process of development. Developmentally significant genetic information therefore cannot be seen as pre-existing the processes that give rise to it. Information is produced from different kinds of resources (one of them is the genome) in the course of the interactive processes of the cell, the organism and the environment. This view fully respects the empirically established evidence about the significance of DNA and its mutations. But the interpretation of the experimental results at the level of the 'basic picture' of the role of the genome within living processes is strikingly different. To replace the 'programme' as the guiding metaphor by the 'system' is much more than a slight change of words or a shift in images. It is rather a totally different view of life, of inheritance, development, embodiment and of the identity of us as living beings, and with that, of the significance of a genetic test result.

One philosophically clarified systems account of the genome,[5] drawing on ideas of Susan Oyama, Gunther Stent, Gerry Webster, Brian Goodwin and others, starts from the assumption that the succession of developmental steps is a result of a complex combination of causal factors, some related to DNA, others not. Rather than being the realization of a plan encoded in DNA sequences, it follows a 'historical' logic, that is, each step can be (ideally) explained from the conditions, structure and dynamic processes of the previous stage. Without a genotypic programme, regularity *emerges*. Some would like to restrict the metaphor of the programme to describe this emerging regularity. But if we take the term programme seriously, this would be inconsistent. 'Programme' implies a difference between the written programme and the programmed phenomena. This difference is exactly what is denied when regularity is an emergent phenomenon. Speaking of a 'phenotypic programme' has no clear logical sense. A second element in a systems approach to genomics is that DNA is not privileged a priori as an ontologically superior or in metaphysical sense 'essential' part. Therefore, developmentally relevant 'genetic information' must be regarded as something that is a *result* of the interactions and processes DNA is involved in, not as information 'encoded' in the sequences of DNA. Information has an ontogeny, as Oyama puts it.

DNA mutations, personal variants of genes that are related to diseases can therefore not be interpreted as 'information for the disease'. They can be correlated with an increased likelihood that a disease may occur and as such they are *indicators* for this increased likelihood (in some case of monogenetic disease even near certainty). However, it would be a misinterpretation to say that mutations are 'prescription for' or a 'gene for' the disease. In the body of the person concerned there is, for example, no information 'for cancer' if somebody is diagnosed with a mutation that increases the likelihood that a type of tumour may occur sometime

5 See details and references in Neumann-Held 1998, Rehmann-Sutter 2000, 2002, 2008 and Neumann-Held and Rehmann-Sutter 2006.

in the future. In the framework of a systemic account of genomics, a cancer-related mutation is not a dangerous factor just waiting in the body or in some parts of the body *at present* to break out (like a time bomb). The frequently used terminology of 'predisposition' still implies the programme genomics' view that information is already present, pre-disposing the body. An expression that is more congenial to systems genomics is 'susceptibility'. Being susceptible, more or less susceptible than the average, does not imply the pre-existence of genetic 'information for …' but refers to variations in the probability that at some point in the future, a constellation will arise whose combination of factors (DNA and other) leads to the development of the disease. I know that for monogenetic disorders this is more difficult to figure out that for polygenetic conditions like familial tumour diseases. But even there – Huntington is a good example – in the time before the disease manifests, the patients can know that they carry the gene that at some point in the future will probably contribute to the manifestation of Huntington's disease, with its characteristic symptoms. But at present, the person's body is not carrying the 'information for Huntington's disease', because this information does not exist yet. What can be seen via a test is the gene that will become involved in the pathogenetic processes leading to the disease.

This difference between programmatic and systemic interpretations of genomics that I have outlined here as ideal types, has a deep impact for those who introduce genetic test results into their worlds of self-understanding and embodiment. It makes a difference whether one sees a mutation that indicates a genetic risk for developing, for example, a cancer as *understood as* a section of the genetic programme, that is, as an instruction to the body to make cancerous tissue, or, in the framework of a systems approach, as a factor that could become involved in a process leading to cancerous tissue. The latter understanding indicates a higher level of likelihood, but it does not imply that the genes in the cells of the body are like little springs wound up to release and make tumours. The body image and the perception of the body are affected by the choice between interpretative patterns of genomics. Hence, genetic hermeneutics matters.

In their book about informed consent, Neil Manson and Onora O'Neill (2007) have demonstrated the shortcomings of the understanding of 'information' as something that could be stored in a container and transmitted from a sender to a receiver over a conduit. They call this the 'conduit/container model of information'. This view is insufficient and reductionist, because it fails vis-à-vis the phenomenology of communication between humans. According to Manson and O'Neill it is perhaps not totally inaccurate but it hides too much. Drawing on Oyama's account of genetic information, they suggest a richer model of information, which is based on agency. Communication is *done* by and between agents, it is a normative affair that presupposes a rich framework of shared norms and shared background commitments, as well as the requisite inferential competences (65). This can be easily applied to genetic communication. The (genetic) information that is transferred from A to B is not a content that was stored in the brains (or notes) of A and sent to B by the means of language and explanation. It is rather something that is *enacted* in the interactive practice of communication between A and B. Mary Terrell White (2007) has drawn attention to the 'hermeneutic' practice of genetic dialogues. Genetic responsibility itself is, as she expresses it, 'a matter of interpretation' (152). This fits well with my point about the effects of the choice between interpretative patterns of genomics (systems or programmes). Obviously it has implications for what we see as a defensible ethical model for genetic communications.

A Needs Based Proposal

When we are looking for a positive ethical model of genetic communication we need to take several points into consideration. *First*, the communicative practice in the realm of genetics is not restricted to the professional-client encounter and can therefore not be covered by a professional ethos of genetic counsellors. Genetic communication of personal genetic information also takes place among relatives. *Second*, the perspective of the clients/patients is not one of passive receivers of information but a perspective of agents who participate in processes of decision making and adjustment. *Third*, genetic information with predictive impact for health has become available in many contexts outside prenatal diagnosis, medically motivated terminations of pregnancies and family planning. It therefore has many different practical implications, ranging from elective embryo transfer in IVF, many different sorts of prevention to improvement of therapies in personalized medicine and self-understanding of oneself as embodied human beings in personal genomics. *Fourth*, the traditional ethos of nondirectiveness and value-neutrality (Bosk 1992 has called it the 'workplace ideology') of genetic counselling does not serve the needs of those counselled. This was never really controversial, even among American human geneticists who most strongly championed nondirectiveness as their 'shop floor ideology' (to use another of Bosk's deconstructive terms). Fraser (1974) observed that: 'Many counsellees come for advice and are disappointed if they do not get it. The counsellor must of course avoid projecting his own personality defects into the situation, but in general he will not be of much help to the counsellee if he maintains an Olympian detachment, concerned only with the statistical probability and not the unique combination of factors entering into the consellee's personal situation' (650). And he endorsed an empathic relationship and an educated awareness of the psychodynamics of counselling in order to help the counsellees find their own good decision. This line of critical awareness of the unhelpful impacts or side-effects of a too rigid, too individualistic or too detached attitude of nondirectiveness has since been further developed into innovative suggestions, as has been outlined above. And *fifth*, the interpretation of genetic information in a concrete situation is not only to the task of understanding the genetic risks relative to the concrete individuals involved. It is more generally a process of 'embodiment of information' that involves cultural backgrounds, family histories and personal experiences that never can be totally value-free. And it also mobilizes interpretative patterns in the shape of 'basic pictures' of the role of genomes in the organism, as we have outlined above with the ideal type contrast between 'programme' and 'systems' approaches to genomics.

My proposal is to take all these aspects into account and to integrate them into an ethics of genetic communication. I assume that there is a fundamental ethical requirement of respect for the autonomy and well-being of those who need to take decisions about their activities. And I assume that this holds for all genetic communication, wherever it takes place, not just for the exchange of information between professional counsellors and their clients. The needs of those who receive or must handle genetic information in some appropriate ways are broader than just being informed about the biological and medical implications of genetic testing and information. This observation is uncontroversial and appears as a constantly repeated theme in discussions about the ethically justified attitude of genetic counsellors and medical geneticists, already in Fraser (1974).

I furthermore assume that the needs of those who receive and must adjust their behaviour make an ethical model of genetic communication ethically defensible. It should not be the dominant ideology of society or some universal account of 'normality' or 'human nature'. This is an ethical assumption that could be argued for in a utilitarian, Kantian, virtue or relationship approach to ethical responsibility. Patients in prenatal genetic counselling for instance need to be listened to, and invited into discussions, where scientific and other 'facts' can be looked at from different angles, rather than being educated (Lippman 1999). They need counsellors who believe what women say when they express their embodied knowledge and accept its validity, rather than consider it something to be corrected. Of course they also need to understand relevant parts of medical and biological information about their fetus, the significance and the limits of the test. And they need to prepare their decision such that it will be their own and they can live with it in the future. The needs in other contexts can be different.

This said I propose a formula: good communication of genetic information enables a good decision or action to be found, all things considered. As a good decision I understand essentially a decision which those responsible or affected can identify and live with. This implies a requirement for the respect of persons as moral subjects who can make decisions about their own lives.

In more detail, the statement combines six ethically critical elements: Good communication is (1) a respectful interaction that (2) enables somebody to find (3) their own (4) good (5) decision or action, (6) all relevant things considered. A few explanations for each element:

(1) Respectful interaction is driven by fully recognizing the other as a subject of a life. The other person in a respectful interaction is a centre of experiences that cannot all be anticipated. The other is not only a receiver of information but a person who needs to be *heard* as an irreplaceable subject who can be vulnerable to many different psychological and social implications and pressures of many kinds, and as a person who has particular needs, goals, values, hopes and fears.

(2) To enable somebody to find a good decision or procedure for action means to provide relevant information, to assist in interpreting and understanding this information in a broader context of life, to make a difficult situation more transparent, to create a situation where a decision or a course of action can be developed without pressure, and to empower them by hearing them into speech (Morton 1985).

(3) A decision or course of action is a person's own if they can identify with it. This does not presume an individualistic account of autonomy but allows other, more inclusive or relational approaches like being in harmony with oneself and with relevant others. The style of finding a decision or course of action that somebody can identify with may differ between persons and situations. Some may prefer a more self-centred approach, others a more other-centred approach; some may proceed more rationally, others more intuitively. Sometimes, telling 'what I would do if I were in your position' is the best starting point in a process that leads to an authentic practice of the other, but in other situations it may be an undue bias. What is important here is less that the decision or course of action is found in a way that accords with one of the established models of moral philosophy. It is rather that it accords with the type of situation and the personal style of moral thinking and feeling. Abby Lippman (1999) mentions that some of her interviewees told the decision story about prenatal diagnosis in retrospect as a story where an original 'feeling', however vague, finally was confirmed with arguments. Perhaps there were other 'feelings' around as well, but one indicated the right direction and helped the woman to identify with the outcome of the decision.

(4) 'Good' is a key word in the formula, indicating that the decision or procedure is more than just functional for reaching certain short-term goals (instrumentally good). A good decision or procedure is in harmony with long-term life projects that are intrinsically worth being striven for. Genetic dilemmas, however, are often situations where not just one long-term goal is relevant, but where different ones may conflict. Then they need to be evaluated and weighed against each other in such a way that the result of the decision-making process seems to be the best possible way forward within the given circumstances, limits and possibilities. Here, the values of the person who becomes the author of the decision are the reference, not the values of the counsellor or of the person who provides genetic information. But sometimes a person wishes to exchange views about values and to broaden their understanding of what is ultimately valuable. Genetic communication therefore is often essentially *about* the concrete understanding of what is relevant in a 'good life' or a 'fulfilled life'.

(5) A decision, action or procedure is a practical response to the situation. It does not necessarily mean the choice of action as one of several 'options', as they are often represented in the image of the 'decision tree'. The decision tree is a metaphor that can help to clarify a situation but is not necessarily sufficiently complex to

represent what is actually at stake for the person. The image of the decision tree with its options as branching points is a rather static representation of practice. People who make difficult 'decisions' may prefer to proceed in smaller steps, each step (one can speak of microdecisions, see Scully et al. 2007) opening perhaps more options or bringing more clarity that is available at a given point in time.

(6) All relevant things should be considered. This often implies a prioritization within an overly complex situation, and it also implies having the relevant information available. Genetics certainly contributes to the set of relevant aspects in those life situations we have been considering here. But relevance is an evaluative term. Not all that seems medically or scientifically relevant is also personally relevant, and vice versa. Genetic communication is a place where relevance *is negotiated* in processes of interpretation and understanding, bringing different perspectives together.

This was quite a long description of an ethical model. We need also a short expression that characterizes it as a distinct approach to the ethics of genetic communication and is still general enough for being interpreted in situation types and specific circumstances. Parallel to the slogan of nondirectiveness, which is a one-word expression, we can say that the suggested model of communicating genetic knowledge is ethically oriented to *allow agency*.[6] Agency is a term that, if carefully examined, covers all six elements of the model. The person needs to be heard and recognized as an agent, that is, as a subject of evaluation, responsibility and moral practice. Agency means that one has room to be responsible and to respond, the space to cope with pressures of any kinds, and that one is free and able to act. The understanding of what is relevant in the situation, of what should be seriously considered, is a resource for performing this capability. Agency implies also that the agent is sovereign in the sense that they can find their own practical response. Somebody is allowed agency if they can evaluate the course of practice with regard to values and long-term life projects such as understandings of a 'good and fulfilled life'.

Allowing agency preserves the best parts of the principle of nondirectiveness: respect and responsible information. But it has no individualistic structure and does not prescribe a detached attitude for those providing genetic information. They are partners in a mutually engaged interaction between persons with different roles, with asymmetric knowledge resources and an asymmetric distribution of decision loads.

To sum up: the ethics of genetic communication in the post-nondirectiveness era is no longer a separate field of professional deontology but appears as a place where the deepest forms of ethics are practically performed by those involved.

6 Lippman (1999, 272) has used this formulation with regard to religious or cultural reasons that can in some instances counter the weight of professional advice and 'allow women agency'.

'The gene' is in a certain sense de-professionalized and again re-professionalized to become an essentially pluri-perspectival entity with a variety of meanings and practical readings, whose trajectory depends on the circumstances and contexts. Local knowledge matters, local experts emerge. Professionals must find their roles and their excellences in relation to them. In mutually responsive communicative interactions they are partners in negotiating and re-negotiating what others see as good and relevant. As we have seen, there is a longer story *before* the claim for a certain right to know or not to know.

References

Ashcroft, R. et al. (eds) (2005), *Case Analysis in Clinical Ethics* (Cambridge: Cambridge University Press).

Biesecker, B.B. (2003), 'Back to the future of genetic counseling: Commentary on "psychosocial genetic counseling in the post-nondirective era"', *Journal of Genetic Counseling* 12, 213–217.

Böhme, G. (1974), 'Information und Verständigung', in E. v. Weizsäcker (ed.), *Offene Systeme I* (Stuttgart: Klett-Cotta), 17–34.

Bosk, C. (1992), *All God's Mistakes: Genetic Counseling in Pediatric Hospital* (Chicago: University of Chicago Press).

Fogle (2000), 'The Dissolution of Protein Coding Genes in Molecular Biology', in P. Beurton et al. (eds), *The Concept of the Gene in Development and Evolution* (Cambridge: Cambridge University Press), 3–25.

Fraser, F.C. (1974), 'Genetic counseling', *American Journal of Human Genetics* 26, 636–659.

Gaff, C.L. et al. (2007), 'Process and outcome in communication of genetic information within families: A systematic review', *European Journal of Human Genetics* 15, 999–1011.

Griffiths, P.E. and Stotz, K. (2006), 'Genes in the postgenomic era', *Theoretical Medicine and Bioethics* 27, 499–521.

Habermas, J. (2003), *The Future of Human Nature* (London: Polity).

Hamilton, R.J. et al. (2005), 'Disclosing genetic test results to family members', *Journal of Nursing Scholarship* 37, 18–24.

Heller, A. and Dinges S. (2006), 'Organisational Ethics – and Their Role in Counselling and Decision-Making Processes for Prenatal Testing', in B. Wieser et al. (eds), *Prenatal Testing. Individual Decision or Distributed Action?* (Wien: Profil), 159–177.

Holm, S. (2005), 'An Empirical Approach', in R. Ashcroft et al. (eds), *Case Analysis in Clinical Ethics* (Cambridge: Cambridge University Press), 201–211.

Human Genetics Commission (2007), *More Genes Direct* (London: COI).

Kapitan, T. (1995), 'Free Will Problem', in R. Audi (ed.), *The Cambridge Dictionary of Philosophy* (Cambridge: Cambridge University Press), 280–282.

Kay, L.E. (2000), *Who Wrote the Book of Life. A History of the Genetic Code* (Stanford: Stanford University Press).

Kessler, S. (1980), 'The psychological paradigm shift in genetic counselling', *Journal of Social Biology* 27, 167–185.

Kessler, S. (1997), 'Psychosocial aspects of genetic counseling. XI. Non-directiveness revisited', *American Journal of Medical Genetics* 72, 164–171.

Koch, L. and Svendsen M.N. (2005), 'Providing solutions, defining problems: The imperative of disease prevention in cancer genetic counseling', *Social Science and Medicine* 60, 823–832.

Latour, B. (1999), *Pandora's Hope. Essays on the Reality of Science Studies* (Cambridge, MA: Harvard University Press).

Lippman, A. (1999), 'Embodied knowledge and making sense of prenatal diagnosis', *Journal of Genetic Counseling* 8, 255–274.

Manson, N.C. and O'Neill O. (2007), *Rethinking Informed Consent in Bioethics* (Cambridge: Cambridge University Press).

Marks, J. H. (1993), 'The Training of Genetic Counselors: Origins of a Psychosocial Model', in D.M. Bartels et al. (eds), *Prescribing our Future. Ethical Challenges in Genetic Counseling* (New York: De Gruyter), 15–24.

McConkie-Rosell, A. and Sullivan J.A. (1999), 'Genetic counseling – stress, coping, and the empowerment perspective', *Journal of Genetic Counseling* 8, 345–357.

Milunsky, A. (1978), 'Prenatal Diagnosis. I. Clinical Aspects', in W.T. Reich (ed.), *Encyclopedia of Bioethics* (New York: Free Press), 1332–1335.

Morton, N. (1985), *The Journey is Home* (Boston: Beacon Press).

Neumann-Held, E.M. and Rehmann-Sutter, C. (2006), *Genes in Development. Re-Reading the Molecular Paradigm* (Durham: Duke University Press).

Niebuhr, H.R. (1963), *The Responsible Self* (New York: HarperCollins).

Porz, R. (2008), *Zwischen Entscheidung und Entfremdung. Patientenperspektiven in der Gendiagnostik und Albert Camus' Konzepte zum Absurden* (Paderborn: Mentis).

Rehmann-Sutter, C. (2000), 'Die Interpretation genetischer Daten: Vorwort zu einer genetischen Hermeneutik', in J. Mittelstrass (ed.), *Die Zukunft des Wissens. XVIII. Deutscher Kongress für Philosophie* (Berlin: Akademie), 478–498.

Rehmann-Sutter, C. (2002), 'Genetics, Embodiment and Identity', in A. Grunwald et al. (eds), *On Human Nature: Anthropological, Biological, and Philosophical Foundations* (Berlin: Springer), 25–50.

Rehmann-Sutter, C. (2006), 'Limits of Bioethics', in C. Rehmann-Sutter et al. (eds), *Bioethics in Cultural Contexts. Reflections on Method and Finitude* (Dordrecht: Springer), 59–79.

Rehmann-Sutter, C. (2008), 'Genetics, A Practical Anthropology', in M. Düwell et al. (eds), *The Contingent Nature of Life: Bioethics and the Limits of Human Existence* (Dordrecht: Springer), 37–52.

Rehmann-Sutter, C. (forthcoming), '"... it is her problem; not ours." – Contributions of Feminist Bioethics to the Mainstream', in J.L. Scully et al. (eds), *Feminist*

Bioethics. At the Center, on the Margins (Baltimore: Johns Hopkins University Press).

Ricoeur, P. (1990), 'Ethique et Morale' (translated by Peter Welsen), in P. Ricoeur (2005), *Vom Text zur Person. Hermeneutische Aufsätze (1979–1999)* (Hamburg: Meiner), 251–267.

Rieh, J.P. and Ray C. (1974), *Conceptual Models for Nursing Practice* (New York: Appleton-Century-Crofts).

Rogers, C. (1942), *Counseling and Psychotherapy: Newer Concepts in Practice* (Boston: Houghton Mifflin).

Scully, J.L. et al. (2007), '"You don't make genetic test decisions from one day to the next" – using time to preserve moral space', *Bioethics* 21, 208–217.

Svendsen, M. (2006), 'The social life of genetic knowledge: A case-study of choices and dilemmas in cancer genetic counselling in Denmark', *Medical Anthropology* 25, 139–170.

Veach, P.M. et al. (2007), 'Coming full circle: A reciprocal-engagement model of genetic counseling practice', *Journal of Genetic Counseling* 16, 713–728.

Walker, M.U. (1998), *Moral Understandings. A Feminist Study in Ethics* (New York and London: Routledge).

Walter, A.P. (1998), 'The Practice of Genetic Counselling', in D.L. Baker et al. (eds), *Genetic Counselling* (New York: Wiley-Liss), 1–20.

Weil, J. (2003), 'Psychosocial genetic counseling in the post-nondirective era: A point of view', *Journal of Genetic Counseling* 12, 199–211.

Weil, J. et al. (2006), 'The relationship of nondirectiveness to genetic counseling: Report of a workshop at the 2003 NSGC annual education conference', *Journal of Genetic Counseling* 15, 85–93.

Wertz, D. and Fletcher J. (2004), *Genetics and Ethics in Global Perspective* (Dordrecht: Kluwer).

White, M.T. (2007), 'Uncertainty and moral judgment: The limits of reason in genetic decision making', *The Journal of Clinical Ethics* 18:2, 148–155.

Whithers, R. (2005), 'Reading the Genes', in R. Ashcroft et al. (eds), *Case Analysis in Clinical Ethics* (Cambridge: Cambridge University Press), 95–114.

Widmer, C. (1996), 'Human Dignity, Nature, and the Sciences of Man', in G. Berthoud et al. (eds), *The Responsible Scholar. Ethical Considerations in the Humanities and the Social Sciences* (Canton, MA: Watson), 19–38.

Wieser, B. (2005), 'Eine Ethik der pränatalen Diagnostik?', in R. Lauritsch et al. (eds), *Das öffentliche Gute. Forschungstag 2004. Klagenfurter Beiträge zur Technikdiskussion*, 107, 25–46.

Wieser, B. (2006), 'Translating Medical Practices: Actor-Network Theory Perspective', in B. Wieser et al. (eds), *Prenatal Testing. Individual Decision or Distributed Action?* (Wien: Profil), 101–129.

Wieser, B. and Karner S. (2006), 'Individualising Decisions. On the Paradoxes of Prenatal Testing', in B. Wieser et al. (eds), *Prenatal Testing. Individual Decision or Distributed Action?* (Wien: Profil), 27–52.

Conclusions

Christoph Rehmann-Sutter and Hansjakob Müller

As the editors of this volume, in this concluding section we will take the opportunity to look back on the various chapters and to highlight some of the most significant conclusions. There are some points that have been clarified and there are still many open questions. Some remain open because they could not be resolved in this book, others have become open through what has been written here and some questions are raised by the dynamics of techno-scientific developments that continue to change the face of genetic medicine and transform the medical and social use of genetic information. The power of these developments should not be underestimated. The ethics of genetic medicine is not in the least the ethics of a field of practice that is already well established and known. The area is evolving rapidly and in directions that can barely be foreseen at the present point in history. Some of the most recent developments in the field demonstrate the speed and fluidity of the development. For instance it has now become possible to sequence the complete genome of a human individual within a few weeks, whereas the first two complete genome sequencing projects took several years. Less than a decade ago, it took hundreds of millions of dollars to sequence a single human genome, but according to present estimates, the cost of the total sequencing of a genome will drop to about 10,000 US-Dollars (Pennisi 2008). But why not focus on health, pick out the most relevant parts of the genome and test them? The cost of whole-genome scans that look at hundreds of thousands or millions of small individual variations in the DNA sequence has fallen to several hundred US dollars. A few months ago, when we drafted the introduction to the book, it was still more than a thousand. Personal genomics has become affordable for many, and competition between companies continues to work in the direction of reducing price and increasing availability. These tests can be individually ordered, not over the counter in the local pharmacy or in a supermarket, but over the Internet, which is special in many ways. First of all it means two things: it is possible to know genetic profiles without personal contact with a counsellor, and it is possible to order them from anywhere in the world. The scan principle, which allows testing for tens of thousands of genetic traits at once, will soon also be offered, applied and somehow also regulated by laws and best practice guidelines, in prenatal and preimplantation genetic testing. We could enumerate many more such rapid developments.

However, there is still an enormous discrepancy between the technical ability to analyze the DNA sequence and the knowledge of the phenotypic significance of variations of its base-composition. The clinical consequences of DNA variations have only so far been evaluated for fewer than 350 human genes (see OMIM Statistics: <http://www.ncbi.nlm.nih.gov>).

The scientific development in the background of these advances on the practical front can perhaps best be referred to as the transition from 'transmission' geneticism which studies the heredity of traits, to developmental genetics and genomics (Barnes and Dupré 2008). The genome is not only the sum total of all coding genes (see the ENCODE project: <http://www.genome.gov/10005107>; Birney et al. 2007). The latest edition of the classic textbook by Bruce Alberts et al., *Molecular Biology of the Cell*, defines the term 'genome' as 'the totality of genetic information belonging to a cell or an organism; in particular the DNA that carries this information' (Alberts et al. 2008, G:15). The 'coding genes', defined as those parts of DNA that code for proteins, are only a tiny fraction of the DNA that is contained in the 23 different human chromosomes. The other parts contain information as well, as recent research, for instance on the regulatory roles of small interfering RNA molecules (MicroRNAs), has demonstrated. And there is also epigenetic information outside the DNA-sequences, for example in the methylation pattern or in histone modifications that regulate gene activity, or in the structure/machinery of all components of this incredibly complex organism of each cell.

Hence, the transition to genomics is not just an increase in scale or quantity. It is a change in research methods, and correspondingly in concepts and views used in molecular biology. Instead of studying only the inheritance of single traits, genomic biology is interested in learning how genomic information functions throughout the entire life cycle, as part of the complex chemical-molecular systems of a cell. It aims to explain not only differences, but also the normal functioning of the body, often using cutting-edge computing power and mathematical models that interrelate many parts of the interactive dynamics of the system. 'Systems biology' has emerged on the scientific landscape. When we compiled this book, the effects of this transition to genomics had just started to hit clinical medicine and public health. The prognostic use of DNA-related information will certainly not stay unaffected.

What Has Been Clarified?

A closer look at the reality of dilemmatic situations related to genetic testing from the perspectives of those involved has revealed a complexity and a dynamic in practical situations that makes it questionable to speak of 'moral dilemmas' in a straightforward sense. The word dilemma implies a situation in a decision-making process, where there are essentially only two realistic options, both of which imply desirable and undesirable outcomes and therefore have moral costs. Testing or not testing? Disclosing the result or not telling at all? Telling it to relatives or just to the patients? The ethical tasks of truth telling are not binary, not just about telling 'it' or not telling 'it', but multifaceted and processual (Langewitz and also Cerny, this vol.). We are in a moral dilemma if we cannot do what we are morally obliged to do without sacrificing other duties or values (for variants of this definition see Sinnott-Armstrong 1995). Clearly, the practice of medical genetics implies many dilemmas of this sort, but, as case studies like the one presented by Winkler and Lyrer in this volume demonstrate, the dilemmatic situation can be seen as emerging within a broader and dynamic context (see Rothman's chapter), which may also allow for other courses of action than those assumed in the depicted dichotomy of the 'dilemma'. The dilemma appears like a frozen and local state of affairs within a much broader texture of dynamic relationships. Decisions can and must be taken, but sometimes there are also ways to proceed that de-freeze the situation and avoid the one heroic act of sacrifice that the dilemma was constructing. The 'disclosure dilemma' as a type of moral dilemma appearing in the practice of genetic counselling and testing has therefore been deconstructed in some way, or at least de-centred. It has proved to be a theoretical abstraction that does not always accurately describe the experiences of caregivers who live a situation in its full complexity. This does not exclude the fact that sometimes, in practice, dilemmas do also occur that can be described in the classical way. This became particularly clear in the contributions of Chadwick, Müller and Kaye et al.

But it is not just the 'dilemma' part of the term 'disclosure dilemmas' that has been remodelled. It is also the 'disclosure' part. The verb 'to disclose' assumes that there is (genetic) information that can be revealed or passed to somebody else. It presumes the availability of a test. But, as the discussions of Tymstra and Schwennesen, Koch and Svendsen show, there are many steps before this. When a test for a certain condition becomes available for clinical use, it represents an offer, which, as such, changes the situation, perhaps dramatically. It introduces an *option to know*, where before no such option existed. If risk screenings are offered, which only reveal whether somebody fulfils 'indications' to test (according to some definition when a test is indicated, however sometimes ambiguous, see Lock's chapter), the next step of disclosure has quite a different appeal, 'taste', and also different ethical connotations. The person is already standing on a medical conveyor belt and the decision is rather about refusing than mandating a more precise test. Disclosure, therefore, is the endpoint of a long story that began somewhere upstream in the chain of events that guide technological developments in society. This chain of events is ethically not neutral, but is beyond the influence of patients and medical geneticists 'on the ground'.

The rights perspective (Chadwick, Miny, both this vol.; Andorno 2004), which the subtitle of our collection positions in a critical light (claiming that we are 'beyond' the right to know/not to know debate), proves to still be relevant and necessary. To see the limits of the rights approach, and to recognize its impacts on the social construction of 'autonomy' does not lead to the abandonment of the rights to know and not to know, but to a contextual view on those rights. The question of whom, in what kinds of situations, has the rights to know and not to know does not lead to a comprehensive understanding of the ethical aspects of decision making about genetic testing. But in many situations generated by genetic tests, they matter. A similar conclusion can be drawn regarding informed consent. Informed consent to testing cannot be the solution to the ethical problem of whether tests are legitimately performed or not. However, testing without informed consent would be highly problematic and infringe the basic rights of those tested. If somebody is supposed to give an informed consent (or refuse), they need to be in a situation of free judgment that is itself a joint social achievement of many who contribute to a situation of decision making (Scully, this vol.). And even the interpretation of legal rights (Wied et al.; Kaye et al.; Steel, all this vol.) is contextual and may involve ambiguities. Tackling the question of how legal provisions can be 'applied' in a given situation is instructive from an ethical point of view, because questions of relevance and values need to be clarified. We could perhaps claim (with Gadamer 1986) that only in concrete and particular circumstances we can understand the laws' 'general' meanings.

A more inclusive picture of autonomy emerges, which is broader and more contextual than the understanding of autonomy as self-determination. Genetic counselling is a highly instructive example for learning more about moral autonomy: an example that involves knowledge and non-knowledge, certainty and uncertainty, self and others, identity and relationships, present and future, memory and expectation, experiences of guilt and responsibility. The study of the preconditions of autonomy could be inspired by the concept of agency, as Rehmann-Sutter (this vol.) suggests. Agency means the capability to act, in the full sense. This capability to act is profoundly dialectical, bound to conditions of dependency and to certain conditions which allow independence.

In a situation of fading exclusivity of genes and of contested symbolisms (Samerski, this vol.), there are still learning steps for all participants, clinicians, consumers, patients, and also for ethicists. Cases and experiences count. Cases contain more than just conditions for the appropriate application of preset ethical values, rules or principles. We can really learn from cases, and we can learn from those who have learnt from cases. Therefore, the ethics of genetics benefits from qualitative studies about the experiences of patients (Porz, this vol.). It is perhaps too banal to say that no general bioethical solution to 'the disclosure dilemma' is possible. We conclude that an ethical understanding of concrete questions that make a situation morally 'dilemmatic' asks for a hermeneutic approach to those socially extended situations where multiple, and sometimes at least partially irreconcilable, commitments and responsibilities emerge. To see what is ethically justified or necessary, also implies a perspective on 'good life'. It is not solely the interpretation of the particular that leads us to ethical recommendations, because decision makers also need to contrast the particular with general ideas of wisdom and justice. From such an interpretation, which combines the particular with the general and may never be complete, ethical recommendations can be developed.

Certainly, this has been a highly subjective collection of points, which have been clarified for us through working on this book. Readers may find other points and see different aspects.

Open Questions

In an evolving field like medical genetics much remains open and could not be treated in this book. We want to highlight some points that need further discussion.

Multi-gene Tests

All considerations in this book started from the assumption that genetic tests are offered and performed for a known disease or disability. They may be influenced by one single gene or by many genes, and they may lead to knowledge of different quality; for some, only knowledge of a higher-than-average risk. But as a direct consequence of a certain 'enumeratism', which is characteristic for genomics (we take this term from Kaneko 2006), in the near future new kinds of tests will become available: tests for a multitude of diseases, desirable and undesirable traits, and risks of many kinds, all at once. They will cover many different kinds of genetic correlations with disease, and tens or hundreds of thousands of markers. Decisions about these kinds of tests will have a very different character to conventional tests. Due to their lack of transparency for the testee, they will be difficult to handle. If used in prenatal settings, they will represent an overall health check that may be easy to accept. However, coping with the implications of the results will be more difficult.

Direct to Consumer Gene Tests

Personal decision making by consumers regarding gene test offers over the Internet represents a new challenge for the personal ethics of self-care. Despite the apparent banality of some components of the presently available test offers (earwax type, eye colour or other known traits, where the genetic test adds no new knowledge), Internet gene tests can give the power of knowledge (genetic information) to individuals who are barely prepared: knowledge that has implications for their future life planning and for other family members, and may cause fears or call forth a false sense of security that may be problematic from a medical point of view. Personal genomics is clearly a business model, based on the fears of many people. It is unclear what kinds of accompanying measures would be needed in order to make the offer of direct to consumer gene tests ethical. Is good genetic counselling possible at all, under these circumstances, considering the limits of available scientific knowledge about phenotypical consequences of single mutations?

The Internet opens an international (business) perspective. Over-the-border ordering of genetic tests and over-the-border provision of genetic information (through personal, password protected websites) is a topic for international medical ethics and governance. Also *medical tourism* needs to be considered. If certain services, for instance PGD or genetic testing of children, are prohibited in one's own country, people who can afford it can go to another country in order to get those services where they are legal. Legal differences, and the pluralism of legal 'solutions' of governance issues in 'biosocieties' open a whole set of questions that touch medical ethics. How can and *should* societies and health care systems handle striking differences between the legal systems? Which ethical points should be considered from an individual point of view?

The Cumulative Perspective of Genetic Test Societies

What kind of society are we living in, when prenatal (or even preimplantation) genetic testing is no longer the exception but becomes the rule? Risk screening and PND, in many countries of the world, has become part of a standard pregnancy care package. Genetic testing is no longer an answer that is selectively recommended under certain, rather rare circumstances of an already known increased risk, but is becoming more and more normal. The offers of risk screening for adults will help to stabilize the social acceptance of prenatal risk screenings, and vice versa. What are the implications of this development towards a normalization of genetic testing for the ethics of parenting? Which approaches to the ethical governance of test offers would be needed? Which capacity building programmes would be necessary, and what role should bioethics play in them?

Genetic Tests and Preventive Medicine

There are two scenarios: risk testing without the possibility of medical prevention and risk testing with the consequent offer of preventive medication. If no preventive medical interventions are available, changes in lifestyle or eating habits, more exercise and other behavioural changes may influence the risk in a positive way. The preventive logic is a good reason to develop extensive offers for genetic risk testing. But how much disclosure of genetic risks is good for people? What are the costs of this knowledge to well-being and contentment? What are the costs to autonomy? In other words, how much value does the freedom to include *irrational* aspects (pleasures that might be unhealthy) in our lives have? For the second scenario, the example of cholesterol is instructive. A recent study shows that certain medications (statins) can reduce the incidence of major cardiovascular events, despite the fact that lipid levels are well below the threshold for treatment with statins according to current prevention guidelines (Ridker et al. 2008; cf. critically Hlatky 2008). This provides a medical reason for preventive consumption of risk-reducing drugs. Analogous situations can arise with genetic risk assessments and preventive medication. The question for public health ethics then is: how much disclosure of risks for preventive reasons is good for people? And what role should interested parties like pharmaceutical companies play in the development of such preventive strategies?

The future may leave gene-centrism behind. Non-genetic factors contribute to the emergence of a disease like genetic factors. But even if we adopt a more integrative view and believe that there is no essential difference between 'genetic' and certain 'non-genetic' information, genetic testing remains special because of practical circumstances. Results can be gained on some ex-vivo body cells. No invasive methods are necessary. In the cells contained in saliva, hair, or scales of their skin, people leave traces of their 'genetic identity' behind, which can be deciphered by high-tech devices. This makes genetics also interesting for *forensic science*. The use of DNA in criminal investigations (Williams and Johnson 2008) provides another list of political and ethical questions, which have not been covered in this book.

References

Alberts, B. et al. (2008), *Molecular Biology of the Cell* (5th edition) (New York: Garland).

Andorno, R. (2004), 'The Right Not to Know: An Autonomy Based Approach', *Journal of Medical Ethics* 30, 435–440.

Barnes, B. and Dupré, J. (2008), *Genomes and What to Make of Them* (Chicago: University of Chicago Press).

Birney, E. et al. (2007), 'Identification and analysis of functional elements in 1% of the human genome by the ENCODE pilot project', *Nature* 447, 799–816.

Gadamer, H.-G. (1986), *Wahrheit und Methode. Grundzüge einer Philosophischen Hermeneutik* (5th edition) (Tübingen: Mohr).

Hlatky, M.A. (2008), 'Expanding the orbit of primary prevention – moving beyond JUPITER', *New England Journal of Medicine* 359/21, 2280–2282.

Kaneko, K. (2006), *Life: An Introduction to Complex Systems Biology* (Berlin: Springer).

Pennisi, E. (2008), 'Number of sequenced human genomes doubles', *Science* 322, 838.

Ridker, P.M. et al. (2008), 'Rosuvastatin to prevent vascular events in men and women with elevated c-reactive protein', *New England Journal of Medicine* 359/21, 2195–2207.

Sinnott-Armstrong, W. (1995), 'Moral Dilemma', in R. Audi, *The Cambridge Dictionary of Philosophy* (Cambridge: Cambridge University Press), 508.

Williams, R. and Johnson, P. (2008), *Genetic Policing: The Use of DNA in Criminal Investigations* (Uffculme: Willan).

Index

Page numbers in *italics* refer to tables.

abortion
  debate 19–20, 23
  following amniocentesis 197–8, 200–1
'Actor Network Theory' 242
age factor
  child *vs* parent consent to predictive tests 114–27
  in prenatal testing 191, 220, 249
Age of Legal Capacity (Scotland) Act (1991) 118
agency 245–6, 252–3, 256
Alberts, B. et al. 262
Alzheimer's disease 65
  APOE gene 66, 67–9
  early-onset 66, 67, 68
  genetics of 66–9
  late-onset 66, 67, 68
    genetic testing for APOE status 71–4
    lay interpretation of risk estimates 75–9
    subjectivity and susceptibility genes 79–80
American Society of Human Genetics (ASHG) 28, 160–1, 162
amniocentesis 132
  'embodiment' of information 249
  legal cases 139–41
  and risk of abortion 197–8, 200–1
  vs chorionic villus sampling (CVS) 133
aneuploidy screening *see* Down syndrome; prenatal testing/during pregnancy (PND) screening
anonymization of biobank information 12–13
Austrian law 135, 141, 148
autonomy 30–1, 100, 101, 208, 263–4
  informing distant relatives 161–2
  and non-disclosure 226
  as relational capacity 239–40, 241
  self-determination and risk determination 93
  'thin' and 'thick' conceptions of 47–8
  see also non-directiveness; prenatal testing/during pregnancy (PND) screening

Balint groups 178
Beauchamp, T. and Childress, J. 30
beneficence 31
  disclosure of prenatal diagnostic options 225–6
  informing distant relatives 162
Bertram, L. and Tanzi, R.E. 67
Biesecker, B.B. 238–9
biobanks 10, 12–13
'blended inheritance' concept 77
BRB v. *JB* 126
breach of contract *see* liability
breaching patient confidentiality 160–1
breaking bad news *see* cancer, communication issues
breast cancer
  false positive tests 86
  mutation-carriers and relatives 160, 163, 244–6, 247–8
  and ovarian cancer 156–8
  and predictive test for colon cancer 55–8
burden and chance, knowledge as 48–9
Burian, R.M. 105

cancer
  communication issues 167–8
    formation of common felt body 175–9
    suggestions for professionals 171–5

what is already known 169–70
predictions concerning 183–9
see also breast cancer
cardiovascular disease
imaging 87
see also hypertrophic cardiomyopathy (HCM); long QT syndrome (LQT); sudden cardiac death (SCD)
carrier status 11–12
'celebrity genomes' 16
Chadwick, R. 10, 13
et al. 9
Chervenak, F.A.
and Chervenak, J.L. 227
et al. 227
and McCullough, L.B. 224, 225
child *vs* parent consent to predictive tests 114–27
Children Act (1989) 126–7
cholesterol levels 87–8
chorionic villus sampling (CVS) 133, 220–1
clinical perspective
carrier status 11–12
child *vs* parent consent to predictive tests 115–16, 122–3, 125
colon cancer, predictive test for 55–8
communication
ethical model of 231–57
see also cancer, communication issues; dialogue
comparative genomics 14
competing risks 186–7
'conduit/container model of information' 252
confidentiality 189
breaching 160–1
consent
informed choice and 100, 192–5, 226–8, 264
open consent concept 17
to predictive tests, child *vs* parent 115–27
corporeal body and felt body 176–7
'cousin in Australia' problem 161–4
Cox, S. and McKellin, W. 70
cut-off point in prenatal testing 194–5, 198, 200–1, 203
CVS *see* chorionic villus sampling
cystic fibrosis (CF) 21, 90, 106

damages awards 147–50
Danish Board of Health, prenatal screening policy 191–203 *passim*
decision making
as distributed action 242–3
genetic counselling as lesson in 99–101
kinship ethics 60–2
need for empirical data on 213–14
patients' context 55–60
responsibility for 201–2
and risk perception 92–3
study methodology 54–5
dependency and vulnerability 247–8
diagnosis 29
diagnostic problems 33
dialogue
bioethics as 205–7
re-modelling 238–41
dietary advice 14–15
direct to consumer genetic tests 35, 265–6
disability
damages awarded for cost of 147–9
rights 13
see also liability
distributed action, decision making as 242–3
DNA tests *see* genetic tests; *specific tests and diseases*
Down Syndrome 90–1, 100, 133, 140, 141
see also prenatal testing/during pregnancy (PND) screening

early detection 85–6
ECG 115, 121, 122, 124–5, 126
'embodied information' 249
'embodied risk' 107–8
Emery, J. 192
emotional distress, damages awarded for 150
empathy/insight 173–4, 209–10
Enright v. *Dr Tse Sak Kwun* 141
epistemologies
misunderstanding of 102–3
social 210–11, 212
Epstein, R.M. 177–8

ethical perspective 16–17, 19–20, 262–4
  child *vs* parent consent to predictive test 116–18, 123–4
  model for communicating personal genetic information 231–57
  patient 244–8
eugenics 27, 28, 235

Falk, R. 98
family history compilation 159
Family Law Reform Act (1969) 118–19, 119–20, 125
felt body 175–9
fetal sex identification 133, 226
Fleck, L. 97, 98
Fluorescent DNA *In Situ* Hybridization (FISH) 132, 221
food and health 89
Fraser, F.C. 233–4, 253
French law 135, 145–6

Gallagher v. *Duke University* 139, 149
Galton, F. 27
gaze in physician-patient communication 175
'gene for' myth 97, 102–3, 105, 106, 251–2
'gene-conforming' lifestyle 89–90
General Medical Council, UK 155
gene(s)
  in colloquial speech 97–8, 99
  as fading scientific fact 98–9
  multi-functionality of 250
  and self 103, 107–9
  as things and causes 104–5
  as threat from within 105–6
genetic counselling 25–7
  constraints 32–5
  essence of 28–31
  ethical problems 19–20
  gene talk critique 103–9
  historical development 27–8
  as lesson in decision making 99–101
  main elements of *30*
  preconditions for 31–2
  reasons for applying for *29*
  room metaphor 19, 23–4
  see also specific issues
genetic determinism 9
'genetic programme' metaphor 250, 251
  vs systemic account 250, 251–2
genetic registers 32
genetic tests 88–9, 261–2
  direct to consumer 35, 265–6
  multi-gene 265
  potential benefits and harms of 185–6
  in pregnancy 90–1
  and preventative medicine 266–7
  reliability and validity of 33
  see also specific tests and diseases
Germany
  law and liability 134–5, 138–40, 142, 145, 146, 147–8, 149, 150, 224
  Nazi 27, 235
Gillick competence 118, 119, 120–1, 125, 126, 127
'Good Medical Practice' principles (GMC) 155

Hagerty, R.G. et al. 169–70
Halpern, S. 68
Hardy, J. 65
harm avoidance principle 167, 186
Harper, P.S. 192
Harris, J. 47–8, 161
HCM *see* hypertrophic cardiomyopathy
health care professionals
  primary care 32–3
  responsibility towards relatives 154–5
  see also cancer
hereditary systemic angiopathy 39–40
  differential diagnosis 40
  misdiagnosis and harmful mistreatment 41–2
  unsolicited disclosure dilemma 41–3, 45–50
Hippocratic Oath 154–5
history
  of genetic counselling 27–8
  'index' patient and family 159
Holm, S. 234
Homo affinitas (relatedness) 62
hope
  provision of 171–2
  subjective definitions of 169–70

Human Genetics Commission, UK 153, 157, 161, 162
human genome sequencing and mapping 9
human genomic databases *see* biobanks
Human Genomic Organization 14, 15
  Ethics Committee 10
  Statement on Pharmacogenetics, Solidarity and Equity 17
Huntingdon's disease
  patient perspective 58–60
  subjective construction of risk 70
  time dimension 252
Husted, J. 11, 16, 47, 48
hydrocephalus 142
hypertrophic cardiomyopathy (HCM) 113, 114
  child *vs* parent consent to predictive test 114–21

identity *see* self
illegal practice, preimplant genetic diagnosis as 144, 224–5
imaginative projection 209–10, 213
imaging technology *see* ultrasound diagnosis
in vitro fertilization (IVF) 92, 132, 234
'index' patient
  and distant relatives 163–4
  and family history 159
individual and collective identity 13–14
individual and collective interests 10, 15, 17
individual and collective moral understandings 211, 212–13
individualism and non-directiveness 235–6
individualized information giving 171–3, 174–5
information flow 206–7
informed choice/consent 100, 192–5, 226–8, 264
insight/empathy 173–4, 209–10
Internet 80, 94, 265
interpretation of genetic information 248–53
  bioethics as dialogue 205–7
  empathy/insight of counsellor 209–10
  empirical data on decision making 213–14
  ethical issues 214, 215
  liability for incorrect 138–9, 143, 224
  moral understandings of counsellor 210–13
  see also 'gene for' myth; gene(s); patient perspectives; risk
IVF *see in vitro* fertilization

Jackson v. *Bumgardner* 135–6, 148
justice principle 31

Kaplowitz, S.A. et al. 169, 172
Kavanagh, A.M. and Broom, D.H. 107
Keller, E.F. 97, 99, 105
Kerr, A. 202
Khachaturian, Z. 65
kinship ethics 60–2
Kirk, P. et al. 171
Kitcher, P. 99
Konrad, M. 47, 48–9, 60, 61

Laurie, G. 155
lay understandings *see* patient perspectives
legal perspective
  child *vs* parent consent to predictive test 118–19, 124–5, 126–7
  disclosure of aneuploidy 224–5
lemon sign 133, 142
Levinas, E. 214
liability
  cases 138–42
  damages awards 147–50
  distinguishing relevant actions 145–7
  distinguishing relevant obligations 143–4
  international comparison 133–6
    see also specific countries
  options for 131–3
  situational distinctions in 136–8
lifestyle 89–90, 94, 115, 121, 122
Lippman, A. 69, 249, 254
location of relatives 62
Lock, M. 202
long QT syndrome (LQT) 113, 114
  child *vs* parent consent to predictive test 122–7
loyalty to family 62

Mack, J.W. et al. 169

Manson, N. and O'Neill, O. 252
Marfan's syndrome 155–6, 163
maternal serum screening/triple test 90–1, 133, 142, 220
Mattocks, C. 15–16
Mayeux, R. 68
McFarlane v. *Tayside Health Board* 136, 137
McLelland v. *Greater Glasgow Health Board* 141, 148
medical tourism 265–6
medicine, importance of genetics in 26
mindfulness-based approaches to communication 178
misunderstandings
  avoidance of 143
  of epistemologies 102–3
moral understandings 210–13
Moss, L. 70
multi-functionality of genes 250
multi-gene tests 265
multidisciplinary approach 32, 185–6

National Institute of Aging (NIA) 65
Nazi Germany 27, 235
needs based approach 253–7
negligence *see* liability
new phenomenology 175–9
newborn screening 11–12, 20–3
Niebur, H.R. 246–7
Nijhout, H. 70
non-directiveness 192–5, 232–8
  alternatives to 238–41
non-disclosure 158–60, 226
non-maleficence principle 31
non-verbal communication 174–5
nuchal translucency test 91, 191, 196, 221, 236
numerical information, patient perceptions of 172–3
nutrigenomics 14–15

open consent concept 17
ovarian cancer and breast cancer 156–8
over the counter/direct to consumer genetic tests 35, 265–6
ownership of genetic information 155–8
Oyama, S. 250–1, 252

pain and suffering, damages awarded for 149
parent *vs* child consent to predictive tests 114–27
Parker, P.A. et al. 170
Parkinson v. *St. James and Seacroft University Hospital NHS Trust* 147, 148
patient perspectives
  breast cancer and predictive test for colon cancer 55–8
  genetic ethics 244–8
  genetic risk 70, 75–9, 172–3, 200–1, 207–9
  see also cancer, communication issues
Personal Genome Project 17
personalized health advice 14–15
pharmacogenetics 14, 15
phenylketonuria (PKU) 20–1
political developments 10–11
polycystic kidney disease (PKD) 159
Polymerase Chain Reaction (PCR)/(QF-PCR) 132, 221, 222
pregnancy *see* prenatal testing/during pregnancy (PND) screening
preimplant genetic diagnosis/prior to conception (PGD) screening 9–10, 11, 132
  as illegal practice 144, 224–5
  non-directive counselling 234
prenatal testing/during pregnancy (PND) screening 90–1, 93, 100, 105–6, 132–3
  and abortion debate 19–20, 23
  case for disclosure 224–6
  case for non-disclosure 226
  current diagnostic options 222, *223*
  development of 219–22
  distributed character of decision making 242
  informed consent 192–5, 226–8
  interpretation of risk figure 197–201
  letting the experts decide 201–2
  non-directiveness 192–5, 233–4, 236
  as routine act 195–6
  social implications of 266
  ultrasound scan 133, 142, 196–7, 221, 222, 227

preventative medicine 266–7
Price, F.V. 197
primary care providers 32–3
prior to conception (PGD) genetic screening *see* preimplant genetic diagnosis
privacy
  'celebrity genomes' 16
  vs national security 11
  vs open consent concept 17
'processes of translation' 193–4, 202–3
psychosocial counselling model 238–40
public debates about science 11
public goods 15
public screening 85–6
public *vs* individual interests 10, 15, 17

qualitative and quantitative aspects of genetic tests 185–6

R (on application of Axon v. *Secretary of State for Health)* 119, 120
R W (A Minor) (Medical Treatment: Court's Jurisdiction) 124–5
Rapp, R. 193–4
Re R (A Minor) (Wardship: Consent to Treatment) 125
Re W (a minor) (medical treatment) 126
Reed, S.C. 28
Reed v. *Campagnolo* 136, 145, 148–9
refusal of treatment by minor 123–7
relatedness (*Homo affinitas*) 62
relational capacity, autonomy as 239–40, 241
relatives
  breaching patient confidentiality 160–1
  breast cancer mutation-carriers and communication with 160, 163, 244–6, 247–8
  'cousin in Australia' problem 161–4
  'Good Samaritan' *vs* 'officious meddler' scenarios 153–4
  health care professionals' responsibility towards 154–5
  kinship ethics 60–2
responsibility 246–7
  for decision making 201–2
  of gene carriers 109, 160
  and predictions concerning cancer 183–9
  towards relatives *see* relatives
REVEAL (Risk Evaluation and Education for Alzheimer's disease) study 71–80
Rieh, J.P. and Ray, C. 240–1
right to know/not to know
  changes in context 9–11
  changes in ethical approaches 16–17, 263–4
  changes in issues 11–16
  and duties 49–50
risk
  competing 186–7
  and decision making 92–3
  'embodied risk' 107–8
  -individualizing screening 86–8
  patient perspectives 70, 75–9, 172–3, 200–1, 207–9
  prenatal tests for Down syndrome 197–201
  'processes of translation' 193–4, 202–3
  and reference class 173
  and responsibility 187–8
  statistical probability and perception of 92, 102–3, 172–3
  time dimension in 187, 252
  see also 'gene for' myth; gene(s)
Rose, S. 70

SCD *see* sudden cardiac death
Schmidt, H. 175–9, 210
Scully, J.L. et al. 50, 53, 236
self/identity
  collective and individual 13–14
  and genes 103, 107–9
sex chromosome aneuploidy 228
social epistemologies 210–11, 212
social impacts 10–11, 266
social science perspective on screening 69–71
solidarity
  and altruism 161
  and equity 16–17
South Glamorgan County Council v. *W and B* 127
standpoint epistemologies 211

statistical probability 71
in decision making 100
REVEAL study 78, 80
and risk perception 92, 102–3, 172–3
sudden cardiac death (SCD) 113–14
see also hypertrophic cardiomyopathy (HCM); long QT syndrome (LQT)
Svendsen, M.N. 193–4, 244–6, 247
Swiss law 135
on genetic testing in humans 225, 226
systemic *vs* programmatic interpretations of genomics 250, 251–2

Tarasoff v. *Regents of the University of California* 160
'technological culture' 94
Templeton, A. 67–8
time dimension
in kinship ethics 61
in risk 187, 252
triple test/maternal serum screening 90–1, 133, 142, 220
trust 172, 186, 201–2
'Tübinger case' 138–9, 224
Tymstra, T. 92

ultrasound diagnosis
cardiac (echocardiogram) 115, 121
of fetal abnormalities 133, 142, 196–7, 221, 222, 227
United Kingdom (UK)
General Medical Council 155
Human Genetics Commission 153, 157, 161, 162
law and liability 135–6, 141, 145, 146, 148, 150
United States (US) 19–20, 21, 22, 23
American Society of Human Genetics (ASHG) 28, 160–1, 162
breaching patient confidentiality 160–1
law and liability 135–6, 139, 145, 148–9
Universal Declaration on the Human Genome and Human Rights (1997) 157, 161
unsolicited disclosure 41–3, 45–50

Veach, P.M. et al. 240
vulnerability and dependency 247–8

Walker, A.P. 232, 233, 234–5, 236–7, 243
Walker, M. 212
Walkin v. *South Manchester Health Authority* 136
Weil, J. 232, 238
et al. 237–8, 239
Wertz, D. and Fletcher, J. 233, 235, 237
whole genome sequencing 15–16, 261
Widmer, C. 246
Wieser, B. 242, 243
and Karner, S. 235–6
withholding genetic information 158–60, 226
wrongful birth claims 146, 147, 148, 149, 150–1
wrongful conception claims 147, 148, 149
wrongful life claims 145–6, 148

Yoxen, E. 69

For Product Safety Concerns and Information please contact our EU representative GPSR@taylorandfrancis.com
Taylor & Francis Verlag GmbH, Kaufingerstraße 24, 80331 München, Germany

www.ingramcontent.com/pod-product-compliance
Ingram Content Group UK Ltd.
Pitfield, Milton Keynes, MK11 3LW, UK
UKHW010955180926
475701UK00004B/376
* 9 7 8 0 3 6 7 6 0 3 1 2 0 *